The New Europe

The European Initiative

Series Editor: PROFESSOR DAVID G. MAYES
National Institute of Economic and Social Research, London, and
Co-ordinator of the Economic and Social Research Council (ESRC) research
project *The European Initiative*.

The late 1980s and early 1990s have produced major events and changes in
Europe which are set to produce fundamental shifts in the economic, political
and social changes throughout the continent. The European Community's
Single Market Programme due for completion at the end of 1992 and the
sweeping political reforms and revolution in Eastern Europe have been the
catalysts. This new series of books has been established to publish the best
research and scholarship on European issues and to make an important
contribution to the advancement of knowledge on European issues.

Professor Mayes is Co-ordinator of a major research initiative on European
issues by the Economic and Social Research Council. The Series, in addition to
publishing the leading contributions made by that initiative, will also publish
other titles drawn from all disciplines in the Social Sciences, including
Economics, Political Science and Sociology.

Titles in the Series:

The European Challenge: Industry's Response to the 1992 Programme
edited by David G. Mayes

The New Europe: Changing Economic Relations between East and West
Susan Senior Nello

The New Europe
Changing Economic Relations between East and West

Susan Senior Nello
University of Siena

HARVESTER
WHEATSHEAF

New York   London   Toronto   Sydney   Tokyo   Singapore

First published 1991 by
Harvester Wheatsheaf,
66 Wood Lane End, Hemel Hempstead,
Hertfordshire, HP2 4RG
A division of
Simon & Schuster International Group

Distributed in North America by
The University of Michigan Press
839 Greene Street, P.O. Box 1104
Ann Arbor, Michigan 48106, U.S.A.

Typeset in 10/12 pt Times
by Inforum Typesetting, Portsmouth

Printed and bound in Great Britain by
BPCC Wheatons Ltd, Exeter.

British Library Cataloguing in Publication Data

Senior Nello, Susan
  The new Europe: changing economic relations
  between East and West. (The European Initiative)
  I. Title   II. Series
  337.094

  ISBN 0-7450-1050-4

---

1 2 3 4 5   94 93 92 91

This book is inevitably dedicated to my three children: Matteo (7), Caterina (3) and Paolo (a little bit older).

Contents

Preface   xiii
Introduction   1
    The main features of non-market economies   2
    Trade between the EC and Central-East Europe up
       until 1989   4
    The new configuration of Europe   5
    Collapse of the central-planning system in 1989 and
       implications for the CMEA   6
    The growing strength of the European community   7
    Difficulties with statistics for Central-East European
       countries   8
    The organisation of the book   9

Part 1   Relations between the EC and Central-East Europe before 1988–89

1   **Historical background**   **15**

    1.1   Introduction   15
    1.2   The CMEA   16
    1.3   Relations between the two blocs up until 1988   17
    1.4   The reasons for the change in CMEA attitude   22
    1.5   Conclusion   23

2   **The mechanisms used by the EC in East–West trade until 1988**   **26**

    2.1   Introduction   26

2.2 The GATT 28
2.3 The application of the Common Commercial Policy
in trade with East Europe 31
2.4 The autonomous trade policy 32
2.5 Sectoral trade agreements 34
2.6 A comment on export-restraint arrangements 40
2.7 The Romanian agreements 41
2.8 Cooperation agreements 42

3 EC anti-dumping and other trade protection measures 48

3.1 Introduction 48
3.2 EC anti-dumping legislation and the difficulty of its
application to non-market economies 49
3.3 Statistics of EC anti-dumping measures against
Central-East European countries 50
3.4 The various steps in the EC anti-dumping procedure 54
3.5 EC anti-dumping rules and comparative advantage 59
3.6 Other EC trade protection laws 60

**4 The EC in a wider context: Cocom and the OECD
consensus on export credits 62**

4.1 Introduction 62
4.2 Technology transfer 63
4.3 Export credits 66

**5 Trade between the European Community and Central-East
Europe until 1989 71**

5.1 Introduction 71
5.2 Intra-CMEA trade and the possibility of switching to
trade with the West 73
5.3 A statistical survey of EC trade with the Central-East
European countries 77
5.4 The structure of EC–USSR trade 80
5.5 The structure of EC trade with the smaller
Central-East European countries 82
5.6 The share of EC member states in trade with
Central-East Europe 83
5.7 Trade between the EC and Central-East Europe in
services 85
5.8 Countertrade 85
5.9 Trends in countertrade and economic transformation
in Central-East Europe 87

5.10 Are Central-East European exports concentrated in
     product groups particularly subject to protection?   88
5.11 Competition from other exporters for EC markets   89
5.12 A disaggregated study of the performance of various
     product groups in EC–CMEA trade   94
5.13 The piecemeal nature of EC trade preferences   96
5.14 Customs union theory   98
5.15 Empirical studies of customs-union effects   99

6 Agricultural trade between the EC and Central-East Europe   107

6.1 Introduction   107
6.2 Common Agricultural Policy (CAP) mechanisms of
     particular relevance to trade with third countries   108
6.3 Other measures since 1988 affecting agricultural trade
     between the EC and Central-East Europe   110
6.4 Agricultural trade concessions to Central-East
     European countries   113
6.5 What the transformation of agriculture in Central-East
     Europe entails   116
6.6 Soviet agriculture   116
6.7 Agriculture in the smaller Central-East European
     countries   122
6.8 The main features of agricultural trade between the
     EC and Central-East Europe   130
6.9 The CAP and agricultural trade with third countries   135
6.10 Indicators of the level of protection for different EC
     agricultural products   135
6.11 A survey of models estimating the impact of the
     CAP on trade with third countries   137
6.12 The impact of the CAP on EC exports to Central-East
     European countries   141
6.13 The impact of the CAP on EC imports from
     Central-East European countries   143
6.14 The outlook for agricultural trade between the EC
     and Central-East Europe   145

Part 2 Economic reforms in Central-East Europe and trade relations with the EC

7 The economic transformation of Central-East Europe   155

7.1 Introduction   155
7.2 Macroeconomic stabilisation   156

7.3   Microeconomic restructuring and systemic change   157
7.4   Social safety nets   159
7.5   The speed of transformation   160
7.6   The sequencing of measures   160
7.7   The transformation process in individual
      Central-East European countries   161

8   Western measures to aid the transformation process in
    Central-East Europe   181

8.1   Introduction   181
8.2   Measures to ease the implementation of stabilisation
      policies   183
8.3   Help for economic restructuring and systemic change
      in Central-East Europe   185
8.4   Contributions to the social safety nets   189
8.5   The European Bank for Reconstruction and
      Development   190
8.6   Why the West should give aid   191
8.7   Assessment of the PHARE Programme   194

9   The tightening links between the Community and
    Central-East Europe   201

9.1   Introduction   201
9.2   Trade and cooperation agreements   202
9.3   The significance of the trade and cooperation
      agreements   204
9.4   Second generation association agreements   205
9.5   The inter-bloc cooperation envisaged by the Joint
      Declaration   208
9.6   Conclusions   209

10   New forms of association and integration in Europe   211

10.1   Introduction   211
10.2   Central-East Europe and the changing configuration
       of the EC   212
10.3   Accession to other 'European' organisations   219
10.4   New associations among Central-East European
       countries   221
10.5   Conclusions   223

11   East–West interfirm cooperation and joint ventures   226

11.1   Introduction   226

11.2   A definition of joint ventures   227
11.3   The objectives of setting up joint ventures   228
11.4   Legislation relating to joint ventures in Central-East
       European countries   229
11.5   Statistics on East–West joint ventures in Central-East
       European countries   230
11.6   Problems with joint ventures in Central-East
       European countries   233
11.7   East–West joint ventures in EC countries   234
11.8   Industrial cooperation agreements   235
11.9   Statistics on interfirm cooperation agreements   237
11.10 Tripartite cooperation agreements   239

12   The implications of German unification for the EC   242

12.1   Introduction   242
12.2   Economic aspects of German unification   243
12.3   The integration of East Germany into the
       European Community   247
12.4   Possible costs of German unification   250
12.5   The special German provisions   251
12.6   Application of EC policies in the five Länder   252

**13   Conclusions: The outlook for economic relations between
       the EC and Central–East Europe   260**

13.1   Is the transition process irreversible?   260
13.2   Western aid measures   262
13.3   Prospects for trade   263
13.4   The new configuration of Europe   265

Bibliography   **267**
Index   **283**

Preface

When this book was begun in 1988 'Eastern European' studies, as they were then called, were a quiet backwater. There were so few publications on links between the European Community and Central-East Europe that there appeared to be a gap in the literature that needed filling. Since then, to use the Delors' expression, 'history has been accelerating'. With the explosion of the subject matter in all directions, few individual authors would now be foolhardy enough to undertake an overall presentation of the topic single-handed. My justification is the so-called Concorde effect – that so much of the book had been written, continuing it seemed worth while. At the time it was impossible to anticipate the amount of updating and rewriting that was to prove necessary, but the initial aim of filling a gap in the literature would seem to remain valid. Even if many aspects of what I have written will inevitably be overtaken by events, none the less much of the material should serve as a starting point or as a key to what is happening next.

So many people helped me in writing this book that I certainly cannot claim the effort to be single-handed, though I accept full responsibility for any errors. I am particularly grateful to Dino Tarditi of Siena University for his kindness in a number of ways, in particular in providing comments, encouragement and in helping me to find the time and funds necessary to carry out the research. Siena University financed most of the project, and allowed me to take five months' sabbatical at the European University Institute to carry out the research.

Though I had worked on both Central-East European economics and European integration, and had long wanted to combine the two, I owe the opportunity for doing so to the extremely propitious climate created by Mario Nuti for comparative economics at the European University

Institute in Florence. He also very kindly managed to find time to comment and create opportunities for discussion.

The research for the chapter on agricultural trade was financed by the Italian National Institute of Agricultural Economics (INEA), and I am grateful to Professor Giuseppe Barbero for providing me with material and allowing me to use some of the results of a study carried out for the INEA.

A special thanks goes to Emir Lawless and Linda Tieri of the European University Institute Library, who helped in numerous ways and kept me informed of all the new material appearing on the topic. Sara Mendosa of Eurostat also very kindly furnished all the statistics on agriculture.

I would also like to thank all the people who provided comments, information, and/or opportunities for discussion, especially Milica Uvalic, Alberto Chilosi, Giovanni Graziani, Giuseppe Are, Harriet Matejka, Marie Lavigne, Michael Tracy, Marvin Hayenga, Wayne Moyer and Patrick McCarthy. I am also grateful to Professor David Mayes of the NIESR and to an anonymous referee who both provided extremely useful comments on earlier drafts of the manuscript.

The research was also based on a series of interviews carried out with national and EC officials. At the EC Commission I am particularly grateful to John Maslen, Renzo Daviddi, Tony Curran, Franco Campoli, and Neville Williams. In London I would particularly like to thank Neil Harvey and Andrew Dickson of the Department of Trade and Industry for numerous interviews and a great deal of information; Peter Davies of the Ministry of Defence; David Wyatt and Janet West of the Export Credit Guarantee Department, and the various people I spoke to at the MAFF. I am also grateful to Mr Kuba of the OECD and to the UN ECE in Geneva for sending information.

I would also like to thank Bill Carroll and Gordon Urquhart for providing me with the chance to try out so much of the material in this book on the unfortunate students of Cornell College, Iowa. The comments and discussions there were invaluable in helping to organise the material, as were the opportunities to present the topic kindly granted by the Johns Hopkins University, the European University Institute, Grinnell College (Iowa) and Iowa State University.

A final thanks goes to my Father for sending so much information; Silvia Paoli without whose Mary Poppins act this book would never have been written, and to my family who felt the upheavals in Central-East Europe more than most people living in Florence.

S. Senior Nello

Introduction

The economic and political transformation of the Central-East European countries(1) is the subject of much current interest, but the pace and unprecedented nature of these changes makes their analysis difficult. The task is not simply one of removing the central-planning apparatus and waiting for markets to appear. Rather, the introduction of market-orientated economies seems likely to take much longer than was first envisaged, and has set in motion a diversification process among the various Central-East European countries. Already, there is a rapidly growing literature dealing with the pitfalls and unforeseen distortions of economic transformation, and suggesting possible policy prescriptions. One of the main aims of this book is to describe the transformation process in the various Central-East European countries and to assess its implications for the level, structure and mechanisms of trade with the European Community(2).

For this purpose a review of the situation prior to change (which occupies the first half of this book) provides a useful starting point. Here, 1988–89 has been taken as a watershed, given that the definitive rupture from the old system occurred then in most of Central-East Europe. None the less, change was evident prior to that date, and subsequently many features of the old system persisted. To understand the transformation taking place a brief description of the main features of non-market economies and their implications for trade is necessary.

The terms 'transformation' or 'change' have generally been used here rather than 'reform', as many Central-East European economists stress that what is occurring is not reform of the system, but, rather, complete rejection of one model and its substitution with another.

1

The main features of non-market economies

Up until 1989, with the possible exception of Hungary, the Central-East European countries could be described as having non-market economies. Essentially, this entails a system based on a vertical hierarchy in which the state owns a large share of the factors of production and makes decisions with regard to resource allocation. This takes place through mandatory central planning, with the state issuing directives from above. The main success indicator is the ability to meet plan targets which are generally set in physical or quantity terms. Prices are centrally fixed and the administration is responsible for identifying consumer preferences in order to determine production and distribution. To ease this task and because of the socialist emphasis on economies of scale, the structure of both industry and agriculture tends to be extremely concentrated. The allocation of resources with centrally fixed prices can only operate if there is some kind of insulation of the central-planned economy from market forces, and this was achieved by means of foreign trade monopolies and non-convertible currencies. This also has the effect of protecting producers from foreign competition.

The structure of output in non-market economies is generally shaped by the development strategy and by ideological considerations. This usually entails the objective of rapid but also selective industrialisation. In particular, precedence is given to military requirements over civilian ones; to investment over consumption; to heavy rather than light industry; to goods rather than services (with the latter not even appearing in the measure used for national income, Net Material Product); and to quantity over quality.

The combination of centralised resource allocation and fixing of prices means that prices in a non-market economy will not necessarily reflect relative scarcity. In general, prices for labour, certain raw materials and energy will tend to be fixed at low levels, while prices on more 'socially unnecessary' products, such as consumer durables, are likely to be relatively high.

A consequence of this price system is that production will not reflect opportunity cost. This tends to encourage systematic waste of resources, in particular of energy, raw materials and labour[3]. As more information emerges from these countries, it is clear that environmental considerations were also routinely neglected. The priority given to the military sector meant that it absorbed a large share of resources, while functioning of the system entailed heavy administrative costs.

The mismatch of demand and supply in centrally planned economies, with shortages on one hand and wastage on the other, has been extensively documented. The early literature (see, for example, the debate between Lange and Hayek and von Mises) generally attributes this situation to difficulties of coordination and information. The lack of information and reliable statistics was confirmed by Gorbachev in 1989: 'We should admit we did not properly know this country we lived in.'(4) However, as Nuti (1990d) points out, the inertia of the system was such that even when information was available (for instance relating to the trend in prices of its energy exports to the smaller Central-East European countries), coordination was often not even attempted.

The waste of resources was possible because the vertical relationship between the state and enterprises failed to resolve the agent-principal conflict in a satisfactory manner. The market and hierarchies approach developed by Oliver Williamson (1986) offers insights into this relationship. The approach is based on the assumptions that individuals are rational within certain boundaries, so they have only limited information, and that they may be opportunist by 'cutting corners for individual personal advantage, covering tracks and the like'. In the case of centrally planned economies this may take the form of enterprises hiding production capacity, for instance by hoarding labour or equipment so that production factors are underutilised. Alternatively, if the state specifies the objectives of the plan in terms of quantity of production output, the enterprise is likely to neglect quality considerations.

An analysis of this 'relationship between the paternalistic state and firm which is its client' is provided by the Hungarian economist, Kornai (1980, 1986a). The basis of this relationship is that everything is negotiable, including the financial position of the enterprise. Because the state was reluctant for firms to go bankrupt, these were kept in business by subsidies, tax concessions, cheap credit, and so on. Given the operation of these 'soft budgetary constraints', the objectives of the enterprises are likely to be best met by rent-seeking behaviour rather than by attempts to increase efficiency or to innovate. In addition, enterprises are encouraged to give in to wage claims of their workers, and to take on foreign loans, knowing that if necessary the paternalistic state will bail them out. Kornai's theories have been at the centre of much controversy, with various economists (see for example Davis and Charemza, 1989), criticising the concept as being loose and challenging the extent to which it can explain the generation of shortage.

None the less the concept of soft budget constraint does help to explain another shortcoming of these economies which became apparent during the second half of the 1980s, namely their increasing lack of monetary discipline. This was reflected in growing budget deficits which were met by expanding the money supply. As a result monetary overhang, or excess liquidity in the household sector, assumed huge proportions in many of the Central-East European countries. Furthermore, a large share of the huge hard-currency debts of most of these countries began as foreign debts taken on by enterprises.

Trade between the EC and Central-East Europe up until 1989

At the risk of oversimplification, at least up until 1989, trade between the EC and the Central-East European countries assumed its unique character because of the following three main groups of factors:

1. system-endemic features of the non-market economies, and especially the combination of centrally-fixed prices, foreign trade monopolies, and incomplete currency convertibility;
2. the hard currency shortages and indebtedness burden (with net foreign indebtedness of Central-East European countries estimated at some $99.2 billion at the end of 1989);
3. the way in which political, economic, military and strategic features of East-West relations were interlinked.

Prior to 1988 a combination of the political climate, hard currency shortages and the Central-East European view that trade with the West was simply an adjunct to central planning, to be kept to the unavoidable minimum, meant that levels of East-West trade were low; and trade with the EC was no exception.

Together, centrally fixed prices and the need to earn hard currency often entailed a temptation to set the export prices of products low. In trading with non-market economies, on the import side one major fear of Western countries was thus that their markets might be flooded by Central-East European products. To meet this threat various measures are adopted: *quantitative restrictions, safeguard measures, anti-dumping measures, and voluntary export restraint agreements.* Though these measures are also used in trade with market economies, the scale on which they are employed, and the forms taken, are different for non-market economies.

On the export side, Western countries often complained of difficulty of access to Central-East European markets, in particular because of the foreign trade monopolies and lack of currency convertibility. The centralised planning system means that there cannot be meaningful reciprocation of Western tariff reductions, so some alternative concession has to be found. This concession often takes the form of a commitment on the part of the Central-East European partner to allow access to its markets, and the most common solution is to encompass this commitment in a bilateral *trade and/or cooperation agreement.* These agreements generally entail the setting up of a *joint committee* to monitor the extent to which the Eastern commitment has been met.

Given the level of indebtedness of Central-East Europe, *export credit subsidies* play a crucial role in encouraging Western exports, and it was estimated that, for example, some 20% of British exports to those countries was covered by such credits in 1988(5).

Finally, the link between political and economic aspects of East–West relations at times led to 'trade denial' measures. These include *trade embargoes and the Cocom* (Coordinating Committee for Multilateral Export Controls) arrangements which were aimed at limiting exports of strategic items to Warsaw Pact countries. Alternatively, when the atmosphere is more favourable, as at present, political and other considerations have lead to the relaxing of Cocom and the granting of *aid measures*.

After 1988, depending on the degree of economic transformation reached by the individual Central-East European country in question, many of these special mechanisms were shed, or amended to bring them into line with the arrangements used in trade with other Western countries. In some cases to encourage the transformation process, and enable the leaders of Central-East European countries to register a foreign policy success, these modifications were made when changes in the Eastern partner's system had been announced but not actually implemented.

The new configuration of Europe

An early consequence of the transformation of Central-East Europe was to undermine the cohesion of the Eastern European economic integration bloc, or the CMEA (Council for Mutual Economic Assistance, also known as Comecon)(6). At the same time, the integration process of the European Community acquired renewed vigour, enabling it to act as a pole of attraction for the newly autonomous Central-East European countries. As will be shown, the interaction of these developments is likely to result in a new configuration of Europe.

June 1988 marks a watershed in this context in that a Joint Declaration of mutual recognition between the EC and the CMEA (Council for Mutual Economic Assistance) was signed, opening the way for a new era of relations between the EC and the countries of Central-East Europe. Essentially, what occurred in 1988 was that the CMEA gave in to the Community on all former points of difference, and to understand how this was possible a brief account of CMEA weakness and growing EC strength is necessary.

Collapse of the central-planning system in 1989 and implications for the CMEA

The weakness of the CMEA is to be explained in terms of the collapse of the central-planning system, and the question which inevitably arises is why such a total and generalised collapse of the central-planning system occurred in 1989. In particular, why was the Soviet Union prepared to relax its influence over its smaller European neighbours?

The poor performance of centrally planned economies had been evident for some time but during the early-1970s freely available Western credits enabled Central-East European imports (especially of technology) to continue, allowing growth to be maintained and reform to be postponed. The net hard-currency indebtedness of Central-East European countries grew from some $4 billion in 1970 to $75.3 in 1982 and $99.2 billion in 1989(7).

By the 1980s the economic and political environment had altered. Credits were becoming more difficult to obtain at a time when the Central-East European countries were increasingly dependent on Western imports for technology. At the same time Central-East Europe was affected by an economic slowdown, with official CMEA statistics indicating a fall in growth for the area as a whole from 4.2% over the 1970–75 period, to 1.4% between 1975 and 1980, and 1% between 1980 and 1985(8). However, as will be explained below, caution should always be used in dealing with Eastern statistics. Aganbegyan (1988, p. 2) argues that Soviet economic growth appears to have ceased between 1978 and 1982 and again between 1980 and 1985, a situation confirmed by Western observers(9). This was particularly critical in a country which had always pointed to its faster growth rate as one of the main indicators of superiority over the capitalist system. The CIA figures for Soviet military spending show an increase in real terms of about 2% per annum in the early-1980s, which would seem to imply a contraction of the non-military economy. Unofficial estimates suggest that GNP fell by 5% in 1989(10).

Soviet exports are heavily concentrated in energy products, and the fall in energy prices over the period between 1986 and mid-1990 meant a loss in foreign exchange earnings estimated at some $6–10 billion per year between 1986 and 1988 (with total hard-currency exports of $28 billion in 1986 (Daviddi, 1990b)).

Further difficulties arose from increasing lack of monetary discipline, with official statistics indicating a rise in the budget deficit from 18 billion roubles (3% of GDP in 1985) to 89 billion roubles in 1989, with the public debt reaching 400 billion roubles or 44% of GDP in 1989(11). Much of the deficit was monetarised, causing the money supply to grow by 18.3% in 1989 on official estimates and by as much as 59% according to some observers. This increase in the money supply contributed to a monetary overhang of 170 billion roubles in 1989 according to official estimates, but which most observers would place at 250 billion roubles or more.

The economic deterioration coincided with Gorbachev coming to power in 1985, and his policy of glasnost enabled the urgent need for change to be admitted. In addition to gold sales, or possible additions to Soviet debt, there were two ways in which resources could be released for the Soviet civilian economy, both of which were of direct relevance to the CMEA.

The first relates to Soviet military spending. In 1987 the CIA raised its estimate for the defence share of GNP to 17–22%. According to certain Soviet estimates, military spending accounted for some 30–40% of Net Material Product, corresponding to some 22–30% of GNP(12). The upward revision of Western estimates is probably mainly due to a failure to realise just how poor overall Soviet performance was.

The second measure entails the introduction of world prices and convertible currencies in intra-CMEA trade, which will be implemented from January 1991. As will be shown in Chapter 5, it is widely agreed that the system of pricing used in the CMEA involved a Soviet subsidy to its smaller neighbours (though there is some debate as to the size of the subsidy) over the 1975–85 period, particularly as these countries paid relatively low prices for energy imports. It is estimated that reform of the intra-CMEA trading system could increase the energy costs of the smaller Central-East countries by up to $15 billion(13).

Although rigidities are likely to remain, especially as intra-CMEA trade accounted for up to 80% of the foreign trade of the smaller CMEA countries, both the carrot and the stick holding the CMEA together have been undermined. Moreover, this occurred at a time when the Community was emerging as a far more united, powerful force.

The growing strength of the European Community

In the mid-1980s European integration revived and the European Community has been undergoing a revolution which entails both deepening and widening processes. The 'deepening' refers to the strengthening of Community policies with, for example, the planned completion of the internal market by 1993, the introduction of economic and monetary union and of political union, including the development of a common foreign policy. The 'widening' process entails the extension of the EC from its present twelve members, probably also to include some of the smaller Central-East European countries such as Hungary, Poland and Czechoslovakia.

This image of growing dynamism on the part of the EC helps to explain why it emerged as a pole of attraction for the increasingly autonomous Central-East European countries. At the same time, by pressing for closer links with the Community, these countries provided an additional incentive for the integration process, encouraging the evolution of a common EC foreign policy stance, and contributing to an awareness of the need for institutional change in the Community. German unity represents the extreme case of this link between developments in the Centre, East and West of Europe.

The EC has also emerged as a major actor in organising aid to encourage the economic and political reconstruction of Central-East Europe. In July 1989 a group of twenty-four Western countries (as well as international organisations such as the World Bank, IMF and European Investment bank) decided to coordinate their aid efforts, under the chairmanship of the European Community. At the same time, the growing interest of Western businessmen was reflected in a boom of East–West joint ventures. This Western response to the transformation process will be described and assessed.

Difficulties with statistics for Central-East European countries

There were immense difficulties in finding reliable statistics for the Central-East European countries, and glasnost has rendered the poor quality of Eastern statistics fully apparent. Many Western observers maintain that discrepancies between Western statistics are equally great, but it is no accident that all the CMEA countries include statistics in their lists of areas for cooperation with the EC, and some are harmonising their systems with that of Eurostat.

As the ECE(14) explains for the Soviet case, the inaccuracy is not '. . . the result of an exceptional intentional distortion of figures in individual years', but, rather, '. . . the persistent application of an unreliable methodology which inevitably leads to large errors in the estimates. These errors may also have been enlarged by arbitrary application of the methodology, but this is probably a secondary issue compared with the inherent weaknesses of the basic methodology.'

In the case of time series, in particular, the application of incorrect methodologies led to huge overestimates(15). Two Soviet statisticians, Selyunin and Khanin (1987), recalculated the industrial production index for the 1928–86 period and found a six-fold increase, rather than the officially reported eighty-nine-fold rise (or nine-fold rise estimated by the CIA).

There appears to have been a further deterioration in Soviet statistics during 1989, with many figures not appearing. Among the smaller Central-East European countries GDR statistics should be treated with caution (though German unification has now eliminated this problem), while after 1981 Romanian statistics lost much of their credibility and from 1986 became virtually non-existent(16). Romanian officials now admit that, for example, the statistics overestimated grain production in 1988 by 69%.

The organisation of the book

Chapter 1 describes relations between the EC and the CMEA and its member states up until 1988. It attempts to explain the path to mutual political recognition, and the gradual CMEA acceptance of the Community view that bilateral links between the EC and individual Central-European countries should take precedence over bloc-to-bloc contacts.

Chapters 2 and 3 describe the traditional mechanisms used by the Community in its trade with Central-East Europe until 1988–89, including quantitative restrictions, sectoral trade agreements, bilateral cooperation agreements between the EC member states and individual Central-East European countries, and EC anti-dumping machinery. Chapter 4 deals with measures applied by all Western countries in their East–West trade which are decided in a wider fora than the EC, namely the Cocom, and the OECD export credit consensus. Indication is given of how all these measures are being adjusted in the light of changes in Central-East Europe.

Chapters 5 and 6 analyse recent trade developments between the Community and Central-East Europe, relying mainly on Western statistics in view of the difficulties described above. The chapters address the question of how East–West trade in Europe has been affected by Western measures such as the creation and successive enlargements of the EC; the Community's system of trade preferences and the Common Agricultural Policy (CAP). Various authors have argued that Western trade measures had little impact on trade with CMEA countries because the trade performance of these countries was decided mainly by internal factors. One of the difficulties with this hypothesis is that it is tricky to find evidence for or against it. Trade flows are the outcome of a number of factors and it is difficult to establish the relative importance of each, the more so the higher the level of aggregation of the trade flow considered. The analysis here draws on customs union theory and recent models of CAP effects on world prices and trade. The results given in the literature generally appear rather more rigorous for agriculture, which is probably largely explained by the fact that the research is limited to a single sector and to relatively (with the emphasis on that word) more homogeneous products.

The second part of the book deals with the changes in Central-East Europe and their implications for trade and economic relations with the European Community. Chapter 7 briefly reviews the economic transformation in process, from Poland's 'big-bang', to the more gradual change in Hungary. In addition to political change, the economic transformation of these countries entails the triple task of domestic and external stabilisation; microeconomic restructuring and privatisation; and the creation of new social safety nets. The contribution of Western aid measures to this transformation process is described and assessed in Chapter 8.

The 1988 Joint Declaration between the EC and the CMEA was followed by bilateral trade and cooperation agreements between the Community and all the Central-East European countries. Association agreements with certain of the smaller Central-East European countries sufficiently advanced in economic and political reform are to follow, while EC membership is an ultimate possibility in a few cases. Hungary has announced a target date for membership of 1995. These tightening links are described in Chapter 9.

The architecture of Europe is changing, and three main types of development or proposal can be distinguished. The first are related to the deepening and widening processes which are transforming the Community. Secondly there are the initiatives to construct a 'European Confederation' or 'Common European House', possibly building on European organisations such as the Council of Europe, or the CSCE (Conference for Security and Cooperation in Europe) with its thirty-five members, including the United States and Soviet Union. Finally, faced with the virtual collapse of the CMEA, there have been a number of proposals for new, smaller integration units among Central-East European countries, one or two of which have actually materialised. Chapter 10 outlines all these new developments and attempts to identify their aims and chances of success.

The economic transformation process is being brought about by the combined efforts of four parties, namely the government and private sectors in both the West and Central-East Europe. One of the main forms taken by private (and sometimes public) initiatives is that of East–West joint ventures. The number of foreign investment projects in Central-East Europe (excluding East Germany) rose from 562 in 1989 to 5070 by June 1990 when there were a further 1500 projects in the German Democratic Republic(17). The Eastern partner often envisaged joint ventures as a means of obtaining technology and know-how, while for the Western partner they offered the prospect of market access and possibly also the opportunity of benefiting from the relatively cheap, well-educated Central-East European labour. Chapter 11 presents statistics about these joint ventures and considers their prospects.

Chapter 12 deals with the implications of German unification for the Community, including the applications of EC measures in the ex-German Democratic Republic; repercussions for the EC Budget; and possible changes in the timetable for admitting further members into the

Community. It is still too early to assess the consequences for EC economic and monetary or political union, though a first reaction has been to strengthen the commitment to integration as a means of ensuring that a united Germany is firmly rooted in Western Europe. ,

Finally a concluding chapter draws the findings of the earlier chapters together and considers the prospects for trade and the possible architecture of a new Europe.

Notes

1. The term 'Eastern Europe', was generally used when that area could be considered as a 'bloc', but it is more correct to describe countries such as Poland, Hungary, the German Democratic Republic and Czechoslovakia as being in 'Central', or 'Central-East Europe' which explains the choice of term generally used here.

    The discussion here relates to the Soviet Union, the German Democratic Republic and the other smaller Central-East European countries (Bulgaria, Czechoslovakia, Romania, Hungary and Poland), with Yugoslavia and Albania generally being excluded.

    For many years the degree of economic reform adopted in Yugoslavia warranted its separate treatment, while its current economic crisis somewhat undermines its claim to be treated as a model for the transformation of other Central-East European countries. Until recently, the European Community (EC) treated Yugoslavia as a Mediterranean country, though, increasingly, as the treatment of Central-East Europe is becoming more generous, Yugoslavia is being included in that category.

    From June 1990 there were indications of change in Albania, with demonstrations and many of the Albanians seeking shelter in foreign embassies being allowed to leave. In December it was announced that political pluralism was to be introduced and, though sufficient transformation had not been achieved, Albania became eligible for the various EC trade and aid measures towards Central-East Europe from mid-1991. None the less, the autarchic policy pursued for many years has meant that trade and economic relations between Albania and the EC and its member states have generally been minimal.

2. Founded by the Treaty of Rome in 1958, the European Community consisted of six members (Belgium, France, the Federal Republic of Germany, Italy, Luxemburg and the Netherlands) up until 1973; of nine members (with the addition of Denmark, Ireland and the United Kingdom) from 1973 to 1981; ten (including Greece) from 1981 to 1985 and twelve (with the inclusion of Spain and Portugal) since 1986.

3. Leading Leontief to describe the system as one of input/input, as reported in Nuti (1990d).

4. Reported in Kaser (1990).

5. House of Commons (1989).

6. By way of shorthand, 'CMEA' or Council of Mutual Economic Assistance is also sometimes used in this book, despite the demise of that organisation in June 1991. The CMEA is also known as Comecon, though this term was generally avoided in Central-East Europe as it is reminiscent of the Cold

War era, being associated with Comintern and Cominform, and because the element of 'assistance' is left out (Nuti 1989).

Only seven of the European members of the CMEA are considered here. The non-European members of the CMEA (Mongolia, Cuba and Vietnam) are excluded from the discussion, as are those countries having only observer status (Angola, Laos, Ethiopia, and North Korea), and Yugoslavia, which only particpates in CMEA activities with regards to certain sectors.

7. ECE figures.
8. These figures are taken from Gati (1990), p. 108.
9. As reported in Åslund (1989), p. 15. The Western observers he refers to are Alec Nove and Michael Ellman.
10. *The Economist*, 6 October 1990.
11. These statistics are taken from Daviddi (1990a and b).
12. These figures are taken from Åslund (1989), p. 15. The main difference between Net Material Product and GNP is that the former does not include services.
13. *The Economist*, 11 August 1990 and 17 November 1990.
14. UN ECE (1989), p. 122.
15. For a more detailed discussion of this question see Kaser (1990) and Segrè (1990).
16. UN ECE (1989).
17. ECE estimates.

PART 1
Relations between the EC and Central-East Europe before 1988–89

1

The Historical background

1.1 Introduction

The current phase in relations between the Community and individual
Central-East European countries dates from June 1988 when a Joint
Declaration was signed between the EC and CMEA(1) which announced the opening of official relations between the two blocs, and
their intention to cooperate in those areas falling within their competence and that are of mutual interest. The process leading to this recognition had taken over twenty-five years and had been characterised by a
series of fits and starts. Just how much ground has been covered is
evident when the Soviet descriptions of the EC in the late 1950s as the
'economic arm of NATO' and 'an organ of West European monopoly
capitalism doomed to inevitable destruction because of its internal contradictions'(2) are borne in mind.

The changed situation in 1988 was the outcome of a process in which
the Central-East European countries gradually gave in to the EC on one
point after another, where previously there had been differences of
opinion. This growing willingness to accept the EC position reflects the
shift in balance of power between the two blocs, a shift which accelerated from the mid-1980s (as will be shown in Chapter 9).

From its creation in 1958 the Community had insisted that the CMEA
was a weaker organisation, pointing to the characteristics and competences of the CMEA to justify its claim. This chapter will therefore begin
with a description of the CMEA, before giving a brief account(3) of the
evolution of relations between the two blocs in order to illustrate how
the EC claim was eventually vindicated. This account will follow the
literature in dividing the relations between the two blocs into three

phases. The first covers the period up to 1972 and was characterised by non-recognition; the second covers the 1972–80 period and was marked by failed attempts at rapprochement; while the process leading to the Joint Declaration of 1988 and beyond dates from about 1983.

1.2   The CMEA

The CMEA was founded in 1949, mainly as a political response to the Marshall Plan, but it only really became active after the signing of the Treaty of Rome, establishing the EC, in 1957. In 1962 Krushchev proposed the establishment of a central planning authority and the endowment of the CMEA with certain supranational powers, but this was contested by several of the smaller Central-East European countries, especially Romania, who feared the reduced national independence implied by the measures. In 1971 the Programme for Further Intensification and Improvement of Cooperation and the Development of Socialist Economic Integration of the CMEA countries was introduced. This set out the guidelines for the integration of the CMEA countries over the following two decades, but in the event only some coordination was achieved, and not the extent of integration envisaged by the Programme.

The introduction of the 1971 Programme coincided with the ending of the transitional period for establishing the EC. This suggests a frequently voiced conclusion(4), namely that integration in the East was often a response or reaction to initiatives to speed up the integration process in Western Europe.

Following van Brabant(5), integration can be defined as 'a process aimed at levelling up of differences in relative scarcities of goods and services by the conscious elimination of barriers to trade and other forms of interaction between at least two different states'. This aim of reducing differences in relative scarcities emerges from an analysis of CMEA policy statements, even though before 1969 the term 'integration' had a pejorative tone implying a new form of capitalist exploitation which was thus only applied to Western efforts.

As an extensive literature discusses, integration in East and West takes very different forms. Up until the recent transformation process the following three main features lent CMEA integration its unique character(6):

1.   Integration was chiefly concerned with the coordination of central plans, especially on matters of trade, as well as the setting up of certain common projects or joint ventures.
2.   The international Socialist division of labour required that inte-

gration be of an infrasectoral rather than sectoral nature to avoid the capitalist tendency towards polarisation between industrialised countries and those producing raw materials.

3. *de facto* Soviet hegemony implied a certain degree of political integration.

Even before the mid-1980s the commitment to integration within the CMEA was less than that of the Community. Right from its early days the EC had a number of supranational characteristics, with its Common Commercial Policy, Common Agricultural Policy, and power to issue Regulations which are directly applicable in member states (in the sense that they do not need to be transformed into national laws). In contrast, there has been no transfer of sovereignty to the CMEA from its member states. As the 1971 Comprehensive Programme states (chapter 1, section 1, paragraph 1):

> Socialist economic integration is conducted on a purely voluntary basis, is not accompanied by the creation of any supranational organisations and does not affect internal planning problems or the financial and accounting activities of organisations.

According to Article IV of the CMEA Charter:

> All recommendations and decisions of the Council shall be adopted only with the consent of the interested member countries of the Council, each country having the right to declare its interest in any question considered in the Council.

This would seem to confirm the view that in its functions and membership the CMEA was far more like the OECD (Organisation for Economic Cooperation and Development) than the EC(7).

The CMEA concluded various agreements such as the cooperation agreements with Yugoslavia (1964), Finland (1973), Iraq (1975), Mexico (1975), Nicaragua (1982) and Mozambique (1985). However, international agreements signed by the CMEA were not automatically binding on CMEA member states, and could not be imposed on them by the CMEA. In effect, the competence to conclude and implement such agreements rests with the CMEA member states, and the CMEA countries appear to have guarded these rights jealously. The outcome is that while the CMEA could have benefited by all the rights that flow from being an international organisation, it was not bound by the concomitant duties(8).

Further differences between the CMEA and the EC arose with regard to their respective memberships. The CMEA included three non-European countries (Cuba, Mongolia, and Vietnam) and there is the obvious difference that the Soviet Union was a member of one of the blocs while the United States was not, which has influenced the way in which relations between the two blocs have developed.

1.3   Relations between the two blocs up until 1988

The first period in relations between the two blocs lasted until about 1972, and was characterised by CMEA hostility towards the EC and a belief that the EC was a temporary phenomenon inevitably doomed to failure because of its internal capitalistic contradictions, so that the best policy was simply to ignore its existence. The ideological justification for this attitude was presented in the seventeen theses on the Common Market published in the journal *Communist* in 1957. Anti-EC propaganda was rife and, far from recognising the Community, the CMEA countries declared their non-recognition and attempted to block EC participation in international organisations and conventions. The first declarations of this type were made by the Soviet Union, Hungary and Poland in the context of the 1968 International Sugar Agreement(9). In 1963 the Soviet Foreign Minister even refused to accept an EC document given to him by the Dutch Ambassador in Moscow. Occasionally, as in 1962 with the thirty-two theses on imperialist integration in Western Europe and Krushchev's speech on 'vital questions of the development of the world socialist system', there was a dawning awareness that the EC seemed capable of surviving as an economic and political reality, though probably the main purpose of these speeches was to encourage closer integration within the CMEA(10).

The second phase in the evolution of EC–CMEA relations dates from Brezhnev's 1972 speech which not only recognised the reality of the Common Market but also opened the way for official contacts between EC and CMEA officials from the summer of 1973. During this phase there were repeated contacts and initiatives to establish relations between the two blocs, all of which met with failure because of set positions on each side. Negotiations were eventually broken off by mutual consent in 1980, which marks the end of this phase.

What brought about this changed policy of the CMEA from 1972, with a willingness to at least try and establish relations with the Community? On the political side it was the era of détente, and preparations were being made for the Conference on Security and Cooperation in Europe (CSCE), so the more open CMEA attitude towards the EC can be interpreted as part of a wider improvement in East–West relations. On the economic side it became impossible to ignore the fact that EC policies, and especially the Common Agricultural Policy, were not only taking effect but were also having repercussions on Central-East European countries. Attacks continued to be made on the EC but it was evident that some working arrangement would have to be found. In addition, the way in which the CMEA proposed to establish links with the Community suggests that this was regarded as a means of strengthening the internal cohesion and integration process of the Eastern bloc.

After approaches first to the governments of the member states holding the EC Presidency in 1973, and then to the EC Commission in 1974, in 1976 the CMEA proposed a framework agreement between the CMEA and its member states and the EC and its member states. This involvement of CMEA member states was a means of getting around the problem of CMEA competences in the matter of international treaties. In the proposed agreement the principles regulating trade between the two blocs were set out, including the insertion of a Most Favoured Nation (MFN) clause, the aim being to reduce obstacles to trade and the granting of trade preferences, and in this way it was hoped that only minor 'particular concrete questions' would be left to bilateral agreements involving the EC and CMEA member states. The framework agreement proposed by the CMEA also included clauses relating to economic, scientific and technological cooperation.

Right from these early initiatives the CMEA insisted that its relations with the EC should be on a bloc-to-bloc basis and that dealings directly between the EC and individual Central-East European countries were to be of secondary importance. This aim can be explained by the dominant position of the Soviet Union within the CMEA and its desire to appear as an equal bargaining partner vis-à-vis the industrially more powerful EC(11).

The CMEA proposal was unacceptable to the EC, as was evident from the Community's counterdraft for an agreement later in 1976. The EC wanted relations between the two blocs to be restricted to general areas such as the exchange of economic information, transport and environmental questions. According to the EC, its member states could not be party to a framework agreement along the lines proposed by the CMEA because this ran counter to Article 113 of the Treaty of Rome. Instead, the Community wanted to give priority to bilateral trade agreements with individual Central-East European States following the transfer of authority for trade matters to Brussels from January 1975.

The EC explained its reluctance to a more extensive framework agreement with the CMEA in terms of the different nature of the two organisations. The EC stressed the intergovernmental rather than supranational character of the CMEA, pointing out that, unlike the EC, the CMEA neither had the power to pursue a common commercial policy nor the legal authority to impose implementation of an agreement on its members(12).

The EC maintained that direct links with the smaller Central-East European countries were preferable in order to take into account the specific characteristics of each country (its level of indebtedness, whether or not it is a member of GATT (General Agreement on Trade and Tariffs), its economic performance, and so on). The Community also feared that bloc-to-bloc dealings would imply Soviet involvement in its relations with the smaller Central-East European countries and would strengthen the bonds between the Soviet Union and its neighbours since that might aid the creation of a counter-vailing power capable of thwarting its own aims in Central-East Europe(13).

Even during this second phase of relations between the two blocs, not only was mutual recognition not reached, but Soviet and Central-East European declarations of non-recognition of the EC continued. In 1974 the Soviet Union succeeded in blocking EC accession to the Convention on the Protection of the Marine Environment in the Baltic Sea Area. During the UNCTAD (United Nations Conference on Trade and Development) negotiations on the Common Fund for commodities, the Soviet Union resisted EC membership of the Common Fund, though ultimately the EC was allowed to contribute capital, but not to vote on decisions that the Fund might take(14).

By the 1980s CMEA attitudes to the EC were mellowing. In the 1982 Protocol to allow EC access to the Convention on Fishing and Conservation of Living Resources in the Baltic Sea and the Belts, only the Soviet Union had doubts, and these were overcome when the member states threatened to withdraw(15). In 1985 there was no opposition to EC participation in the Convention on the Protection of the Ozone Layer.

In the absence of recognition up until 1988, various *ad hoc* arrangements emerged. After the transfer of authority for trade matters to the EC level from 1975 the Central-East European countries and EC member states continued their bilateral relations by transforming their previous trade agreements into cooperation agreements (as will be discussed in Chapter 2).

Although official CMEA trade policy was against bilateral agreements(16), individual East European countries did sign a number of sectoral agreements with the EC for sectors which were particularly sensitive for the Eastern partner. These implied a certain *de facto* recognition as Lysén (1987, p. 96) argues:

> It must be illogical not to consider the fact of entering into contractual
> relations with a non-recognised organisation – giving rise to rights and
> obligations between the parties – to amount to an implied recognition of
> that organisation's international legal personality and powers pertaining to
> the agreement.

Furthermore, non-recognition did not stop various smaller CMEA members having as active and frequent dealings with the Community as did many countries which have missions accredited to the EC(17).

Though it is difficult to define a precise date, the third phase of relations between the two blocs dates from roughly 1983 and is characterised by a more open, pragmatic CMEA attitude towards the EC. From 1983 Hungary and Czechoslovakia began discussions with the EC aimed at extending their trade links beyond existing sectoral agreements, and there were indications from the CMEA that it wished to resume the dialogue abandoned in 1980. In June 1983 a communiqué at the CMEA Summit Meeting in Moscow announced the willingness of CMEA members to sign an 'appropriate' agreement between the CMEA and EC in order to develop the economic and trade relations already existing between members of the two blocs. During a visit of the then EC President, Craxi, to Moscow in May 1985, Gorbachev announced that it was time to initiate relations with the EC, and to search for a 'common language' insofar as the EC countries act as a 'political entity'(18). Later in 1985 the Secretary of the CMEA sent a letter to the President of the Commission proposing the negotiation of a document of a general nature between the two blocs, such as a mutual declaration of official recognition. The CMEA had gone a long way towards meeting the EC objections to the 1976 framework agreement.

A delay then occurred as the Community wished to establish the principle of the 'parallel approach', by which bilateral relations between the EC and CMEA member states could be developed simultaneously with relations between the two blocs. This was accepted by the CMEA in 1986.

A further stalemate then arose over the geographical application of the Joint Declaration. All EC agreements with third countries contain a territorial clause establishing that the agreement holds for all territories in which the Treaty of Rome is applied. The Treaty contains special provisions for West Berlin, thus including a territorial clause in an agreement implied that West Berlin formed part of the Community. This created problems for CMEA countries because of the Four-Power Agreement, and, for example, Soviet refusal to accept a territorial clause meant that the fisheries agreement negotiated in 1977 was never concluded. Although territorial clauses had been included in certain sectoral agreements, the CMEA at first maintained that this would not be possible in the case of the Joint Declaration because of its general rather than specific nature and because no time limit was involved. Ultimately, when it became evident that the Community was not prepared to give way on this point the CMEA accepted the 'Hungarian Formula' used for the earlier sectoral agreements. This entailed including a territorial clause in the agreement without specifically mentioning West Berlin by name, and then proceeding to an exchange of letters between the parties, with the CMEA reasserting the validity of the Four-Power Agreement, and the Community acknowledging receipt of the letter.

1.4   The reasons for the change in CMEA attitude

In the past, CMEA attitudes to foreign policy have generally been similar, if not indistinguishable, from those of the Soviet Union. Why then did the Soviet Union abandon its long-standing insistence on bloc-to-bloc relations and accept the EC view that there should be bilateral dealings between the Community and individual Central-East European states?

Structural aspects of the trade between the EC and individual Central-East European countries largely explain the impasse in negotiations up until 1988. There is an asymmetry in the importance of East–West trade for the EC and the CMEA, with the CMEA generally accounting for only 6–7% of EC trade (roughly the same fraction as countries such as Sweden or Switzerland), while the EC accounted for roughly 20% of CMEA trade.

Trade with the Community is far more important for the smaller Central-East European countries than for the Soviet Union, and the agricultural exporters in particular (Hungary, Poland, Bulgaria and Romania) were in favour of normalisation. In contrast the main Soviet exports are oil, gas and raw materials which were little affected by tariffs or quotas, and for which alternative markets could be found. In consequence the economic interest was not sufficient to overcome the Soviet Union's political and ideological objections to recognition of the EC, while on the other hand the Community also had little incentive to make concessions.

The Community attitude was also influenced by the fact that after 1973 a trade surplus emerged with the Central-East European countries, and the high level of hard-currency debt of certain of these countries created uncertainty about exporting to them(19). From 1980 this surplus was transformed into a deficit.

The change in Soviet (and hence CMEA) attitude is to be explained by economic factors and by a new pragmatism in international relations. Economic factors include the stagnation of CMEA countries during the 1980s; the slump in EC–CMEA trade over the 1984–87 period; the deterioration in Soviet terms of trade from 1986; and reaction to the renewed integration process of the EC and especially the proposed completion of the Single European Market from 1993(20). As will be shown in Chapter 9, the Central-East European countries were concerned, in particular, that changes in the EC system of quotas and of product specifications from 1993 might affect their exports to the

Community, thus they desired closer links to discuss ways in which the damage would be limited and possible gains could be shared.

Political factors also played a role in bringing about the changed CMEA attitude to the Community. Though the initial impetus for the change predates Gorbachev's coming to power (he became Secretary General of the Communist Party of the Soviet Union in March 1985), the new attitude bears the stamp of perestroika. In particular, there was the realisation that trade would have to be redirected away from loss-making areas such as the developing areas and the CMEA, towards developed countries which could offer it much-needed technology and know-how(21).

The European opposition to the 1981 US embargo also softened Soviet attitudes to the Community(22). Better relations with the EC were probably regarded as a means of reducing the risk of Western sanctions on exports of grain and technology to Central-East Europe and of encouraging a more moderate stand with regard to the Cocom lists.

The CMEA move may to some extent also have represented a recognition of the status quo, and a rather belated attempt to regain some control over the individual initiatives taken by various smaller Central-East European states. As will be discussed in Chapter 2, in 1980 Romania signed what is effectively a fully fledged trade agreement, and from the early 1980s other smaller CMEA countries had been negotiating similar arrangements with the Community. The Soviet Union was extremely worried about these 'autonomist' initiatives(23). Not only did it fear isolation, but the Soviet Union also wanted to avoid being left behind its smaller Central-East European neighbours in obtaining the economic benefits to be had from closer links with the Community.

Finally, it seems likely that to increase its chances of joining GATT the Soviet Union attempted closer links with the EC and the United States to overcome their opposition(24).

1.5 Conclusion

The 1988 declaration is important as a symbol, marking the end of one long process (the path to mutual official recognition between the two blocs) and the beginning of another. It reflects the relaxing of tension, and the 'normalisation' of relations between the two blocs. Normalisation is here taken to mean the possibility of discussing problems; the negotiation of agreements if necessary; the end of attempts to hinder EC participation in international organisations; and the establishment of formal relations, which generally entails accrediting diplomatic missions(25).

As a result of normalisation, the way was open for an explosion of links at all levels and in various forms between the Community and Central–East Europe. This process of rapprôchement seems to have gathered its own accelerating momentum. Although the Joint Declaration envisaged cooperation at bloc-to-bloc level, this was soon overshadowed by the importance of emerging bilateral relations and especially the trade and cooperation agreements, association agreements and possible membership of the EC on the part of some of the smaller Central-East European countries. The relaxing of tension eased the path for German unification and enabled the EC to play a major role in organising and coordinating Western measures to aid the transformation process in Central-East Europe. In this accelerating process the Joint Declaration is perhaps coming to be seen simply as one of a series of milestones, but it retains its significance as one of the first, opening the way for later measures.

Notes

1. In the presentation here, unless specifically stated that the EC refers to the present twelve members (EC(12)), the statistics reflect the changing membership of the Community (see Note 2 of the Introduction). Internal German trade (i.e. that between the German Democratic Republic and the Federal Republic of Germany) is not included in the statistics of trade between the two blocs.
2. See Marsh (1978), p. 26.
3. For a more complete account see Bel (1988); Chapman (1986); Chiusano (1985); Friessen (1976); European Parliament Document 1–531 (1982); Marsh (1978); Maslen (1986); Matejka (1988); Riishoj (1985); Tosi (1987); Verny (1988); and Wilczyński (1980), UN Doc. ST/LEG/SER.D/3, pp. 338–9.
4. Lysén (1987); Matejka (1988).
5. Van Brabant (1989), p. xxi.
6. These three categories were suggested by Maciejewski and Nuti (1985).
7. Pinder (1986), pp. 11–12.
8. Cutler (1987), p. 266.
9. Groux and Manin (1984), p. 20.
10. See Marsh (1978), p. 27.
11. Marsh (1978), p. 63.
12. The EC objections are also voiced in the Irmer Report of the European Parliament (1982), which states:

    The degree of integration and the powers of Comecon for instance cannot be compared with those of the Community; the EC has exclusive powers to pursue a common commercial policy whereas Comecon has no such powers. Admittedly, Comecon as an institution may conclude agreements but it has no legal powers whatsoever to impose the implementation of such an agreement on its members.
13. Peter Marsh (1978), p. 56.
14. Cutler (1987), p. 265.

15. Lysén (1987), p. 103.
16. Cutler (1987), p. 263.
17. John Maslen (1983), p. 334.
18. As described in European Report No. 1137 of 5 June 1985.
19. For an account of factors contributing to the impasse in relations between the two blocs for so long see Palankai (1990).
20. For an account of these factors see Nuti (1988).
21. Matejka (1988), p. 15.
22. Verny (1988), p. 17.
23. T. Schreiber (1985).
24. Matejka (1988), p. 15.
25. The Joint Declaration did not itself involve setting up diplomatic missions between the two blocs, but in the summer that followed, all the Central-East European countries except Romania (which subsequently did so) requested to set up diplomatic missions with the EC. In June 1990 the Community announced that it intended to set up a mission in Hungary, followed by Poland and other Central-East European countries.

2
The mechanisms used by the EC in East–West trade until 1988

2.1   Introduction

The EC used various mechanisms such as quotas, selective safeguards, sectoral agreements and cooperation agreements in its trade with Central-Europe up until 1988, all of which have been substantially modified since then. These modifications reflect fundamental changes in economic relations in Europe; and a description of the instruments used by the EC up until 1988 aids an understanding of the significance of what has happened subsequently.

Certain of the measures used by the EC, such as quotas and selective safeguards, were designed to meet the specific difficulties of trade with non-market economies. Depending on the degree of transformation reached in the various Central-East European countries, from 1988 onwards these instruments are being altered or eliminated. Because the form taken by these mechanisms is circumscribed by the GATT (General Agreement on Trade and Tariffs), this chapter will begin with a description of GATT arrangements to accommodate trade with non-market economies.

The smaller Central-East European countries have frequently accused the EC of protectionism, and in particular they have argued that the creation and successive enlargements of the Community have had adverse implications on their own exports in sectors such as agriculture, steel and textiles. As a result all these countries signed agreements covering these sectors with the Community despite the problem of political recognition. The limited nature of the concessions granted in these agreements, and the fact that the Community used more quotas in its trade with the CMEA than any other group of countries led the Central-

East European countries to claim that they occupied a low position in the EC's 'hierarchy' of preferences.

The question of EC protectionism will be taken up in more detail in Chapters 5 and 6, but here there will be a brief analysis of the instruments used by the EC on its imports of manufactured products from Central-East Europe(1) which form the basis of many of these accusations. Since 1988 the EC has partly responded to these claims by improving market access (for example by offering more favourable terms in sectoral agreements and by reducing or abolishing quantitative restrictions on imports from Central-East Europe) as part of its programme to encourage the transformation process in Central-East Europe.

The legal justification for EC protectionist measures is to be found in the Treaty of Rome and in its subsequent interpretation. Articles 110–116 of the Treaty set out the goals of the common external commercial policy of the EC and the procedures for its implementation, but ambiguities in the text mean that there is a certain leeway for interpretation. The overall impression of these objectives is what Pelkmans (1984, p. 221) describes as a 'conditional but determined readiness to lower external Community protection and liberalise world trade at large'. However, the conditionality has been given rather broad interpretation with, for example, the European Court arguing in 1979 that the Treaty 'does not form a barrier to the possibility of developing a commercial policy aimed at regulation of the world market for certain products'(2). This is virtually a blank cheque for the use of non-tariff barriers in some sectors.

At the same time, at least up until the late 1980s, EC trade policy appeared to be rather piecemeal and incoherent. A wide variety of measures were adopted, some by the EC member states, and others at the EC level, with no clear logic behind the division of authority. The multitiered system of preferences which was used for trade with third countries distinguished not only between major regional groupings of countries but also within them. As a result, although in general the Central-East European countries seemed justified in claiming that they occupied a low position in the hierarchy of EC preferences, this was not true of the German Democratic Republic and/or certain Central-East European textile and clothing imports, access to EC markets was often easier than for LDC (less developed countries) suppliers(3).

The main reason for the incoherence of EC trade policy was the relatively slow pace of European integration during the 1970s and early-1980s. In particular, the EC member states were reluctant to transfer authority for trade and other matters to the Community level. This took the form of delaying implementation of the Common Commercial Policy, challenging the Community's interpretation of the Treaty in certain cases, and devising means to retain *de facto* responsibility for commercial matters in others. For example, Community competence to carry out an investigation before implementing safeguard measures was only established in 1982; the application of the Common Commercial Policy in trade with Central-East Europe was delayed from 1970 to 1973 and again to 1975; and responsibility for export credits still remains a matter of dispute. When the Community assumed exclusive responsibility for trade agreements in 1975, the EC member states introduced bilateral cooperation agreements with Central-East European countries which acted as trade agreements to all intents and purposes. Harmonisation of trade measures often proceeded at a slow pace, as was evident in the case of quantitative restrictions, while in some cases the incentive to standardise measures came mainly from extra-EC sources such as the OECD for export credit measures, or the GATT for introduction of a common anti-dumping code. As will be explained in Chapter 9, only in the mid-1980s did the Community regain impetus in its integration process.

The EC decision-making process also contributed to the lack of coherence in trade policy. In order to reach common positions mutual bargaining is necessary and compromises must be reached. For example, the Treaty specifies that trade agreements are decided by the Council on recommendation from the Commission, and during this process there are numerous opportunities for special interests to exert pressure. Approaches such as public choice or regulation theory would seem to offer more appropriate instruments for explaining these phenomena(4), as many decisions concerning the common commercial policy would appear irrational by the single actor model.

Following an account of the GATT framework as applied to non-market economies, this chapter describes the introduction of the Common Commercial Policy in trade with Central-East Europe, and the quantitative restrictions, sectoral agreements, and bilateral cooperation agreements adopted by the EC in trade with the CMEA up until 1988.

2.2   The GATT

The aim of the GATT is to work towards free international trade, especially through a reduction in tariffs. When a country joins the GATT it receives the benefits of trade concessions already negotiated within that framework on the basis of the MFN (Most Favoured Nation) principle. In return the country has to offer 'equivalent' concessions.

In 1986 at Punta del Este the GATT members launched the Uruguay Round negotiations. This was the eighth round of trade negotiations carried out by the GATT, and by far the most ambitious. In addition to reductions in tariffs and non-tariff barriers, the aim of the Uruguay

Round was to extend fair trade disciplines and to liberalise trade in sectors such as agriculture, textiles, services and natural-resource-based products, which had been largely exempt from GATT rules and regulations. Rules on intellectual property and foreign investment were to be drawn up, while certain GATT articles and codes were to be redrafted in order to improve dispute procedures and enable better surveillance of members' trade policies. Some 108 countries (including a number of less-developed countries hoping for membership) participated in the negotiations.

Czechoslovakia was a founder member of the GATT and did not have a special protocol of accession when it signed the GATT agreement in January 1948. It did, however, remain a 'sleeping member' of GATT, not participating in trade rounds, nor requesting fulfilment of other members' obligations(5). Poland (1967), Romania (1971), and Hungary (1973) are members, though all three had special protocols to account for what at the time was considered their non-market status. Bulgaria has had observer status since 1967, and is negotiating accession. The Soviet Union gained observer status in May 1990 and the question of whether it should become a full member has been the subject of heated debate(6). Poland has been able to re-negotiate its GATT membership to reflect its move towards a market-orientated economy, and other smaller Central-East European countries would like to do the same. The GATT does not provide a clear definition for distinguishing between market and non-market (state-trading) economies. The existence of this 'grey area' has been the source of much contention among certain Central-East European countries who have maintained that as a result it was not clear what reforms they would have to introduce to classify as market-orientated economies.

As an extensive literature shows(7), the GATT system was essentially conceived for market-orientated economies, and many of the main principles which GATT members are supposed to observe lose their meaning when applied to trade with non-market economies. This is especially true with regard to the principles of *tariff reductions, reciprocity* and *non-discrimination*.

Tariff concessions are only effective as an instrument of trade liberalisation if they are reflected in the prices at which imports are sold, and this is not necessarily the case in a system where prices are fixed administratively. Moreover, neither Poland nor Romania had import tariffs when they joined(8), so it was evident that some other provision would have to be found.

Reciprocity implies that the concessions made by the parties involved should be more or less balanced. Where market economies are concerned this generally involves matching tariff reduction with tariff reduction. As tariff reductions have little meaning in the context of non-market economies, alternative concessions have to be found and, as will be shown, these are 'difficult to estimate *ex ante* and to monitor *ex post*'(9).

Non-discrimination, or the granting of MFN status, becomes almost impossible to monitor in a system where decisions concerning import levels are taken as administrative measures by state-trading associations having a monopoly.

To meet these problems, GATT requires that non-market economies make alternative concessions to reciprocate the benefits they receive under the MFN clause. The Polish protocol of accession to GATT contained a commitment to increase Polish imports from GATT members at an annual rate of 7%. In the Romanian protocol of accession there was a commitment to 'develop and diversify' its trade as well as a 'firm intention' to increase Romanian imports from GATT members as a whole at a rate not slower than the overall growth of imports provided for in its five-year plans. When Hungary joined in 1973 it stressed the shortcomings of the import commitment approach, argued that market forces were already playing a role in its economy, and demonstrated that it had a functioning tariff system, so it became a GATT member on the basis of tariff concessions. However, in the working-party session on its protocol, Hungary did undertake to increase its imports from GATT members.

However, each of these formulae to guarantee a certain level of market access to centrally planned economies suffers from difficulties(10). In the case of Poland, because growth in imports was based on the preceding year's trade, there was a disincentive to increase imports beyond the target amount. Moreover, the commitment was fixed in current prices and a particular currency, so it was liable to be affected by inflation and exchange-rate changes. Both the Romanian and Hungarian commitments suffer from vagueness. In addition, the Romanian commitment is based on the provisions of the plan, so it could be the subject of manipulation.

There are two GATT provisions aimed at meeting the fear that non-market economies might flood Western markets with low-priced exports. These are the right to maintain discriminatory quantitative restrictions, and to apply 'selective' safeguard measures on a discriminatory basis where exports from non-market economies threaten to cause injury to domestic producers. As Patterson (1986, p. 191) points out,

> While the market economy prefers discriminatory quantitative restrictions which are justified on the basis of mere risk of market disruption, the non-market economies view the discriminatory quantitative restrictions as a greater evil than selective safeguards because of the formers' potentially far-reaching adverse precedents.

The GATT accession protocols of Poland, Hungary and Romania have permitted the use of quantitative restrictions under certain conditions, provided that the discriminatory element does not increase, and is 'progressively relaxed' (Poland) or 'removed' (Romania and Hungary). There has been considerable controversy as to what this commitment implies and how quickly elimination of quantitative restrictions should take place, as the discussion of the EC experience will show.

De jure, all GATT members are entitled to MFN status. The bilateral trade agreements existing up until 1974 between EC member states and CMEA countries had generally contained MFN clauses relating to tariff matters. Subsequently, as a matter of principle the Community refused to extend these concessions in a blanket fashion to the CMEA as a whole, but in practice MFN status was granted to each of the Central-East European countries individually. For non-GATT members such as the Soviet Union and Bulgaria MFN status was given *de facto*, but not *de jure*, which was largely a question of negotiating tactics since if the status were granted *de jure*, it would no longer be a concession.

2.3   The application of the Common Commercial Policy in trade with East Europe

According to Article 113 of the Treaty of Rome, after the ending of the traditional period the Community was to assume responsibility for matters relating to the Common Commercial Policy:

> particularly in regards to changes in tariff rates, the conclusion of tariff
> and trade agreements, the achievement of uniformity in measures of
> liberalisation, export policy and measures to protect trade such as those to
> be taken in the case of dumping or subsidies.

In the face of opposition from both the EC member states and Central-East European countries the Commission postponed the deadline for introduction of the Common Commercial Policy vis-à-vis state-trading countries from 1970 until 1973 and again until 1975. From that date bilateral trade agreements between EC member states and Central-East European countries expired and the Community set out the broad lines of its future policy in the 1974 'general model for trade agreements' or 'memorandum'. A copy of this memorandum was sent to each of the CMEA countries and contained the following elements(11):

1.   the willingness of the Community to conclude trade agreements with individual CMEA member states;
2.   the reciprocal allocation of the MFN (Most Favoured Nation) clause;

3. the reduction of quotas (except those falling under the Common Agricultural Policy (CAP));
4. *ad hoc* provisions for payments and trade financing;
5. joint committees were to be set up to supervise the agreements.

The Community's offer to sign trade agreements with individual CMEA countries from 1975 was met with silence at the time (apart from China and, later, Romania) owing to the political recognition problems. The Community announced that in the absence of such trade agreements, decisions would be taken unilaterally and would not be subject to negotiation; this is the basis of the so-called autonomous trade policy. In essence, this policy relates to the quantitative restrictions on imports from Central-East European countries.

2.4   The autonomous trade policy

As Peter Marsh (1978, p. 50) describes, the autonomous trade policy clearly represented the lowest common denominator in that it simply put a 'Community label on existing national trade legislation'. The bilateral trade agreements between EC member states and Central-East European countries had contained lists of import quotas on sensitive products. Rather than trying to harmonise these restrictions, they were incorporated *en bloc* and virtually unchanged into Community legislation.

These quantitative restrictions are significant on a number of counts. Firstly, as described above, these were permitted by GATT in trade with state-trading countries under certain conditions. These quotas therefore acquired a symbolic value, acting almost like a stigma of still remaining a non-market economy. Not surprisingly, then, reduction or elimination of these quantitative restrictions appears as one of the earliest measures used by the Community to encourage the transformation process in Central-East Europe.

Secondly, the autonomous trade policy represents an example of the weakness of the Community at the time, and of the ability of the EC member states to resist harmonisation or transfer of authority to the EC level. As will be shown, the completion of the Single Market from 1993 would seem to require radical revision of the system of quotas, and this has probably contributed to the willingness of the EC countries to remove quotas in trade with Central-East Europe.

Finally, these quotas formed part of the gamut of protectionist measures used by the EC, so their reduction or elimination from 1988 onwards marks a step in the direction of new and closer trade relations with Central-East Europe. To illustrate how this is the case, and the likely impact of eliminating these quotas, a detailed description of the system is useful.

In accordance with the Common Commercial Policy, the Community is responsible for the lists of restrictions of each of the member states and for the liberalisation lists. When the last national restriction against a particular product is dropped, the Commission adds that product to the liberalisation list and it becomes subject to the surveillance and safeguards procedures for goods coming from GATT members(12). Regulation 3420/83 (amended by 2273/87) sets out the lists of national quotas for imports not liberalised at EC level, as well as the procedure for amendment of these lists. By 1 December of each year the EC Council has to decide on the lists for the following year. For countries having joint committees, these lists are negotiated directly each year in the joint committee meeting, though the annual decision leaves a margin of 20% either way at the discretion of each EC member state concerned. Apart from the annual Council decisions, the Commission (if necessary in consultation with the East European Countries Consultative Committee), can make a number of amendments to the lists(13).

Although since 1988 the liberalisation process has gained a new impetus, even before that date the commitment to liberalisation of these lists set out in the 1974 memorandum was generally met. According to John Maslen (1983, p. 327), the decision usually liberalised the quotas by 1.5–3.5%. As a result of some 7600 Nimexe headings of the Community's common customs tariff, about 1420 were partially or totally under quantitative restrictions in at least one member state in 1985 compared with some 1570 in 1975(14). Italy is the EC country with most quantitative restrictions on trade with East Europe, having 992 restrictions up until 1988, and 500 in 1989. The change in tariff nomenclature introduced in the lists since January 1988 renders recent comparisons extremely difficult, as well as creating a certain amount of practical confusion(15).

Up until the recent measures, the Community maintained more quantitative restrictions in its trade with the CMEA than with any other group of countries. According to the EC Commission, some 3–5% of actual trade between the EC and Central-East Europe was affected by such restrictions, the exact percentage varying according to the product and country in question, but the impact on potential trade, or trade which would take place in the absence of such restrictions is much greater. Many of the restrictions are on textiles (reflecting the operation of the Multifibre Agreement), footware, chemical products, some electronic components, toys, glassware and ceramics, some wooden products, certain agricultural goods and the metallurgy sector, and thus the restrictions, at least in some cases, were of considerable importance to the Central-East European country concerned.

However, the fact that many quotas remained unfilled is often taken as evidence for a widely held view in the West that quantitative restrictions are of greater political than economic significance. As a response to non-recognition, the Community may have wanted to retain the possibility of according less-favourable treatment to Central-East European countries. The right to discriminate is considered an important bargaining counter. During the interviews Western trade officials described these quotas as 'relics of the past' maintained in response to local pressure to preserve employment, and did not consider them to be very important. One official even suggested that Central-East European insistence on this issue was because quotas may act as a scapegoat in cases where low trade levels were in fact due to poor economic performance in the Eastern country.

Because these quantitative restrictions operate at the national level, the problem of re-export to other EC member states arises. According to Article 115 of the Treaty of Rome, as interpreted by Decision 433/87 of the Commission, a member state can apply to the Commission for permission to introduce protective measures, or surveillance of intra-Community imports of these products.

The application of Article 115 is inextricably linked to that of Article 113. Once a common commercial policy with free circulation of products within the Community is established, Article 115 should become redundant. According to the EC Commission, it will not be possible to retain these lists of national import restrictions after 1992. Either imports will have to be liberalised, or, if they are sensitive, Community-wide restrictions will have to be introduced. A problem arises in that applying certain national restrictions across the Community would increase the level of protection and so run counter to GATT principles. Some EC countries, such as the Federal Republic of Germany, the Netherlands and the United Kingdom are pushing for virtual or complete liberalisation by 1992, but others, such as Italy, are concerned for sensitive items such as certain textile or footware products. The Commission is considering the possibility of alternative policies, such as voluntary export restraints, for these products.

2.5   Sectoral trade agreements

The sectoral trade agreements between the Community and Central-East Europe were an early symbol of the growing influence of the EC. Despite the problem of political recognition, economic necessity forced all the smaller Central-East European countries except Albania and the German Democratic Republic (for which such arrangements were often rendered unnecessary by the special German provisions described in Chapter 12) to sign agreements of this type. As Tosi describes (1987,

p. 61), these agreements were essentially 'low profile', and were described as 'technical agreements' to minimise their political significance. Table 2.1 sets out the agreements in various industrial sectors, while those relating to agriculture are presented in more detail in Chapter 6.

As will be illustrated, these agreements are all in sectors in which not only the EC but all industrial countries depart from the GATT principle of non-discrimination (Articles I and XIII), and the GATT mandate of applying tariff rather than non-tariff barriers. The agreements belong to what are often referred to as 'grey area' measures because they violate the spirit if not the letter of GATT. One of the aims of the Uruguay Round is to bring these sectors more effectively under GATT rules and regulations.

Easier market access through improved terms of these agreements constitutes another important element of the EC package to aid the

Table 2.1 Industrial* trade agreements between the EC and CMEA members as of 31 March 1988

CMEA partner	Product	Type of agreement	Duration
Romania	Industrial products[1]	Trade	1981–86
Bulgaria	Textiles	VER	1987–91
Czechoslovakia	Textiles	VER/MFA	1987–91
Hungary	Textiles	VER/MFA	1987–91
Poland	Textiles	VER/MFA	1987–91
Romania	Textiles	VER/MFA	1987–91
GDR	Textiles	Import quota	1987–present
Bulgaria	Steel	ERA – price monitoring system[2]	1979–89
Czechoslovakia	Steel	ERA – price monitoring system	1978–89
Hungary	Steel	VER – price monitoring system	1978–89
Poland	Steel	ERA – price monitoring system	1978–89
Romania	Steel	ERA – price monitoring system	1978–89
Soviet Union	Kraftliner and board	ERA – and minimum prince undertaking	1983–88

Notes:
* The agricultural agreements are presented in Chapter 6.
[1] Excepting steel and textiles.
[2] While price monitoring systems do not imply export restraint, they are operated by means of bilateral consultations during which the admissible level of exports is indicated.

Symbols (see text for further explanation):
ERA – export restraint arrangement.
VER – voluntary export restraint.
MFA – Multi-fibre arrangement.

Source: Harriet Matejka (1990). The table is based on GATT, developments in the trading system October 1987–March 1988, L/6366, 12 August 1988, EC Documentation Service Data Bank.

transformation process in Central-East Europe. Even though the concessions at times appear limited, considerable opposition has been encountered from EC producers.

2.5.1 Agreements and arrangements in the agricultural sector

The first instance of positive integration or policy to be implemented at the EC level was the Common Agricultural Policy, which came into effect from 1967–68. This had immediate repercussions for some of the smaller Central-East European countries which had traditionally exported agricultural products to EC countries, forcing them into a response. All the smaller Central-East European countries except the German Democratic Republic and Albania signed agricultural arrangements with the Community between 1965 and 1980. More recently, export restraint agreements setting quotas for exports of sheep, goatmeat and calves to the EC have been signed with smaller Central-East European countries.

In 1977 the decision of the Community to introduce a Common Fisheries Policy and to claim a 200-mile maritime economic zone led to negotiations with the Soviet Union, the German Democratic Republic and Poland. Although the Soviets played down the significance of this, the Community considered the negotiations an important milestone in the path towards political recognition(16).

2.5.2 Textile agreements

In 1976 Romania signed a textile agreement with the Community which was followed by textile agreements with Poland, Hungary, Bulgaria, Czechoslovakia and China.

The EC applies the MFA (Multifibre Agreement) régime in its textile trade with those Central-East European countries which are GATT members. Bulgaria has an MFA-type agreement, and to all intents and purposes receives MFA treatment. Up until 1990 EC policy towards textile imports from the Soviet Union and the German Democratic Republic was slightly more rigid (for example with regard to quotas and flexibility arrangements) than for the other Central-East European countries.

The first Multifibre Agreement was signed in 1974, though it was predated by the short-term and long-term agreements of the 1960s. Further MFA Agreements followed in 1977, 1981 and 1986, each covering five-year periods.

Following the implementation of MFA I in 1974 there was a delay in working out a common EC position. Imports grew rapidly before the Community had time to evolve Community-wide arrangements with major suppliers. The EC was under additional pressure because of the adjustment towards increased specialisation within the Community(17). These factors, to a large extent, explain the timing and nature of the textile agreements with individual Central-East European countries.

The MFA permits seven industrial countries or groups of countries (that is eighteen countries, considering the EC member states separately) to impose restrictions on imports from over thirty countries, but it also imposes obligations on these industrial countries. In particular, they have to implement structural adjustment policies, and to adhere to the provision of Annex B which specifies base levels, annual growth rates and flexibility of quotas. The annual growth rates of imports subject to restraints are set at not less than 6%, though lower rates are permitted in cases of market disruption. The flexibility provisions allow for carry-over and carry-forward of quotas, and also include a 'swing provision' enabling certain quotas to be exceeded provided they are counterbalanced by other reductions elsewhere.

The number of products covered by the MFA has gradually been extended. Whereas MFA I included textiles and clothing made from wool, man-made fibres, cotton and blends thereof, MFA IV also covered products made from vegetable products and blends of vegetable and silk fibre which compete with textiles made from other fibres.

The concept of market disruption represents the key to understanding how the MFA operates in practice. Market disruption is defined as the occurrence of a substantial increase in imports of specific products from particular sources at prices below those prevailing in the importing country. For there to be market disruption these increases must cause 'serious damage' or actual threat to domestic producers. Market disruption is also defined on a cumulative basis so restraint is possible even when a country's share of imports is very small.

According to Article 4 of the MFA, in cases of market disruption, bilateral agreements are permitted and these agreements may contain departures from the norms set out in Annex B. These departures usually take the form of growth rates lower than 6%, and denial of flexibility under the swing and carry-over provisions.

However, as Sampson (1987) points out, 'market disruption' is usually understood to be a result of low-priced imports rather than the fact of their mere existence as in the case of the MFA. Moreover, he illustrates that there is a great deal of bureaucratic discretion in deciding whether there has been 'serious damage' to domestic producers. Importing industrialised countries have adopted extremely complex systems of product classification, rendering it virtually impossible to identify the industry claimed to be threatened. For instance the EC product classification covers some ninety-nine product categories, which are sub-divided into four groups, the first two of which contain the most sensitive items(18). As a result, importing countries have a virtual blank cheque to introduce bilateral agreements. Under Article 4 of the MFA, the EC has negotiated bilateral agreements with twenty-one developing and six Central-East European countries. It is not surprising that Cline (1987, p. 152) describes the MFA as tending to become 'an arrangement that mattered far less than the implementing bilateral agreements under its aegis'.

In addition to the EC quotas, there are also quotas applying on some textile and clothing products at the level of individual EC member states(19). Reporting in 1984 the UNCTAD found 377 Community quotas (127 of which were on sensitive items) and twenty-eight national quotas applying in individual member states. Given that each of the Community-level quotas is broken down into national subquotas, the total number of quotas faced by the twenty-seven countries with bi-lateral agreements with the EC was over 3000.

As part of the Uruguay Round negotiations, the United States pro-posed that textile trade be brought under GATT regulations. The US countries favour a system of global quotas, but the Community would like to see progressive liberalisation of the MFA by gradually disman-tling existing market access restrictions. A necessary condition of this reform would be the reinforcing of GATT rules and disciplines with regard to safeguards, anti-dumping, counterfeiting and subsidies.

The 1986 agreements between the Community and Poland and Hung-ary were due to expire in 1990. As will be described in Chapter 9, other trade concessions had been given to the two countries, so it was decided to render the treatment of textile imports less anomalous. In February 1990, the EC Commission proposed that imports from Poland would be increased by 20% by value and the rise would apply to twenty or more categories of textiles. For Hungary the increase would be about 13% and apply to some fifteen categories.

A new textile agreement covering the 1990–92 period was also signed with the Soviet Union in 1990. It is a voluntary export restraint agree-ment according to which textile exports to the EC may rise from their 1989 volume of 10,000 tonnes to 48,000 tonnes.

2.5.3   *Steel agreements*

Czechoslovakia and Hungary signed agreements for steel with the Com-munity in 1978, and similar agreements with Bulgaria, Romania and Poland followed.

These agreements have to be interpreted against the background of world steel trade which has been characterised by a spiral of 'rebound' protectionism in which measures imposed by the United States are followed by those of the Community, and so on.

The reasons for the crisis in world steel have been described extensively elsewhere, and include the evolution of production techniques; the emergence of new low-cost, steel-producing countries such as Japan in the 1960s and South Korea and Brazil subsequently; falling transport costs; declining investments in some high steel-consuming industries, and reduced use of steel in some sectors, such as automobile production.

Following the 1967–68 recession, falling prices and rising imports led the United States to introduce the first steel export restraint arrangements in 1968. The 1973 oil crisis led to a sharp drop in the demand for steel, and between 1974 and 1976 EC steel imports from third countries rose from 4.9 to 11 million tonnes, while exports fell from 30.1 to 23.2 million tonnes(20).

Even though EC steel policy is decided within the framework of the European Coal and Steel Community (ECSC) Treaty of 1951, the main mechanisms by which it still operates emerged in response to this crisis. From 1977 minimum prices were introduced for certain steel products, and non-binding 'guidance' prices for others. The Davignon Plan at the end of 1977 extended the number of products falling under both the minimum and guidance price systems and introduced voluntary production quotas for certain products. With regard to imports, EC anti-dumping machinery was strengthened, and bilateral agreements were negotiated with major suppliers. The calculation of anti-dumping duties was facilitated by the introduction of the list of minimum prices for most products covered by the ECSC. Under this procedure temporary anti-dumping duties were introduced for six categories of steel products coming from seven countries, including three in Central-East Europe(21).

Bilateral agreements were signed with the fifteen main suppliers of steel to the Community, who together accounted for 80% of EC steel imports. Among these were the agreements with the smaller Central-East European countries listed above. Under these arrangements quantitative limits on exports were set at 1976 levels, and the exporting country was committed to respect prices which were slightly below the ECSC guidance prices. In return for these agreements, the EC suspended pending anti-dumping actions and agreed not to open new procedures if the arrangements were respected(22).

The bilateral agreements have been renewed annually. Between 1981 and 1984 they entailed a reduction of exports to the EC of 12.5% in relation to the 1980 level, and subsequently of 10%. In 1987 and 1988 there was to be no increase in steel imports from Central-East European countries to the EC, though in 1989 a 3% increase was permitted. In the context of measures to aid the transformation of these countries, in 1990 the quotas were raised by 15%. A fall in EC steel consumption by 3% in 1990 led Community producers to request a 3% reduction in quotas for 1991, but eventually it was decided to leave the import ceilings for Central-East Europe unchanged at 2.657 million tonnes.

For many years the Central-East European countries were unable to meet their import ceilings, and in 1990 for instance only 75% of the quotas were used. To ease this situation, it was agreed that product-specific quotas would be partially replaced by overall import quotas from 1991.

2.6 A comment on export-restraint arrangements

Export-restraint arrangements, such as those described above, between the EC and individual Central-East European countries have been growing in importance as a protectionist 'grey area' measure over the last decade and have been the subject of much controversy.

Voluntary export restraints (VERs), such as the textile agreements described above, entail an export restriction which is imposed unilaterally by the exporting country from the formal point of view, but which in fact is introduced in response to pressure from the government or industry in the importing country. These VERs are essentially bilaterally negotiated agreements and, according to Kostecki (1987, p. 426), 'the claim that they are unilateral rests on a legal nicety'.

Orderly market arrangements (OMAs), such as the sheep and goat-meat arrangements between the EC and individual Central-East European countries, consist of government-to-government arrangements which specify rules with regard to export-supply management, consultation and the monitoring of trade flows. These OMAs can be defined as a subcategory of export restraint arrangements (ERAs). The latter include not only government-to-government OMAs, but also arrangements with the direct participation of industry.

In all these types of arrangement the export restraint involved may entail quotas and/or minimum export prices. A distinction between VERs and ERAs is that the latter explicitly recognise the bilateral nature of the arrangement and elimination or modification of the export restraints requires the consent of both parties.

As a general comment on all these arrangements, though they appear to be an improvement on the autonomous setting of policy, it must be questioned how far they are in fact 'voluntary'. Often, the exporter has only the choice of accepting the demands made by the importing country (or group of countries in this case) or losing its place on that market. As emerges from the discussion above, the threat of EC anti-dumping activities was a major motive for the Central-East European countries' acceptance of steel agreements.

2.7 The Romanian agreements

Interpreting the acceptability of sectoral agreements widely, in addition to its textile and steel agreements, in 1980 Romania signed a trade agreement with the EC covering other industrial sectors and establishing a joint committee. The agreement was originally for five years, but was rolled over, as is a frequent practice with such agreements. The aim of introducing these agreements separately was to avoid the appearance of a fully fledged trade agreement and to conform to the official CMEA view that sectoral but not general trade agreements were acceptable.

Though the agreement did not entail tariff concessions, it committed the EC to abolishing or suspending certain quantitative restrictions on imports from Romania, in particular of some chemicals, fertilisers, glass and ceramics. In return, Romania was to increase and diversify its imports of EC products. The terms offered by the EC in the Romanian trade agreement were relatively favourable partly for political reasons in an attempt to lure Romania to the West and encourage the process of internal economic reform.

In 1983 a Contact Group on Agriculture was also established between Romania and the EC and this meets to discuss trade in certain agricultural products.

Romania was interested in a follow-up to its 1980 agreement which would also cover agricultural products and contain elements of cooperation. Initially, the Community found the Romanian demands for reductions in quantitative restrictions excessive and was concerned about the large and growing Romanian trade deficit with EC countries. Moreover, the Community did not feel that Romania had met the commitment made in the 1980 agreement to increase and diversify imports from the EC. Not only had Romanian imports from the EC fallen, but the Community also criticised the quality of economic information from Romania. The internal political situation in Romania under Ceausescu, and especially the destruction of villages and the resettlement of the rural population, was another source of tension and led the EC to break off negotiations for a new agreement with Romania in March 1989. Following the fall of the régime in December 1989, diplomatic relations were re-established, the 1980 agreement was reapplied and negotiations leading to the 1990 agreement were begun.

2.8   Cooperation agreements

Speaking of the implementation of the Common Commercial Policy
vis-à-vis state-trading countries, John Pinder wrote in 1974: 'The Commission's long march down the route outlined in the Treaty of Rome
will soon have reached its destination and it looks as if on arrival not
much will be found.' This was especially true of the agreements for
'economic, scientific, industrial and technological cooperation' between EC member states and Central-East European countries up
until 1988. These agreements provided a means by which the EC member states could resist the transfer of authority to the Community, a
resistance which was only overcome in 1988 when the EC itself began
signing trade and cooperation agreements with the Central-East European countries.

The bilateral cooperation agreements of the EC member states are
also a direct consequence of the political recognition problem. In the
absence of the bloc-to-bloc relations sought by the CMEA countries
from 1972, direct links with the EC member states were preferred to
agreements with the Community. As will be shown in Chapter 9, the
trade and cooperation agreements signed by the Community from 1988
are therefore an indication of its growing power vis-à-vis both its member states and the CMEA.

2.8.1   *Cooperation agreements defined*

As their name suggests, these agreements for 'economic, scientific, industrial and technological cooperation' cover a wide range of topics.
They are long term, generally lasting for ten years, though some have no
time limit. They represent official statements of intent concerning the
development of cooperation, and provide a framework in which economic activity can take place. These agreements contain the following
elements(23):

1. A declaration of mutual interest in cooperation and of the intention
    to promote cooperation between the enterprises and organisations
    of the two countries.
2. A specification of the economic sectors and areas of research where
    cooperation is to take place.
3. A definition of the forms of cooperation which are of particular
    interest to the two parties, for example coproduction and specialisa-
    tion, the establishment of joint ventures, and so on.
4. Provisions for the establishment of joint committees which meet
    annually to implement the agreement. At times working parties for

particular economic sectors or areas of cooperation may also be established.

2.8.2 *The debate between the EC and its member states over respective competences*

The view of EC member states was that Community responsibility should be restricted to the functions listed in Article 113, and responsibility for government-level cooperation agreements was not among these. The Commission strongly challenged the idea that this list of competences is exhaustive. In particular, the Commission pointed to the decline of the tariff on industrial products, and the emergence of new commercial instruments(24) as evidence that Community powers would need to be more extensive to be effective in implementing the Common Commercial Policy.

The upshot of the debate over respective competences was that while in 1975 the Community assumed responsibility for all trade agreements, cooperation agreements remained the responsibility of the member states, and the authority of the Community over these agreements was limited to where they affected trade. This division of authority was never accepted by the Commission. At the time it put forward various proposals, such as the negotiation of framework agreements which would complement agreements already contracted by the member states, or coordination of the various bilateral government-level cooperation agreements by the Commission, but these did not meet the approval of the member states. Instead, what was agreed was the establishment of an information and consultation procedure for cooperation agreements between the member states and Central-East European countries. This procedure, which was set up in accordance with Council Directive 74/393 of July 1974, has the following aims:

1. to ensure that intergovernmental cooperation agreements conform to the common policies of the EC;
2. to encourage exchanges of information;
3. to assess the value of measures which the Community might adopt to encourage cooperation agreements.

In order to implement this procedure a special committee of high-ranking civil servants drawn from each of the member states and from the Commission was established and meets at regular intervals. According to EC officials, in the past the procedure often proved to be not very efficient because of the reluctance (or failure) of the member states to consult or provide information about their agreements (25).

**2.8.3   *The common interest of the EC member states and CMEA
countries in maintaining direct bilateral links***

A European Parliament Document of December 1979(26) illustrates
that, with the exception of Ireland, which had agreements only with
Poland and the Soviet Union, and the German Democratic Republic,
which had no agreement with the Federal Republic of Germany because
of the special German provisions described in Chapter 12, all the, then
nine, EC members had agreements with all the Central-East European
countries considered here. The Irish case can be explained by the low
level of business with Central-East Europe.

Virtually all these cooperation agreements were signed in the 1973–74
period, suggesting a common reaction to the EC decision to end bilateral trade agreements involving its member states. There seems to
have been a kind of bandwaggon effect in an attempt to avoid being left
out of the potential benefits that these cooperation agreements might
offer. More importantly, it seems likely that the EC member states and
Central-East European countries shared an interest in using these cooperation agreements to substitute their earlier trade agreements and
maintain their bilateral commercial links.

In most cases the EC member states entered these cooperation agreements in response to pressure from Central-East European countries.
These countries favoured the direct bilateral dealings with individual
member states permitted by cooperation agreements, not only because
of the political recognition problem, but also because this seemed to
offer more chance of gaining special concessions for their country.

Unless obliged to do so by the Treaty, EC member states were frequently reluctant to create new Community instruments or align themselves to common policies(27). More specifically, on the question of
relations between the EC and Central-East Europe, Connie Friessen
(1976, p. 97) describes the UK case:

> The British Department of Trade and Industry, the Export Credit
> Guarantee Department and the European Trade Council have played
> important roles in facilitating British trade with the East. . . . These agencies
> give no evidence of encouraging the Commission to play an active role.

**2.8.4   *The cooperation agreements and Article 113 of the Treaty of
Rome***

There have been several cases in which clauses in individual
government-level cooperation agreements of the EC member states
were challenged as running counter to Article 113 of the Treaty. In
particular, on a number of occasions individual member states (Italy, the

Federal Republic of Germany and the Netherlands) included Most-Favoured-Nation clauses in bilateral agreements, and, strictly, the granting of such concessions should fall within the competence of the Community(28). A few intergovernmental cooperation agreements also contained provisions to grant import permits for products arising from cooperation projects (such as the agreement between Italy and Romania of 1973 and that between the Netherlands and Poland of 1974). The Franco–Soviet Agreement of 1974 contained a clause designed to encourage sales of Soviet products in France, while a number of government-level agreements between Greece and various Central-East European countries were also the subject of questions in the European Parliament(29).

However, it was rare that the member states challenged EC authority so flagrantly. As one national official stated, owing to the small number of people involved and club-like nature of the information and consultation procedure, the representatives of each of the EC member states knew what was acceptable at EC level, so they could anticipate to ensure that cooperation agreements between their government and third countries did not contravene EC regulations.

The real problem, therefore, appeared to be another, namely: whether the cooperation agreements of the member states conformed to the spirit, and not just the letter, of Article 113. For example, as Connie Friessen (1976, p. 96) said of the 1974 ten-year United Kingdom–Soviet Agreement:

> It was an obvious attempt by both parties to circumvent the implications of the EC's common commercial policy. Even though the cooperation agreement takes advantage of the legal loopholes, it represents a violation of the spirit of EC policy.

In one area in particular cooperation agreements seemed to run counter to the spirit of Article 113 and that was in the activities of the joint committees set up to monitor the implementation of the agreements. Levcik and Stankovsky (1979, pp. 140–1) describe the changing function of the joint committees in the following words: 'a body whose functions had originally been limited primarily to handling grievances is being transformed into an instrument to take positive action to promote trade and cooperation'.

The results of a study carried out elsewhere(30) would seem to belie the notion that in signing cooperation agreements, Western governments simply created the framework for cooperation and left to individual firms the practical business of carrying out East–West trade and cooperation. Instead, governments were involved in an ongoing process of export promotion for their firms with one of the major aims of joint committees being to raise actual levels of East–West trade.

As will be shown in Chapter 9, since 1988 with the signing of trade and cooperation agreements between the Community and individual Central-East European countries the debate about respective competences of the EC and its member states in regard to cooperation agreements seems to have been largely resolved in favour of the Community. The EC now has joint committees with all the Central-East European countries except Albania, with all the increased information and ability to check on the activities of its member states that this implies. None the less, the EC member states can continue to sign bilateral cooperation agreements with Central-East European countries, and though agreements at the EC level take precedence, these bilateral agreements can still serve a useful political function as an expression of goodwill or solidarity towards the Central-East European country in question.

Notes

1. The question of agricultural protectionism is taken up in Chapter 6.
2. Reported in Pelkmans (1984), p. 221.
3. According to Yannopoulos (1985a).
4. For examples of this approach applied to CAP decision-making see Moyer and Josling (1990) or S.M. Senior Nello (1985b).
5. As described in Pissula (1990).
6. In particular the United States opposed GATT membership. See also the debate between van Brabant (1990) and Brada (1989).
7. See, for example, Kostecki (1979); Patterson (1986); Bolz and Pissula (1986, 1990); Matejka (1990a).
8. Poland and Romania introduced tariff systems after joining GATT, in 1974 and 1976 respectively.
9. Hirsch (1988), p. 468.
10. As Patterson (1986), pp. 188–9, points out.
11. As described in the Klepsch Report of the European Parliament (1974).
12. In accordance with Regulation 1765/82. This applies to eleven state-trading countries, including the Soviet Union and its several smaller Central-East European neighbours. Regulation 3420/83 applies to all these countries, as well as to China.
13. According to Maslen (1986, p. 345), forty-three such decisions were taken in 1984, sixty-three in 1985 and seventy in 1986, almost all of which were directed towards liberalisation.
14. This figure was reported by K. Taylor (1977). Each year, actual levels of imports are examined to see how far quotas were used and where concessions could be made. Concessions entail either abolishing restrictions, enlarging quotas, or introducing quotas for imports which were previously non-liberalised.
15. Nimexe was originally used for historical reasons, because it had been adopted in EC member states. The earlier agreements with East European countries were set out in Nimexe, and problems now arise because, as a result of the change in nomenclature present headings do not correspond to those set out in the agreements.

16. Peter Marsh (1978), p. 61.
17. As Cline (1987), p. 150, points out.
18. Described in Majmudar (1988), pp. 125–6.
19. EC Regulation 4136/86 sets out the procedure by which the quotas at EC level are broken down into subquotas for the member states, with Benelux counting as a single member state (see Sarre, 1988, p. 235).

    The Community also operates a 'basket exit' mechanism so that if imports from a specific country reach a specified percentage of all EC imports of that product in the preceding year, the EC can call for consultations to arrive at an agreed quota level, or impose a quota unilaterally if agreement is not reached.

    Under the MFA, an 'anti-surge' procedure also operates for highly sensitive products. This permits regulation of the level of imports in previously underutilised quotas to prevent sharp and substantial increases in imports of those products.
20. Irmer Report of the European Parliament (1982), p. 15.
21. As Wetter (1985), p. 488 reports.
22. Described in Wetter (1985), p. 488.
23. This definition is based on the work by Litvak and McMillan (1974), and Levcik and Stankovsky (1979).
24. The European Court of Justice confirmed the Commission opinion of the importance of new commercial instruments in its 1975 decision on export credit subsidies (see OJ C, No. 268, of 22 November 1975, pp. 18–23). For a more detailed account of this debate see Lysén (1987).
25. See, for example, the answer given by Mr Hafercamp on behalf of the Commission on 16 July 1984 to Written Question No. 353/84 reminding the EC member states of their 'procedural and material obligations'.
26. Document of the European Parliament of 31 December 1979.
27. As described in Pinder (1979).
28. These examples are all taken from the Schmidt Report of the European Parliament (1978).
29. See, for example, written questions 75/83 and 723/83 from Mr Beyer de Ryke on the Greek–Soviet agreement.
30. S.M. Senior Nello (1985a).

3

EC anti-dumping and other trade protection measures

3.1   Introduction

In the past it was frequently claimed that EC anti-dumping measures were used as a protectionist device, and that their application in trade with Central-East Europe was particularly vigorous. It was also argued that the way in which anti-dumping rules were applied to non-market economies placed these countries at a disadvantage vis-à-vis other exporters to the Community.

The aim here is to assess these claims, which will first entail an illustration of why it is difficult to apply the concept of dumping to non-market economies. As will be shown, this helps to explain why in the past Central-East European countries figures so frequently in EC anti-dumping cases. As certain Central-East European countries become far enough advanced in the economic transformation process, it seems likely that they will cease to be considered non-market economies for the purpose of anti-dumping rules, so that this disadvantage will disappear.

The chapter then goes on to consider the claims of protectionism by reviewing the relevant statistics and analysing the EC anti-dumping procedure in some detail. From the statistics it emerges that the number of anti-dumping cases involving Central-East European countries has declined since 1985. In part this seems to reflect the changed international environment and growing technological gap of the Central-East European countries. However, a further reason is that the main emphasis of EC anti-dumping policy appears to have shifted to high technology, so that countries such as Japan and the NICs (newly industrialised countries) are increasingly involved.

It is often maintained that the openness of the EC anti-dumping procedure acts as a guarantee of it not being used in a protectionist way. For example, Pelkmans (1984, pp. 248) argues:

> A considerable part of the procedure is public, while criteria are known, and the considerations underlying every duty are to be published in the ˊ Official Journal. Such a procedure greatly reduces the constituency politics that might turn anti-dumping policy into a protectionist device that it shouldn't be.

While this may remain true for the most part, certain examples remain difficult to explain away. One such instance was mentioned in Chapter 2, when the threat of EC anti-dumping machinery to regulate steel imports was used to encourage the smaller Central-East European countries to sign bilateral sectoral agreements with the EC(1).

Aside from illustrating the specific difficulties arising in the case of non-market countries, the description of the anti-dumping procedure here shows that the EC authorities have a certain amount of discretion or flexibility in applying the legislation. As the EC authorities are subject to pressure from EC producers and rely on them for information, there would seem a potential, at least occasionally, for giving the interests of domestic producers special consideration.

3.2   EC anti-dumping legislation and the difficulty of its application to non-market economies

EC anti-dumping legislation(2) which is based on Article 113 (Common Commercial Policy) for the EC and Article 74 for the ECSC is a sphere where authority is very much in the hands of the EC rather than its member states. This legislation draws heavily on the GATT Articles relating to dumping (Article VI) and to subsidies (Articles XVI and XXIII), as well as the agreements to implement these Articles.

According to EC legislation, dumping is said to occur when the price of an export to the EC is lower than the 'normal value'. EC anti-dumping procedures are never opened by the Commission acting on its own initiative, rather it is always at the request of one or more producer who represents the 'Community industry'. If the dumping is found to cause injury or threat of injury, and the 'interest of the Community' so requires, the EC Commission may impose an anti-dumping duty, though in most cases it simply insists on a price undertaking from the exporting country involved.

The first stage in any anti-dumping procedure is to determine the 'normal value' of the product. In the case of market economies, the 'normal value' is generally based on the price actually paid or payable for a like product in the country of origin or exportation(3). Dumping therefore usually refers to unfair price discrimination which entails selling products on a foreign market at a price which is lower than that of the domestic market.

This concept of dumping implies that it is somehow possible to compare the domestic price on the producer's market with the price on the foreign market. Herein lies the problem for application to non-market economies, and both EC and GATT law recognise that the domestic price in a non-market economy may not be an appropriate basis for an anti-dumping procedure.

Following the GATT, the EC therefore applies special rules for the calculation of normal value in the case of non-market economies(4). This entails selection of an analogue country which can be used to derive a normal value. This is then compared with the export price charged by the country being investigated.

As a result, as will be shown below, the charge of dumping against a non-market country will depend not only on its own pricing policy, but also on the way prices are set by the producer in the analogue country. Not only does the non-market producer have no say in the setting of prices in the analogue country, but the producer chosen may be a potential competitor, suspicious of the Community's anti-dumping measures, and therefore reluctant to give the necessary information about prices. Moreover, the choice of analogue country will to some extent influence the chances of finding a dumping margin on the part of the non-market economy.

A second difficulty arises because the way in which 'normal value' is calculated for non-market countries does not allow for the possibility that lower prices in the non-market economy might effectively reflect more efficient production techniques (especially in view of the priority at times given to export industries) rather than the whole complex of distortions arising from centrally fixed prices. This question will be taken up in more detail below.

Regulation 1766/82 specifies which countries fall into the category of non-market economies for the purpose of EC anti-dumping measures. There has been some discussion as to whether the list is exhaustive(5). Use of the list has the advantage of reducing uncertainty, but because the criteria for deciding whether a country is non-market are not laid down, the countries concerned have no indication of the degree of economic change that would be necessary to remove them from the list.

3.3　Statistics of EC anti-dumping measures against Central-East European countries

Over the 1970–82 period there were 315 EC anti-dumping actions of which 122 concerned Central-East European countries. Table 3.1 sets out the number of anti-dumping procedures opened against Central-East European countries each year since 1980, both in absolute terms and as a percentage of total procedures. Table 3.2 indicates the product and, where possible, the outcome of some of the anti-dumping procedures opened against CMEA countries since 1985. The fall in the number of cases involving Central-East European countries since 1985 is evident from the tables. The share in EC anti-dumping procedures of Central-East European countries which are GATT members does not seem to be noticeably different from those which are not.

At the time of German unification there were five EC anti-dumping cases involving the German Democratic Republic, two of which had led to the application of duties, while the others entailed price undertakings. When a customs union was created with the German Democratic Republic in June 1990, the Community agreed to suspend the two anti-dumping duties in force.

EC anti-dumping investigations tend to occur in batches of countries, which is not surprising as investigations are carried out in response to a claim on the part of Community manufacturers that they have been injured by price-cutting on the part of non-EC suppliers. Such injury is far more likely to occur when several countries are attempting to supply the EC market.

As Table 3.3 shows, in most cases proceedings led to a price undertaking on the part of the Central-East European country, though in some cases anti-dumping duties were applied. In 1983 duties were applied on imports of unwrought nickel from the Soviet Union; lithium hydroxide

Table 3.1 EC anti-dumping cases initiated each year since 1980 involving Central-East European countries

Country	1980	1981	1982	1983	1984	1985	1986	1987	1988
Bulgaria	–	1	–	–	2	1	–	–	1
Czechoslovakia	–	8	5	3	4	1	2	–	1
GDR	–	6	6	2	3	2	3	–	1
Hungary	1	5	1	1	4	1	–	1	1
Poland	–	6	1	1	4	1	–		1
Romania	–	4	3	3	2	2	1	2	2
USSR	1	3	3	3	4	1	1	2	1
Central-East European total	2	33	19	13	23	9	7	5	8
All countries' total	25	48	58	38	49	36	24	39	40
Central-East Europe as % of all countries	8	69	33	34	47	25	29	13	20

Source: Annual Report of the Commission on the Community's Anti-dumping and Anti-subsidy Activities, various years.

Table 3.2 Anti-dumping procedures initiated against imports from Central-East Europe since 1985 by product

Product and year	Countries involved	Outcome
1985		
Flat glass	R, B, H, Czech. (and Yugoslavia)	Undertakings
Acrylic fibres	R	
Portland cement	GDR, P (and Yugoslavia and Spain)	No injury
Deep freezers	GDR, USSR (and Yugoslavia)	Undertakings
1986		
Potassium permanganate	Czech., GDR (and China)	Undertaking
Polyester fibre	GDR, R (and Turkey and Yugoslavia)	No injury
Urea	Czech., GDR (and other 5 countries)	Undertakings
Ferro-silicon	USSR	Undertaking
1987		
Urea (extension)	R (of 6 countries)	Undertaking
Polyester fibre	R (of 5 countries)	
1988		
Calcium metal	USSR	Still investigating
Welded tubes (iron and steel)	R (and Yugoslavia)	Still investigating
Barium chloride	GDR	Still investigating
Methenamine	R, P H, B, Czech. (and Yugoslavia)	Still investigating

Key: R, Romania; B, Bulgaria; H, Hungary; P, Poland.
Source: Adapted from information given by the EC Commission.

Table 3.3 Outcome of anti-dumping investigations involving Central-East European countries

	1980	1981	1982	1983	1984	1985	1986	1987	1988
No. of undertakings	25	3	25	11	16	2	13	4	–
Imposition of definitive duties	4	–	3	7	–	–	–	1	1
Imposition of provisional duties	3	–	10	10	3	1	3	4	3
No dumping	–	1	1	–	–	–	1	–	–
No injury	–	–	5	4	–	8	2	2	–
Concluded for other reasons	3	–	–	–	1	–	–	–	–

Source: Annual Report of the Commission on the Community's Anti-dumping and Anti-subsidy Activities, various years.

from the Soviet Union; choline chloride from the German Democratic Republic and Romania; hardboard from Czechoslovakia and Poland; and artificial corundum from Czechoslovakia. In 1984 duties were applied on imports of angles, shapes or sections of iron or steel from the German Democratic Republic; on hardboard from the Soviet Union; on copper sulphate from Poland; on electric motors from various CMEA countries; and on freezers from the Soviet Union in 1986.

Where anti-dumping duties are applied they operate as a form of variable levy which prevents foreign suppliers undercutting the price of domestic manufacturers. Not only does the variable-levy system operate regardless of how inefficient the domestic producer may be, but it also runs the risk of encouraging collusion among foreign suppliers since the option of cutting prices to increase market share is no longer open. EC legislation sets the maximum anti-dumping duty which can be imposed equal to the margin, but unlike in most other GATT members (and notably the United States) the duty may be set at a level lower than that of the margin if this is sufficient to remove the injury. In practice, duties are often set at much lower levels than the margin (especially since 1983) and, for instance, in the case against potassium permanganate imports from the German Democratic Republic, Czechoslovakia and China, which ended in 1986, the anti-dumping duty imposed was 20% even though the margin found was 45–102%. Similarly, in the case of imports of bicycle chains from China and the Soviet Union, which ended in 1986, the duty was 28% and the margin, 69.28–95.40%.

Table 3.4 indicates the value of imports from Central-East European countries which are affected by anti-dumping measures as a percentage of the total value of imports from these countries.

As Table 3.5 shows, the sectors most affected were chemicals, engineering, wood and paper, textiles, iron, steel and other metals, though the severity of the measures varied according to the sector involved. In

Table 3.4 Value of EC imports subject to anti-dumping measures in 1986

(a) Country	(b) Value of imports subject to anti-dumping measures (1000 ECUs)	(c) Total value of imports (1000 ECUs)	(b) as % of (c)
Bulgaria	394	548,836	0.07
Czechoslovakia	21,970	2,107,765	1.04
GDR	8,125	1,625,728	0.50
Hungary	10,321	1,887,964	0.50
Poland	5,215	2,947,278	0.18
Romania	5,670	2,482,673	0.20
USSR	9,336	13,157,677	0.07

Source: Vandoren (1988).

Table 3.5 Investigations initiated against Central-East European countries by main economic sector

	1980	1981	1982	1983	1984	1985	1986	Total
Chemical and allied	1	14	15	3	12	2	5	52
Textiles	–	–	2	–	–	1	2	5
Wood and paper	–	2	–	–	5	–	–	7
Mechanical engineering	2	12	–	–	1	2	–	17
Iron and steel								
(EC and ECSC)	–	1	–	1	1	–	–	3
Other metals	–	–	2	2	–	–	–	4
Other products*	–	4	–	7	4	4	–	19
Total	3	33	19	13	23	9	7	107

* This includes: flat glass, horticultural glass, sanitary apparatus, ice skates and upright pianos.
Source: Annual Report of the Commission on the Community's Anti-dumping and Anti-subsidy Activities, various years.

various European Parliament Reports(6) CMEA countries are also accused of dumping in the road and maritime transport sectors, and it is maintained that EC undertakings are gradually being excluded from the market. According to these reports, CMEA enterprises collaborate with Western firms or set up their own branch offices within the EC, and then undercut the freight rates operating in the EC member states by as much as 50%. With regard to maritime transport, it is estimated that the CMEA countries (mainly the Soviet Union) accounted for some 35% of North Atlantic sea traffic. This is said to be the result of lower Soviet freight rates which are permitted by low labour costs and the state bearing the costs of depreciation and insurance.

According to the Irmer Report of the European Parliament (1982, p. 23), cases of dumping involving Central-East European countries generally have the following characteristics:

(a) Normally the products involved are simple to manufacture, using techniques that are already well established in the West.
(b) The products are often manufactured in the West in relatively uncompetitive conditions, by Western undertakings which are less modern than the most recent East European production centres.
(c) Dumping complaints are normally made when the products from the Eastern bloc have already acquired a large market share to the detriment of domestic producers in the West.

3.4 The various steps in the EC anti-dumping procedure

The EC anti-dumping procedure for imports from non-market economies entails the following:

1. the selection of a 'like product' and an 'analogue' market-economy country;
2. the selection of the criterion for calculating normal value in the analogue country;
3. the calculation of export price;
4. the comparison of export price and normal value 'on a comparable basis as regards the physical characteristics of the product, quantities and conditions and terms of sale'.

3.4.1   *The choice of 'like product' and 'analogue' country and the calculation of normal value*

The choice of analogue country and the calculation of normal value in that country are closely linked as the Commission will only consider analogue countries for which the assessment of normal value is likely to yield a reasonable result(7).

The EC has a certain leeway in the choice of which analogue country and criteria to apply. In making its choice the Community relies on information from the parties concerned, that is, the Community industry which lodged the complaint, as well as exporters and importers. The Community industry has the right to suggest an analogue country and suitable criteria, though these may be challenged by the exporters and importers. In the last resort the choice lies with the Community authorities. In practice, exporters and importers rarely challenge the choice of analogue country and in the case of Central-East European countries this is often because they find it difficult to obtain information about the analogue market economy(8).

After the inquiry the EC publishes the criteria on which the analogue country was chosen, and according to Vandoren (1988, p. 200), those appearing most often are as follows:

1. similarity of the scale and techniques of production;
2. similarity of the access to raw materials;
3. an adequate level of internal competition or control of domestic prices;
4. the low level of protection;
5. physical similarities of the producer;
6. in some cases the analogue is the only producer;
7. the level of economic development of the analogue country.

In practice the determining criterion would seem to be the willingness of producers in the analogue country to cooperate with the Community authorities in their inquiry. Often producers are suspicious because EC anti-dumping measures might be applied to them as well. Furthermore, the confidential information they supply may have to be rendered non-confidential and public in some form.

Unlike the situation within the United States, the last criterion, that of economic development, is rarely used by the Community, which tends to stress microaspects, and finds the link between the state of an industry and the state of an economy somewhat tenuous. Between 1980 and 1986 the analogue countries used most often in cases concerning state-trading countries were: Austria (twelve times), the United States (twelve times), Yugoslavia (ten times), Spain (nine times), Norway (four times) and Japan (four times). As can be seen, the countries chosen generally have higher levels of income than the non-market countries under investigation. As Evans (1990) points out, on the one hand the higher level of income of the analogue countries may imply lower costs because of a higher level of technological development, and this is admitted. However, the possibility of lower costs because of a lower level of development in the non-market economy (for example because of cheaper labour costs) is ruled out.

Normal value is calculated on the basis of one of the three following criteria:

1. the price at which the like product of the analogue country is actually sold (a) for consumption on the domestic market, or (b) to other countries including the EC;
2. a constructed value of the price of the like product in the analogue country;
3. the price actually paid or payable in the EC adjusted if necessary to include a reasonable profit margin.

In most cases involving non-market economies the actual price on the domestic market of the analogue country tends to be used, and 3 above never appears to have been applied.

Central-East European countries criticise the EC because it is difficult for them to know in advance which analogue country will be used. This makes it difficult to ascertain how prices should be adapted to avoid the finding of a dumping margin. They maintain that they are at a disadvantage vis-à-vis producers in market economies, because, according to EC procedure, the determination of dumping for market economies is established with reference to domestic price or the production costs of the exporter. As Hirsch (1988, p. 475) points out, this implies that with an 'impartial enquiry, fairly conducted' which is based on actual costs, an exporter in a market economy who is not dumping has a good chance of proving his innocence. Moreover, to avoid charges of dumping, the producer in a market economy has the choice of raising export price, or reducing domestic price. In contrast, in a non-market economy normal value is based on prices in the analogue country and these are beyond the control of the non-market producer.

In addition, if the non-market economy wishes to challenge the charge of dumping, it must do so on the basis of information about the normal value in the analogue country. Because by definition the analogue country is a potential or actual competitor, it will have little interest in supplying that information and, furthermore, as Denton (1987, p. 222) points out, will have 'an adverse interest in the outcome of the case from the non-market economy's point of view'. This may help to explain why Central-East European countries often concentrate their attention on other phases of the anti-dumping procedure and in particular on the question of whether injury has been caused, a choice justified in that in practice the extent of injury (if any) seems to carry more weight than the size of margin in deciding the scale of anti-dumping measure to apply.

3.4.2 *Export price*

In establishing whether dumping has occurred the normal value then has to be compared with the export price. For this purpose either the actual or a constructed export price is taken. The latter is used where there is no export price, or where countertrade is used, thus it is particularly relevant to the case of Central-East European countries. The constructed price is generally based on the first resale to an independent buyer.

3.4.3 *'Fair comparison' of export price and normal value*

In most EC anti-dumping cases against Central-East Europe a margin of dumping is established. The latter is based on the difference between normal price and export price (using weighted averages if necessary), though, following GATT, the EC regulations require that these two are placed 'on a comparable basis as regards the physical qualities of the product, quantities and conditions of sale'.

The way in which these adjustments are carried out is the subject of much controversy. Community legislation sets out the adjustments to be made to allow for fair comparison in some detail, but a certain amount of discretion remains. At times it is claimed that whereas in calculating the export price, certain overheads and expenses are deducted, they are added in to calculate the normal value(9). This different treatment increases the dumping margin and has led to claim that the EC is breaching the principles set out by the GATT.

The response of the Commission is that two issues are being confused: the construction of normal value and export price, and the comparison of the two. This does not answer the objection that fair comparison would seem to require correspondence in the way in which export price and normal value are calculated.

The question of adjustment for the inferior quality of Central-East European goods to ensure fair comparison is often raised. On some occasions the Commission has allowed these shortfalls in quality to be taken into account in calculating normal value, as, for instance, in the 1982 Soviet upright pianos case and the 1982 case of photographic enlargers from Poland and the Soviet Union.

3.4.4 *Injury*

Even when a case of dumping is proven, anti-dumping duties cannot be imposed unless there is a finding of actual material injury, threat of material injury or material retardation to EC producers. Of these, to date the third, material retardation of the establishment of an EC industry, has never been used. Threat of injury has only been used once, in the 1985 procedure against imports of Portland cement when the conditions for threat of injury were not found.

In establishing whether injury has occurred, EC legislation requires that the injury must be caused by the dumped imports to 'Community industry' producing a 'like product'. Furthermore, it must be shown that the injury requires protective measures.

Three factors must be taken into consideration in deciding whether injury has occurred: the volume of dumped imports, their price and their consequent impact on the Community industry concerned.

A practice sometimes used by the Community authorities which is severely criticised by the exporters involved is to compare the export price with a 'target price' which it is reasonable for the EC producer to charge, rather than with the actual price. Using this method the extent of price undercutting found is sometimes substantial as it may be argued that dumping practices have depressed the Community price.

In calculating injury to Community producers, the volume of dumped imports is calculated on a cumulative basis. This procedure is sometimes challenged by countries accused of dumping whose share of the EC market is relatively small.

3.4.5 *Community interest*

Where dumping and injury are established a duty can only be imposed if it is called for by the 'Community interest'. The latter is defined in terms of the 'interests of consumers and processors of the imported product' and the 'competitive situation within the Community market'. In general it would seem that in interpreting the 'Community interest', more weight is given to producers than consumers. None the less, in many cases this criterion has been applied in a way which alleviates the severity of EC anti-dumping measures. For example, in the 1986 case of ball and tapered rollings from Poland, Romania and the Soviet Union, it was decided that the 'Community interest' did not require continuation of the proceedings.

Since 1984 a system of five-year *ex officio* reviews of all anti-dumping cases which ended in duties or undertakings has been in operation. Central-East European observers(10) sometimes complain that the procedure for carrying out these reviews requires that the 'Community industry' concerned be informed, but not the other affected parties (notably customers).

3.5   EC anti-dumping rules and comparative advantage

As was seen above, the EC anti-dumping procedure is based on the principle that distortions in the price structure of non-market economies mean that the prices on the domestic market cannot be taken as an indication of normal value. Instead, normal value is based on prices in an analogue country. An unfortunate corollary of this approach is the view that the intrinsic inefficiency or 'irrationality' of the price structure of non-market economies means that they can never produce at costs lower than those of the analogue countries. The possibility of Central-East European countries having a comparative advantage in certain types of production is not admitted.

There are several reasons why Central-East European countries might have a comparative advantage in the production of certain goods(11). For example, there may be low labour costs resulting from an abundant supply of relatively well-trained labour. Alternatively, there may be advantages accruing from Western technology as the Central-East European countries became industrialised later and so may have been able to avoid some of the pitfalls experienced by the West.

Hirsch (1988) quotes a case in which the Soviet Union asked for a 15% allowance to take account of differences in the costs of producing electric motors between the Soviet Union and Yugoslavia due to economies of scale and rationalization. This was rejected by the EC authorities on the grounds that 'the concept of "economies of scale" is specific to market economies and there is not reason to consider it valid in countries where trade is a monopoly and where domestic prices are fixed by the state'(12).

Similarly, in the same case a request for an allowance of 20% to take account of lower Soviet labour costs was rejected because this would imply reliance on Soviet costs and 'that country does not have a market economy'(13).

Another case which raised these issues was that brought by the United States against importation of golf cars from Poland(14). These were produced in Poland using technology from the aircraft industry, since the production of golf cars was a sideline for the Polish aircraft industry. In the West it is unlikely that such a high degree of production and technology would be used in the production of golf cars. However, during the hearings it was established that the use of such efficient machinery to produce golf cars was the result of Poland's desperate need to earn hard currency, and that it implied inefficiency elsewhere in the system.

EC anti-dumping legislation is based on the concept of an analogue country because it is believed that the non-market country cannot show effectively that it can produce the goods cheaper than can the analogue country; if such proof were possible, the analogue-country rule would be superfluous. There would seem to be an inherent flaw in the rules(15).

3.6   Other EC trade protection laws

Given the nature of state intervention in centrally planned economies, in theory the EC could at times apply anti-subsidy measures to these countries, but in practice the anti-dumping instrument has always been used.

The safeguard procedure is used to protect the EC from excessively low prices or market disruption. In such cases import licences can be partially or wholly suspended, thus limiting or preventing imports from third countries. However, the safeguard procedure has hardly ever been used as it is considered a double-edged weapon, running the risk of retaliation. Moreover, unlike anti-dumping measures, it generally has to be applied in a non-discriminatory way. A notable example of its use was the EC suspension of beef imports from 1974 to 1977.

In 1984(16) a 'new commercial instrument' was introduced by which the EC can take measures with regard to 'illicit commercial practices'. This measure is modelled on section 301 of the US Trade Agreements Act. Whereas previously EC trade policy instruments were designed to avoid injury to domestic producers, the 1984 measure is aimed at protecting EC trade interests in third countries.

Notes

1. Wetter (1985).
2. EC anti-dumping rules are based on two Council Regulations of 1984 amended by further Regulations of 1987 and 1988 (No. 2176/84, in OJ 1984, L 201, ECSC 2177/84, 1761/87 and 2423/88 of 11 July 1988).
3. In certain cases where the domestic price is unreliable (for example because of state subsidies), an alternative price may be taken.
4. Regulation 1681 OJ 1979, L 196/1.
5. According to Vandoren (1988, p. 205, note 22), objections of this type were reported on numerous occasions, including the following cases: imports of incandescent lights and tubes from Czechoslovakia, the German Democratic Republic, Hungary and Poland in 1980; freezers from the Soviet Union in 1986; mechanical alarm clocks from Czechoslovakia, the German Democratic Republic and the Soviet Union in 1981.
6. See, in particular, the following European Parliament Documents: Schmidt (1978), Jung (1979), De Clercq (1981), Irmer (1982) and Seeler (1986).
7. Denton (1987), p. 211.
8. Vandoren (1988), p. 200.
9. See, for example, Norall (1986).
10. Piontek (1985).
11. Described in some detail by Wilczyński (1969).
12. Council Regulation 864/87, OJ L83 of 27 March 1987, p. 4.
13. *op. cit.,* p. 5.
14. Denton (1987).
15. This point is discussed in some detail by Denton (1987).
16. Regulation 2641/84.

4

The EC in a wider context: Cocom and the OEDC consensus on export credits

4.1   Introduction

The Western trade mechanism most closely associated with the Cold War era is the Cocom (the Coordinating Committee for Multilateral Export Controls) which entailed limits on exports of 'strategic' items to Warsaw Pact countries. The European Community has never even had the right to observer status in the Cocom, and the implementation of the Cocom restrictions varies considerably among EC member states, so posing problems for completion of the Single Market.

Another area in which the role of the Community has been relatively limited is in the context of export credit subsidies. According to a 1975 decision of the European Court, export credits were an instrument of commercial policy and so fell within the competences of the Community. None the less, there has been little harmonisation of the export credit practices of the EC member states (though there has been a considerable degree of coordination) and the Community does not yet possess its own export credit instrument. It does, however, represent its member states in the OECD which is the main form in which export credit subsidies and related measures are decided.

In both contexts the Community has pressed for a more active role. In the case of Cocom the urgency has gone out of the Community's request with regard to the smaller Central-East European countries, but the Iraqi example suggests that there may be a continuing role for Cocom, with the main focus on potentially unstable third world countries.

As will be shown, for many years the United States was not in favour of greater participation of the Community in Cocom, especially as there had been growing tension with West Europe as to the utility of the restrictions and the extent to which changed circumstances had rendered them obsolete. This divergence of opinon can largely be explained by the difference in the importance of Central-East Europe as an export market (especially for manufactured products) for the United States and Western Europe.

Export credit subsidies and investment guarantees are of great importance in trade with Central-East Europe, enabling Eastern imports to continue despite hard-currency shortages, and reducing the risks for the Western partner. It is estimated that, for example, some 20% of UK trade with these countries is covered by export credit guarantees(1). These measures are an important element of the Western aid package (the PHARE Programme) to aid economic and political transformation in Central-East Europe and, in the context of this Programme, the proposal to introduce Community export credit measures has again been revived. Despite political opposition it seems likely that this will ultimately be agreed, given the Community's growing role in coordinating national measures and its participation in international organisations such as the European Bank for Economic Reconstruction and Development (BERD, discussed in Chapter 8) concerned with such measures.

4.2 Technology transfer

Cocom, which is an informal committee of Nato composed of Japan and the main Nato members, is the international forum in the West for discussion of technology transfer. There is no treaty covering Cocom, and the implementation of measures agreed is carried out voluntarily by its member states. The main functions of Cocom are to maintain lists of strategic items, in the export of which the Soviet Union, the smaller Central-East European countries, Afghanistan, China, Mongolia, North Korea and Vietnam are subject to embargo and/or monitoring.

The evolution of Cocom has been largely influenced by changes in US attitudes(2). During the 1950s and a part of the 1960s the United States wanted to minimise exports to the Warsaw Pact countries, and the Cocom restrictions entailed some 360 products subject to embargo, 90 subject to quantitative restrictions and a further 100 which had to be monitored.

In the late-1960s the United States pronounced in favour of an extension of trade, including that with the Central-East European countries, but insisted on a tightening of controls on exports of military or technological potential. For this purpose three Cocom lists were compiled, relating to the export of:

1. atomic energy materials and facilities;
2. munitions;
3. industrial goods of potential military use.

Export of many items on the first two lists is banned completely, and it is the third list which is subject to most attention. In order to sell an item on the Cocom list to a country that had been a member of the Warsaw Pact, an export licence has to be obtained. For the most sensitive items, granting of an export licence will be decided at a Cocom meeting in Paris by means of 'general exception' applications. For less sensitive items an export licence will be granted by the trade ministry in the country concerned 'at national discretion', possibly after consultation with the defence or foreign affairs ministries.

A further change in US policy occurred during the 1970s, culminating in the 1979 US Export Administration Act which aimed at preventing exports of know-how or advanced technology to Central-East European countries because of the risk of reducing or eliminating the 'temporary technological advantage' enjoyed by the United States. Though the Western European countries criticised the United States for attempting to apply its national legislation extraterritorially, at the time they largely adhered to the more rigid US Cocom line. This can be explained by the reaction to the Soviet invasion of Afghanistan and the political climate of the era of Brezhnev and his immediate successors. Between 1982 and 1984 additional Cocom restrictions were introduced, especially in the computer and telecommunications fields.

However, from the mid-1980s there was growing strain between Western Europe and the United States. This can be demonstrated by the apparent slowness of the United States to react to Gorbachev's initiatives, the increasingly central role played by the EC in East–West affairs, and the suspicion that Cocom might simply be helping the United States to maintain certain technological advantages vis-à-vis the West as well as Central-East Europe(3). For example, there were differences of opinion over the export of telecommunications equipment, such as telephone exchanges using optical fibres. At the October 1989 Cocom meeting the United States found itself in an isolated position, facing united European and Japanese requests to free the lists.

In part these differences may be said to reflect the EC's much higher level of dependence on trade with the CMEA countries than that of the United States. Moreover, the composition of trade was very different, with grain exports being especially important for the United States, while Europe is more concerned with exports of industrial plant and equipment (as will be shown in Chapter 5).

The effectiveness and the utility of applying the Cocom lists to Central-East Europe were increasingly subject to challenge. As various studies carried out during the 1970s and early 1980s illustrated(4), the main Central-East European interest was in products with relatively low R and D content which are difficult to define as having a high strategic interest. These products accounted for a large percentage of EC exports to CMEA countries(5). According to the Seeler Report of the European Parliament (1982), one result of Cocom has been to force CMEA states into developing their own technologies in fields such as offshore drilling or robots for car production to reduce dependence on the West. A Trade and Industry Committee Report of the House of Commons(6) not only found clear cases in which Cocom had been breached, but also convincing evidence that the Cocom restrictions hindered the process of economic reform in Central-East Europe, encouraged high technology exports from other parts of the world, and entailed a considerable loss of business for EC firms. One businessman maintained that in the absence of regulations, some business could be doubled or even tripled. The explosion of East–West joint ventures since the late-1980s and the new investment programmes of the Central-East European countries lent greater urgency to EC requests for increased freedom of exports of these products.

At the Cocom meeting of February 1990, agreement was reached on a number of issues. There was to be an easing of Cocom restrictions on exports of computers, telecommunication products and machine tools. As in the case of China, trade controls were to be loosened in respect of Poland, Czechoslovakia and Hungary, provided these countries introduced 'credible' controls to prevent the re-export of these products to the Soviet Union (though it is doubtful how effectively these controls can be monitored). The difference in opinion between the United States and Europe (in particular Germany) re-emerged over treatment of the Soviet Union, which was ultimately excluded from the relaxed restrictions. The unification of Germany, with the pre-existing trade links between the German Democratic Republic and other Central-East European countries is also posing difficulties for Cocom.

At the February 1990 agreement it was also agreed to cut the deadline for obtaining an export licence through the 'general exception' procedure in Paris from twelve to eight weeks. Thirteen per cent of all applications have to follow this procedure, and businessmen have complained frequently about the time lag involved, especially since in practice the deadline is suspended if any question is raised, so that the waiting period could be as long as six months or a year(7).

The meeting also established that there would be a new review of the Cocom lists. The last complete review had taken place in 1984, and since then there has been a one-quarter rotating review of the lists each year. As many businessmen have pointed out(8), especially in the computer industry, a review period of four years is longer than the life-cycle of many products. The 1988 Hänsch Report of the European Parliament called for publication and further reduction of the lists, as well as the simplification of control procedures in order to avoid uncertainty and unnecessary bureaucracy.

The EC has never been a member of Cocom, and has never had observer status or even the right to automatic access to the Cocom lists, despite recommendations by the European Parliament that the Community should insist on a more active role in this sphere(9). However, the United States does not appear enthusiastic about the prospect of greater EC participation, possibly because of the stronger bargaining position that this might entail for Western European countries. Certain EC member states also appear to share this reluctance to include the Community.

However, the responsibility of individual countries for implementing Cocom restrictions not only leads to differences in application (in terms of ease and time necessary to obtain export licences) vis-à-vis Central-East European countries, but also in technology transfers between EC member states(10). This would seem incompatible with completion of the Single Market from 1993, and from that time either there will have to be harmonisation of the legislation of member states, or uniform application of the Cocom restrictions.

4.3 Export credits

The reintegration of the Central-East European countries into the world economy implies an increase in the levels of trade and investment. On the Western side the private sector will be largely responsible for taking decisions regarding trade and investment, though governments can influence these decisions by a number of measures, including those related to export credit subsidies and foreign investment guarantees.

Export credit subsidies are generally granted by special government-backed agencies which are permitted to lend to foreign purchasers at interest rates below market levels. In France, for instance, is the Banque Française pour le Commerce Extérieur, and in Britain is the Export Credit Guarantee Department. In certain other countries the loan is granted by commercial banks, but interest rate payments are subsidised by a transfer from the government to the bank.

There is a risk that, particularly in times of recession, countries will use export credit subsidies to favour their own businessmen. This has the effect of distorting competition, and may even lead to an export credit war. The risk is thought to be particularly grave in the case of business with certain Central-East European countries as their foreign currency shortages and high levels of indebtedness encourage extensive use of export credits.

To meet this risk, export credit matters are raised at the EC, OECD and GATT levels, though today by far the most important forum for international discussions on export credit matters is the OECD. This has the obvious advantage over the EC of including the United States, Japan and other major industrialised countries.

The form and extent of subsidies on exports (including export credit subsidies) is limited by GATT. The most recent GATT rules for export credits are contained in its Code for Subsidies and Countervailing Duties which came into effect from 1979. This Code contains an explicit reference to the arrangements agreed in the OECD and states that any 'export credit practice which is in conformity with those provisions is permitted by the GATT'.

Alongside discussions on technical questions, the Community represents the member states in the OECD forum, where the individual EC countries have observer status only. This representation has provided the stimulus to a considerable degree of coordination. None the less, much responsibility for export credits remains in the hands of the EC member states despite a 1975 decision of the Court of Justice(11) that export credit subsidies were an instrument of commercial policy and so fell within the competences of the Community listed in Article 113 of the Treaty.

Unlike the GATT, the OECD does not have the power to establish legally binding international treaties, so the arrangements agreed in the OECD forum take the form of a gentleman's agreement or consensus. The first OECD consensus was agreed in 1976 and related to interest rates, maturities and other loan conditions. In 1978 detailed guidelines to implement this consensus were drawn up (the Arrangement on Guidelines for Officially Supported Export Credits) and the membership of the consensus was extended.

The consensus guidelines set out the limits on terms and conditions of government-backed export credits of two years' duration or over(12). These limits are set out on a three-tier basis, in accordance with the GNP per capita of the importing country concerned. The lowest income countries are granted the most favourable conditions(13). Until 1982 the Soviet Union and all the smaller Central-East European countries were in the intermediate category, but subsequently the Soviet Union, the German Democratic Republic and Czechoslovakia were moved into the highest tier.

From 1983 a tightening of the consensus was agreed which established a new system for countries with interest rates lower than the specified minimum, and introduced a new automatic adjustment mechanism for minimum interest rates(14). This confirmed the overall tendency of the consensus to move in favour of tighter controls of export credit subsidies and the general opinion seems to be that the OECD arrangements have been successful in confining some of the worst excesses. It has also contributed to increased transparency and discipline in reporting. However, several problems remain, as a European Parliament Document(15) explains: 'Rapidly rising, but also diverging interest rates have meant widening and varying gaps between market rates and "consensus" interest rates and hence a great increase in the interest rate subsidies by certain countries in particular.'

Although extremely difficult to prove, there does seem to be evidence that at least some government-backed loans were made at rates below those of the consensus(16). This would seem the case for the Italian loan to the Soviet Union in December 1988, which was the subject of much criticism.

Community representation of the member states has meant that a common EC position has to be worked out. This takes place in the Policy Coordination Group for Credit Insurance, Credit Guarantees and Financial Credits(17), which is responsible for carrying out the EC information and consultation procedure in matters of export credit subsidies. All new credits of over five years' duration must be submitted to this procedure(18).

According to those involved (i.e. the Commission and national officials and the representatives of some banks), the consultation procedure works fairly efficiently and, as well as enabling exchange of information, has led to a certain convergence of opinion among member states. Though at times the Commission has difficulty in obtaining information from the member states, it is felt that ultimately it generally succeeds. The member states usually go a considerable way towards meeting the complaints made against them in this group, and although ultimate redress is possible within the EC Council, this is rarely necessary.

Turning specifically to Central-East Europe, from 1988 a number of large credit packages were signed with individual EC member states. For instance, in addition to the Italian–Soviet accord mentioned above, a consortium of FRG banks led by the Deutsche Bank AG also agreed a financial package with the Soviet Union(19). Subsequently, however, as will be shown in Chapter 5, the delays in Soviet payments have entailed considerable difficulties for Western credit agencies. The PHARE Programme has also entailed export credit packages on the part of the twenty-four OECD countries for Hungary and Poland, with ceilings being set at 2850 million ECU for Poland and 1640 million ECU for Hungary in February 1990, though these two figures include a certain amount of overlap(20). All these credits relate to exports of Community products, and a Hungarian proposal to extend EC export credits to sales of Hungarian agricultural products to the Soviet Unuon met with little support in the Community. As will also emerge from other examples, the form taken by Western-aid measures is not always immune from considerations of self-interest.

Notes

1. House of Commons Trade and Industry Committee (1989), p. XIV.
2. Tosi (1989).
3. These differences were reflected, for example, in the sharp exchanges over the gas pipeline (in particular during the Ottawa Summit of 1978) and the fact that US sanctions against the Soviet Union following events in Afghanistan and Poland were only matched by an EC commitment not to undermine these sanctions.

   For a more detailed account, see, for example, Bertsch (1985), Schiavone (1985) and Woolcock (1982). According to Schiavone, though the compromise reached among Cocom members in July 1984, concerning trade in computers, software and telecommunications, resolved some of the differences between the United States and Western Europe, many perplexities remain.
4. See, for example, Fallenbuchl (1983), Levcik and Skolka (1984), and Zaleski and Wienert (1980).
5. See Tosi (1989).
6. House of Commons *op. cit.*, pp. xvi–xvii.
7. House of Commons Trade and Industry Committee Second Report (1989), p. xvi.
8. House of Commons *op. cit.* p. xvi.
9. See, for instance, European Parliament Toussaint Reports, 1988 and 1989.
10. See Tosi (1989).
11. See OJ No. C 268 of 22 November 1975, pp. 18–23.
12. The consensus divides official support into pure cover, which relates to export credits guaranteed or insured by the government, and official financing support, which includes credits given by the export credit agency or those subsidised by the government. The matrix of minimum interest rates applies only to official financing support. In addition, the consensus does not extend to the terms and conditions of insurance or guarantees, but only to export credits which benefit from such terms or guarantees.

    Certain 'derogations' from the rules of the consensus, and 'deviations' from normal practices are permitted, on condition that other participants in the consensus are notified. The latter are then allowed to 'match' the deviation or derogation. From 1982 a no-derogation amendment was passed which implied a commitment on the part of participants not to avail of the possibility of derogations. However, they did retain the right to match derogations and since 1983 most derogations have been of this form, matching either commitments made before the amendment, or granted by countries not participating in the consensus.
13. The conditions relate to the percentage of the contract which can be covered by cash payments (15%); maximum repayment terms (eight-and-half years or ten years for poor and some intermediate countries) and a matrix of minimum interest rates, broken down by duration of credit and group of countries concerned.
14. With the new system, changes in the matrix were tied to changes in the weighted averages for government bond yields for the five countries making up the special drawing rights of the IMF (International Monetary Fund).

    The automatic system entailed increases in minimum interest rates, so causing problems for countries such as Japan, the Federal Republic of

Germany and Switzerland which had intererst rates below the minima. It was therefore agreed that when commercial rates of interest fell below the minima, a 'commercial interest reference rate' would be calculated and any participant in the OECD consensus could provide export credits in that currency at that rate. In practice, considerable problems have arisen from the operation of this dual system with interest rates which could be subsidised for some currencies and not for others. Moreover, agreement on what level of 'commercial interest reference rate' is acceptable has proved difficult.

15. The Delorozoy Report, p. 15.
16. Crane and Kohler (1985), p. 374.
17. Established by a Council Decision of 27 September 1960.
18. See Council decisions of 14–15 May 1962, 26 January 1965, 25 July 1967, 73/391/EEC of December 1973 and 76/641/EEC of 27 July 1976.
19. As reported in ECE (1988), p. 379.
20. In the sense that many ceilings were fixed for the two countries. These figures are taken from J.M.C. Rollo *et al.* (1990).

5

Trade between the European Community and Central-East Europe until 1989

5.1   Introduction

An analysis of trade between the EC and Central-East Europe up until 1989 is interesting *per se*, but it is also essential to address the questions of how far intra-CMEA trade is now likely to be switched to East–West trade, and the extent to which the creation and successive enlargements of the European Community affected trade with Central-East Europe.

At the 45th Summit of the CMEA in January 1990, the need for radical reform of intra-CMEA trade was agreed, and it was decided to use world prices in this trade from January 1991 and to pay deficits and surpluses in convertible currencies. Essentially, intra-CMEA trade consists of a swap of Soviet energy products for agricultural products and manufactures from its smaller neighbours. The use of world prices will add greatly to the energy bills of the smaller Central-East European countries, causing an additional strain at a time of already difficult adjustment. The first part of this chapter will describe these changes in some detail as they provide the key to understanding likely developments in trade with the West.

This is followed by a statistical survey of EC–CMEA trade in which the main trends, chief partners and structure of this trade are identified. There is also a brief account of trade in services, which received low priority as long as the Central-East European countries were centrally planned, but which is now expected to grow in importance. A feature traditionally associated with East–West trade, but which is becoming increasingly common in the trade of OPEC and developing countries, namely countertrade, is then discussed and the likely impact of the economic transformation on this form of trade is assessed.

Up until 1989 a number of authors argued that measures such as the creation of the EC or its granting of trade concessions would have little impact on the level of trade with Central-East Europe. This was said to be because the level of trade with the West was decided by factors internal to the CMEA and its member states. The starting points for this argument were the traditional difficulties experienced by the CMEA countries in producing exportables. The products available for export were generally characterised by an inappropriate commodity structure, and poor quality and marketing as a result of 'systematic inefficiency and the negative feedback of international imbalance through the lack of essential imports'(1). The lack of essential imports chiefly concerned machinery, equipment and know-how, but also consumer goods which could help provide incentives. This situation was coupled with the concepts of socialist international division of labour and of a policy to limit trade with the West.

The unfavourable commodity structure of CMEA exports was said to be reflected in the concentration in product groups for which international demand was weak; there were relatively high levels of protection and they were particularly subject to competition, not only from the NICs (newly industrialised countries), but also from the EC and among the Central-East European countries themselves(2).

In order to examine the hypothesis that EC–CMEA trade depends chiefly on internal factors, this chapter analyses the commodity structure of that trade and compares the export performance of Central-East European countries with that of other exporters to the Community. The results here would seem to lend support to the hypothesis. However, as will emerge from the second part of this book, depending on their success in achieving economic transformation, changes in the export supply situation of the various Central-East European countries can be expected.

The body of economic theory which attempts to assess the impact of organisations such as the European Community (and its trade concessions) on trade with third countries is customs union theory. The final sections of this chapter give a brief account of customs union theory and of empirical studies of EC–CMEA trade based on this approach.

As will be shown, the results of these empirical studies yield certain insights, but are not very satisfactory. A major shortcoming is that trade flows are the outcome of a combination of factors and it is difficult to isolate the effect of just one of these, the more so the higher the level of aggregation considered. This is one reason why the empirical analysis of the impact of EC policies in a single sector, agriculture, generally yields far more robust results (though this also depends on the greater changes brought about by the EC in agriculture than in other sectors), as the next chapter will show. Further difficulties for the analysis of EC effects also' arise from the rather piecemeal nature of EC trade preferences.

This chapter relies almost exclusively on Western statistics, given the difficulties in finding reliable statistics for these countries, as explained in the introduction to this book.

5.2 Intra-CMEA trade and the possibility of switching to trade with the West

In assessing how far the Central-East European countries are going to be able to switch their trade to the West, account has to be taken of the system of pricing used for intra-CMEA trade as well as the composition and level of that trade.

Up until 1975 prices in intra-CMEA trade were fixed for the period of the coming five-year plan on the basis of average world market prices over the preceding five years according to what was known as the 'Bucharest Formula'. Following the first oil crisis, a three-year average (1972–74) was used in 1975 and from that year the 'Moscow Formula' was adopted which entailed annual adjustment in prices to reflect a rolling average of world prices for that commodity over the previous five-year period. From the beginning of the 1960s most prices were set in terms of the transferable rouble, which was simply an accounting device, and not transferable even within the bloc. The transferable rouble accounts were supplemented by dollar accounts in the case of a few goods which were considered marketable in the West. The basis of the system was essentially bilateralism, and surpluses settled in transferable roubles amounted essentially to low-interest or interest-free loans.

As mentioned above, the Soviet Union traditionally exports mainly gas, oil and raw materials to the smaller CMEA countries in return for imports of agricultural products and industrial goods. It is widely agreed that the system of pricing used in the CMEA involved a Soviet subsidy to its smaller neighbours over the 1975–85 period, though there is considerable debate as to the size of that subsidy. The increases in the prices of Soviet energy exports to other CMEA countries lagged behind the rise in world prices. Marrese and Vanous (1983) argued that the subsidy element also included the Soviet Union paying higher prices for manufactures than these would have fetched on world markets. However, Koves (1983) maintained that the two authors failed to take account of the fact that the Soviet Union had imposed an inefficient economic structure on its smaller neighbours which *inter alia* was more energy-intensive, thereby offsetting the possible benefit of cheaper Soviet energy. Dietz (1985) questioned the use of world prices as a yardstick in the case of CMEA manufactured goods, especially for goods not traded on world markets, and suggested that the relatively high prices of manufactured goods in intra-CMEA trade could reflect the higher costs of producing manufactured goods in those countries.

The concentration of Soviet trade in a few product groups implies a particularly important role for terms of trade developments. In 1986 the fall in oil prices implied a deterioration in the Soviet terms of trade by 39% (3), causing Soviet export receipts to fall by almost $8 billion over the 1985–86 period. In 1987 a slight improvement in oil prices was more than offset by a fall in gas prices (gas accounting for roughly 20% of total Soviet exports, and a third of fuel exports). Again in 1988 fuel prices fell by 15% while cereal prices rose, causing a 14% fall in the Soviet terms of trade. At the same time Soviet domestic demand for petrol and petrol products was rising, while there were growing difficulties with production. The obsolete equipment was proving increasingly inadequate for ever more difficult extraction in Siberia, and pipelines needed renewal. In 1989, according to official Soviet statistics, crude oil production fell by 2.7%, but the decline reached 6.8% by the third quarter of 1990 compared with the same period a year earlier. According to the ECE, the volume of Soviet oil exports could fall by 42% from its 1989 level of 70 million tonnes by the mid-1990s. The worsening of terms of trade and the difficulties of energy production were major factors contributing to the deterioration of the Soviet economic situation in the late 1980s.

Within the CMEA, the fall in energy prices from 1986 transformed Soviet surpluses with the other Central-East European countries into deficits in most cases(4). The use of the transferable rouble and bilateral clearing in CMEA trade implied an incentive to the smaller CMEA countries to reduce their surpluses with the Soviet Union and in 1987 there was a fall in the Soviet share of the exports of all the smaller Central-East European countries except Romania and Bulgaria.

Reduced deliveries on the part of smaller Central-East European exporters also help to explain why in the first nine months of 1989, compared with the same period in 1988, Soviet cereal imports from the West increased by 21%, while those from other CMEA countries fell by 15% (5). Over the same period meat imports from the West increased by 231% and fell by 20% from the CMEA.

The USSR preferred to import from Western countries because, unlike the smaller Central-East European countries, at least up until recently these were prepared to offer export credits. However, even for Western exporters it has become virtually impossible to do business without government-backed guarantees from Western export credit agencies. Whereas in the past the Soviet Union had an excellent record of payment, by May 1990 a lag in payments of some 10% of the total value of Soviet imports was estimated(6).

In part, these delays may be due to the confused situation which followed the ending of the monopoly of the Ministry of Foreign Trade and allowed some 14,000 enterprises and foreign trade organisations to participate directly in foreign transactions. Not only do these lack experience, but it would appear that they are still often subject to central directives in regard to import orders, and these frequently take insufficient account of the enterprise's hard-currency holdings(7). The fact that state trading organisations were among the worst offenders (such as Soyuzhimexport which is responsible for foreign trade in chemicals and household goods) could point either to the level of bureaucratic disarray reached, or to a more fundamental cash-flow problem. The increase in imports was essentially decided by the central government as a means of combating growing unrest, and, at least in the short run, there appears to be some difficulty in finding the hard currency necessary to pay for these imports.

One means of meeting these and other Soviet economic difficulties was by reforming the system used in trade with Central-East Europe so as to obtain hard currency for Soviet energy exports. Gorbachev talked of CMEA reform as early as March 1985, and at a CMEA meeting of 1987 only the Romania of Ceausescu denied the need for change. The fragility of the CMEA became fully apparent at the 45th CMEA Summit in Sophia in January 1990 when a declaration was signed calling for radical renewal in the shortest time possible, despite the dissent of Cuba which announced that it was prepared 'to defend socialism, if necessary with arms'. The reform eventually decided upon entailed substituting the system based on the transferable rouble with trade at market prices and in convertible currencies from January 1991.

Initially it was estimated that the adoption of world prices and convertible currencies in intra-CMEA trade could increase the energy bills of the smaller Central-East European countries by at least $6 billion in 1991(8), but the higher oil prices in 1991 could lead to this figure being more than doubled.

At the same time the UN embargo on Iraq implied considerable losses for Hungary, Czechoslovakia, Bulgaria and Poland. Iraq has foreign debts with these countries which were being repaid in the form of oil exports. The respective debt figures were: $1.3 billion for Bulgaria, $500 million for Poland, $1.7 billion for Romania, and Hungary has estimated that it stands to lose $500 million(9). These countries have requested compensation for these losses from the Group of Twenty-Four western countries.

As early as July 1989 a bilateral agreement was signed between Hungary and the Soviet Union which entailed trade in world prices between the two countries. The Hungarians were prepared to accept a short-term deterioration in their terms of trade, believing in the longer term that they could avoid the waste in fuel implied by low-cost Soviet energy supplies, while less reliance on Soviet outlets would stimulate the technological adaptation necessary to sell on world markets. During the first six months of 1990 Hungary succeeded in reducing its exports to the CMEA by almost one-third, and increasing those to the West by 17%. However, a number of Hungarian companies were unable to find alternative markets to replace the Soviet Union, and face bankruptcy.

The question which arises is how far 'intra-CMEA' (if such a term can still be used) trade is likely to survive these changes. Despite measures to reduce consumption (such as price rises of 30% in Poland, 66% in Hungary, though the rise had to be halved in the face of popular protest, and rationing in Bulgaria), the energy requirements of Central-East Europe will continue to rise. However, although the Soviet Union has certain advantages in terms of geographical proximity and existing links, production difficulties are increasingly affecting supplies. This was evident, for example, by oil exports to Hungary being cut off for six days in September 1990, and Czechoslovakia being told that there will be a 3 million tonne reduction in Soviet oil supplies in 1991.

The scale of the adjustment task necessary to switch to trade with the West is enormous. According to ECE estimates, in 1988 intrabloc trade for the European CMEA countries accounted for 55% of their exports and 58% of their imports (see also Table 5.1). In the case of raw materials and energy products the percentage rose to 90%, while for engineering products and consumer goods the percentage was lower at 40–50%(10). Moreover, these countries participated in a number of common projects, and forty years of intra-CMEA trade encouraged the development of certain common norms and standards as well as separate technologies in some areas.

None the less, early indicators suggest that despite the difficulties involved, the intra-CMEA trade is declining rapidly. All these countries require imports of Western technology and know-how to renovate their economies. Moreover, Western products are generally of the quality requested, competitively priced, technologically advanced and delivered on time with no problems of servicing and spare parts. According to a

Table 5.1   The Soviet share in the trade of the smaller Central-East European countries (percentages based on $ values)

	Imports			Exports		
	1985	1986	1987	1985	1986	1987
GDR	39.7	40.2	42.4	38.0	37.5	36.0
Poland	37.8	36.8	35.9	30.1	31.2	29.3
Czechoslovakia	45.8	45.5	43.0	43.5	43.5	41.0
Hungary	30.0	30.9	28.6	33.5	33.9	33.1
Romania	22.4	19.8	22.4	17.4	15.4	21.4
Bulgaria	59.0	56.2	57.1	55.7	56.6	61.1

Source: Eurostat.

study carried out by four Western research institutes(11), in fifteen years EC exports to Central-East Europe could be greater than those to the United States. The future export performance of the Central-East European countries lies in their capacity to restructure their economies and adapt production to Western markets, but pronouncements about the speed and extent to which this is possible would appear premature.

5.3 A statistical survey of EC trade with the Central-East European countries

The EC is far more active in foreign trade than the CMEA, accounting for some 35% of world imports and 37% of world exports in 1986, compared with the equivalent figures for the CMEA of 8.6% and 9.1% (12). The scale of EC–CMEA trade is relatively limited, amounting to only some 2–3% of all world trade over the 1979–87 period (Table 5.2).

What immediately becomes apparent from any analysis of EC–CMEA trade is the asymmetry of its importance. In 1986, for example, the EC accounted for 31% of all CMEA imports from third countries, while the CMEA accounted for only 7% of extra-EC imports (see Tables 5.3–5.4).

Over the 1979–87 period the ECU value of EC imports from the CMEA rose by 113% (or an average annual increase of 16.3%). This was greater than the corresponding 88% increase for Class I countries (Western industrial countries(13)), the 60% rise for Class 2 (developing countries) or the 78% growth in total extra-EC(12) imports over the same period. However, if the period is broken down, between 1984 and 1987 EC imports from the CMEA fell by 33%, compared with a 3% rise in imports from Class 1 countries, a fall of 28% from Class 2 countries, and an overall fall in extra-EC imports of only 12%. As will be explained below, the performance of the EC imports from Central-East Europe after 1984 reflects the fall in price of energy products, which account for a large share of CMEA exports to the EC.

However, even if energy products are excluded, the CMEA share in EC imports rose by only 3% between 1984 and 1987, which was the same as for less-developed countries, and less than the increase (7%) for developed countries (Class 1) or for extra-EC imports as a whole (6%).

In 1987 the EC accounted for 13% of total CMEA exports, but the EC share of CMEA exports to industrialised countries was 67%, as compared with the 20% of EFTA, the 7% of the United States and the 5% of Japan.

Over the 1979–87 period EC exports to the CMEA grew by 45% (an average of 2.9% per year), which was slower than the growth in exports

Table 5.2   Total EC trade with Central-East Europe (million ECU)

	1958	1960	1965	1970	1975	1980	1985	1986	1987	1988	1989
USSR											
Exports	386	604	563	1415	5064	7808	12509	9875	9189	10113	12592
Imports	477	706	1066	1554	4064	11382	20710	13158	13128	12988	15511
balance	–91	–101	–503	–139	1000	–3573	–8201	–3283	–3939	–2875	–2919
*GDR**											
Exports	57	95	177	219	494	865	947	1073	1086	1264	1664
Imports	61	91	166	230	519	951	1832	1626	1390	1400	1636
balance	–4	3	11	–10	–25	–86	–884	–553	–304	–136	28
Poland											
Exports	197	209	315	604	2745	2892	2733	2389	2332	2756	3953
Imports	229	278	438	689	1733	2805	3572	2948	2907	3360	3855
balance	–32	–69	–123	–85	1013	87	–839	–559	–575	–604	98
Czechoslovakia											
Exports	136	178	283	565	1068	1405	1966	1944	2078	2170	2388
Imports	143	184	281	478	874	1544	2272	2108	2055	2211	2556
balance	–7	–6	2	87	194	–139	–306	–164	23	–41	–168
Hungary											
Exports	72	134	195	416	980	1619	2486	2450	2373	2354	2988
Imports	70	103	198	372	713	1430	2014	1888	1996	2158	3393
balance	2	32	–4	44	267	189	473	562	376	196	405
Romania											
Exports	56	105	256	500	1105	1772	1157	987	651	614	692
Imports	72	111	224	462	989	1826	2910	2483	2489	2234	2536
balance	–16	–7	31	38	116	–55	–1753	–1496	–1178	–1620	–1844
Bulgaria											
Exports	30	63	152	231	689	805	1639	1472	1453	1406	1465
Imports	33	50	127	191	222	507	586	549	517	462	528
balance	–2	13	25	40	466	299	1053	923	936	944	937
Albania											
Exports	2	4	9	15	37	64	101	65	56	–	–
Imports	1	1	2	8	26	57	76	125	56	–	–
balance	1	4	7	7	11	7	25	–60	1	–	–
*Total smaller CMEA**											
Exports	550	788	1387	2550	7118	9422	11029	10380	10029	10564	13150
Imports	609	818	1436	2430	5076	9120	13262	11727	11350	11825	14509
balance	–59	–30	–49	120	2042	302	–2233	–1347	–1321	–1261	–1354
*Total CMEA**											
Exports	936	1392	1949	3965	12183	17231	23539	20254	19217	20746	25742
Imports	1086	1524	2502	3982	9141	20501	33972	24884	24479	24884	30015
balance	–151	–131	–553	–18	3042	–3271	–10433	–4630	–5262	–4138	–427
Internal German trade											
Exports	191	228	302	660	1286	2097	3551	3502	3210	3487	3920
Imports	204	267	315	545	1096	2210	3430	3209	3575	3273	3482
balance	–14	–39	–14	115	190	–113	121	293	–365	214	438

* Excluding internal German trade.

Source: Eurostat.

Table 5.3 The share of Central-East European countries in EC trade (per cent)

	EC(12) exports			EC(12) total imports			Extra-EC imports		
	1958	1975	1988	1958	1975	1988	1958	1975	1988
USSR	1.1	2.0	1.1	1.3	1.5	1.4	2.0	3.1	3.4
GDR	0.2	0.2	0.1	0.2	0.2	0.2	0.3	0.4	0.4
Poland	0.6	0.1	0.3	0.6	0.7	0.4	1.0	1.3	0.9
Czechoslovakia	0.4	0.4	0.2	0.4	0.3	0.2	0.6	0.7	0.6
Hungary	0.2	0.4	0.3	0.2	0.3	0.2	0.3	0.5	0.6
Romania	0.4	0.2	0.1	0.2	0.4	0.2	0.3	0.7	0.6
Bulgaria	0.1	0.3	0.2	0.1	0.1	0.1	0.1	0.2	0.1
Smaller Central-East Europe	1.6	2.9	1.2	1.6	1.9	1.3	2.5	3.7	3.1
Total Central-East Europe	2.7	4.9	2.3	2.9	3.5	2.7	4.5	6.9	6.4
Internal German	0.5	0.5	0.4	0.6	0.4	0.4	0.9	0.8	0.9

Source: Adapted from Eurostat.

Table 5.4 The EC share in trade of the Central-East European countries (per cent based on $ values)

	Imports			Exports		
	1985	1986	1987	1985	1986	1987
USSR	12.2	11.5	14.4	18.1	13.2	11.4
GDR	20.2	15.9	15.5	19.6	18.2	15.8
Poland	18.5	17.0	18.1	22.6	23.6	23.4
Czechoslovakia	9.5	9.7	10.6	9.0	9.6	9.5
Hungary	21.6	22.5	24.3	16.0	17.3	19.7
Romania	10.1	11.6	10.2	24.6	26.1	24.1
Bulgaria	8.4	9.4	9.5	6.4	6.4	4.9

Source: Eurostat.

to Class 1 countries (104%), Class 2 countries (74%) or overall extra-EC exports (88%). Over the 1984–87 period EC exports to Central-East Europe fell by 13%, with only the LDCs (Class 2) performing worse with a 21% fall, at a time when the exports to Class 1 countries rose by 8%.

The EC share in total CMEA imports fell from 15% in 1979 to 7% in 1984, but recovered slightly to 11% in 1987. The share of Central-East European countries in total extra-EC exports fell from 8% in 1979 to 5.6% in 1987. The CMEA percentage in exports of other major industrial countries, or country groupings, also fell over the same period, from 6.7% to 5.3% for EFTA, from 3.1% to 0.9% for the United States and from 3.1% to 1.4% for Japan.

5.4   The structure of EC–USSR trade

As can be seen from Tables 5.5 and 5.6, the composition of EC trade with the Soviet Union and with the smaller Central-East European countries is very different, so it is usual in the literature to treat the two separately.

Table 5.5   The composition of EC–Soviet trade (per cent)

	Exports			Imports		
	1979	1984	1987	1979	1984	1987
SITC 0	6	13	9	1	1	1
SITC 1	1	1	0	0	0	0
SITC 2	2	2	2	10	5	10
SITC 3	1	1	1	61	84	70
SITC 4	0	1	1	0	0	0
SITC 5	14	11	17	9	3	5
SITC 6	37	34	33	12	4	8
SITC 7	35	31	29	3	1	3
SITC 8	4	5	6	0	0	1
SITC 9	1	2	3	3	2	1
Total 0–9	100	100	100	100	100	100

Key:
SITC 0: Food.
SITC 1: Beverages and tobacco.
SITC 2: Crude materials, inedible, except fuels.
SITC 3: Mineral fuels, lubricants and related materials.
SITC 4: Animal and vegetable oils, fats and waxes.
SITC 5: Chemicals.

SITC 6: Manufactured goods classi-fied chiefly by material.
SITC 7: Machinery and transport equipment.
SITC 8: Miscellaneous manufactured articles.
SITC 9: Commodities and trans-actions not classified according to kind.

Source: Eurostat.

Table 5.6   The composition of EC imports from the smaller Central-East European countries (1987) (per cent)

	Poland	Hungary	Czech.	Romania	GDR	Bulgaria	Total smaller CMEA
SITC 0	21	24	7	5	3	13	6.8
SITC 1	0	1	0	0	0	5	0.4
SITC 2	11	10	12	3	6	8	10.0
SITC 3	16	4	9	35	5	20	42.2
SITC 4	0	0	0	0	0	0	0.1
SITC 5	6	10	10	5	16	11	6.8
SITC 6	19	18	30	14	27	19	14.9
SITC 7	11	11	13	7	23	8	7.7
SITC 8	16	21	15	31	19	13	10.1
SITC 9	1	2	2	1	0	4	1.1

Key: *see* Table 5.5.
Source: Eurostat and adapted from OECD data (for the total of smaller CMEA countries so there may be some discrepancies for the total).

The Soviet Union is by far the most important Central-East European partner in trade with the Community, accounting for 48% of all EC exports to the CMEA in 1987. The Soviet share in EC exports was the largest for all product groups, and in six out of the ten SITC (Standard International Trade Classification) categories, the Soviet Union absorbed over 50% of EC exports to the CMEA.

As in the case of overall Soviet trade, that with the EC is largely an exchange of oil and oil products for manufactures and agricultural goods, causing Graziani (1987) to describe this trade as having a relatively high degree of complementarity(14).

In 1987 manufactured goods accounted for some 33% of EC exports to the Soviet Union, and exports of these goods to the Soviet Union amounted to 16% of all EC exports to the CMEA. Other important categories were machinery and transport equipment (29% of all Soviet imports from the EC in 1987), and chemical products (17% in 1987). However, over the 1979–87 period the share of manufactured goods, machinery and transport equipment fell, possibly reflecting the overall economic slowdown, the effect of Cocom, and the Soviet policy of giving preference to imports from the CMEA during the early 1980s(15). Imports of miscellaneous manufactured products rose to 3% in 1987, reflecting the policy of making consumer goods more readily available to the Soviet population. The share of agricultural products in EC exports to the Soviet Union grew from 6% in 1979 to 13% in 1984 and was 9% in 1987 (as will be discussed in the next chapter).

Mineral fuels (mainly crude oil and petroleum products) accounted for 70% of Soviet exports to the EC in 1987, having reached a peak of 84% in 1984. In 1987 imports of mineral fuels from the Soviet Union accounted for 38% of all EC imports from the CMEA. Raw materials (SITC 2 and 3) together accounted for 80% of Soviet exports to the Community in 1987 (and almost 90% in 1984).

The Soviet Union is also the main CMEA exporter of other categories to the Community such as chemicals, manufactured goods (SITC 6), machines and transport equipment, and miscellaneous manufactured items (SITC 8). However, the share of manufactured products fell from 12% in 1979 to 4% in 1984 and 8% in 1987.

The importance of the EC in Soviet imports from the West (52% in 1987) is less than for the smaller Central-East European countries (73% for Czechoslovakia, 68% for Poland, and 71% for Hungary). The EC absorbed some 67% of Soviet exports to the West in 1987 which was also lower than the equivalent percentage for any of the smaller Central-East European countries except Hungary (64%) or the German Democratic Republic if internal German trade is excluded (62%). The EC share in Bulgarian exports to the West rose to 80%, with 70% for Poland and Romania, and 69% for Czechoslovakia in 1987.

5.5 The structure of EC trade with the smaller Central-East European countries

The ECU value of EC exports to the smaller Central-East European countries grew by 5% in 1988 and by 30% in the first nine months of 1989 compared with the same period in 1988. The ECU value of EC imports from those countries rose by 4% in 1988 and 20% in the first nine months of 1989 compared to a year earlier. These increases followed two years in which both imports and exports to these countries had fallen.

If internal German trade is added to GDR trade with the rest of the Community, the German Democratic Republic occupied first place in trade with the EC, in regard to both exports and imports (or deliveries and purchases, as referred to in internal German trade) among the smaller Central-East European countries. Among the other smaller Central-East European countries the share in EC exports was highest for Poland, followed by Hungary, while the share in EC imports was greatest for Poland, Romania and Czechoslovakia in that order (see Tables 5.2 and 5.3).

As Table 5.6 shows, mineral fuels (SITC3) represented the largest category of EC imports from the smaller Central-East European countries, especially for Romania, Bulgaria and Poland. Apart from Polish coal, and some Czech coal and GDR lignite, this category consisted largely of re-exports of refined petrol products on the basis of crude oil imports from the Soviet Union and/or OPEC(16). The three countries having particularly large shares of mineral fuels in their exports to the Community were also those most concerned to earn hard currency in view of their foreign debt situation, while the recourse to energy products reflects the difficulties of these countries in producing manufactured goods of sufficient quality for Western markets.

The other main categories of exports of the smaller Central-East European countries to the EC were manufactured goods (SITC 6 and 8), raw materials, machinery and transport equipment, chemicals and agricultural goods.

The share of intermediate goods in the exports of the smaller Central-East European countries (28% in 1985) is higher than the corresponding figure for the Soviet Union, as is the share of final manufactured products (26% compared with 2% in 1985)(17). In 1986, intermediate products, iron and steel products (18.8% of all exports to the EC), non-ferrous metals (7.3%), textile yarn and fabric (3.4%) and chemicals (9.7%) all figured strongly(18). Important among final products were clothing (18.1%), footwear, furniture, and scientific and optical instruments.

As in the Soviet case, EC exports to the smaller CMEA countries were concentrated in machinery and transport equipment, manufactured goods and chemicals (see Tables 5.7 and 5.8).

5.6 The share of EC member states in trade with Central-East Europe

As Table 5.9 shows, among the EC member states, the Federal Republic of Germany was by far the main trading partner with Central-East Europe. Excluding internal German trade, the Federal German Republic accounted for 45% of EC exports to Central-East Europe, and for roughly 30% of imports in 1987(19). Italy was next in importance,

Table 5.7 The composition of EC exports to the smaller Central-East European countries (1987) (per cent)

	Poland	Hungary	Czech.	Romania	GDR	Bulgaria	Total smaller CMEA
SITC 0	9	3	5	5	8	3	5.6
SITC 1	1	1	1	0	4	1	1.1
SITC 2	3	4	6	10	7	3	4.8
SITC 3	1	0	0	1	1	2	0.8
SITC 4	1	0	0	0	0	0	0.4
SITC 5	24	22	19	21	18	21	21.3
SITC 6	19	26	15	36	18	20	20.8
SITC 7	32	33	43	15	35	42	35.5
SITC 8	7	9	9	10	7	6	7.9
SITC 9	3	2	2	1	2	2	1.8

Key: *see* Table 5.5.
Source: Eurostat and adapted from OECD data (for the total of smaller CMEA countries so there may be slight discrepancies for the total).

Table 5.8 Changes in EC exports to the smaller Central-East European countries by product group over the 1979–87 period (%1987/%1979)

	Poland	Hungary	Czech.	Romania	GDR	Bulgaria
SITC 0	0.8	0.6	0.7	1.0	0.7	0.4
SITC 1	1.0	0	1.0	0	1.0	1.0
SITC 2	0.8	0.8	0.9	3.3	1.4	0.5
SITC 3	1.0	0	0	0.1	1.0	2.0
SITC 4	1.0	0	0	0	0	0
SITC 5	1.3	1.1	0.8	1.4	1.0	1.1
SITC 6	0.7	1.0	0.8	1.2	0.8	0.6
SITC 7	1.1	1.0	1.3	0.4	1.1	1.6
SITC 8	1.8	1.3	1.3	2.0	1.8	1.2
SITC 9	1.5	1.0	2.0	1.0	2.0	1.0

Key: *see* Table 5.5.
Source: Adapted from Eurostat.

with 20% of EC imports and 15% of exports, followed by France (15% of imports and 13% of exports), and the United Kingdom (12% for both imports and exports). Together, these four countries covered some 80% of EC trade with Central-East Europe.

Belgium and the Netherlands each absorbed 7% of all EC imports from the CMEA in 1987, and 5% and 6% of exports. The share of Spain, Portugal, Greece, Ireland and Denmark in EC–CMEA trade were all under 5%.

In 1987, 9% of all FRG imports came from Central-East Europe (excluding the German Democratic Republic), which represents a fall compared with 1979 or 1984 (both 12%). In 1987, FRG imports from these countries were concentrated in three main product groups: mineral fuels (34% of all FRG imports from the CMEA), manufactured goods falling under SITC 6 (19%), and miscellaneous manufactured goods in SITC 8 (13%).

Over the 1979–87 period, total FRG imports rose by 66%, while those from Central-East Europe increased by only 29%. The declining share of Central-East Europe in FRG imports was largely due to a loss of markets for manufactures, as FRG imports of mineral fuels from the CMEA rose by 19% over the 1979–87 period (at a time when total FRG imports in this category fell by 35%).

Following the pattern of all EC countries, FRG exports to Central-East Europe were concentrated in the three categories of machinery and transport equipment, manufactured articles (SITC 6) and chemicals. West German exports to Central-East Europe rose more rapidly than for other EC member states, with, for instance, FRG exports of machinery and transport equipment (SITC 7) rising by 46% over the 1979–87 period compared with 26% for the EC as a whole. None the less, this

Table 5.9 Main EC partners in EC–CMEA trade (per cent)

| | Imports | | Exports | |
	1979	1987	1979	1987
Benelux	5	7	5	5
Denmark	3	2	2	1
FRG	32	30	40	44
Greece	2	2	1	1
Spain	3	5	2	2
France	14	15	18	13
Ireland	1	1	0	1
Italy	19	20	12	15
Netherlands	7	7	5	6
Portugal	1	1	0	0
UK	14	12	14	12
EC(12)	100	100	100	100

Source: Eurostat.

increase was slower than that of total FRG exports of SITC 7 (107%).

The share of Italy in EC exports to Central-East Europe also rose from 12% in 1979 to 15% in 1987. The main Italian import from these countries was mineral fuels, which accounted for 45% of all Italian imports from the CMEA in 1987, having reached a peak of 54% in 1984. Italian imports of this category from the CMEA rose by 94% over the 1979–87 period.

French exports (particularly of manufactured goods (SITC 6) and machinery and transport equipment) to the CMEA fell by 7% over the 1979–87 period, while both British imports and exports rose less quickly than the EC average. As a result of North Sea oil, the share of mineral fuels in all UK imports from Central-East Europe in 1987 (21%) was less than for the EC as a whole (44.8%).

5.7   Trade between the EC and Central-East Europe in services

Non-factor services (transport, travel, and other services(20)) account for a relatively small share of East–West flows, though an increase is expected due in part to the proliferation of East–West joint ventures in which services play a substantial role.

The annual ECE *Economic Survey of Europe* provides estimates for 'net services plus transfers' between Central-East European countries and Western industrialised countries, but stresses that for certain countries a great deal of estimation is necessary. According to the ECE, the Soviet Union and smaller Central-East European countries had an overall deficit of $3.7 billion in total net services plus transfers (including estimated net interest payments of CMEA banks) in 1988. If allowance is made for the deficit as a result of investment income (the bulk of which is accounted for by interest payments on foreign debt), the CMEA countries had a surplus in non-factor services with the West, possibly of the order of $4.0–4.5 billion. According to IMF data, in 1987 Poland achieved a large net surplus on shipment and travel with Western industrialised countries, while Hungary obtained a substantial surplus on travel, but a deficit on shipment.

5.8   Countertrade

The term 'countertrade' covers a wide range of trade practices (the most important of which are described below), all of which involve some kind of reciprocity: goods and services are accepted as full or part payment for other goods or services.

Differences in definitions used and lack of reliable data give rise to considerable variations in estimates of the volume of countertrade. Many estimates place the share of countertrade in total world trade in the order of 10–30% (21). There seems to be widespread agreement that the share of countertrade in total trade rose in the early 1980s and, following a period of relative calm, has begun to increase again in recent years. The IMF figure of 1% of total world trade in 1980 rose to 10% in later estimates, while the GATT estimate for 1985 was 8% (22).

Various forms of countertrade can be identified. *Barter* is essentially a spot arrangement involving a straight exchange of two sets of goods, and often no cash is involved.

Counterpurchase entails the Western partner providing goods and services in return for its exports over a set period of time (typically one to five years). Two separate contracts specifying deliveries and payments are used, and the value of the counterpurchase may be less, equal to, or greater than the value of the Western exports.

In general, the counterpurchase agreement takes the form of a binding contract, though at times a more general framework understanding is used. The contract generally involves a penalty clause to ensure that the Western partner fulfils the commitment to buy the counterpurchase goods. *Evidence accounts* may be used to avoid having to balance each Western export sale with a counterpurchase deal. These record all trade between the parties over a certain period, typically a year.

Buy back is a longer-term arrangement (often five to ten years) which frequently has a high value per transaction and in which the original sale is of plant, equipment or an infrastructure project. These sales are often financed by long-term loans, which may also be government-backed. Repayment takes the form of goods produced with the equipment, at times supplemented with deliveries of other goods. The exporter often purchases other goods over and above the value of the original sales.

Buy-back was particularly prevalent in Western trade with the Soviet Union during the 1970s, and a typical example was the delivery of pipelines by the FRG company, Mannesmann, to the Soviet Union in return for gas from Siberia. During the 1980s tighter credit conditions and the austerity measures introduced in Central-East European countries led to a decline in the use of buy-back.

Another form of industrial compensation (i.e. investment against goods, as opposed to commercial compensation, which involves goods against goods) which has been growing in importance in East–West trade in recent years is that of *offsets*. These are essentially industrial cooperation agreements and, as will be shown in Chapter 11, since the late-1980s these have generally taken the form of joint ventures in the context of Central-East Europe. An essential feature of offsets is that the Western partner agrees to incorporate local products in the final product, either by subcontracting or coproduction, thereby offsetting part or all of the Eastern partner's procurement costs.

Finally *switch trading* may be used to finance trade. This involves the Eastern partner agreeing to pay for Western goods by delivering products to a third country. The latter in turn pays the Western supplier in hard currency.

5.9   Trends in countertrade and economic transformation in Central-East Europe

The Central-East European countries were no exception to the overall rise in the use of countertrade in recent years, and the literature generally attributes this to shortages of convertible currency and the foreign trade reforms. During the 1980s the burden of servicing the foreign debt, and reduced export prospects resulting from recession, protective measures and difficulties in selling their products in Western markets (poor quality, inadequate marketing, etc.) implied increased recourse to countertrade as a 'second best' solution which enabled imports from the West to continue while reducing the amount of foreign currency required. Moreover, countertrade may be used to circumvent debt servicing obligations. Agreements with creditors often entail that a certain proportion of hard-currency earnings has to be used to service the foreign debt. Countertrade which is not registered by the Central Bank may represent a means of getting around this obligation(23).

Alternatively, countertrade can be regarded as the 'discount' that the Western partner had to pay to enter the Central-East European market. For example, Amann and Marin (1989) explain the specific case of barter as a rational response to market distortions: the Eastern partner uses barter to overcome informational or marketing barriers to entry in Western markets, while entry to the Eastern market is conditional on accepting barter.

Two aspects of the economic transformation in Central-East European countries have provided an added incentive to use countertrade. The first is the decentralisation implied by foreign trade reforms. The number of operators who participate in trade has increased and the self-financing requirements mean that hard currency is needed to pay for imports. One way round this constraint is to offer the Western partner payment in the form of countertrade. A major drawback is that the quality of the products offered in countertrade often seems to be diminishing: if the Eastern partner can sell its products directly in the West for hard currency it will. Moreover, previously, with foreign trade

monopolies the products of one enterprise were often offered as countertrade goods for another foreign trade organisation, but this is becoming increasingly difficult with the direct participation of enterprises
in trade.

Secondly, economic transformation and the restructuring of Central-
East European countries has increased the demand for technology and
know-how. Whereas during the 1970s Western export credits represented a major form of financing technology transfer, in the late-1980s
there has been growing resort to the joint ventures described in Chapter
11 which represent an institutionalised form of countertrade.

There is considerable debate about the advantages and disadvantages
of countertrade. On the one hand it is argued that it represents a way
round the constraint imposed by hard-currency shortages and is an acceptable alternative to a non-trade situation. Moreover, industrial compensation is seen as a means of acquiring technology and know-how, and
improving the range and quality of Eastern products available for
export.

Against this, international organisations such as the OECD and
GATT sometimes argue that countertrade encourages bilateralism, and
runs against the principle of open and multilateral world trade. Counterpurchase and barter are at times accused of mitigating the pressure for
structural adjustment. Moreover, when the quality of products offered
in return is poor, the Western partner incurs a cost. A criticism of
industrial compensation is that it may be insufficiently flexible and, if
market conditions alter, the Western partner could incur heavy losses.
Although international trade based on traditional cash transactions
would seem preferable, the widespread use of countertrade by Central-
East Europe and less-developed countries suggest that at least in the
short run this is not possible in view of their financial and trade
difficulties.

5.10 Are Central-East European exports concentrated in product groups particularly subject to protection?

Olechowski and Sampson (1980) estimated that EC *ad valorem* tariff
rates were particularly high for product groups such as textiles, ceramics,
glass, machinery and equipment. Leaving aside energy products and raw
materials (which, as shown above, are particularly important in the Soviet case), Tables 5.5 and 5.6 indicate that these sectors figure strongly
among the exports of the Central-East European countries to the
Community.

As emerged from Chapters 2 and 3 of this book, protection frequently
takes the form of non-tariff barriers (NTBs) such as variable levies,

quotas, voluntary export restraints, and so on(24). A study carried out by Olechowski and Yeats (1982) found that in 1976 some 78% of textile imports were covered by NTBs, followed by machinery (73%) and shoes (58%). According to the study, 27% of all exports from CMEA countries were affected by quotas or restrictive licensing arrangements, while only 8–9% of those from developing or developed countries were. They also found that minimum price restrictions affected 6.6% of total exports from CMEA countries, as compared with less than 0.5% from developed and developing countries. The incidence of variable levies and health and sanitary regulations was found to be less for the CMEA than for the developed and developing countries, though the impact of export restraints (3% for CMEA exports) was greater (1% developed and 0.3% developing).

The study also broke non-tariff barrier frequency and coverage indices down by individual Central-East European countries, and found Hungary, Poland and Bulgaria to be particularly affected by these barriers. For example, 97.8% of Hungary's trade faced some kind of barrier with over one-third of the restraints taking the form of quotas or restrictive licensing arrangements. These covered 44% of total Hungarian exports, while minimum prices covered a further 25%, and the variable levies of the CAP (discussed in the next chapter) covered a further 14%. According to the study, 37% of Bulgaria's exports to the EC were covered by quotas and licensing, a further 16% by minimum prices, and 12% by variable levies. For Poland 39% of exports to the EC were found to be covered by quotas and licensing, 8% by minimum prices, and a further 7% by variable levies.

A more recent study by the UNCTAD (UNCTAD, 1986) of all developed market economies found that, in 1984, 33% of all imports were covered by some form of non-tariff barrier, with the percentage rising to 58% for clothing and 74% for textile yarns and fabric.

However, one difficulty with this type of study is that statistics on the frequency and coverage of NTBs do not necessarily give an indication of their protectionist effect. For instance, according to the EC Commission many of the quotas on imports from Central-East Europe had not been fully utilised.

5.11 Competition from other exporters for EC markets

Tables 5.10–5.16 set out the results of a market-share analysis comparing the performance of EC imports from Central-East Europe with those from other main countries and country groupings over the 1975–87/8 period. The limitations of market-share analysis are well known: trade flows are influenced by a whole series of factors and the approach cannot establish the relative importance of each. None the less, the approach does provide some indication of the relative performance of different exporters to the Community.

An indication of the change in market share can be given by the following simple index:

$$x = \frac{\% \text{ EC imports at end of period}}{\% \text{ EC imports at beginning of period}}$$

with x greater, equal or less than 1 according to whether the market share has increased, remained the same or fallen.

As can be seen from Table 5.12, the share of the smaller Central-East European countries for all product groups fell most (0.7), followed by

Table 5.10 Changes in EC imports from the smaller Central-East European countries by product group over the 1979–87 period (%1987/%1979)

	Poland	Hungary	Czech.	Romania	GDR	Bulgaria
SITC 0	1.4	1.0	1.2	0.7	0.4	0.7
SITC 1	0	1.0	0	0	0	1.3
SITC 2	1.0	1.3	0.9	0.8	1.2	1.1
SITC 3	0.6	0.8	1.0	0.9	1.3	0.9
SITC 4	0	0	0	0	0	0
SITC 5	2.0	1.3	1.4	1.7	1.1	1.6
SITC 6	1.0	1.0	0.9	0.9	1.0	0.9
SITC 7	0.9	1.0	0.9	1.4	1.1	0.9
SITC 8	1.6	1.0	1.1	1.4	1.0	1.4
SITC 9	1.0	2.0	1.0	–	0	4.0

Key: see Table 5.5.
Source: Adapted from Eurostat.

Table 5.11 Market share of different countries and country groups in EC(12) imports (1988) (per cent)

	Total EC imports	Extra-EC imports
EFTA	9.73	23.34
N. America	8.26	19.80
ACP(66)	1.86	4.47
Mediterranean Basin	3.25	7.79
European CMEA	2.68	6.42
Smaller CMEA	1.28	3.07
USSR	1.40	3.35
Japan	4.47	10.70
Selected NICs*	3.62	8.67
OPEC	3.43	8.22

* Hong Kong, Indonesia, Malaysia, Philippines, Singapore, South Korea, Taiwan, Thailand.
Source: Adapted from Eurostat.

the United States (0.8) and the Soviet Union whose share remained unchanged. The greatest increase was for Japan (2.4%), though the market share remained small at 4.4% in 1987. The intra-EC share and that of EFTA also rose by 1.2% and 1.8% respectively.

The greatest fall in market share for the smaller Central-East European countries over the 1975–87 period was for animal and vegetable oils (0.1) (though EC imports of these from Central-East European countries were relatively limited), followed by machinery and transport

Table 5.12   Change in market share of total EC(12) imports (1975–88)

	Total EC imports			Extra-EC imports		
	%1975 %1958	%1988 %1975	%1988 %1958	%1975 %1958	%1988 %1975	%1988 %1958
EFTA	0.85	1.24	1.05	1.08	1.49	1.61
N. America[1]	0.69	0.80	0.55	0.88	0.97	0.85
ACP(66)	0.56	0.50	0.28	0.72	0.61	0.43
Mediterranean						
Basin	0.59	0.71	0.84	0.91	0.85	0.91
Eur. CMEA	1.17	0.95	1.11	1.62	1.06	1.72
Smaller CMEA	1.18	0.66	0.79	1.52	0.80	1.22
USSR	1.20	0.91	1.09	1.69	1.10	1.69
Japan	3.09	2.10	6.48	3.94	2.53	9.97
Selected NICs[2]	1.12	2.29	2.56	0.86	1.90	1.64
OPEC	1.30	0.24	0.32	1.67	0.29	0.49

Notes:
[1] US and Canada.
[2] Hong Kong, Indonesia, Malaysia, Philippines, Singapore, South Korea, Taiwan, Thailand.
Source: Adapted from Eurostat.

Table 5.13   The 1987 market share in EC imports by SITC Group* (per cent)

	Intra-EC	EFTA	N. America	Japan	European CMEA	Smaller CMEA	USSR
SITC 0–9	58.0	9.8	7.8	4.4	2.8	1.4	1.4
SITC 1	77.7	9.7	7.9	0.1	0.8	0.6	0.2
SITC 2	36.0	12.6	17.3	0.3	4.7	2.0	2.7
SITC 3	27.2	9.2	2.6	0.1	11.4	2.0	11.4
SITC 4	66.6	2.3	4.9	0.9	0.6	0.5	0.1
SITC 5	72.9	9.7	8.5	1.9	1.9	1.2	0.7
SITC 6	64.1	16.7	3.6	1.6	2.4	1.8	0.8
SITC 7	62.9	8.6	10.7	10.8	0.7	0.5	0.2
SITC 8	56.1	8.2	7.4	4.9	2.3	2.1	0.2
SITC 9	45.6	17.0	13.4	1.1	2.3	1.2	1.1

* Apart from SITC 0, food and live animals, which is dealt separately in the next chapter.
Key: *see* Table 5.5.
Source: Adapted from OECD data.

Table 5.14   Changes in market share of EC(12) imports over the 1975–87 period by SITC group (%1987/%1975)

	Intra-EC	EFTA	N. America	Japan	European CMEA	Smaller CMEA	USSR
SITC 0–9	1.2	1.8	0.8	2.1	0.9	0.7	1.0
SITC 1	2.8	8.1	0.6	1.0	1.0	1.0	1.0
SITC 2	1.5	1.0	0.9	0.6	0.9	1.0	0.9
SITC 3*	1.5	10.2	1.0	1.0	1.8	1.5	1.9
SITC 4	1.6	0.7	0.8	1.0	0.1	0.1	–
SITC 5	1.0	1.2	0.8	1.2	0.8	0.8	0.9
SITC 6	1.0	1.3	0.6	0.6	1.0	1.0	1.1
SITC 7	0.9	0.9	0.8	2.2	0.5	0.5	0.7
SITC 8	0.9	1.0	1.0	1.1	0.6	0.6	1.0
SITC 9	1.0	0.8	0.7	1.6	1.0	0.8	1.6

* The OPEC share in EC imports of SITC 3 fell from 72.3% in 1975 to 35.1% in 1987.
Key: *see* Table 5.5.
Source: Adapted from OECD data.

Table 5.15   The 1987 market shares in EC imports for selected products (per cent)

	Textiles, yarns etc. SITC 65	Iron and steel SITC 67	Furniture SITC 82	Clothing SITC 84	Footwear SITC 85
Intra-EC	67.4	74.8	75.5	49.7	69.7
EFTA	8.4	14.2	9.9	3.5	2.7
CMEA[1]	1.5	3.3	7.2	3.7	2.7
of which:					
USSR	0.2	0.6	0.3	–	–
Yugoslavia	0.7	1.0	1.8	3.5	2.4
N. America[2]	2.7	1.0	1.3	0.7	0.1
Japan	2.3	1.0	0.3	0.4	0.1
Selected (8) NICs[3]	4.8	0.6	2.5	17.3	13.9
China[4]	2.3	0.1	0.4	3.1	1.9
India	2.0	–	–	2.1	0.8
Pakistan	1.3	–	–	0.7	0.2
Morocco	0.4	–	–	1.9	0.4
Tunisia	0.2	–	–	1.9	0.1

Notes:
[1] European CMEA.
[2] US and Canada.
[3] Thailand, Malaysia, Singapore, Philippines, Indonesia, S. Korea, Taiwan and Hong Kong.
[4] Mainland China.
Source: Adapted from OECD data.

equipment (0.5) miscellaneous manufactured products (0.6) and chemicals (0.8). For the Soviet Union the greatest fall over the period was in transport equipment (0.7), followed by chemicals (0.9).

Turning to selected sensitive product groups, as shown in Table 5.16,

Table 5.16 The change in market shares in EC imports for selected products over the 1975–87 period (per cent)

	Textiles, yarns, etc. SITC 65	Iron and steel SITC 67	Furniture SITC 82	Clothing SITC 84	Footwear SITC 85
Intra-EC	0.9	1.0	–	0.7	1.0
EFTA	1.3	1.3	–	0.9	0.8
CMEA	0.8	1.0	1.1	0.6	0.6
of which:					
USSR	0.7	1.2	3.0	–	0.6
Yugoslavia	3.5	3.3	–	8.8	2.0
N. America	0.5	0.5	1.3	0.5	1.0
Japan	1.9	0.2	3.0	0.8	0.5
Selected (8) NICs	1.4	3.0	6.3	1.0	2.6
China	2.3	–	4.0	7.8	3.2
India	1.8	–	–	2.3	4.0
Pakistan	1.2	–	–	7.0	0.5
Morocco	1.0	–	–	3.8	1.0
Tunisia	1.0	–	–	2.7	–

Key: *see* Table 5.5 for SITC definitions and more precise country descriptions.
Source: Adapted from OECD data.

between 1975 and 1987 the Central-East European countries lost more of their market share in textiles (0.8) and clothing (0.6) than any other country or country group apart from the United States. In contrast all the Asian countries considered (mainland China, Japan, India, a group of eight NICs (newly industrialised countries) and Pakistan, in that order) increased their share in EC imports of textile yarns and fabrics, as did Yugoslavia and the EFTA countries. The share of Tunisia and Morocco remained stable. With regard to clothing, Japan and the EFTA lost ground, but all the other Asian countries considered increased their share, especially mainland China (7.8) and Pakistan (7.0). Yugoslavia (8.8), Morocco (3.8) and Tunisia also did exceptionally well (2.7).

The share of Central-East Europe in EC imports of footwear also fell by more (0.6) than that of the EFTA countries, while the shares of intra-EC imports, the United States, and Morocco remained unchanged, and those of Yugoslavia and India increased.

The CMEA share in EC iron and steel imports remained unchanged over the 1975–87 period, as did that of intra-EC trade. The shares of the United States (0.5) and Japan (0.2) contracted drastically over this period, while those of Yugoslavia and the group of eight NICs and, to a lesser extent the EFTA countries, increased.

With regard to furniture the market share of Central-East European countries rose (1.1) between 1975 and 1987, largely because of the huge increase (3.3) in the (still small) Soviet share. However, that of China and the selected NICs increased by even more (4.0 and 6.4 respectively).

5.12   A disaggregated study of the performance of various product groups in EC–CMEA trade

Eurostat (1990) has carried out a disaggregated study of the thirty main exports and imports in EC–CMEA trade by 3–5 digit SITC group. In so far as sufficient information was available, the study distinguishes the various product groups according to whether over the 1979–87 period there was (a) an increase in their unit value in ECU and in the quantity traded; (b) an increase in quantity; but fall in unit value; (c) a fall in quantity but not unit value; and (d) a fall in both quantity and unit value. The results are presented in Tables 5.17 and 5.18.

Table 5.17   The performance of selected product groups in EC imports from Central-East Europe over the 1975–87 period

Increase in unit value and quantity imported

SITC no.	Product description	% extra EC imports 1987	% total EC imports 1987
821	Furniture, parts thereof	29.3	2.3
3330	Crude petrol	12.4	8.4
7810	Passenger motor vehicles excluding buses	5.7	1.9
682	Copper	9.7	1.1
684	Aluminium	4.7	0.4
749	Non-electric machine parts	4.3	0.4
3414	Petroleum gases	11.2	2.5
24821+24831	Lumber sawn etc.	16.2	3.2
674	Iron, steel univ. plate sheet	15.4	1.0

Increase quantity imported but fall in unit value

SITC no.	Product description	% extra EC imports 1987	% total EC imports 1987
3344	Fuel oils, nes.	48.2	6.8
34131	Liquefied petroleum gas	27.7	2.1
28209	Iron and steel scrap	59.4	0.6
5112	Cyclic hydrocarbons	27.7	0.6
3343	Gas oils	48.8	8.3
562	Fertilisers manufacture	17.0	0.8
33419	Other light petrol oils	35.1	3.8

Fall in quantity imported, but increase in unit value

SITC no.	Product description	% extra EC imports 1987	% total EC imports 1987
011	Meat, fresh, chilled, frozen	20.3	1.7
85102	Footwear, leather	10.5	0.7
322	Other non-agglomerated oils	13.4	2.0
672	Iron, steel, primary forms	22.6	0.7

Fall in quantity and in unit value

SITC no.	Product description	% extra EC imports 1987	% total EC imports 1987
97101	Gold for non-monetary uses unworked and half-worked	2.2	0.3

Table 5.18 The performance of selected product groups in EC exports to Central-East Europe over the 1975–87 period

Increase in unit value and quantity imported

SITC no.	Product description	% extra EC imports 1987	% total EC imports 1987
582	Products of condensation, etc.	10.8	1.7
598	Misc. chemical products	10.7	2.0
724	Textile, leather machinery	9.4	2.3
653	Woven man-made fibres, fabric	11.4	1.0
583	Polymerisation etc. products	9.6	2.4
6514	Synthetic fibre yarn bulk monofil	16.9	1.1
515	Organic, inorganic compounds, etc.	9.1	1.3
6783	Other iron, steel tubes	41.3	1.8

Increase quantity imported but fall in unit value

SITC no.	Product description	% extra EC imports 1987	% total EC imports 1987
6782	Iron and steel seamless tubes	39.5	3.1
0412	Other unmilled wheat, etc.	49.3	2.3
743	Pumps nes. centrifuges, etc.	7.1	1.1
043	Barley unmilled	37.8	0.8
6784	Highpressure conduit	71.0	2.1

Fall in quantity imported, but increase in unit value

SITC no.	Product description	% extra EC imports 1987	% total EC imports 1987
87483	Other electronic measuring equipment	8.4	1.2
674	Iron, steel, univ. plate sheet	17.3	4.0
745	Non-electrical machine tools	8.1	1.2
723	Civil engineering equipment	6.1	0.9
591	Pesticides, disinfectants, etc.	18.0	1.3
744	Mechanical handling equipment	8.2	1.2
7721	Switchgear equipment, etc.	18.0	1.3
728	Other machinery for special industries	10.7	3.8
749	Non-electrical machine parts accessories	6.5	1.8
01111	Bovine meat with the bone in	12.3	0.1
7849	Other parts for vehicles	1.4	0.6
736	Metal-working machine tools	16.4	3.3
741	Heating, cooling equipment	9.5	1.7

With regard to EC imports from Central-East Europe, the first thirty products covered roughly 62% of all EC imports from those countries in 1986, with the seven categories of energy products on the list alone accounting for 42.7% of EC imports.

From the study it emerges that the only products for which the quantity of EC imports from Central East Europe fell were for meat, footwear, other agglomerated oils, iron and steel in primary forms, and unworked and half-worked gold for non-monetary purposes. Agricultural products, footwear, and ECSC are sectors in which EC levels of protection are relatively high. The quantity of all other energy products imported by the EC from Central-East Europe rose, even though the unit value of many of these fell. Both the unit values and the quantities increased for products such as furniture, sawn lumber, vehicles apart from buses, non-electrical parts of mechanical engines, copper and aluminium.

There was less concentration among the EC exports to Central-East Europe with the first thirty 3–5 digit SITC groups covering no more than one-third of total EC exports to Central-East Europe, and no single product group amounting to more than 3.5% of EC exports to the CMEA.

Among the product groups in which the quantity of EC exports to Central-East Europe rose over the 1979–87 period, manufactured articles of SITC 6 figure most frequently (five groups), followed by chemicals (SITC 5, four groups), followed by agricultural commodities and machinery and transport equipment (two groups each). In contrast, nine of the thirteen categories which experienced a decline in quantity over the 1979–87 period fall under SITC 7 (machinery and transport equipment) and virtually all these reductions relate to machinery. Given the requirements of the Central-East European countries, this decline is particularly grave.

The share of high-technology products in EC exports to Central-East Europe rose from 4.1% in 1979 to 6.2% in 1987. Over the 1979–85 period, EC exports of these products to the rest of the world rose on average by 15% a year, while those to the CMEA either fell (by 5% between 1980 and 1985) or rose at a slower rate (13% a year if only those years in which there was an increase are considered). The Cocom lists probably contributed to the slower growth of the exports to CMEA countries.

5.13 The piecemeal nature of EC trade preferences

In assessing the effect of the Community on trade with Central-East Europe, account has to be taken not only of the overall impact of the formation of the EC, but also of the regional nature of the EC's approach to trade preferences. The EC has evolved a multi-level tier system of preferences between the world's main trading blocs, but at times also within those blocs. Olechowski and Sampson (1980) distinguish three levels of preference: countries receiving (a) no preference; (b) generalised preferences; and (c) specialised preferences.

The countries receiving no preference are limited to receiving MFN-treatment, while generalised preferences are taken to refer to the GSP, which Romania received from 1974, and which was extended to other smaller Central-East European countries from 1990. Up until 1988 the specialised preferences were those granted to the six EFTA countries, the sixty-six ACP countries under the Lomé Agreements (some of which had previously benefited from the Yaoundé agreements), and the countries covered by the EC's Mediterranean policy.

According to Olechowski and Sampson the group of countries receiving 'no' preference in 1976 accounted for 39% of all EC imports from third countries and included countries such as the United States, Japan, Canada, South Africa, Australia and New Zealand, in addition to the CMEA countries with the exception of Romania. According to Olechowski and Sampson, countries receiving only MFN treatment faced an average weighted *ad valorem* tariff of some 8.9% for agricultural products, and 8.2% for manufactures which was almost double the corresponding average rates of 5.2% and 4.3% for countries receiving no preference.

As will be shown, the situation has changed drastically since 1989 for various Central-East European countries, but even before that there were numerous exceptions to the 'hierarchical' structure of EC preferences. For example, in addition to the privileged treatment of the German Democratic Republic, Yannopoulos (1985a, pp. 457–8) found that:

> although in most cases the Socialist countries of Eastern Europe as a group are non-preferred suppliers, nevertheless in the case of textiles and clothing the outward processing arrangements that they maintain with the EC give them better market conditions to Community markets than LDC textile exporters constrained by the MFA.

As will become evident below, these exceptions, and the rather piecemeal character of EC commercial policy complicate the assessment of the effects of that policy on trade with third countries. Various features of the EC decision-making process account for this lack of coherence in commercial policy. In the first place there is the blurring of responsibility between the Community and its member states, described elsewhere in this book, which results in a two-tier structure of policy. Moreover, the balance is not stable, but appears to be shifting in favour of the Community(25).

Secondly, even where competences are firmly in the hands of the Community, many decisions regarding the Common Commercial Policy seem irrational by the standards of single-actor model. In order to reach common positions, mutual bargaining is necessary and compromises must be reached. For example, the Treaty specifies that trade agreements are decided by the Council on recommendation by the Commission. During this process there are numerous opportunities for special interests to exert pressure, and for internal conflicts to spill over into the external field.

Finally, trade between the EC and third countries will be affected by the changing membership of the Community.

5.14   Customs union theory

Customs union theory provides the theoretical underpinning of assessment of the effects of the formation of the EC, though the literature (26) points to various divergencies between theoretical analysis and empirical studies.

Following Robson (1987, p. 13) three main features of a customs union can be identified, namely, that tariffs are eliminated on intragroup trade; that a common external tariff is applied on trade with third countries; and that customs revenue is apportioned among partners according to some commonly agreed formula.

The difference between a customs union and a free trade area is that whereas the former implies a common external tariff, the latter allows national tariff differences on trade with third countries to continue, but entails rules of origin to limit intragroup trade to products originating or mainly produced in that area.

At the time of the negotiations on the Treaty of Rome, the United Kingdom proposed a free trade area, but this was explicitly rejected by the original six members in favour of a customs union.

The main aim of customs union theory is to identify the welfare effects of the creation of a customs union. Changes are likely to occur on the demand and supply sides, as well as in the terms of trade. The literature often makes the distinction between dynamic effects (such as those relating to the economies of scale, technological progress, increased competition and so on), and static effects (which are usually taken to refer to the stylised trade effects described below), though the distinction is blurred and not very helpful(27).

With regard to the impact on trade, various possible effects can be distinguished.

1. *External trade creation* which entails an increase in exports from third countries to the customs union if the national tariffs previously adopted by some partner countries were higher than the common external tariff. *Internal trade creation* implies replacing expensive domestic production with cheaper imports from the partner country.
2. *Trade diversion* or the replacement of low-cost imports from third suppliers with more expensive imports from a partner country.
3. *Trade destruction* which occurs in a situation where imports from partners cannot substitute for former imports from third countries. Distinguishing between internal trade diversion (what is usually meant by trade diversion) and external trade diversion (the replacement of union trade by that with higher-cost third countries), van Brabant (1989) defines trade destruction as a combination of both(28).

4. There may be *balance of payments adjustments* because the change in tariff usually implied by the formation of the customs union will alter the current account of partner countries thereby inducing adjustments (e.g. of exchange rates) with implications for trade with third countries.
5. Finally, there may be *supply-side diversion*(29) entailing the substitution of exports to third countries with exports to partner countries.

The study of customs-union formation has also been extended to include possible trade reactions by other major participants in world trade(30). Various policy reactions are possible: the country affected by the formation of the customs union can do nothing, risk a trade war or begin negotiations.

The founding fathers of GATT accepted the not intuitively obvious idea that the creation of the EC would contribute to the freeing of world trade, and events would seem to have proved them largely right (31). The Dillon and Kennedy Rounds which roughly halved industrial tariffs can be regarded as partly a reaction to the formation of the EC, while the prospect of the European Single Market from 1993 is a major reason behind EFTA's interest in the European Economic Area, and the demands of smaller Central-East European countries for closer association with the Community.

5.15 Empirical studies of customs-union effects

As there are already extensive surveys of empirical estimates of the impact of EC formation(32), the discussion here will be limited to studies which specifically deal with the implications for trade with Central-East European countries.

The difficulties encountered by empirical estimates of the effects of customs unions are well documented(33), so attention will simply be drawn to the limitations of the *ex-post* 'residual-imputation' approach used by the studies presented below. These are based on information about the actual integration situation, and attempt to quantify, by reference to various explanatory factors, the likely development of the economies concerned in the absence of the customs union. The integration effect is then calculated as a residual, or the difference between what actually happened and what was projected to happen in the *anti-monde* in which the customs union was absent. The difficulty lies in correctly formulating the *anti-monde*. Moreover, because the approach is based on an unknowable *anti-monde*, it cannot be tested against experience in the way an analytical model can, so ultimately the evaluation of the estimates made on the basis of this approach is largely a matter of judgement about how plausible are the simplifying assumptions about the *anti-monde*.

Balassa proposed a method which uses the *ex-post* income elasticity of demand for imports on the assumption that in the absence of integration this elasticity would have remained constant. The *ex-post* income elasticity of demand is defined as the ratio of the average annual rate of change in imports to that of GNP, both expressed in constant prices. The method consists of comparing these elasticities for intraarea and extraarea trade for periods before and after the integration. Under *ceteris paribus* conditions a decline in the income elasticity of demand for extraarea imports indicates trade diversion. Alternatively, a rise in this elasticity for intraarea imports indicates gross trade creation (increases in intraarea trade), while an increase in these elasticities for imports from all sources indicates overall trade creation.

As several authors have noted(34), there are various drawbacks with the approach such as its dependence on choice of base period, and neglect of supply-side effects. Sellekaerts (1971, 1973) also spells out the limitations of treating trade effects as a residual in the specific context of this model. The *ceteris paribus* assumptions dictate that there is no change in autonomous prices, exchange rates or in trade flows as a result of the dynamic effects of integration, but in practice it is very difficult to distinguish between autonomous and integration-induced price changes, or to assess whether dynamic effects of integration are being picked up in the residual.

The results of a study carried out by Balassa in 1975 comparing the pre-integration period of 1953–59 with two post-integration periods (1959–65 and 1965–70) found a rise in the income elasticity of demand for intra- and extra-EC imports, taken together, indicating trade creation, while trade for extraarea imports only remained unchanged.

The study then goes on to assess the impact of the EC on various other countries, or groups of countries, including the CMEA. Distinction is made between the 'Common Market effect', competitive effect and price effect.

The 'Common Market effect' indicates the amount of trade diversion or expansion which is likely to affect a particular third-country supplier (or supplying area) to the EC, calculated on the basis of the performance of the 'average' supplier to the Community. The 'Common Market effect' is the algebraic difference between two estimates of EC imports from that third-country supplier: (a) the amount of EC imports from that supplier had the EC not been formed – for this purpose the estimated rate of growth of all third-country suppliers to the EC during a given pre-integration period is applied to the actual value of EC imports from that particular supplier (e.g. the CMEA) in a given base year; (b) the hypothetical level of imports from that supplier in a post-integration period which would have resulted if imports (in constant prices) from the supplier were changing at the same rate as the actual average change in all EC imports from third countries. If the difference between these two estimates is positive it indicates that the particular supplier realised exports to the EC greater than would have been predicted on the basis of the performance of the 'average' supplier to the Community and without the creation of the EC.

However, the 'Common Market effect' is a potential effect which says nothing about whether the third-country supplier actually experienced the amount of trade creation or trade diversion calculated as being 'most likely'. It is the 'competitive effect' which indicates whether in fact the supplier in question exported more or less to the EC than could be predicted from the performance of the 'average' supplier to the EC. The 'competitive' effect is measured by the difference between the actual imports (in constant prices) of the particular supplier area and the second estimate above. The total effect will be composed of the 'Common Market effect', competitive effect and price effect.

Balassa's 1975 estimates suggest that the CMEA countries suffered a negative 'Common Market effect' over the 1959–70 period. If the 'Common Market effect' is expressed as a percentage of total EC actual imports (in constant prices) from the supply area in question(35), the negative effect on the CMEA is second only to that of the category 'other developed countries' (see Table 5.19).

The trade diversion, as measured by the 'Common market effect' suffered by CMEA countries, was found to be greatest for manufactures (SITC 6 and 8), food, beverages and tobacco (SITC 0, 1 and 07) and chemicals. The particularly adverse effect on CMEA countries can be

Table 5.19   The Common Market effect as a percentage of 1970 actual exports (valued in 1959 prices)

Product group	CMEA	USA	UK	EFTA*	Other developed countries	Non-associated LDCs
Food, beverages and tobacco	–16.9	–18.1	–11.0	–33.5	–21.7	–23.5
Raw materials	–1.8	–2.1	–3.5	–2.5	–2.5	–3.9
Fuels	+19.4	+40.0	+25.2	+26.9	+2.1	+16.8
Chemicals	–18.7	–14.2	–18.6	–17.6	–8.6	–41.5
Machinery	+35.2	+48.7	+75.2	+73.7	+10.0	+9.4
Transport equipment	+16.2	+17.0	+24.8	+13.6	+1.9	+21.1
Other manufactures	–18.2	–15.1	–29.2	–27.6	–11.5	–26.6
All sectors	–4.0	+5.1	+8.4	–1.6	–8.0	+0.3

* Continental EFTA.

Source: Yannopoulos (1985b) who bases his calculations on Balassa (1975, pp. 393–8).

attributed to the concentration of their exports (51% of all CMEA exports to the EC in 1970) in the three product groups where the negative 'Common Market effect' is greatest for all third-country suppliers. These relatively modest gains in areas of trade creation (such as machinery and transport equipment) could reflect internal supply constraints in the Central-East European countries.

Balassa found competitive gains for the Central-East European countries for all product categories except fuels and chemicals. The competitive gain was greatest for foodstuffs (and especially live animals, meat products and fuels) coming chiefly from Hungary, Romania and Bulgaria, and raw materials from the Soviet Union.

The total effects for all exports from the CMEA to the EC were found to be positive, indicating that these exports were greater than could have been predicted on the basis of the performance of all third-country suppliers to the Community, and on the assumption that the EC had not been formed.

The same approach was used by Sellekaerts (1971), who, in addition to the base year 1959, presents alternative estimates using the average value of EC imports from a specific extraarea supplier over the 1958–60 period. On the basis of estimates of *ex-post* income elasticities of demand for imports, Sellekaerts found evidence for extraarea trade creation in raw materials, fuels, machinery and transport equipment over six- seven- and eight-year periods up until, and from, 1959 (including 1959). The evidence for other sectors was less clear, but there appeared to be extraarea trade diversion for chemicals and manufactures when seven- and eight-year periods prior to, and after, 1959 were considered, and for food over six- and seven-year periods up until, and from, 1959.

Empirical studies using the two alternative bases and for the 1959–66 period were also carried out for each of the Central-East European countries. The estimated 'Common Market effects' were found to be positive for the total exports to the Community from Yugoslavia, Bulgaria, Romania, Hungary and the German Democratic Republic, indicating that their exports were concentrated in sectors in which trade creation was found. The competitive effect for these countries was also positive, indicating that they performed relatively better than 'average' suppliers to the Community, so that their share in EC imports from third countries rose. Large positive total effects were found for Bulgaria, Hungary, Romania and Yugoslavia. The total effect for the German Democratic Republic was positive, but smaller, partly because of a negative price effect, but also because the trade flow analysed excluded internal GDR trade and thus was relatively small.

In addition to the limitations mentioned in connection with the Balassa results, a major drawback of this study was the early period

(1959–66) it considers, as many EC policies, and in particular the Common Agricultural Policy, were not fully operative. Thus, for example, Sellekaerts found no evidence for trade diversion of EC food imports from any of the smaller Central-East European countries. The total effects for Czechoslovakia and Poland were found to be negative. Czechoslovakia experienced a negative competitive effect for all sectors except raw materials, and the positive competitive effect of the latter was achieved only at the cost of a negative price effect. Sellekaerts attributes Czechoslovakia's poor competitive performance largely to the inefficiency of its foreign-trade sector. Poland was also found to have a negative competitive effect overall, especially in food, fuels, chemicals and manufactures.

Several computations were made for the Soviet Union, covering the 1959–64 and 1959–65 periods, as well as that from 1959–66. These indicated a positive 'Common Market effect', a large negative competitive effect, and a price effect which was negative in fuels, chemicals, transport equipment, and (over six- and seven-year periods from 1959) machinery. The negative competitive effect was found to be particularly large in food (this issue is taken up in the next chapter), manufactures, chemicals (over six- and seven-year periods from 1959), fuels and raw materials (over seven- and eight-year periods from 1959).

Yannopoulos (1985b) also carried out an empirical study of the impact of the Community system of trade preferences on the exports of Central-East Europe to the Community. This used the EFTA countries as a 'control' group in view of the fact that prior to the first enlargement of the Community (in 1973) EFTA and the CMEA faced similar conditions of market access to the Community, whereas subsequently the EFTA countries acquired preferential treatment.

Yannopoulos used the double standardisation procedure suggested by Young (1972). Differences in the export performance of the CMEA and EFTA in EC markets were attributed to three groups of factors: (a) changes in relative competitiveness which have occurred since the preferences were granted; (b) different rates of demand growth in the EC and the rest of the world; and (c) the trade preference. The aim was to isolate the impact of the first two groups of factor so that the effect of the trade preference can be calculated as a residual.

The impact of the EC's growth in demand is first isolated by deflating the growth of EFTA exports to the Community by the rate of growth of CMEA exports to the EC. The effect of changes in the relative competitiveness of the EFTA and CMEA is then separated by deflating the ratio of the rate of growth of the EFTA to the rest of the world, by the rate of growth of CMEA exports to the rest of the world, and by using this ratio to deflate the first. This can be expressed as the ISEP (index of standardised export performance), which is defined as:

$$ISEP = (Ebg/Eng): (Ebr/Enr)$$

where E = the rate of change of exports, b = beneficiary group (EFTA), n = non-beneficiary group (CMEA), g = the preference-granting area (EC) and r = the rest of the world.

If the value of this index is found to be greater than 1 it may reflect the positive impact of the trade preference, and could be taken to represent gross trade creation. However, apart from the difficulty of determining whether effects other than those of trade preferences are picked up in the residual, the index is very sensitive to the base year chosen, as well as to the level of aggregation. In particular, there should be a sufficient degree of disaggregation to reflect the structure of preferences. The piecemeal nature of EC preferences described above renders this particularly difficult.

Calculating this index for EFTA and CMEA exports for all product categories taken together over the 1973–82 period, Yannopoulos found a value of less than 1 for the ratio (15.8/18.2): (14.5/12.8). This suggests that the performance of CMEA exports to the EC was slightly more favourable than could have been predicted on the basis of their relative competitiveness vis-à-vis EFTA exporters, and on the basis of demand growth within the EC. Results are also presented for the textile and clothing sectors, but they are less interesting for the study here as they relate to what GATT defines as the 'Eastern Trading Area', which includes certain Asian countries such as China, Vietnam, Mongolia and North Korea.

Yannopoulos (1985b) also estimates the impact of the enlargement of the Community to include Greece on imports from Central-East European countries including Yugoslavia. He found that over the period from 1980 (the last pre-accession year) to 1983 (January–June), the EC share in Greek imports rose by 25% while that of Central-East Europe fell by 50%. Similarly, the EC share in Greek exports rose by 18% while that of Central-East Europe fell by 43% over the same period.

The change was found to be particularly dramatic for agricultural trade (and especially beef), with the EC share in Greek agricultural imports rising from 40% to 78% over the period considered while that of Central-East Europe fell from 22% to 2%.

Though Yannopoulos admits that additional information would be necessary to attribute these changes to EC enlargement, the scale of reorientation of agricultural trade would seem to suggest a case of trade diversion.

By way of conclusion, there seems to be a need for additional disaggregated studies, and the data provided by the Eurostat would appear useful for this purpose. The approach described above, which was suggested by Yannopoulos (based on Young), might offer a possibility, though it would be necessary to break this data down by country and link it to information on trade concessions by country and product group.

Notes

1. Maciejewski and Nuti (1985), p. 23.
2. Graziani (1987).
3. Unless otherwise stated the statistics in this paragraph are taken from ECE and especially ECE (1988) and ECE (1989).
4. For a more detailed account see Frantseva (1990).
5. *Agra Europe*, 16 March 1990.
6. *The Economist*, 19 May 1990.
7. *The Economist*, 19 May 1990. When enterprises earn hard currency it is deposited with the Vneshekonombank (State Bank for Foreign Economic Affairs) which then opens credit to them. It is reported that the credit offered is a matter of negotiation and may bear little relation to the hard-currency holdings of the enterprise. When delays in payment began, it would appear that the Vneshekonombank refused to accept responsibility for the debts of enterprises and foreign trade organisations. None the less, many Western suppliers continued their deliveries so the situation worsened.
8. *The Economist*, 11 August 1990, and 17 November 1990.
9. European Report No. 1615, 20 September 1990 and *The Economist*, 17 November 1990.
10. Kokushkina (1990), p. 3.
11. The BIPE, the IFO, Prometeia and Cambridge Econometrics, as reported in Saryusz-Wolski (1990b).
12. Unless otherwise stated, in Sections 1–5 of this chapter the statistics are all taken from Eurostat, and especially Eurostat (1989).
13. Class 1 includes the EFTA and other West European countries, the United States and Canada.
14. Two trade flows are complementary if the composition of exports of one country is almost the mirror image of the structure of imports of the other.
15. According to Graziani (1987), p. 84.
16. According to Graziani (1987), p. 88.
17. Estimates based on UN Commodity Trade Statistics.
18. Excluding internal German trade.
19. The coverage of other services includes: insurance, trade earnings, banking, advertising, other business services, construction, communication, film broadcasting and patents.
20. As reported by the Club de Bruxelles (1988), p. 24.
21. Gwiazda (1990), M. Wülker-Mirbach (1990).
22. As reported by the Club de Bruxelles (1988), p. 24.
23. M. Wülker-Mirbach (1990).
24. The Community's justification for using such measures is based on a 1979 interpretation of the European Court, reported in Pelkmans (1984, p. 222). According to the Court, the objectives of the Community entailed a conditional readiness to lower EC external protection, though this did not rule out the possibility of the Community developing a commercial policy

aimed at regulation of certain products, which seems an open invitation to the use of non-tariff barriers.

25. In addition to the debate about cooperation agreements and export credits, until 1982 member states were responsible for safeguard clauses, and they also retain responsibility for VERs, though these are overridden by those at the Community level.

26. See, for example, Pelkmans and Gremmen (1983), Pomfret (1988).

27. Robson (1987), p. 32, El Agraa (1985), p. 117.

28. Holzman (1985, 1987) maintained that the creation of the CMEA entailed trade destruction, though this was achieved through foreign trade monopolies and inconvertible currencies rather than an explicit common external tariff.

29. El Agraa (1985).

30. See, for example, Pelkmans (1984).

31. Pelkmans (1984), Yannopoulos (1985a).

32. See Sellekaerts (1973), Robson (1987), and Pomfret (1988) and the references therein.

33. See, for example, El Agraa (1985), Robson (1987) and Pomfret (1988).

34. Balassa (ed.) (1975), Clavaux (1969) Sellekaerts (1971, 1973).

35. This form of presentation follows Yannopoulos (1985b).

6

Agricultural trade between the EC and Central-East Europe

6.1   Introduction

There is by now a huge literature on the impact of the Common Agricultural Policy (CAP) on agricultural trade with third countries (1). The relatively high levels of EC support prices have transformed the Community from a net importer to a major net exporter of many temperate foodstuffs (see Table 6.1), while the successive enlargements of the Community have entailed considerable trade diversion. This has stimulated protests from agricultural exporters, including Poland and Hungary. On the other hand it is frequently maintained that the Soviet

Table 6.1 The positions of the EC and European CMEA and USSR in world agricultural trade[1] (per cent)

| | EC[2] | | | | European CMEA | | | | USSR | | | |
| | Imports | | Exports | | Imports | | Exports | | Imports | | Exports | |
	(a)	(b)	(a)	(b)	(a)	(b)	(a)	(b)	(a)	(b)	(a)	(b)
1970	41.7	28.8	27.7	11.8	8.8	10.7	7.5	9.1	4.4	5.4	2.0	2.4
1975	38.5	21.8	30.8	12.1	10.8	13.7	6.1	7.8	7.2	9.1	1.2	1.5
1980	38.0	20.5	33.5	15.6	10.8	13.9	4.7	6.0	7.1	9.1	0.6	0.8
1984	34.5	17.5	32.1	14.5	11.4	14.3	4.7	5.9	8.7	10.9	0.7	0.9
1985	36.3	17.9	34.5	15.8	11.0	14.2	4.9	6.3	8.6	11.1	0.7	0.9
1986	43.6	20.9	35.6	17.0	8.0	11.5	3.9	6.2	5.7	8.3	0.6	1.0

Notes:
[1] SITC 0 and 1, Food, beverages and tobacco.
[2] EC 6, 9 and then 12, with the 1986 figures reflecting the accession of Spain and Portugal.
(a) Share of all world trade.
(b) Share in world trade excluding intra-EC trade.
Source: Adapted from UN Commodity Trade Statistics.

Union, as a major food importer, has been able to benefit from subsidised sales of EC surpluses.

The aim here is to assess the validity of these claims. First I will give a
brief description of how the CAP mechanisms affect trade, and a survey
of agriculture in the Soviet Union and smaller CMEA countries in order
to explain their trade performance, and examine how this might be
altered by the reforms in progress. Then follows a short analysis of the
main features of EC–CMEA agricultural trade.

The impact of the CAP on East–West trade will be analysed using the
results of empirical estimates of EC levels of protection for various
products, and of models estimating the impact of CAP liberalisation on
world agricultural prices and trade. A market shares analysis will also be
carried out despite the limitations of this approach. Finally, the outlook
for East–West agriculture in Europe will be considered in the light of
such developments as the GATT negotiations and the single Market
from 1993.

No attempt has been made to apply a model of CAP effects to the
specific case of EC–CMEA agricultural trade. This is partly because the
speed and extent of change in Central-East European countries, together with its ongoing nature, suggest that such an effort is premature
and likely to be instantly outdated (as indeed is any attempt to study
these economies at present). Problems also arise concerning the reli-
ability of statistics in these countries.

Further difficulties of this type of approach arise from the previous
(and in some cases, present) centrally planned nature of these economies. This means that assumptions of market clearing could not be
made, as there was generally a mismatch between supply and demand,
with shortages on the one hand, wastage on the other and very few
reliable statistics about either. This was the case even for foreign trade
given the non-convertibility of currencies, and foreign-trade associations
occupying monopoly positions.

6.2   Common Agricultural Policy (CAP) mechanisms of particular relevance to trade with third countries

There are numerous descriptions of how the CAP support-price system
operates(2), thus only a brief indication of its main features will be given
here. The actual legislation implementing the system and the termin-
ology used vary according to the product but there are many common
features. The system described in the next paragraph is for cereals, but
the instruments used for many other products (such as beef and veal,
sugar, dairy products) are based on the same principles.

Essentially, the Council of Ministers fixes a target price each year which represents the desired return for producers. Threshold prices are also set and these are minimum entry prices for imports from third countries. The threshold price is equal to the target price minus the transport costs from a fixed port of entry. Above threshold prices, imports from third countries are relatively freely available. Finally, there are floor prices or intervention prices which set a minimum level below which market prices should not normally fall. In order to prevent actual market prices falling below intervention prices, intervention agencies in each of the member states buy up eventual surpluses of the product.

With regard to imports to the EC, there are four main systems for covering the difference between fluctuating world prices and internal EC prices. The first uses of *variable levies* which cover the difference between the lowest-offer price on world markets and the Community entry price or threshold price. The protection offered to EC producers by the variable levy system is complete in so far as it is impossible for farmers to undercut the threshold price, regardless of how competitive they are. Variable levies apply on cereals, milk and dairy products, sugar and some Mediterranean products such as rice and olive oil.

A second group of products is covered by *ad valorem duties* which charge a certain percentage of the import price as a tax. In this case the protection offered to EC farmers is less than for variable levies since changes in the competitiveness of third-country producers relative to those of the EC will be felt by EC consumers. Sheepmeat and oilseeds are based on this system.

For a third group of products, including live cattle and beef, pigmeat and poultrymeat, *a combination of variable levies and customs duties* is used.

Finally, for goods such as wine and fruit and vegetables, *customs duties and a reference (minimum import) price* are applied. If a third country offers the product at prices below the reference price, countervailing duties are imposed. In general, reference prices are set at levels closer to world levels than are threshold prices, and reference prices can be regarded as a form of floor price above which customs duties provide the means of protection.

On the export side *export refunds* may be used to enable EC goods to compete on world markets if EC prices are above world levels.

It is necessary to bear in mind that although the price-support and market-management measures constitute the basis of the EC system for most products, in most cases additional measures are used and these also have repercussions on EC trade with third countries. For example, *subsidies* are paid to reduce storage costs or to encourage consumption, as in the case of butter, or skimmed milk powder for fodder. *Deficiency payments* are used for oilseeds and other minor crop products, while *variable and annual premiums* operate in much the same way as deficiency payments operate for sheepmeat. As will be shown below in the context of EC agricultural trade concessions, there are also *seasonal barriers* for certain products, and *special preferences* for associated countries. In addition there are a whole host of *national measures*, in particular relating to taxation, credit and investment. For certain products there are *quotas* on the level of production, and *set-aside*, or payments to leave land unused, are also adopted on a limited scale. Finally, *quantitative restrictions* apply to imports of certain agricultural products, particularly from CMEA countries.

During the 1970s inflation was relatively high and demands on the part of farmers for compensation for their higher costs were usually met by the Council of Ministers agreeing large annual increases in support prices (see Table 6.2). As is well known, this contributed to growing self-sufficiency for the main temperate products(3), surpluses (shown in Table 6.3) and rapidly rising expenditure on the Guarantee Section of the FEOGA (European Agricultural Guarantee and Guidance Fund) Budget.

By the mid-1980s the situation was unacceptable and a series of measures was taken to reform the CAP. Pressure for this reform came from two main sources: the financial burden imposed by the CAP on the Community Budget was no longer acceptable; and third countries affected by the CAP were beginning to make their requests for change felt, especially in the GATT negotiations described below.

As it was widely agreed that the price cuts necessary to bring supply in line with demand were politically unacceptable, a combination of measures was resorted to(4). This is not the place for a detailed discussion of this question but various authors(5) have shown that the reforms were limited in scale, riddled with practical difficulties and unlikely to contribute substantially to the basic problem of bringing EC prices in line with world levels.

6.3   Other measures since 1988 affecting agricultural trade between the EC and Central-East Europe

Many features of the trade and cooperation agreements signed between the EC and individual Central-East European countries affect agriculture. As will be shown in Chapter 9, an essential feature of all these agreements was the progressive removal of quantitative restrictions applied by EC member states on imports from the CMEA country concerned. Some of these quantitative restrictions applied to agricultural products including tomatoes, lettuce, green beans, processed potatoes, honey, preserved fruits, grapes, citrus fruit juice, and, for a limited time when EC products are in season, to certain horticultural products.

Table 6.2 Average annual rate of change (per cent) in the agricultural prices (target or equivalent prices) fixed by the EC Council of Ministers

Year	ECU[a]	Prices in national currency	
		in nominal[b] terms	in real[c] terms
EC(6)			
1968–9	–1.3	–0.7	–
1969–70	0	0	–
1970–71	0.5	1.5	–
1971–72	4	4	–
1972–73	4.7	4.8	–
EC(9)			
1973–74	6.1	7.2	2.2
1974–75	15.5	17.8	6.9
1975–76	8.6	12.2	–2.3
1976–77	9.1	12	3.4
1977–78	4.9	7.5	–0.6
1978–79	2.4	7.5	0.1
1979–80	1.2	7.4	–2.9
1980–81	4.9	4.5	–3.9
1981–82	9.3	13.3	0.9
EC(10)			
1982–83	10.3	10.5	0.6
1983–84	4.3	6.6	–2.5
1984–85	–0.4	3.3	–3.5
1985–86	0.1	1.8	–4.5
1986–87[d]	–0.3	2.2	–
1987–88[d]	–0.2	3.3	–
1988–89	0	1.6	–
1989–90[e]	–0.1	1.2	–

Notes:
[a] Common prices in ECU (intervention price or equivalent) weighted by national agricultural production.
[b] Common prices in ECU converted into national currency at green rate including all adjustments to the green rate included in the price decisions or taking place in the previous year.
[c] Using GDP deflator.
[d] During the transition period the number of products under common price regimes in Spain and Portugal is very limited, so the calculation of the EUR 12 average is meaningless.
[e] Estimates of the effects of Commission price proposals. Common prices in ECU are converted into national currencies using the green rates resulting from the Commission's proposals, or in the case of floating currencies, the calculations are based on the agrimonetary situation of the week 6–12 December 1989. Account is also taken of the alignment of Spanish and Portuguese prices with common prices following from accession measures.

Source: The Agricultural Situation in the EC, various years, and *Agra Europe*, 21 December 1989 for the 1989–90 proposals.

Table 6.3 The quantity of EC agricultural goods in public storage (1000 t)

	30/11/83	30/11/85	30/11/86	31/12/87	31/12/89
Common wheat	6806.4	3890.4	2475.3	2395.5	2264.1
Non-breadmaking common wheat	14.0	8012.3	6084.6	1722.0	229.7
Barley	1672.9	4650.7	3792.8	3585.8	2989.9
Rye	311.5	1108.2	1147.9	754.9	1239.1
Duram wheat	736.8	986.2	1022.5	2027.5	1017.4
Maize	–	–	190.4	22.3	865.9
Sugar	–	–	15.7	–	–
Olive oil	120.7	75.4	283.1	311.1	130.8
Skimmed milk powder	957.2	513.8	846.8	593.6	21.9
Butter	636.3	1018.1	1279.3	888.4	4.8
Beef carcases	301.4	588.9	452.5	537.2	107.2
Boned beef	88.7	214.2	219.5	216.6	51.0
Pigmeat	–	25.8	0.1	–	–

Source: The Agricultural Situation in the EC, various years.

The 1988 trade and cooperation agreement between Hungary and the Community included a clause allowing for 'the possibility of granting each other reciprocal concessions on a product by product basis' for agricultural goods in view of what was recognised as the fundamental importance of agricultural trade for Hungary (6).

At meetings of the joint committees established between the Community and the Central-East European country in question agricultural issues are often raised. For instance during the 1989 meeting the Hungarians asked for an increase in Hungarian exports of sheepmeat and cheese to the Community, and the application of normal duties on Hungarian wine. Similarly, at the 1989 Polish–EC joint committee meeting the question of Polish sheepmeat exports to the Community was raised. The Hungarians also suggested setting up joint working parties with the EC to examine questions of agricultural policy, including the implications of the Single Market (on issues such as new standards for packaging).

The cooperation envisaged by the agreements also extends to the agricultural sector. For example, there is to be cooperation with Hungary in the veterinary area. One aspect of this cooperation is to encourage the establishment of East–West joint ventures in the CMEA country, and some of the largest of these joint ventures relate to agriculture. For instance, the Italian group Ferruzzi–Montedison signed three deals in the Soviet Union involving investments worth slightly over $2 billion in November 1989. The largest of these entailed converting some 500,000 hectares near Stavrapol into a modern agricultural enterprise covering the entire productive cycle. Another example is the joint venture between the FRG branch of Tetra Pak and the Hungarian savings bank

OTP to manufacture food packaging. It was hoped that this could raise Hungarian sales of dairy produce, and possibly triple sales of fruit juice (7).

As will be described in Chapter 9, many aspects of Western aid measures for Central-East Europe relate to agriculture. In addition to food aid to Poland, the Soviet Union and Romania, assistance in developing the agricultural sector is to be given to Poland, Hungary, Bulgaria and Romania. There was to be easier access to Western markets for agricultural goods, and in addition to eliminating all remaining quantitative restrictions on imports from Hungary and Poland, the Community agreed to extend GSP (General System of Preferences) treatment (which Romania already enjoyed) to all the other smaller Central-East European countries from 1990, as will be described below.

6.4   Agricultural trade concessions to Central-East European countries

For many years Central-East European countries argued that they occupied a low position in the hierarchy of EC trade relations with third countries, which they maintained placed them at a disadvantage vis-à-vis exporters in many Mediterranean and developing countries, and forced them to compete on the same (if not less favourable) terms as such major agricultural exporters as the United States, Argentina, Canada or Australia.

The EC reaction to this complaint was that the Central-East European countries could hardly expect otherwise given their refusal to recognise the Community until 1988. Furthermore, in the case of temperate foodstuffs, the economic importance of EC trade concessions to other third countries should not be overestimated as the quantity of the product on which the concession applies is often relatively small or because access tends to be limited to seasons when imports do not compete with EC production (8).

From 1988 onwards the situation appears to be so reversed that the African, Caribbean and Pacific (ACP) countries party to the Lomé Conventions have expressed fears at the extent of concessions being given to Central-East Europe.

Even before 1989 the Community had granted certain agricultural trade concessions to Central-East European countries. As described in Chapter 2, despite the non-recognition of the EC, the implementation of the CAP from 1967 to 1968 had immediate repercussions for some of the smaller Central-East European countries which had traditionally exported agricultural products to EC countries, forcing them into a response. In 1965 Poland negotiated with the Community over conditions for imports of Polish agricultural products. This was followed in 1968 by talks between Hungary and the EC over imports of pork to the Community. In each case the negotiations resulted in the so-called 'agricultural arrangements' which consist of an exchange of letters between the Commission and the ministry and appropriate trade organisation in the Central-East European country. These arrangements entail a commitment on the part of the EC not to apply supplementary levies on imports of the product in question, while the Central-East European country concerned agrees not to export at prices below the sluice-gate price. As Table 6.4 (which is by no means exhaustive) shows, between 1965 and 1980 'agricultural arrangements' were signed with all the smaller Central-East European countries except the German Democratic Republic (which instead had special German provisions) and Albania, and they cover various products including poultry, eggs, wine and different kinds of meat.

Over the 1980–82 period agricultural agreements were signed with Poland, Romania, Hungary, Bulgaria and Czechoslovakia, and in 1987 a further agreement was signed with the German Democratic Republic. These agreements take the form of voluntary export restraints and fix annual quotas of sheep- and goatmeat, though allowance is made for consultation with the exporting country. New agreements on sheepmeat were signed in 1990.

Similar agreements for young calves for fattening were signed with Hungary, Poland and Romania in 1988. There have been a number of complaints on the part of EC producers that prices have been depressed by increased deliveries of bull calves from Central-East Europe. For

Table 6.4 Agricultural arrangements and agreements between the EC and East European countries

Arrangements to respect EC prices	
Wine	Bulgaria (1971), Hungary (1970), Romania (1970)
Pigmeat	Bulgaria (1971), Hungary (1968, 1971), Poland (1968), Romania (1970)
Tomato concentrate	Romania (1970)
Cheese	Bulgaria (Kashkaval, 1971), Hungary (Kashkaval, sheep cheese, 1971), Romania (Tilsit, 1989; Kashkaval 1969)
Sunflower oil	Bulgaria, Romania (1970)
Eggs and poultry	Romania (ducks and geese, 1969; eggs, 1975), Poland (chicken and geese, 1968), Bulgaria (chicken, geese and eggs, 1972)
Voluntary export restraint agreements with quotas	
Sheepmeat and goatmeat	Bulgaria (1980), Czechoslovakia (1980), GDR (1987), Hungary (1980), Poland (1980), Romania (1980)
Young calves for fattening	Hungary (1988), Poland (1988), Romania (1988)

Source: Adapted from information supplied by the EC Commission.

instance, between June and August 1990, the price of Friesian calves dropped from £130 to £60. It is claimed that many of these calves enter the Community illegally via East Germany (9).

Romania received GSP (General System of Preferences) treatment and this was extended to Poland and Hungary from January 1990 and subsequently also to Bulgaria, Czechoslovakia, Yugoslavia and East Germany (for a brief time before unification). The GSP covers some 320 products and involves tariff reductions of 20–50%. As shown in Table 6.5, the concessions on products covered by variable levies were more limited. According to W. Von Urff (1984, p. 5);

> The concessions made under the Generalised System of Preferences mainly refer to commodities which are of minor importance to European agriculture. Normally the preference consists of a reduced tariff, the amount of which – even after reduction – varies in close positive correlation to the degree of competition with the Community's internal production.

The concessions proposed by the Commission met with opposition from the Council of Ministers and the EC farm lobby. As a result the measures shown in Table 6.5 are less generous than the Commission's first proposals(10). Moreover, a number of products which are exported in substantial quantities by Poland and Hungary to the Community were included in the 1989 GSP list, but not in that of 1990(11). In addition, the effect of the concession on soft fruit is limited by seasonal concessions, and the zero duty on pigmeat is reduced by the existence of variable and supplementary levies(12). The Commission proposed more favourable terms for certain fruit and vegetables from 1991(13).

Table 6.5 EC agricultural trade concessions for Hungary and Poland from 1990 under the General System of Preferences

Rabbit meats and offals	7%
Strawberries	13%
Sour cherries	11%
Apple juice (subject to certain constraints)	12%
Powdered peppers (capsicum)	4%
Canned duck or goose liver	11%
Raspberries (depending on whether fresh/frozen, with/without sugar)	9–18%

50% rebate in the existing import levy within the following quotas:	
63% ducks	3000 t
75% ducks (in pieces)	25,000 t
Frozen pork hams	4000 t
Cured hams (bacon)	2000 t
Sausages (dry or for spreading)	4000 t
Sausages (cooked, not liver)	1500 t
Canned pork products	6800 t

Source: Agra Europe, 1 December 1989.

6.5   What the transformation of agriculture in Central-East Europe entails

Despite variations from country to country, it is possible to identify certain common features of what the transformation of agriculture will entail. This should not, however, be taken to imply that the agriculture of all these countries will undertake all these changes, which include the following:

1. The elimination of subsidies and the freeing of prices both of agricultural products and of agricultural inputs. Higher retail food prices are likely to dampen domestic demand, while the removal of subsidies on inputs will add to costs.
2. With the exception of Poland, the agriculture of most of these countries is dominated by large cooperatives and state farms carrying out diverse activities. In many cases these are too large and have to be broken up into smaller units. There may be a role for cooperatives, but the system of property rights would have to be altered. In some cases state enterprises could be transformed into joint-stock agribusiness firms.
3. The question of property rights has to be decided, not only with regard to land ownership, but also to livestock, machinery, buildings and equipment in the case of collective farms which are being dismantled.
4. Restructuring of the industries producing farm inputs, and of the processing and distribution industries, is necessary and in many cases this would entail breaking up monopoly and monopsony power.
5. Improvements in machinery, equipment, breeds, seeds, fertilisers and training are needed, although to an extent which varies according to country (ranging from Romania and the Soviet Union at one extreme to Hungary at the other).
6. The share of the working population in agriculture will have to be reduced. The figures of 44% in Romania, 30% in Poland, 20% in Hungary and 11% in the German Democratic Republic are far higher than the equivalent 4% for the EC.
7. Agriculture must be made more environment-friendly.
8. The question of how and whether to protect agricultural imports must be decided.

6.6   Soviet agriculture

There is a huge and rapidly expanding literature on Soviet agriculture(14), so here only two (interrelated) questions of particular significance for East–West agricultural trade will be raised: why perestroika has so far failed to overcome the traditional weakness of Soviet agriculture, and what is the outlook for Soviet food imports, especially of grain. Following the Soviet Union's first major incursion onto world markets in 1972, grain imports have grown rapidly, for example, the Soviet Union now accounts for some 20% of all world wheat imports.

The poor performance of Soviet agriculture is well documented. Yields are low, for example amounting to only 1.83 tonnes/ha for cereals and 12.1 tonnes/ha for potatoes in 1987, compared with equivalent figures of 4.4 and 27.4 for the EC as a whole, or of 4.9 and 16 for Hungary.

It is estimated that some 20% of output of cereals (30–40% for some products) is lost between the harvest and transformation(15). Meat losses amount to some 1 million tonnes during the transformation process alone. As will be shown in Chapter 7, this situation deteriorated further in 1990. If these losses could be reduced, it is estimated that half the annual import requirements (of some 30–40 million tonnes) of grain would be eliminated. Sixty per cent of the planned increase in food production by 1995 was due to come from reduced wastage.

There is a rapid rural exodus (for example of 4.5 million people in eight years in the Russian Republic, leading to the complete abandonment of 3000 villages), while the rural mortality rate of those of working age is 20% higher than the Soviet average, and infant mortality is 50% higher. In twenty-five years, agriculture has lost some 22 million hectares, of which roughly half have been absorbed for industrial ends, but 6 million hectares have been completely abandoned.

These developments occurred despite heavy investment in agriculture. According to Segrè (1989b), agriculture accounted for some 20% of total investment over the 1976–80 period, though the share fell to 17.2% in 1986.

One of the most fundamental principles of the Soviet Union has been to guarantee food supplies to the population at low prices. This goal has to be seen against a background of slow increases, and large variations in production from year to year on the one hand, and, on the other, rapid increases in income(16) coupled with relatively high income elasticity for certain products (notably meat(17)) and a growing population. Wädekin reports that over the 1980–86 period official incomes grew by 22% and total agricultural output by 17%, but between 1986 and 1989 incomes grew by 22% and agricultural production by only 2%. It is estimated that the Soviet population grew by some 54 million between 1959 and 1979, and has since *been growing at some 2–3 million per year(18). According to the Soviet academician, Nazarenko, the Soviet Union will require food supplies (at current prices) worth some 205–210 billion roubles by 1995 as compared with 142 billion in 1989(19).

There are large regional disparities in the growth of both agricultural production and population. The Soviet population itself rose over the 1983–87 period by 3% and gross agricultural production by 6%(20). However, the change in agricultural production over the 1986–88 period compared to that of 1981–85 in Uzbekistan was –0.3%, while population growth over the period from the end of 1983 to the end of 1987 was 11.8%. The equivalent figures for Armenia were –4% for agricultural production and 3.5% for population.

According to official statistics, the Soviet Union was able to increase per capita meat consumption from 20kg in 1960 to 65kg in 1988, but it has not reached the goal of 70kg set out in the 1972 Food Programme(21). However, Soviet measures include all kinds of fat, hooves, etc., thus to render these weights compatible with those used in the West they would have to be reduced to 60% of their present value (Wädekin, 1990). Regularity of supplies, quality and presentation of foodstuffs remained unsatisfactory and reached crisis proportions in 1990 (as will be discussed in Chapter 7).

Four kinds of retail outlet operate in the Soviet Union: the state shops, the para-state consumer cooperatives, the kolkhoz markets and the illegal black market. Prices are subsidised in the state shops, but supply is insufficient. This is partly due to a large share of products which should have gone to state shops being sidetracked into other legal and illegal retail outlets (Wädekin, 1990). In the uncertain situation theft and hoarding became ever more prevalent and, as will be explained, in 1990 various Republics (including the Ukraine, Uzbekistan and Tadzikistan) limited or stopped exports of foodstuffs from their territory. The long-standing problems of poor distribution and wastage were aggravated by the breakdown in the old command system.

Rationing of products in the state distribution network became increasingly widespread, and before the price reform of April 1991 prices on kolkhoz and black markets were often up to thirty times higher (and even more for certain products). For instance, whereas in the state shops eggs (when they could be found) cost between 90 copecks and 1 rouble, the price on the kolkhoz markets was 15–30 roubles in October 1990 and the difference for pork was 1.90 and 25 roubles(22). According to official statistics, the average income in 1990 was 270 roubles per month, although at least 71 million have less than 100 roubles per month. On average 40% of household expenditure is on food and drink (excluding alcohol)(23).

The ability to obtain foodstuffs or other products became increasingly dependent on the extent to which individuals could afford to pay prices on the kolkhoz and black markets; their position and the degree of privileged access this allowed; and personal contacts (for instance family in the country) and the goods they could offer in barter (Wädekin, 1990).

To improve or simply to maintain standards of food consumption the Soviet Union had to resort increasingly to international markets. The share of imports in consumption between 1960 and 1987 rose from 0.2% to 13.7% for cereals, from 1.5 to 6.6% for meat, from 0.6 to 19.7% for butter, and from 3.8 to 22.5% for vegetable fats(24). The very large increase in grain imports reflects the precedence given to livestock production. The annual average level of cereal imports rose from 14.5 million tonnes over the 1970–75 period to 26.4 million over the 1976–81 period and 35.4 from 1982 to 1988. Moreover, a growing share of these imports has been coming from the West, and this is largely due to the reluctance of traditional suppliers such as Hungary and Bulgaria to continue exporting when large Soviet deficits emerged as a result of the worsening in Soviet terms of trade between 1986 and mid-1990 (as explained in the last chapter).

Clayton (1985) obtained quite convincing results in a regression between net grain imports and domestic production instability. However, to obtain a complete picture other factors would have to be taken into account, including world production and prices, the Soviet terms of trade, total Soviet export earnings, the impact of procurement, and the quality of Soviet agricultural production. In the immediate future, as will be explained below, the decisions of the Soviet leadership are likely to prove a major factor in determining the level of grain imports.

In view of rapidly rising production costs (by some 25% on sovkhoz (state farms) and 17.3% on the kolkhoz (collective farms)) over the 1980–87 period(25), and despite some hidden inflation, in order to keep retail prices of basic foodstuffs stable the state had to increase its subsidies on agricultural products to a planned 95 billion roubles for 1990. The overall budget for agriculture and the food industries rose from some 25 billion roubles in 1980 to a planned 116.5 billion for 1990 when it is expected to account for 47.4% of the total Soviet Budget(26).

Despite differences in emphasis, there is widespread agreement among Soviet and Western observers that system-endemic causes are to blame for poor Soviet agricultural performance, although adverse climatic features also contributed. The causes include: insufficient producer incentives (arising in part from the price system); lack of dependable supply and poor quality of inputs resulting in hoarding and low productivity; poor rural infrastructure and vast distances between centres of production, conservation and transformation; emigration of the best-trained labour supply to the cities; inadequate buildings, storage facilities, etc.; and the structure and organisation of the agricultural sector.

6.6.1 *Perestroika and Soviet agriculture*

There have been various attempts to meet these difficulties, including the unsuccessful 1982 Food Programme, and the application of perestroika to the agricultural sector from 1985. With Gorbachev's report to the Plenum of the Central Committee of March 1989, and the measures introduced in April 1989, the main elements of this first phase of agricultural restructuring became evident.

In his 1989 speech, Gorbachev stressed that although all kinds of agriculture including 'peasant' farms ('private' was still a taboo word) and individual private plots were to compete on the same terms, the sovkhoz and kolkhoz were to remain the 'main path' to agricultural development. However, the sovkhoz and kolkhoz were to be transformed into genuine cooperatives operating to a large extent on a leasehold basis. The sovkhoz and kolkhoz could lease any means of production, including land, to socialised organisations or enterprises, but also to individuals or groups of individuals. The Decree of 7 April 1989, relating to leasing allowed land to be leased from five to fifty years or more, with the possibility of contracts being passed on to members of the family.

Other reform measures introduced during this first phase of perestroika include increased autonomy for the basic agricultural production units with regard to 'planning, production, price formation, production measures and the distribution of income'(27). The *quid pro quo* for this autonomy was tighter financial constraints, with the threat that farms which failed to balance their budgets within two to three years would be refused loans, 're-organised' or wound up. The tax system was to be revised, and there was to be a vigorous programme to improve rural living conditions and infrastructure, by building roads, hospitals, sport and cultural facilities, etc., improving social insurance and pension schemes and relaunching small-scale industry and food processing.

The management of the agro-industrial sector was to be restructured with decentralisation of most authority for the day-to-day management of the sector(28). Orders were no longer to be met by the old bureaucratic means of detailed official norms and control of careers, but instead there was to be increased reliance on indirect and incentive methods, such as preferential supply and loan arrangements.

In 1987 it was announced that the mechanism and criteria for determining prices would be reformed. However, although from January 1990 there was a reduction in the number of products for which purchase prices were fixed, changes in the retail prices for basic foodstuffs did not occur until April 1991.

It was subsequently decided that Soviet farmers producing wheat and oilseeds above previous average levels were to be paid in hard currency which could be used to pay for imports of consumer goods, machinery or equipment. Initially this measure was limited to state farms, but its possible extension to cooperatives, or even individuals operating in the agricultural sector, were to be considered. The major shortcoming with this project was the enormous quantity of wheat or other products which had to be sold to the state in order to be able to purchase imports. For instance Segrè (1990a) calculates that to be able to buy an American combine harvester worth $150,000, the sovkhoz would have to sell the wheat produced from some 800 hectares.

In February 1990 the Soviet Parliament passed a new land law and in March 1990 a law on property was passed. In their final form both these laws represented compromises, not only with conservatives opposed to complete acceptance of the idea of private property, but also with the Republics anxious for greater decentralisation of power.

The land law envisaged perpetual, hereditary leasing of land, though land could not be sold, divided, rented or given away, and the use of salaried workers was forbidden. The various Republics are to be responsible for implementation of the law and to decide on many of its details, such as the maximum size of holding allowed. The kolkhoz would be responsible for the allocation of land, while local Soviets would resolve any disputes arising and could revoke the lease if the land were exploited badly or insufficiently. In this way both the kolkhoz and the local authorities still retained a considerable degree of authority. The sovkhoz and kolkhoz would also be able to own land permanently (whereas in the past they 'utilised' land and the harvest belonged to the state).

Various inconsistencies in these agricultural reform measures can be cited. For instance, it is difficult to see how financial discipline was to operate until prices were freed or there was direct access to markets. It is doubtful how much independence enterprises had in fact gained when much of their production still had to be sold to the state at prices which were more flexible, but fixed to a large extent. The early experience of leasing was not very successful. Although officially the number of sovkhoz and kolkhoz with leasing contracts rose from 15,000 (30% of the total) in 1988 to 18,000 in 1989, in practice only a very small proportion of total land is involved(29). The kolkhoz and sovkhoz remained in a position to dictate many of the terms of leasing, while almost daily the Soviet press cited examples of bureaucratic obstruction to leasees, for instance in rendering it difficult for them to obtain machinery, inputs or credit.

In addition to the general motives for resistance to reform, additional reasons emerge in the case of agriculture. Soviet agricultural policy has followed a cyclical development, with encouragement of private initiatives when times are especially hard, only to block them when the peasants appeared to be earning too much, and there is a fear that this time, too, the policy may be shortlived. Again there is a reluctance, as a result of lack of experience, to undertake riskier forms of production. There remains a widespread prejudice against 'kulaks' and resentment against the 'speculators' or 'profiteers' who have been able to benefit from the situation of uncertainty and shortages.

From 1990, the question of agricultural reform was mainly discussed in the context of plans to tackle the overall reform of the Soviet economy. As will be shown in the next chapter, the Shatalin Plan pronounced in favour of the privatisation of the sovkhoz and kolkhoz, but the reform package agreed in October 1990 relegated the decision on private property to the Republics.

In December 1990 the Russian Parliament voted a land law allowing for private property. However, in its final form this also represented a compromise in that conditions were imposed; for instance resale had to be to local authorities and could only take place after ten years.

At the same time Gorbachev announced a series of measures to meet the food crisis. The main objective was to maintain food supplies at the 1989 level, which would *inter alia* entail imports of 1.5 million tonnes of meat and 500,000 tonnes of butter(30). As will be discussed in connection with food aid, a list of Soviet food requirements was also presented at the Paris CSCE meeting of November 1990. Conditions for foreign joint ventures were to be improved, and the Soviet government proposed, subject to the approval of the Republics, to place 3–5 million hectares at disposal for use as private plots(31).

As will be shown in Chapter 7, the question of reform of Soviet agriculture, like that of the economy as a whole, has become inextricably linked to the power struggle between the Union and the Republics. The scope for reduced wastage (as in the Polish case) and a greater role for private agriculture would seem to offer the best prospects for early improvement in Soviet agricultural performance. However, given the uncertain outlook, the deteriorating domestic supply situation and the growing food requirements, it seems likely that Soviet dependence on food imports will rise in the short-to-medium run.

6.7 Agriculture in the smaller Central-East European countries

Growth in agricultural production was slower in the 1980s than the 1970s in all Central-East European countries except the German Democratic Republic (see Table 6.6), reflecting the overall economic slowdown of these countries and the austerity measures taken at the time(32). In particular, hard-currency shortages and the debt situation meant limitation on imports of high-quality agricultural equipment and spares.

Table 6.6 Trends in East European agriculture

	Bulgaria	Hungary	GDR	Poland	Romania	Czech.	USSR
Annual % change in:*							
Gross ag. production							
1971–75	2.2	3.1	2.2	3.2	4.9	3.8	2.5
1976–80	2.1	2.9	1.4	0.6	5.4	2.7	3.0
1981–85	1.2	2.1	1.6	–0.5	2.0	1.9	1.1
1986–90 (plan)	1.6–1.9	1.4–1.9	1.5	2.3	6.1–6.7	1.3	2.7
1986	11.7	2.4	–	5.0	12.9	0.6	5.3
1987	–4.3	–1.0	1.6	–3.0	2.3	0.9	0.2
1988	–0.1	4.5	–4.0	0.6	2.9	2.2	0.7
Ag. investment							
1981–85	–0.1	–2.4	–3.6	–6.9	5.8	3.4	1.9
1986	–12.1	6.9	5.8	0.4	–3.2	3.1	6.4
1987	13.0	21.4	8.6	3.5	–2.4	–1.9	2.3
Employment in ag.							
1976–80	–2.7	–0.5	–0.3	0.5	–4.6	–1.4	–1.2
1981–85	–2.6	–0.9	1.1	–0.8	–0.5	–0.2	–0.3
1986	–2.1	–4.6	0.5	–1.2	0.1	–0.6	–0.9
1987	–3.4	–3.9	0.1	–0.8	0.1	–0.8	–0.4

* The five-year figures are annual averages for each five years as compared with the preceding five-year period.
Source: ECE Economic Survey of Europe, various years, and Lhomel (1989) who bases her employment statistics on Vacic (1988).

The slower growth of the 1980s occurred despite agriculture being given a higher priority in many of these countries (for example investment in agriculture rose in all these countries over the 1981–85 period compared to the previous five-year period), in contrast with the 1970s when agriculture was simply regarded as a springboard for industry(33).

As Segrè (1989a) reports, the new priority has rendered agriculture in the various Central-East European countries more homogeneous, a development which is also evident in the structure of agricultural production in these countries. As in the Soviet Union, rising consumer expectations and incomes have increased the demand for higher quality food, especially meat. As a consequence, with the sole exception of Romania, the share of livestock in total production has gradually increased over the last twenty years.

Partly because of this increase in livestock production, some of the smaller Central-East European countries have problems in meeting their requirements of animal feedstuffs, and are heavily dependent on imports from the West. Limited hard currency to pay for these imports during the 1980s has meant that at times, particularly in Poland and Romania, it has been necessary to slaughter livestock. For instance, Lhomel (1989) reports a 15% reduction in the Polish pig herd, and a 25% reduction in poultry between 1980 and 1987. The German

Democratic Republic was a major importer of cereals and animal foodstuffs from the EC and experienced no decline in its imports during the 1980s, while Czechoslovakia succeeded in reducing imports of cereals and animal foodstuffs, though without any corresponding decline in meat production.

As can be seen from Table 6.7, the worsening of agricultural performance in the 1980s was reflected in a large negative trade balance for the six smaller CMEA countries taken as a group. Table 6.7 also shows considerable differences in the trade performance of the smaller Central-East European countries, and these differences have to be taken into account in assessing longer-term prospects. It is possible to distinguish a 'southern' group of countries (Bulgaria, Romania and Hungary) in which, traditionally, agriculture has played a predominant role, and which were generally exporters of agricultural products. Even this generalisation has to be qualified since, for example, many Romanian agricultural exports were achieved only at the expense of rationing and shortages on the domestic market, while Bulgarian imports of cereals contributed greatly to its problem of foreign indebtedness. Poland is also an important agricultural exporter, though this is probably a reflection of the desperate need to earn foreign currency to service the Polish foreign debt, and the difficulties of producing enough manufactured goods of sufficient quality for export. In contrast, Czechoslovakia is more industrialised and agriculture occupies a less important position.

Table 6.7 Total agricultural trade of the Central-East European countries (annual averages, million $)

	Bulgaria	Hungary	GDR*	Poland	Romania	Czech.	USSR
Exports							
1971–75	919.6	1025.3	203.5	764.0	679.4	303.3	2028.4
1976–80	1572.2	1813.8	446.5	1079.4	1242.1	481.3	2547.0
1981–85	1715.9	2068.9	462.5	797.0	956.4	574.2	2512.6
1986	1659.1	1878.0	497.8	987.7	880.2	612.2	2463.9
Imports							
1970–75	340.9	600.3	1255.9	1136.8	490.2	1083.2	5114.1
1976–80	556.2	1109.1	2125.9	2370.0	1334.0	1776.9	12365.1
1981–85	836.6	811.3	2152.1	1836.7	881.5	1748.6	19456.7
1986	1091.4	858.5	1909.8	1310.2	729.3	1868.4	15379.4
Trade balances							
1971–75	578.8	425.0	–1052.4	–372.8	189.2	–779.9	–3085.7
1976–80	1016.0	704.7	–1679.3	–1290.6	208.2	–1295.6	–9819.1
1981–85	879.3	1257.6	–1689.6	–1039.7	74.9	–1174.4	–16944.1
1986	567.7	1019.5	–1412.0	–331.5	150.9	–1256.2	–12915.5

* Excludes trade between the GDR and FRG.
Source: ECE Economic Bulletin for Europe (1988), which uses FAO data.

6.7.1 The agriculture of each of the smaller Central-East European countries

In *Poland* the private sector accounted for 77% of the utilised agricultural land, 82% of net final production and 86% of total value added(34). Until the recent reforms Polish agriculture was therefore anomalous both when compared to the rest of the Polish economy and to agriculture in other Central-East European countries, so it was frequently quoted as an example in the debate on the possible coexistence of different systems. In order to resolve this anomalous situation, in post-war Poland a cyclical pattern of trial and error emerged with periodic attempts at rapid socialisation of agriculture being followed by the abandoning of these attempts because of their excessive social and economic cost. The uncertainty engendered by these changes in policy together with the precarious future and low priority given to private initiatives in agriculture greatly contributed to the problems of Polish agriculture.

In 1985 the average size of a Polish farm was 4.9 hectares; and 58.9% of the country's 2.8 million farms were less than 5 hectares. In addition land holdings were fragmented, often with up to nine non-contiguous plots. This, together with poor infrastructure, meant that rural poverty was endemic. Two-thirds of small farms rely on salaries of at least one member of the family from the non-agricultural sector, while the lack of shops in some areas also contributes to the widespread recourse to subsistence farming(35).

Finally, for many years the dependence of Polish agriculture on a corrupt and inefficient system of collection, transformation and distribution entailed losses and poor quality of products. Farmers faced the monopsonic power of a purchasing system based on huge regional co-operatives, while processing was concentrated in units which were too large, too far from farms and based on obsolete technology. As a result, for instance, producing 11,500 million litres of milk in 1987 Poland appeared to be one of the largest European dairy producers, on a par with the Netherlands. However, only 30% of this milk was of sufficient quality to conform with the norms imposed by the Polish dairy industry, and only 21% was actually processed(36). As a result in 1987 Poland had to import 33,000 tonnes of butter and 44,000 tonnes of cheese. Similarly, meat on the domestic market suffered from short supply, mediocre quality and little variety.

From April 1989 production prices for farmers were freed, and minimum prices were introduced for staple agricultural products in order to guarantee farm profitability and lift rural incomes to urban levels. In August a free market in the agricultural and food sector was introduced and nearly all subsidies on food were abolished(37). Inflation was 740%

in 1989, with food prices in December 1989 being 878% higher than the same month a year earlier. In December retail prices for bread and sugar were seventeen times above the previous year, pork – 18.2 times, beef – 14.5 times and dairy products about 14 times(38).

The Mazowiecki stabilisation programme (described in Chapter 7) hit agriculture particularly hard, with profitability being reduced by higher farm taxation and increasing production costs (in part because although the monopolies of farm inputs continued, their subsidies were eliminated). By mid-1990 the prices received by most farmers were below world levels, while high retail prices and the stabilisation measures meant that internal demand for many foodstuffs was dampened (by an estimated 10–15% in the first quarter of 1990). Chilosi (1990) reports a 41% fall in production in the food industry in January and February compared with the corresponding months a year earlier. Demonstrations by farmers in July 1990 caused the agricultural minister to lose his office, and there has been a virtual schism of Rural Solidarnosc.

According to official Polish statistics, in 1990 agricultural production fell by 1.4%, with arable production unchanged and a 3.2% decline in livestock production. The latter reflects reduced demand, and an eightfold increase in input prices during the year, while prices for agricultural products rose by four times. The use of artificial fertilisers fell by 16.5% in 1990 and that of pesticides by nearly one third.

The grain harvest reached a record level of 28 million tonnes in 1990, a 3.9% increase over the 1989 volume. The wheat harvest for 1990 was expected to be some 8.2 million tonnes(39). In June 1990 the largest Polish food trader, Rolimpex, requested the government to export 1 million tonnes of grain of which 500,000 tonnes were wheat(40). The EC Commission had to be reassured that none of this formed part of the 1.5 million tonnes of wheat granted to Poland as part of the PHARE aid package, and agreed not to deliver the further 300,000 tonnes committed unless it was needed by Poland.

In the past, Poland had generally imported some 1.5 to 2 million tonnes of wheat a year, and the changed situation can be attributed partly to reduced wastage and to higher prices dampening domestic demand. Previously, bread had been used to feed livestock as it was cheaper than other animal feeds, but the reduction in subsidies on bread meant that this was no longer the case. According to some estimates, there could be a net reduction in Polish wheat consumption of some 30% (41).

Milk production of 15,755 litres in 1990 was 1.1% down on 1989 levels, following a 3.6% increase in 1989. Subsidies continued on skimmed milk powder but not fresh milk, thereby encouraging butter production so that some 50,000 tonnes of butter had to be placed in public stocks by the end of 1989(42).

The government was also obliged to make intervention purchases for pigs in March 1990, and subsequently for grain(43). Subsidies on fertilisers and whole milk were partially reinstated, but the government maintained that it could not afford to introduce the guaranteed minimum prices being requested by many farmers. One of the main requirements for improved agricultural performance is the restructuring of production of farm inputs, and of the purchasing and processing systems. In order to improve farm structure, the low-interest purchase of land is being encouraged.

From 1990 the liberalisation of foreign trade and the elimination of quantitative restrictions led to a rapid increase in agricultural imports, particularly on the part of small private firms and individuals. While this increased competition, Polish farmers argued that they were placed at a disadvantage vis-à-vis other agricultural exporters, and particularly the EC. Though there would seem to be a case for introducing some limited form of protection (possibly through tariffs), the risk of discouraging the urgently needed restructuring of Polish agriculture should also be taken into account.

The USDA has estimated that by 2000 Poland could be a net meat exporter, especially of pork and, to a lesser extent, beef, but that net import requirements of grains and oilseeds would continue(44). These results are based on the assumptions that the productivity gap between Polish and West European agriculture closes by a half, that Polish agricultural prices reflect world levels, and that there is positive income growth.

Hungarian agriculture has generally been regarded as a success over the last fifteen years. During the 1960s, as a legacy of the policy of Nyers, there was widespread recognition of the fundamental role that agriculture played in the Hungarian economy, and of the need to render agriculture efficient by importing high-quality inputs from the West, including machinery, livestock breeds, and seeds. At the same time there were successive measures to liberalise the statutes of agricultural co-operatives which meant that the sector was at the forefront of the reform process when the New Economic Mechanism (NEM) was introduced in 1968. The virtual disappearance of peasant farms at this time was largely compensated by the importance attached to the private plots of cooperative members, and with the revival of reform in the late-1970s the cooperative members were able to extend their private initiatives into other branches of industry and the services(45). As a result Hungary has been able to develop a system of marketing and processing which places it at an advantage vis-à-vis other Central-East European countries as regards the quality and presentation of agricultural produce.

Since 1985 agriculture has grown on average by 2% per year while the overall economy has declined so that the share of agriculture in GNP has risen. However, difficulties for the sector arose from the reduction of state subsidies to agriculture from 34,000 million forints in 1987 to 32,000 million in 1988 and 24,300 million in 1989. As a result, for example pork retail prices rose by 35% in January 1990, causing a fall in consumption of 15%. At the same time feed costs were rising, bringing about a decline in the pig population to the levels of the 1970s(46).

Changes will have to be implemented in the structure of Hungarian agriculture and though there may be a continuing role for cooperative farms (with altered property rights), changes in the state farms are likely to prove necessary, possibly transforming them into joint-stock agribusiness firms(47). However, the capital for investment (especially in view of the tight credit situation) or foreign partners willing to participate in joint ventures are not always forthcoming(48). The issue of property rights is also likely to prove difficult to resolve.

Despite being a member of the free-trading Cairns group of the GATT, in 1990 Hungary still applied import licences on about 70–75% of all agricultural products by volume, and about 60% of the product list. The exceptions were mainly processed food products, fruit and vegetables and tropical products.

Hungary was especially affected by Soviet payment difficulties and the virtual ban on imports of wine to the Soviet Union as part of Gorbachev's campaign against alcoholism. In order to ease its foreign debt burden and because of its reluctance to continue exporting to the Soviet Union, Hungary is attempting to increase its food exports to hard-currency countries.

As a basically industrial country, the level and diversity of *Czechoslovakian* agricultural production must be regarded as satisfactory. Self-sufficiency rates of some 90% have been reached for most major products, though at times this has been attained only at the cost of bans on exports and entailed making agriculture the most heavily subsidised sector of the economy. The average size of cooperatives was 2597 hectares in 1987 and these accounted for 80% of arable land, while state farms with an average size of 6162 in 1987 accounted for a further 10–12% of arable land (49). The high levels of nitrate and phosphate pollution will have to be reduced.

Bulgaria is the Central-East European country in which, according to the statistics available, the agricultural sector declined most rapidly, despite heavy investment, and during the 1980s performance remained poor (see Table 6.6). An inadequate irrigation system and a series of bad harvests led to grain imports which greatly added to the problem of foreign debt(50). At the end of the 1980s the socialised sector accounted for nearly 85% of arable land, with an average farm size of 3.9 thousand hectares. In 1990 de-monopolization of distribution and processing was begun, and in February 1991 a privatisation law was introduced, and consumer prices for foodstuffs were liberalised.

Romanian agriculture is in a drastic state of underdevelopment, with chronic shortages of capital, energy and fertilisers. This is largely due to Ceausescu's policy of industrialisation which included the famous 'resettlement' programme designed to narrow the gap between rural and urban development, and create a 'new socialist man' very different from the traditional Romanian peasant(51). As has now become apparent, despite the continuing scarcity of statistics, the industrialisation policy was not only unsuccessful, but starved the agricultural sector of resources.

The *German Democratic Republic* will be discussed in connection with the question of German unification, but it should be noted that without the German Democratic Republic, the agricultural trade deficit of the smaller CMEA countries during the 1980s shown in Table 6.7 would virtually be eliminated.

6.7.2   *Prospects for agriculture in the smaller Central-East European countries*

Bearing in mind that the stage of transformation reached varies considerably among the smaller Central-East European countries, the question arises as to how this transformation is likely to affect their agricultural trade.

Various factors suggest that the demand for agricultural products is unlikely to rise, at least in the short run. The removal of subsidies means higher retail food prices; stabilisation measures are likely to imply lower incomes; and industrial restructuring will involve higher levels of unemployment. Shortages of foreign exchange will continue to impose a check on imports of agricultural products and inputs, especially in view of the indebtedness situation of many of these countries, and of the huge increase in their energy bills expected from 1991 (as explained in Chapter 5).

The Polish example has illustrated how the reduction of wastage may have a positive impact on supply. Against this, however, must be set the disruption associated with at least the initial stages of transformation, and the USDA has estimated that the gross agricultural output of the region could fall by 1% in 1990 and even more in 1991(52). Despite this fall in output, the USDA suggests that exports from the area might rise because of the desperate need to earn foreign currency.

In the longer run, there is potential for increased production. For instance, yields of cereals are 3.5 tonnes/hectare in Poland and 4.5–5.5 in Hungary as compared with up to 8 tonnes/hectare in similar areas in

Western Europe (53). Despite variations, in many areas such as Eastern Bulgaria and Romania, the soil is considered to be very fertile. Finally, when compared with the small, fragmented farms in many areas of Western Europe, if the question of property rights can be successfully resolved, the legacy of collective farms could leave the smaller Central-East European countries with a more favourable farm structure.

6.8 The main features of agricultural trade between the EC and Central-East Europe

As is often noted, there is asymmetry in the importance of East–West trade for the EC and CMEA, and this asymmetry applies also in the case of agricultural trade. In 1986 the EC accounted for 10.8% of CMEA agricultural imports and 26.8% of exports(54). The corresponding figures for the EC were 1.7% of all imports and 2.5% of all exports (see Tables 6.8, 6.9 and 6.10). Leaving aside intra-EC trade, the CMEA 7 accounted for 4.3% of Community imports from third countries, and 9.1% of exports in 1986.

As can be seen from Table 6.11, the EC agricultural trade deficit was turned into a surplus in most years after 1980. This was due to the increase in Soviet grain imports especially after 1980. It should be noted

Table 6.8   EC agricultural exports to the CMEA (million ECU)

Year	(a) Ag. exports EC(12) to CMEA	(b) Ag. exports EC* to CMEA	(c) (b) as % total EC ag. exports	(d) Annual % change in (b)	(e) (b) as % total EC(12) exports to CMEA
1962	138	117	2.6	–	–
1965	250	213	3.5	13.9	12.8
1970	301	249	2.6	67.1	7.6
1975	518	401	1.8	–19.6	4.3
1978	754	560	1.8	4.1	5.4
1979	1093	919	2.6	64.1	7.1
1980	2173	1924	4.7	109.4	12.6
1981	3480	3518	6.8	82.9	19.2
1982	2304	2208	4.1	–37.2	12.9
1983	2558	2421	4.2	9.6	12.2
1984	2415	2300	3.6	–5.0	10.9
1985	2593	2505	3.7	8.9	11.0
1986	1756	–	2.5	–29.9	8.7
1987	1376	–	1.9	–21.6	7.2
1988*	1507	–	2.0	9.5	–

* Eurostat SITC Rev. 2 became Rev. 3.
Source: Adapted from Eurostat.

Table 6.9   EC agricultural imports from the CMEA (million ECU)

Year	(a) Ag. imports EC(12) from CMEA	(b) Ag. imports EC* from CMEA	(c) Annual % change	(d) (a) as % total EC(12) imports from CMEA
1962	450	430	–	–
1965	561	519	23.3	22.4
1970	756	736	–0.5	19.0
1975	992	917	1.7	10.9
1978	1100	1004	6.9	8.0
1979	1021	1002	–0.2	6.0
1980	1085	944	–5.7	5.3
1981	1081	1060	12.3	4.7
1982	1156	1107	4.4	4.2
1983	1212	1159	4.7	4.1
1984	1447	1375	18.6	4.0
1985	1591	1525	10.9	4.7
1986	1417	–	–7.1	5.7
1987	1483	–	4.7	6.1
1988	1518	–	2.4	–

Source: Adapted from Eurostat.

Table 6.10   The share of East-Central European countries in total EC(12) agricultural imports (per cent)

	CMEA	USSR	Hungary	Poland	Romania	Bulgaria	GDR	CSSR	Intra EC
1962	4.3	1.0	0.6	1.6	0.5	0.3	0.1	0.3	31.6
1965	4.1	0.5	0.8	1.5	0.6	0.4	0.1	0.3	35.5
1970	4.3	0.5	1.0	1.2	0.7	0.4	0.2	0.3	43.6
1975	2.9	0.2	0.7	0.7	0.5	0.2	0.4	0.2	50.5
1980	2.0	0.1	0.6	0.7	0.2	0.1	0.1	0.1	54.7
1985	1.9	0.2	0.6	0.7	0.1	0.1	0.1	0.2	58.8
1986	1.7	0.2	0.5	0.6	0.1	0.1	0.1	0.1	61.5
1987	1.7	0.2	0.5	0.7	0.1	0.1	0.4	0.1	60.7
1987% %1962	0.4	0.2	0.8	0.4	0.2	0.3	0.4	0.3	1.9

Source: Adapted from Eurostat.

that the particularly high level of cereal imports in 1981 coincides with the EC commitment not to undermine the US embargo.

Despite variations from year to year, the share of the CMEA 7 in all EC agricultural exports changed little over the period, from 2.6% in 1962 to 2.0% in 1988 (see Table 6.8). The equivalent share in extra-EC agricultural exports was 7.6% (4.6% for the Soviet Union) for 1987, but this percentage rose to 19.8% for cereals and cereal preparations (SITC 04) and 20.9% for animal feedstuffs (SITC 08). The CMEA share in

Table 6.11   The agricultural trade balance of the EC(12) with the USSR and the smaller Central-East European countries (million ECU)

	Imports from USSR	Exports to USSR	USSR trade balance	Central-East Eur.(6) trade balance	Total European–CMEA trade balance
1962	104.4	31.1	−73.4	−238	−312
1965	64.5	45.5	−19.0	−292	−311
1970	85.7	41.7	−44.0	−410	−455
1971	106.1	41.0	−65.1	−395	−460
1972	70.8	95.7	24.9	−505	−480
1973	56.1	191.5	135.4	−613	−478
1974	67.4	183.0	115.6	−493	−377
1975	75.3	186.6	111.3	−585	−474
1980	74.3	1092.8	1018.5	70	1089
1981	82.5	1774.2	1691.7	708	2399
1982	89.1	1356.5	1267.4	−118	1148
1983	88.2	1754.6	1666.4	−319	1346
1984	123.5	1595.3	1471.8	−503	968
1985	139.6	1742.1	1602.5	−600	1002
1986	123.3	1081.5	958.2	−619	339
1987	123.1	829.5	706.4	−814	−108
1988	122.3	800.5	678.2	−689	−11

extra-EC exports of dairy products was only 4.7%, 2.7% for meat and live animals, and 5.7% for fruit and vegetables in 1987.

The variations from year to year in EC exports to the CMEA can be partly explained by the shortcomings of agriculture in the Soviet Union and certain other CMEA countries outlined above, as well as by austerity measures attempting to limit hard-currency imports. However, it is also because East–West European agricultural trade is relatively modest in size so that a single transaction may have a considerable impact on the statistics. Moreover, as foreign trade associations were responsible for much of Central-East European trade, transactions tended to be fairly large. This can be illustrated by the example of a contract between the Italian firm Cerealmangimi, and the Exportkleb of Moscow, which entailed furnishing 300,000 tonnes of grain worth about 29 million ECU to the Soviet Union in 1987. The impact of this order on trade statistics is evident when it is recalled that total Italian grain exports to the CMEA were worth less than 5 million ECU in 1986.

From Tables 6.8 and 6.9, 1986 emerges as a particularly bad year for Central-East European agricultural trade, with imports from the EC falling by 29.9% and exports to the EC by 7.1%. The explanation lies in the fall in energy prices and the reaction of the Soviet Union which 'preferred to adapt its imports from Western industrialised countries which were payable in hard currency to its reduced export earnings rather than compensate for these losses with new hard currency debts'(55).

The main Central-East European importer of agricultural products from the EC is undoubtedly the Soviet Union and, as Table 6.12 shows, its share in these imports rose from 22.5% in 1962 to 36.1% in 1975 and 53.2% in 1988. Between mid-1988 and mid-1989, the Soviet share in EC exports to the CMEA amounted to 67% of cereals, 76% of dairy products, 48% of meat, and 41% of sugar and honey. Poland is the second major importer but as Table 6.12 shows, its share fell from 23.0% in 1975 to 17.1% in 1988, probably reflecting the overall economic slowdown and stabilisation measures. Between mid-1988 and mid-1989 the Polish share in EC exports to the CMEA was 52% of coffee, tea, cocoa and spices (SITC 07), 38% of animal feedstuffs, 20% of meat, and 17% of cereals.

The country which accounted for the largest share (37.9%) of CMEA agricultural exports to the EC in 1988 was Poland, followed by Hungary whose share in CMEA agricultural exports to the EC rose from 12.8% in 1962 to 32.2% in 1988, reflecting the relatively successful agricultural performance described above.

With regard to the EC members, as Table 6.13 shows, France was the main exporter and the third most important importer in 1986, and the Federal Republic of Germany is the main importer and the second major exporter, reflecting its geographical proximity to, and a historical tradition of trade with, the East. Italy emerges as a major importer, while the United Kingdom's exports to the CMEA grew from 2.39% to 14.54% in 1986. Ireland and Greece also increased their exports rapidly after joining the EC.

As Table 6.14 shows, cereals and animal feedstuffs (SITC 04 and 08) accounted for 51.1% of all EC agricultural exports to the CMEA in 1988, with 75% of these exports going to the Soviet Union. The share of dairy produce rose from 2.7 in 1976 to 15.6 in 1988. Other important EC

Table 6.12 The share of individual Central-East European countries in total EC(12)–CMEA agricultural trade (per cent)

	Imports				Exports			
	1962	1970	1975	1988	1962	1970	1975	1988
USSR	23.2	11.3	7.6	8.1	22.5	14.0	36.1	53.2
GDR	1.0	3.9	11.8	2.3	24.6	10.0	10.0	9.8
Poland	37.7	29.8	25.1	37.9	12.3	24.6	23.0	17.1
Czechoslovakia	6.7	7.2	6.2	8.7	11.6	26.9	10.6	7.8
Hungary	12.8	22.2	24.5	32.2	16.7	14.3	9.3	4.2
Romania	11.6	16.3	18.4	5.9	4.4	4.7	4.8	1.7
Bulgaria	7.0	9.1	6.3	4.4	5.4	4.7	6.0	5.9

Source: Adapted from Eurostat.

Table 6.13   The share of individual EC countries in EC(12)–Central-East European agriculture trade (per cent)

	Imports			Exports		
	1976	1981	1986	1976	1981	1986
FRG	32.94	39.69	37.89	20.77	21.55	24.49
Italy	28.23	25.37	24.49	10.47	5.12	3.11
France	20.12	14.91	13.03	41.28	34.98	33.04
UK	8.71	5.10	5.76	2.39	11.10	14.54
Netherlands	3.30	4.41	4.52	12.92	12.87	5.01
Belgium/Lux.	4.66	6.42	4.53	6.82	6.64	1.40
Greece	n/a	2.66	2.14	n/a	3.50	5.81
Denmark	1.90	1.42	4.44	5.72	2.37	4.35
Ireland	0.11	0.06	0.06	0.60	1.55	3.66
Spain	n/a	n/a	2.27	n/a	n/a	3.75
Portugal	n/a	n/a	0.86	n/a	n/a	0.83

Source: Adapted from Eurostat.

agricultural exports to the CMEA are fruit and vegetables (9.3%) and meat and meat preparations (8.8%). Table 6.14 also illustrates that meat and live animals together accounted for 46.6% of CMEA exports to the EC in 1988, with fruit and vegetables, and also fish, proving important. The substantial cereal and animal feed imports to the CMEA coupled

Table 6.14   The structure of EC–CMEA agricultural trade (per cent)

	Imports			Exports		
	1976	1981	1988	1976	1981	1988
00	24.2	22.5	16.5	2.7	0.3	1.1
01	38.1	38.9	30.1	9.8	15.1	8.8
02	1.7	1.9	2.2	2.7	6.6	15.6
03	7.1	7.1	13.8	3.1	1.2	4.0
04	2.0	1.9	2.7	39.8	39.8	43.2
05	20.7	20.8	24.1	12.1	6.0	9.3
06	1.3	2.2	3.2	14.1	15.3	2.5
07	0.6	0.7	2.0	6.2	0.7	3.8
08	2.6	2.2	3.4	7.7	11.1	7.9
09	0.6	0.6	1.9	1.9	3.6	3.8

Key:
SITC   product:
00   live animals
01   meat and meat prep.
02   dairy and eggs
03   fish, crustaceans and molluscs
04   cereals and prep.
05   fruit and veg.
06   sugar + honey
07   coffee, tea, cocoa and spices
08   feedstuffs
09   misc. food

Source: Adapted from data from the FAO *Trade Yearbook*, various years.

with the exports of meat and live animals suggests that livestock fattening is an important source of hard currency for the Eastern European
countries.

6.9   The CAP and agricultural trade with third countries

As EC agricultural prices are generally above world levels(56), domestic
consumption is discouraged and domestic production stimulated, thus
tending to increase exports and reduce imports. The EC taken as a
whole is large relative to the world market, so that these changes in the
volume of trade will have repercussions on the *level* of world prices.
Price-support policies generally render agricultural goods less scarce in
the rest of the world and so have tended to depress world prices.

As will be shown below, the level of EC protection varies according to
product, and this is likely to affect the *structure* of EC trade and relative
prices in the world market.

The system of import levels and export subsidies increases the
stability of agricultural prices in the EC. Not only does greater price
stability act as an incentive to increase production, it also reduces the
necessity for EC farmers to spread risks by diversifying production.
Against this, however, as the results of certain studies shown below also
indicate, EC policies have added to the price *instability* of certain agricultural products in the rest of the world(57).

6.10   Indicators of the level of protection for different EC agricultural products

There have been numerous studies to estimate the level of EC (and
other) agricultural protection, and a whole series of measures has emerged. The results of the various studies are not directly comparable, even
when the same measure is used, because of differences in prices taken,
products covered, definitions and years considered, and so on. Each of
the measures taken suffers from certain weaknesses, and there is considerable debate about which is the most appropriate. If, however, the
results of various empirical studies estimating the level of protection are
closely examined, a hierarchy in the level of protection for different EC
products emerges(58). This can be seen from Table 6.15.

The *nominal protection rate* reflects the degree of divergence between
the domestic and world price for a product. This measure is subject to
considerable limitations in that estimates of nominal protection tend to
be based on prices which do not actually prevail in any market. Not only
are actual market prices in the EC frequently lower than target prices,

Table 6.15   Estimated hierarchy of different product groups according to various measures frequently used to measure EC protection

Nominal Protection Rate 1978–79 1980–81	Producer subsidy equivalent 1988	Support measurement unit 1989
Butter	Sheepmeat	Milk
SMP	Milk	Beef
Olive oil	Beef	Cereals
Beef & veal (live animals)	Wheat	Sugar beet
Maize		Rice
Barley		Rapeseed and soya
Durum wheat, oilseeds		
Common wheat		
White sugar		
Pigmeat		
Husked rice		

Source: Adapted from the *Agricultural Situation in the European Communities*, and the *Eurostat Yearbooks* for the level of nominal protection, the OECD for producer subsidy equivalents, and *Agra Europe*, 27 October 1989 for support measurement units.

but the third country offer prices used for the calculations are minimum prices, so in practice these could often be higher. Moreover, as explained above, EC preferential trade agreements mean that substantial quantities of agricultural products are imported at reduced rates of levy or duty. Furthermore, large-country effects are not usually taken into account (such as the effect of the CAP in generally lowering the prices prevailing on world markets). A further shortcoming is that nominal protection rates are incomplete and do not take account of many of the policies described above which affect EC agricultural trade flows.

Producer subsidy equivalents (PSEs) (and their counterpart, consumer subsidy equivalents) represent an attempt to meet this last criticism. These are important not only as a measure of protection, but also because of the role they have played in international trade negotiations.

PSEs can be defined as the subsidy that would be necessary to replace all the agricultural policies actually used in a country and leave farm revenue(59) unchanged. One of the great advantages of PSEs is that they are flexible, and can be adjusted to include different policies, or to leave some out.

The OECD (1989) estimated that the level of EC protection as measured by PSEs increased from an average of 35% over the 1979–81 period to about 52% in 1986, and attributed most of the increase to CAP market price support. According to the OECD, between 1979–81 and 1986 the rise in protection was faster in the crops sector (33–66%) than for livestock (33% to roughly 47%).

This is not the place to enter into the debate about PSEs but a few of their shortcomings should be mentioned. The first relates to the treatment of world price, since the estimates depend very much on the time period considered, and the 1987 OECD calculations ignored large-country effects. Secondly, PSEs entailed aggregating policies which have very different effects on trade, so the impact of, say, a 10% reduction in PSE would have a very different impact on trade, depending on the policy mix reflected in the PSE(60). A further weakness of PSEs is in the treatment of supply-control measures, such as the EC milk production quotas, and Tangermann, Josling and Pearson (1987) suggest that the use of such measures should be credited in a lower value of PSE.

The *Support Measurement Unit (SMU)* proposed by the EC Commission represents an attempt to meet some of these difficulties by taking account of variations in world price levels, and of supply-control measures, while excluding factors independent of agricultural policies.

Allowing for variations according to measure used, year and study, as Table 6.15 shows, the level of EC protection is highest for dairy products such as butter, cheese and skimmed milk powder, olive oil, beef and sheepmeat. Wheat and coarse grains occupy an intermediate level, while protection is lower on pigmeat, rice, oilseeds, poultry and sugar. Finally (though not presented in Table 6.15), the level of protection is lowest on fruit and vegetables and is zero on grain substitutes such as manioc.

6.11   A survey of models estimating the impact of the CAP on trade with third countries

Table 6.16 presents some of the results of various recent models which attempt (*inter alia*) to estimate the effect of liberalisation of EC agricultural trade on world agricultural price levels(61). These models help to provide an answer to the question 'what are the effects of the CAP?' by presenting an alternative scenario in which EC agricultural protection is partially or wholly removed.

The results obtained by the different models are not directly comparable because of differences in the base years, countries considered, sources of data, underlying assumptions and definitions, and so on(62). None the less, taken together they provide some indication of the direction and relative size of changes in world price levels for different agricultural products as a result of CAP liberalisation.

In many of the studies (OECD, Valdés and Zietz) it is assumed that changes in policies elsewhere and the consequent changes in world prices will have no impact on policies in what were then considered centrally planned economies. The OECD study therefore limits itself to calculating the change in value of CMEA imports (an increase of $39.5

Table 6.16 Estimates of the impact of EC agricultural trade liberalisation on world market prices

Model	Base period	Number of countries	Type of EC trade liberalisation	Model characteristics and comments	Commodities	% change in world prices	
Tyres and Anderson (1984)	1980	24	100% unilateral	PE dynamic	Wheat	13	
					Coarse grain	16	
					Rice	5	
					Ruminant meat	17	
					Non-ruminant meat	1	
						Unilat.	*Multilat.*
OECD (1987)	1979–81	11	10% unilateral all OECD multi-lateral	PE, CS	Milk	2.81	4.42
					Beef	0.90	1.49
					Pork	−0.01	0.33
					Poultry	−0.8	0.30
					Sheep-meat	1.53	2.18
					Wheat	−0.10	−0.11
					Coarse grain	−0.23	−0.31
					Sugar	0.55	0.99
					Rapeseed	0.42	0.79
					Soyabean	−0.98	−1.03
					Wool	0.20	0.01
					Rice	0.01	0.05
						ag.	*All sectors*
Kristoff and Ballinger (1989)	1984	8	100% ag. 100% all sectors	PE, endog. exchange rates, 2 composite non. ag. goods	Wheat	1.6	5.0
					Corn	0.2	2.7
					Soya	−5.4	−4.9
					Rice	6.6	13.2
					Sugar	29.1	33.4
					Dairy	20.0	25.5
					Beef	12.9	14.7
					Poultry	4.9	7.2
						Stan-dard run	*CPE run**
Matthews (1985)	1981	191 countries	Unilateral 100%	PE, CS	Wheat	0.7	1.2
					Barley	2.9	5.7
					Maize	0.5	0.7
					Rice	0.1	0.1
					Sugar	6.0	8.0
					Beef	3.9	5.1
					Pork	4.0	8.1
					Mutton	5.0	6.9
					Poultry	3.2	4.4
					Butter	10.5	15.4
					SMP	7.5	10.7
					Oil cake	−7.9	−10.7
					Veg. oils	5.0	6.4

Model	Base period	Number of countries	Type of EC trade liberal- isation	Model character- istics and comments	Com- modities	% change in world prices	
						1990	2000
Frohberg, Fischer and Parikh (1988)		20 and ROW	*Unilateral* gradual reduction in CAP price support 1982–86	GE dynamic recursive links national models	Wheat	6.8	8.7
					Rice	5.9	1.5
					Other cereals	7.4	3.7
					Beef & sheep- meat	11.1	6.9
					Dairy	18.9	14.9
					Other animal products	4.8	5.2
					Protein feeds	2.9	0.3
					Total ag.	6.2	4.5
						1986	
Burniaux RUNS (1988)		10	*Unilateral* CAP dis- mantling 1980–86	GE urban/ rural sectors 13 ag. 5 non- ag. groups, some behav- ioural equations reflecting price rigidities	Wheat	10.8	
					Cereals	19.9	
					Sugar	12.2	
					Meat	14.7	
						Unilat.	*Trilat.*
Mahé and Moreddu MISS (1988)	1978–79	4 + ROW	25% unilateral and trilateral (+ US and Japan)	PE, CS	Cereals	2.1	2.9
					Oilseeds	0.6	0.6
					Cereal substi- tutes	1.1	2.1
					Beef	2.8	6.1
					Pigmeat and poultry	1.5	2.9
					Milk	6.1	9.7
					Sugar	1.9	3.3
Koester (1982)	1980		100% unilateral	Model used by Valdés and Zietz, PE, CS	Oats	19.7	
					Barley	14.3	
					Wheat	9.6	
					Maize	2.2	
Sarris and Freebairn (1983)	1980	13 + ROW	100% unilateral and multi- lateral	PE single sector	Wheat	11% (multilat.) 9.1% (unilat.)	

Table 6.16   continued

Model	Base period	Number of countries	Type of EC trade liberal-isation	Model character-istics and comments	Com-modities	% change in world prices
Sarris (1988)	1981–83	49	Multilat. and unilat.	PE, CS	Wheat	–9.3 (multilat.) 3 (unilat.)

Key:
PE = partial equilibrium   DC = developed country
GE = general equilibrium   LDC = less developed country
CS = comparative statistics   ROW = rest of world

million, or 0.2%) as a result of a 10% reduction of agricultural assistance on all products in all OECD countries.

Matthews (1985) compares a standard run in which the CMEA countries are assumed to have the same price elasticities of demand and supply as the rest of the world (–0.4 and 0.4) and a simulation in which the elasticities of CMEA countries were assumed zero, as shown in Table 6.16.

An alternative assumption that is sometimes made about centrally planned economies was that a set amount of funds was allocated to imports in the five-year plans, so that any alteration in price would lead to a corresponding adjustment in quantity imported.

According to the 1984 Anderson and Tyres study, multilateral agricultural trade liberalisation would result in a loss in export earnings of $4.1 billion for the CMEA countries. It is estimated that EC liberalisation would reduce Soviet imports of wheat by 500,000 tonnes, and coarse grains by 300,000 tonnes. Soviet consumers were found to benefit by about $2 per capita from EC protection. In a later (1988) article using 1980–82 as the base period, a phased EC liberalisation over the 1988–92 period is found to cause a short-run reduction in net welfare of $(1985)1.6 billion and an increase in producer welfare of $(1985)4.5 billion for 'centrally-planned Europe', while in the longer run (by 1995) these countries would experience no change in net welfare, but an increase in producer welfare of $(1985)9.5.

Sarris finds that a unilateral EC liberalisation leads to reduced variability of world wheat prices by 8.5%, while the corresponding figure for multilateral liberalisation is 32.2%. According to Tyres and Anderson, a unilateral EC liberalisation will lead to a reduction in the coefficient of variation from 0.51 to 0.25 for wheat, and from 0.21 to 0.14 for coarse grain. The Sarris result assumes that stocks of world wheat average zero, but Josling (1980, 1981) has shown how the variability of world stocks affects world wheat prices, and cites the Soviet example. The 14 million tonnes (net of exports) purchased by the Soviet Union in 1972–73 occurred at a time of adequate stocks and surpluses, but the 1973–74 purchases coincided with a fall in LDC production, and were a 'major reason why the export price increased by 70% over the year' (1980, p. 31).

The IIASA FAP model (Frohberg *et al.*, 1988) assesses the impact of unilateral CAP liberalisation on a number of variables for CMEA countries. The model uses price elasticities of supply and demand calculated by the FAO. It is estimated that, for example in 1970 prices, the impact on CMEA countries respectively in 1990 and 2000 will be: −0.1 and −0.3 for agricultural GNP; 0.0 and −0.1 on human consumption; 6.9 and 11.8 on the CMEA agricultural trade balance; −5.4 and −3.1 on the terms of trade; and −0.3 and −0.6 on the level of agricultural self-sufficiency.

A difficulty with many of these estimates is that the CMEA countries are generally treated as bloc, and distinction is not made, for example, between a major agricultural importer such as the Soviet Union and an exporter such as Hungary. Furthermore, all the studies predate 1989, so new simulations would be necessary to take account of the subsequent transition of these economies.

6.12 The impact of the CAP on EC exports to Central-East European countries

As Table 6.7 shows, the main Central-East European agricultural importers were the Soviet Union, East Germany, Czechoslovakia and Poland and, for all of these, cereal and/or feedstuff imports were important. The results of the models shown in Table 6.16 indicate that EC policies depressed world prices by up to 13% for wheat and 16% for coarse grains (Anderson and Tyres, 1984), though most estimates are lower in the range of 7–11% (Frohberg, Fischer and Parikh, 1988; Burniaux, 1988; Koester, 1982; and Sarris and Freebairn, 1983).

The CAP therefore entails a considerable saving in foreign currency for CMEA agricultural importers, but it is extremely difficult to assess the values of this saving even ignoring possible policy reactions, partly because of the special price system used in intra-CMEA trade up until January 1991 (see Chapter 5) and, in the case of trade with the EC, because of the export refund system.

Though by the end of 1989 EC intervention stocks had been reduced to 8.6 million tonnes for cereals, 4800 tonnes of butter and 160,000 tonnes of beef, in the past, as Table 6.3 shows, these levels were much higher(63). In order to reduce these surpluses, on occasion these foodstuffs were sold to third countries (and in particular to the Soviet

Union) at what were attacked as being excessively low prices. The debate about sales of cheap butter to the Soviet Union even reached the popular press, and the 1981 Aigner Report of the European Parliament cites a number of occasions when such sales occurred, including 200,000 tonnes in 1973. In 1988, for instance, the EC sold 340,900 tonnes of butter to the Soviet Union, mostly at a price of $583/tonne, which is roughly half the GATT minimum export price. A Special Report of the EC Court of Auditors in 1990(64) quoted other examples, including a sale of 900,000 tonnes of wheat to the Soviet Union in February 1989 with an export refund of 71 ECU/tonne in a week when a refund bid of 61.9 ECU/tonne to another destination was regarded as too high.

The Aigner Report criticised this type of sale as often not being covered by budgetary appropriations and, given that they occurred at times when massive Soviet demand had unbalanced world markets, the deals were said to take place at prices which were 'inappropriate to the market situation and advantageous to the importers'.

In setting the level of export refund, management committees in the European Commission take into account likely future developments in world prices for the product in question, the cost of intervention storage and the political issues related to the size of intervention stocks as well as 'the supply–demand balance within the Community, the cost to the budget, political pressures from the third country to which the product is to be exported and the state of the domestic processing industry'(65). In addition, the Commission may differentiate the level of export fund by destination.

As a result of this discretion in setting the level of export refunds, the Commission and national governments are subject to intense lobbying by traders and importing countries. In particular, although the Commission has an interest in containing the level of spending on export refunds, according to Western trade officials involved, as the major world importer of cereals and meat the Soviet Union has in the past proved an extremely able bargaining partner, and if the EC wanted to export it often had little choice but to accept the price requested by the Soviet Union as there are few other buyers on this scale on world markets.

There is evidence that the recent weakening of the CAP intervention system for products such as cereals, beef and dairy products has been associated with increasing recourse to export subsidies as a means of maintaining internal EC prices stable. For instance, expenditure on export refunds for cereals grew from 1175 million ECU in 1980 to 2773 million ECU in 1989(66).

A further issue that should be mentioned is the link between surpluses and food aid. Though not a justification for the accumulation of further surpluses, they undoubtedly predisposed the Community towards giving aid to Poland, the Soviet Union and Romania. There is already evidence that the EC farm ministers are presenting the needs of Central-East Europe as a reason for a more expansionary agricultural policy(67). However, not only would this run counter to EC GATT obligations (as will be explained below), but an expansionary EC policy would have long-term effects in creating further excess productive capacity, while presumably the requirements of at least many of the smaller Central-East European countries are transitional, lasting only for the short to medium run.

6.13 The impact of the CAP on EC imports from Central-East European countries

The CMEA countries which were traditional exporters of agricultural products, especially Hungary and Poland, frequently criticise the 'protectionist' nature of the CAP. For instance, a Hungarian delegate to the UNCTAD (UNCTAD, 1980) maintained that the CAP had caused a 30% fall in Hungarian agricultural exports to the Community over the 1973–76 period. The suspension of beef and cattle imports to the Community after 1974 was held to be particularly damaging as these accounted for 52% of CMEA agricultural exports to the Community. Similarly, Poland maintained that its bacon industry had been built up to a large extent on the basis of the EC market (and especially the United Kingdom) and that introduction of the CAP meant that Polish exports were virtually reduced to speciality products. These countries also complain about reduced export earnings on third markets because of the lower level and greater instability of world agricultural prices resulting from the CAP.

Many of the statistics presented here lend support to these claims. In addition to the transformation of the EC from a net importer to a net exporter of the major temperate agricultural foodstuffs, the successive enlargements of the EC have entailed considerable trade diversion, with the share of intra-EC imports in total agricultural imports rising from 31.6% in 1962 to 60.7% in 1987.

The EC levels of protection are highest for certain livestock products including beef and sheepmeat and, as has been illustrated, these account for a large share of the agricultural exports of CMEA countries. However, as Tables 6.4 and 6.5 show, in some cases the smaller Central-European countries have obtained EC trade concessions for these products, even though the quantities on which these concessions obtain are usually very limited. The results of various studies suggest that EC protection of pigmeat, which is of particular interest to Polish exporters, is lower than for most other agricultural products.

The results of the models presented in Table 6.16 indicate that while in some cases the CMEA agricultural exporters may have been able to benefit from lower world prices for animal feedstuffs and cereals as a result of the CAP(68), this advantage was frequently more than offset by the even greater reduction in prices of certain meat products.

The limitations of market-share analysis are well known(69). None the less, taken in conjunction with the other results presented here, a more complete picture of EC–CMEA agricultural trade emerges.

An indication of the change in market share can be given by a simple index:

$$x = \frac{\% \text{ EC imports at end of period}}{\% \text{ EC imports at beginning of period}}$$

with x greater, equal or less than 1 according to whether the market share has increased, remained the same or fallen.

Table 6.11 shows that over the 1962–87 period the share in all EC agricultural imports fell for all Central-East European countries (0.4), though the fall was least for Hungary, and most for the Soviet Union and Romania (0.2) followed by Bulgaria and Czechoslovakia (0.3). These differences probably reflect the differing agricultural performances of these countries described in sections 6.6 and 6.7 above, and the Czech aim of increasing self-sufficiency, even though at times this necessitated export bans. The CMEA share in extra-EC agricultural imports fell from 6.2% in 1962 to 4.7% in 1988 (0.8).

Table 6.17 illustrates that the CMEA share in imports of food and beverages (SITC 0 and 1) over the 1970–86 period fell slightly for the world (0.9) and EFTA (0.7), the fall in EC share (0.5 for all imports and 0.6 for extra-EC imports) was slightly greater than those of EFTA and the world, but in line with the fall for all developed countries (0.5). The fall in intra-CMEA import share (0.6) was largely due to the Soviet grain imports from the West after 1972 and there was an increase in the import share of less-developed countries (1.1).

Table 6.17 The share of the CMEA countries in imports of food, beverages and tobacco (SITC 0 and 1) (per cent)

	World	DCs	LDCs	CMEA*	EFTA	EC**	
1970	8.8	3.8	4.4	42.2	9.0	4.5[a]	8.0[b]
1975	10.8	3.0	8.5	27.7	6.9	3.4	7.3
1980	10.8	2.2	4.0	19.6	6.6	2.1	5.2
1985	11.0	1.9	5.3	20.8	5.9	2.0	5.2
1986	8.0	1.8	4.8	25.2	6.5	2.3	4.9
% 1986							
% 1975	0.9	0.5	1.1	0.6	0.7	0.5	0.6

Notes:
* European CMEA.
** Reflects changing EC membership.
[a] All trade.
[b] Excluding intra-EC trade.
Source: Adapted from UN Commodity Trade Statistics.

Table 6.18 The share of CMEA countries in imports of various products (per cent)

EC(12) total imports	SITC no.	CMEA share 1975	1987	%1987 %1975
Live animals	00	12.1	8.3	0.7
Meat, etc.	01	7.2	4.6	0.6
Dairy, etc.	02	0.8	0.3	0.4
Cereals, etc.	04	0.2	0.5	2.5
Veg. and fruit	05	2.6	1.7	0.7
Sugar, etc.	06	1.4	2.1	1.5
Coffee, etc.	07	0.4	0.4	1.0
Feedingstuff	08	0.6	0.6	1.0
Misc.	09	0.3	0.8	2.6
SITC 0:	EC(12)	2.5	2.5	1.0
	EFTA	5.5	9.2	1.7
	OECD	2.6	1.8	0.7

Source: Adapted from OECD data.

Table 6.18 is based on OECD data for various agricultural products and the 1975–87 period. While the CMEA share of all EC agricultural imports (SITC 0) remained the same over this period, that of the OECD fell (0.7), while that of the EFTA rose (1.7) with the main EFTA increase coming from the Soviet Union (2.7), followed by Poland and ⁓Hungary (2.1).

The decline in EC import share was greatest for dairy products (0.4), meat and meat products (0.6), live animals (0.7), and fruit and vegetables (0.7), the first three of which were precisely the products which emerge elsewhere in this study as having the highest EC levels of protection.

6.14 The outlook for agricultural trade between the EC and Central-East Europe

The prospects for future East–West agricultural trade in Europe depend on demand and supply conditions in world markets, in Central-East European countries and in the EC.

Predictions about future developments in world agricultural markets are beyond the scope of this study, apart from noting that if the warnings of a changed trend in climatic conditions due to the greenhouse effect are well-founded, major Western exporters such as the EC and the United States may have less potential for agricultural (and especially grain) exports to the Soviet Union and for food aid.

The situation in the Central-East European countries depends very much on the outcome of the transformation process. In some countries, notably the Soviet Union and Romania, little improvement can be expected in the short to medium run because of the time required to decide on and/or implement reform, the initial disruption arising from change, and the further lag before results are obtained.

The measures taken by the EC to assist the CMEA countries play an essential role. Hard-currency shortages and austerity measures constituted a major check on CMEA imports of agricultural products and inputs in the 1980s, and debt relief could do much to ease the situation in the 1990s. As described above, a main element of the 'PHARE' programme is assistance to agriculture and especially the modernisation of food production, processing and marketing. The trade and cooperation agreements between the Community and individual Central-East European countries generally entail cooperation in agriculture as well as improved access for certain agricultural commodities to EC markets, and the 'second generation' association agreements will represent a further step in this direction. Analogously, the integration of East Germany into the Community, and accession of other smaller Central-East European countries (and especially of Hungary and Poland) seem likely to lead to increased surpluses and higher budgetary costs, but this might be considered to be the price to pay for the political advantages of eastward enlargement of the Community.

Turning to the EC, two developments are of special relevance in determining the prospects for agriculture. The first is the Single Market from 1993 and the question of whether this will lead to additional trade diversion. In particular, the agrimonetary system which has enabled price increases in national currencies higher than the 'common' prices agreed in ECU involves a series of border taxes and subsidies (monetary compensatory amounts) on intra-EC trade, and thus would seem to require reform before January 1993.

Secondly, there is the issue of CAP reform in the light of the Uruguay Round GATT negotiations aimed at bringing agriculture more effectively under GATT rules and disciplines(70). A conflict was soon to emerge with the United States proposing a 'zero option' which entailed the elimination of all trade-distorting subsidies and barriers to market access for agricultural products over a ten-year period, and the EC response that it was first necessary to stabilise world markets. The 'free-trading' Cairns group of fourteen agricultural exporters (of which Hungary is a member and Poland has observer status) first took a stand similar to that of the United States, but then tried to find a middle way (71).

Although agreement was reached in April 1989 in Geneva on short-term and long-term objectives with regard to agricultural trade liberalisation, the EC in particular subsequently interpreted the terms of the agreement in a way which made them less biting(72). The United States then proposed that frontier protection and domestic support be reduced by 75% and export subsidies by 90% in the period to 2000. An EC offer to reduce the level of protection of its agricultural sector by an aggregate 30% over the 1986–95 period led to a breakdown in negotiations in December 1990. In January 1991 the Agricultural Commissioner, Mac-Sharry, presented proposals for a radical reform of the CAP, but the opposition this encountered from the EC member states did not bode well for continuation of the GATT Round.

What would be the implications for the Central-East European countries of at least partial agricultural trade liberalisation if the Uruguay Round were to succeed? The result of the models in Table 6.18 give some indication of the higher world prices that agricultural importers, and especially the Soviet Union, would have to pay. Central European agricultural exporters such as Hungary would stand to gain from these higher prices, but in estimating the benefits account should be taken of the EC agricultural trade concessions for these countries.

It is also open to question how far the Central-East European countries would be able to take advantage of easier access to EC markets for agricultural products where they would be competing with some of the world's major agricultural producers. Although their geographical proximity to major EC markets is an advantage, only Hungary is at present capable of producing agricultural products at the level of quality and presentation generally required by EC consumers. However, the time required for other Central-East European producers to overcome this shortcoming is probably less than in the case of many industrial products.

Notes

1. A problem arises in choosing among the various definitions of agricultural products. Most of the statistics for EC–CMEA trade presented here are based on Eurostat which identifies agricultural products with the SITC Section 0, which is food and live animals chiefly for food, and so excludes tobacco and drinks which fall under SITC 1. The FAO definition is slightly different, covering most of SITC 0 but excluding SITC 03, that is, fish. For the UN Commodity Trade Statistics, agricultural products are defined as SITC 0, 1, 21, 22, 232, 261–5, 268, 29 and 4.
2. See, for instance, Harris, Swinbank and Wilkinson (1983).
3. In the early years the Community was self-sufficient only in dairy products, but self-sufficiency was reached for wheat in 1973, sugar in 1977, beef and veal in 1980 and coarse grains in the early-1980s. As the Bureau of Agricultural Economics of the Australian Government (1985, p. 19) explains, this increase in self-sufficiency was due to an increase in production by 2% per annum while consumption was rising by only about 0.5%. According to

Dûchene, Szczepanik and Legg (1985, p. 55–6) the EC was the world's largest exporter of meat, dairy products, beverages, barley, wheat flour, and potatoes; it was second for sugar, eggs and every individual meat; and it was fourth for wheat and oilcakes.

4. In 1984 *production quotas* were introduced for milk, and from that year a *restrictive price policy* was adopted, which has generally entailed freezing or cutting all intervention prices in ECU each year. However, as Table 4.2 shows, the *agrimonetary system* by which the 'common' ECU prices are converted into national currencies has operated in such a way as to convert these reductions (or freezes) in ECU prices into moderate increases in national currencies (described in more detail in Senior Nello (1985b)).

   At the same time the *intervention system was weakened* for many products, with, for example, limits being imposed on the quantities of butter and skimmed milk powder being accepted for intervention, a shorter intervention period for cereals, and the intervention price being reduced for beef. More stringent quality controls, and a *coresponsibility levy* were also introduced for cereals.

   In February 1988 the Council of Ministers approved a package of measures for CAP reform which included the application of *'automatic stabilisers'* aimed at limiting expenditure on support of markets and prices; a *set-aside* scheme; and measures to encourage *early retirement*. In addition, there were to be *budgetary guidelines* to limit the annual growth in the Guarantee Section of FEOGA to 74% of the growth in the GNP of the Community. Structural funds were to be doubled, including those under the Guidance Section of FEOGA, the European Social Fund, and the European Regional Development Fund.

   The 'stabilisers' entailed fixing maximum guaranteed amounts for products such as cereals, oilseeds and protein feeds. If these were exceeded there was to be a reduction in support prices. For cereals there was also to be a further 3% coresponsibility levy in addition to the basic levy of 3% already applying. For a more detailed account of these measures see Avery (1988) and Tracy (forthcoming).

5. Hartmann and Schmitz (1988); Koester and Terwitte (1988); and Tangermann (1989).

6. Article 6 of the Agreement, EC Commission (88) 1332, final of 21 September 1988

7. *Agra Europe*, 3 March 1990.

8. See Matthews (1985).

9. *Agra Europe*, 31 August 1990.

10. For example, there will be no reduction in duty on exports of horses for slaughter, and potato starch with a 50% cut in import duty will only be allowed in a quota of 5000 tonnes (*Agra Europe*, 1 December 1989).

11. The most notable example is jam, on which duty was reduced from 26% to 6% in 1989, but for which no reduction was foreseen for 1990. Other duties were actually increased, as for example boarmeat (from 0% to 3%), honey (25% to 27%) and mushrooms (8% to 16%) (*Agra Europe*, 3 October 1989).

12. Neville-Rolfe (1989).

13. Including blackcurrants, redcurrants, cherry preparations, cucumbers and gherkins from 1991.

14. See, for example: J. Brada and K.-E. Wädekin, ed. (1988); E. Cook (1985); Di Leo (1986); D. Gale Johnson and K. McConnell Brooks (1983); A.

Giroux (1984, 1986 and 1989); K. Hartford (1987); B.F. Johnston (1989); S. Hedlund (1984); E.-L. Littmann (1989); A. Segrè (1989a and 1989b); Sorbini and Segrè (1989); and K-E. Wädekin (1989).

15. In his speech to the Plenum of the Central Committee of 15 March 1989 Gorbachev puts grain losses at an annual average of some 15–20 million tonnes, with almost as much again being lost during storage and processing. All the statistics in this paragraph are taken from Gorbachev's speech.

16. Income grew by an estimated 24% between 1975 and 1983.

17. Western estimates of the income elasticity for meat range from 0.7 to 0.9, while some Soviet estimates are above unity.

18. According to Clayton (1985), p. 1044.

19. *Agra Europe*, 23 February 1990.

20. The statistics in this paragraph are taken from Wädekin (1990).

21. The 1988 figure is based on USDA (1989). According to Segrè (1989b), certain Soviet estimates are much lower at 45 kg. According to Jampel and Lhomel (1989) in 1987 per capita consumption of meat and meat products in kilos was 64.1 for the Soviet Union, 74 for Bulgaria, 78.3 for Hungary, 66.3 for Poland, 99.4 for the GDR and 89 for Czechoslovakia.

22. All these prices are taken from *La Repubblica*, 20 October 1990.

23. Wädekin (1990).

24. As Segrè reports (1989b), p. 884.

25. Segrè (1989b).

26. As reported in *Agra Europe,* 30 March 1990.

27. Resolution of the Council of Ministers of the Soviet Union of 5 April 1989 on the restructuring of economic relations in the agro-industrial sector of the Soviet Union.

28. See Pouliquen (1990) for a more detailed account of these measures, and of their decentralising effect.

29. As Segrè (1989b), p. 889, points out.

30. As announced by the Prime Minister, Ryzkhov on Soviet television on 2 December 1990.

31. *Il Sole 24 Ore*, 5 December 1990.

32. For instance, 1988 Polish agricultural production in constant price terms was only 100.7% of the 1978 level, but overall net material product in 1988 was just 99–99.4% of the 1978 level.

33. For a more detailed discussion, see for example Lhomel (1989) and Segrè (1989a).

34. Pouliquen (1987).

35. As Pouliquen (1987) points out, the picture which emerges from the statistics for farm size is perhaps excessively negative in that account is not taken of land which is let, and the concentration of usage is greater than the concentration of ownership. Moreover, as he illustrates, in response to government policy which deliberately favoured the larger farms (through selective mechanisation, more advantageous credit terms, fiscal incentives, etc.) the share of farms over 10 hectares grew from 12.6% in 1970 to 16.3% in 1985 when they accounted for 45.1% of all utilised agricultural land. This occurred despite an increase in land prices over the period.

36. Lhomel (1989).

37. In 1988 a state subsidy of 2327 million zlotys had been necessary to limit increases in prices of essential foodstuffs (Jampel and Lhomel, 1989).

38. *Agra Europe*, 2 March 1990.

39. *Agra Europe*, 20 July 1990 and 22 March 1991.

40. European Report No. 1601, 6 July 1990.
41. *Agra Europe*, 20 July 1990.
42. As reported in *The Economist*, 21 April 1990.
43. N. Cochrane (1990), oral presentation at the 'World Conference for Soviet and East European Studies', Harrogate, 21–26 July.
44. *Agra Europe*, 26 January 1990.
45. Csizmadia and Székely (1986); Cristofoli (1981); and Lhomel (1989).
46. *Agra Europe*, 8 June 1990.
47. Csaki (1990).
48. This appears to be the case for the Kornye combinat, with its 2000 employees and 6500 hectares, as described in *Agra Europe*, 8 June 1990.
49. *Agra Europe*, 11 May 1990.
50. See, for example, ECE (1988) and Wyzan (1989).
51. For an account of this policy see Ronnas (1989).
52. *Agra Europe*, 20 July, 1990.
53. *Agra Europe*, 20 July 1990.
54. UN Commodity Trade Statistics, FAO definition of agricultural commodities, values in $.
55. European Parliament, Seeler Report (1986), p. 22.
56. With a few exceptions (for example during the world commodity boom of 1973–75).
57. This question is discussed in more detail in U. Koester (1982); P.M. Schmitz (1984), pp. 29–81; M.D. Bale and E. Lutz (1979), pp. 512–16; S.J. Turnovsky (1978).
58. For a more detailed account see S.M. Senior Nello (1990b).
59. Much of the literature refers to leaving income unchanged, but as Peters (1989a, 1989b) illustrates, the PSE is essentially a revenue concept.
60. To get around this problem Tangermann, Josling and Pearson (1987) suggest that a narrower definition of PSEs should be used in trade negotiations. The Canadians, McClatchy and Cahill (1988), have also developed a trade diversion equivalent, but it is somewhat unwieldy and raises practical difficulties about how it could be used in international trade negotiations.
61. For a description of earlier models see *inter alia* Buckwell *et al.* (1982); Mahé and Moreddu (1988); Stoeckel (1985); and the Bureau of Agricultural Economics (1985); Matthews (1985).
62. As discussed in more detail in Tarditi *et al.* (1988).
63. *Agra Europe*, 26 January 1990.
64. The Management and Control of Export Refunds. Court of Auditors Special Report, No. 2, 1990.
65. Aigner Report (1981), p. 10.
66. *Agra Europe*, 2 March 1990.
67. *Agra Europe*, 26 January 1990.
68. In assessing the scale of this benefit, account has to be taken of the extent to which these inputs are imported from the West, and again, for intra-CMEA trade, the special price system used.
69. See, for example, Matthews (1985).
70. In theory GATT rules should apply to agricultural as well as industrial goods, but reflecting the interests of the United States when the GATT was established (Ford Runge and Stanton, 1988), a number of exceptions for the agricultural sector have always been tolerated. Subsequently there has also emerged a tendency to ignore GATT rules about when these exceptions should apply. In addition, many new instruments (such as import

levies, and voluntary export restraints) have evolved since the GATT was founded, and are now considered 'grey area measures' because of the uncertainty as to whether they contravene basic GATT principles. Finally, there are virtually no GATT rules applying to health and sanitary measures which can act as non-tariff barriers.

71. See Tracy (forthcoming) and Saccomandi (1988) for more detailed accounts.

72. According to the EC Commission, 1986 was the base line not only for the short-run, but also for the long-run objectives, so the Community could obtain credit for the various reforms introduced over the 1986–88 period and no additional measures would be necessary before 1990. This was at odds with all other participants who agreed on 1989 as a base year for the long-run objectives. Moreover, in 1986 world prices for many agricultural products were relatively low, implying correspondingly higher support levels. The long-term objective for the EC was set out in ECU rather than national currencies, and the agrimonetary system generally implies that prices in national currencies are higher than ECU support prices.

PART 2

Economic reforms in Central-East Europe and trade relations with the EC

7

The economic transformation of Central-East Europe

7.1   Introduction

The economic transformation of Central-East European countries can be broken down into three main elements: macroeconomic stabilisation (both internal and external); economic restructuring, systemic change and privatisation; and the creation of social safety nets. As will emerge repeatedly during this chapter, these economic tasks overlap each other and with social and political issues.

While the application of the central planning model lent a certain similarity to Central-East European economies in the past, their underlying conditions were very different in terms of resources, production methods, trade patterns and policies. The economic transformation process has compounded these basic differences by setting in motion a diversification process. Though the agenda for change has many common elements in the various countries, the extent, speed and sequence of its implementation varies considerably. Distinction is usually made between the 'big bang' approach adopted in Poland (though the bang does not appear to be so big when compared with the East German experience), and Hungary's more gradual transformation. The Soviet Union also represents a case apart, in that the process of economic transformation has become intrinsically linked to the nationalities question.

The need for change springs from the system-endemic shortcomings of centrally planned economies described in the introduction to this book. Earlier attempts to meet these difficulties ranged from the GDR model of 'technocratic fine tuning' to the measures aimed at the introduction of economic decentralisation in Hungary in the 1960s and 1970s. As Marrese (1988, p. 5) describes, the latter was based on the belief that the negative features of central planning can be eliminated by replacing centrally-determined plan targets and supply allocations for enterprises with a market-guided system based on profit-sharing for enterprise managers and workers. In this model, the central planners would guide the market along lines consistent with central preferences via control of taxes, subsidies, interest rates, access to credit and foreign currencies, import licenses and foreign exchange multipliers.

By the mid-1980s these attempts to reform the system from within had been discredited and, following certain initial hesitation on the part of the Soviet Union and Czechoslovakia, all these countries announced their intention to move towards market-orientated economies.

Given the differences of the transformation process from country to country, each of the Central-East European countries will be discussed individually. First, however, certain common elements of change will be indicated, as well as the importance of sequencing the measures correctly.

7.2   Macroeconomic stabilisation

Most of the Central-East European countries face an immediate need for stabilisation policies. Domestically, this entails the elimination of inflationary pressures, both where these are open (such as the 1989 Polish hyperinflation), or in the form of repressed inflation (rising excess demand which remains in the hands of the population as excess liquid assets (Nuti, 1986)). With regard to external balance, a stabilisation programme is required when net export earnings are no longer adequate to service foreign debt(1). Table 7.1 sets out the levels of net and gross hard-currency indebtedness of the various Central-East European countries.

Economic transformation may contribute to inflationary pressures through the reduction of product subsidies; the ending of the CMEA trading system (by raising the price of energy for the smaller Central-East European countries); devaluation; and the likely increase in public spending on infrastructure and unemployment benefits.

Though a detailed analysis of the question is beyond the present scope(2), the transformation process requires that use of direct regulation to achieve macroeconomic objectives be replaced to a large extent by indirect regulation via macroeconomic instruments such as monetary, fiscal and exchange rate policy. In particular it is necessary to reduce budget deficits and end their monetisation, and to move towards unified exchange rates at realistic levels. As a pre-condition for the successful operation of these measures, more reliable statistics have to be made available.

In the Central-East European context the introduction of monetary

Table 7.1 Gross and net debt of Central-East European countries in convertable currencies (billion $, end of years)

	Bulgaria	Czech.	GDR	Hungary	Poland	Romania	USSR	Total
1970	0.7	0.3	1.1	0.8	1.2	1.0	1.6	6.7
1975	2.7	1.0	5.2	3.1	8.4	2.9	15.4	38.7
1980	3.6	4.5	13.6	9.1	24.1	9.6	25.2	89.7
1985	3.5	3.3	13.6	11.8	29.7	6.6	31.4	99.8
1987	6.2	5.1	19.2	17.7	39.2	5.7	40.2	133.4
1988	7.6	5.2	20.2	17.3	39.2	2.3	42.5	134.3
1989**	8.1	5.0	21.7	17.3***	38.9	–	42.9	133.8
*Net debt**								
1970	0.6	–	0.9	0.6	0.9	1.0	0.6	4.6
1980	2.9	3.3	11.6	7.7	23.5	9.3	16.6	74.8
1987	5.1	3.5	10.2	16.2	36.2	4.3	26.2	101.7
1988	5.9	3.6	10.3	16.0	35.6	1.5	27.2	100.0
1989**	6.8	3.4	11.0	16.1***	35.2	–1.5	28.3	99.2

Notes: * Reflecting assets with BIS-reporting banks.
** Estimates.
*** Readjusted to $20.7 for gross debt and $18 for net dept by the Hungarian authorities (see text).
Source: *Economic Bulletin for Europe*, vol. 40, no. 3, 1988.

discipline requires the creation of independent central banks, a commercial banking system, financial markets for bonds and shares (and especially for government bond markets to help end the monetisation of public deficits) and adequate monetary instruments(3).

The fiscal system and its administration also require reform to increase transparency, reduce subsidies, cut spending on administration (and on defence in the case of the Soviet Union), reform the system of taxation (substituting taxes on income and value added for turnover tax) and widen the tax base. In particular, it would be necessary to ensure uniform tax treatment for different enterprises and individuals 'to divorce the fiscal process from its past associations of arbitrariness, instability and negotiability' (Newbery, 1990, p. 83). This would contribute to breaking the 'tutelage' (Hare, 1990a) relationship between state and enterprises and for that reason is likely to encounter resistance.

Wage restraint is also essential in the Central-East European context and, for instance, Poland introduced a system of partial wage indexation (30%, then rising to 60%) and additional taxation of firms granting wage increases beyond certain limits.

7.3 Microeconomic restructuring and systemic change

Economic restructuring entails correction of all the distortions arising from central control of pricing and the allocation of resources. This is achieved by demonopolisation, privatisation, the end of mandatory planning and the liberalisation of prices, trade and of the capital and labour markets. There has to be a greater role for consumer sovereignty, while enterprises must be given more responsibility for decisions relating to inputs, prices, products and clients. In other words enterprises have to be transformed from mere administrative units that implement the plan, and until this is achieved a domestic supply response will not be forthcoming (Nuti, 1990d). In order to introduce these measures an adequate legal framework with regard to property rights, contracts, competition and company law is required.

Greater flexibility of wages, and labour mobility will have to be encouraged. In the past low wages led to hoarding of labour, and much of this hidden unemployment will have to be acknowledged as open unemployment. The restructuring of industry will also require reallocation of labour. However, as Newbery (1990, p. 88) points out for the case of Hungary, restructuring will entail development of the retail sector and, it should be added, services in general, these being among the easiest sectors to enter. Increased labour mobility is likely to require new policies with regard to housing.

Trade liberalisation entails measures such as the reform of the CMEA trading system; direct participation of enterprises and individuals in foreign transactions; the elimination of quotas and licensing on imports; removal of those subsidies and tax concessions on exports which run counter to GATT principles; freeing of foreign travel restrictions; introduction of currency convertibility, and relaxation of capital account transactions. Many of these measures have already been implemented by various Central-East European countries, while the introduction of others is constrained by foreign debt and balance of payments considerations. A strong argument in favour of trade liberalisation is the contribution it makes to the creation of competition.

The literature on privatisation is expanding rapidly (see, for instance, Prodi, 1990; and Grosfield, 1990), and here it is impossible to do more than indicate some of the main issues. Privatisation has a strong political element as a means of reducing the role of a state considered too powerful and possibly corrupt. Its appeal lies in creating vested interests in the new order, thereby rendering the transformation process difficult to reverse. Privatisation can act as a powerful weapon in breaking down the tutelage relationships between state and enterprises. Efficiency arguments are generally used in favour of privatisation, though the distributive effects are likely to be greater(4) and, unless flanked by other measures such as demonopolisation or trade liberalisation, privatisation alone may be insufficient to raise efficiency.

At times the initiative for privatisation may come from the enterprise managers themselves who see it as a means of increasing their salaries, freedom of operation or even wealth. This may lead to abuses such as the 'spontaneous' or 'wild' privatisation carried out largely by the nomenklatura in Poland and Hungary before the relevant legislation was tightened. This form of privatisation entailed no compensation to the state for the sale of its assets, and lacked procedures to ensure that assets were correctly valued and transactions took place in open, competitive conditions.

The valuation of assets represents one of the chief difficulties of privatisation, given the price system and lack of transparency in the way in which subsidies and the tax system operate in a centrally planned economy. The risk of distortions and inequitable outcomes resulting from underestimating the value of assets could jeopardise the whole transformation process by undermining popular support.

Poland and Czechoslovakia have both introduced voucher schemes, which entail giving vouchers that can be used to purchase state-owned enterprises to a part of the population (all citizens over eighteen in the case of Czechoslovakia). In Czechoslovakia these vouchers can be used directly in auctions of state-owned firms, but in Poland the vouchers must be placed in privatisation funds. Payment of a registration fee is necessary to use a voucher in Czechoslovakia to ensure that those taking part have an interest in buying shares. The advantages of vouchers are that they may enable the privatisation process to proceed more rapidly and they help to overcome the difficulty of finding purchasers for state assets. Against this, such schemes have the drawback of not helping to reduce the budget deficit. This together with the belief that most state firms can be sold explains why Hungary did not adopt vouchers.

An alternative means of finding purchasers is to encourage wide-scale sales of state assets to foreigners, preferably in the form of joint ventures. This would probably contribute to inflows of technology and know-how, especially in the form of management and marketing techniques. However, as Portes (1990) points out, there have already been accusations of Western firms 'carpetbagging' or 'profiteering' in the sense that they have been snapping up assets cheaply.

Other possibilities include management buy-outs, the liquidation of enterprises and sale or lease of their assets, or that banks or other financial institutions hold a substantial share of assets, at least temporarily. For instance, one of the forms of privatisation adopted in Poland entails an initial phase of control by the Treasury, which will subsequently sell shares to set up joint-stock companies.

7.4   Social safety nets

An inevitable consequence of economic transformation is the acceptance of bankruptcies, unemployment and greater inequalities of income.

The question of how much unemployment can be tolerated is central to the debate about the speed at which transformation should take place, which is discussed in the next section. None the less, even with more gradual change governments will have to provide adequate social se-curity measures (and especially unemployment benefits), while trying to ensure that these do not destroy incentives.

7.5   The speed of transformation

One of the central debates about the transformation process is whether change should be gradual, proceeding step-by-step, or whether sudden and immediate change or a 'big-bang' approach (also referred to in some Eastern literature as 'shocking' [*sic*] therapy) is preferable.

The more gradual approach, such as that adopted by Hungary, allows for the possibility of adjusting policies as the situation alters, but there is also the risk that the transformation process might lose momentum, or leave tutelage relations intact(5). There will probably also be more op-portunity for reabsorbing labour if restructuring proceeds more slowly, thus keeping unemployment figures lower.

One of the main arguments in favour of speed is that the reform measures are all interlinked, forming a 'seamless web'(6). However, there is the risk that the 'big-bang' approach may lead to overshooting with excessively high levels of bankruptcy and unemployment, and large falls in living standards, as many economists have claimed happened in Poland. The disruption of supply could create bottlenecks throughout the economy, while the fall in real wages and depressed demand could impair the chances of recovery *inter alia* by causing fiscal imbalance, thereby threatening the basic objective of the stabilisation policy to combat inflation. There is a danger that the degree of 'belt-tightening' required of the population could exceed the threshold of political toler-ance, thereby discrediting the transformation process, and encouraging backsliding or even reversal of policies.

7.6   The sequencing of measures

If a big-bang approach is adopted, many measures will be implemented simultaneously, but in the case of gradual change correct sequencing of measures may provide the key to the success of the programme. Unfor-tunately, economic theory provides relatively little guidance with regard to sequencing and there is a need for further research in this area. There does, however, seem to be a certain amount of agreement that institutional features play an important role in deciding which sequence is appropriate for the country in question.

There now also seems to be consensus that domestic macroeconomic stabilisation should come first, otherwise restructuring could be affected by inflationary pressures hindering economic decisions and distorting income distribution. The problem of valuation of assets provides a strong argument for carrying out stabilisation and price liberalisation before privatisation, and for rejecting the proposal that privatisation should be used to absorb the monetary overhang(7).

Opinions differ as to whether demonopolisation and restructuring should come before privatisation. There is a risk that state monopolies may simply be replaced by private ones and that if the process of demonopolisation is delayed, it could encounter even more opposition at a later stage. On the other hand, for political motives it may be preferable not to delay privatisation too long, but in this case it is essential that an effective competition policy be introduced.

The 'conventionally preferred order' (Portes, 1990) based on the experience of economic liberalisation in less developed countries generally entails a preference for liberalising the goods market before that of factors (and especially the capital market) and liberalising the current account before the capital account of the balance of payments (since otherwise there is a risk of capital inflows causing undesired appreciation of the exchange rate).

There is also some debate as to when it is desirable to introduce currency convertibility and liberalise current transactions. While such measures would contribute to competition, there is the risk that the simultaneous domestic and external adjustment required might prove excessive and strain political tolerance. The likely impact on the smaller Central-East European countries of dismantling the CMEA trading system illustrates how real this risk is. The introduction of currency convertibility would also require huge devaluations which could add to inflationary pressures and undermine stabilisation measures. For this reason Hare (1990b), for example, argues that Hungary should first adapt to domestic liberalisation before attempting full trade liberalisation.

7.7 The transformation process in individual Central-East European countries

7.7.1 Poland

From 1989 Poland began to implement a series of measures based on the 'big-bang' approach for moving towards a market-orientated economy.

This first entailed the freeing of 90% of all prices, the ending of most subsidies, and the introduction of an internally convertible currency for current transactions.

The combination of these measures and excessively generous wage concessions led to inflation of 740% in 1989(8). To meet this situation in January 1990 an IMF-agreed stabilisation programme was introduced, and this constitutes the first stage of the Balcerowicz Programme (named after the Finance Minister). The aim of the January measures was to eliminate both open hyperinflationary pressures and repressed inflation, with the latter being achieved by keeping wage increases below those of prices. The second stage of the Balcerowicz programme dates from mid-1990 and entailed industrial restructuring to bring the Polish economy more in line with that of Western Europe. Central to this second phase was the privatisation law ratified in July 1990.

As a result of the stabilisation programme, in January 1990 real incomes fell by 24% compared with December and living standards, as measured by the level of consumer expenditure in constant prices, fell by 35%. The figure for the fall in living standards probably represents an overestimate as shortages in the past had implied a misallocation of expenditure and time (in queues)(9) and because comparison was made with 1989, a year of hyperinflation in which wages grew rapidly. With respect to 1987, the fall in real wages was only 2–3%(10). The dampening of demand following the austerity measures led to a slowing of inflation from 78% for January to 24% in March and 3.5% in July 1990.

According to official Polish statistics, GDP fell by 12% in 1990, after a rise of only 0.2% in 1989. It was estimated that industrial production fell by 26%(11), but these statistics refer only to the state sector. Unemployment rose from 55,800 in January to 700,000 in July 1990 and reached 6.1% of the labour force by the end of the year.

However, if account is also taken of the private sector the outlook is more favourable. It is estimated that the output of the private sector may have grown by 50% in 1990, increasing from 11% of GNP in 1989 to 18% in 1990(12). In 1989 employment in the private sector may have grown by 500,000 bringing the total to 1.8–2 million people. Growth has been particularly prevalent in the service sector (with new retail outlets, restaurants, etc., springing up), but much of this activity forms part of the black economy and thus does not appear in the statistics.

Largely as a result of its low value, the zloty remained relatively stable, and exports rose by 40% in 1990 resulting in a hard-currency surplus of $3.8 billion. However, over the past five years the hard-currency surplus of roughly $1 billion and foreign remittances of a further $1.5 billion have been insufficient to service the net foreign debt, so that much interest has not been paid, and has had to be capitalised either through rescheduling arrangements or *de facto*(13).

Progress was made in reducing the budget deficit, but whether this continues will depend on the political will of the government to continue wage restraint, and the extent to which economic decline is reflected in lower tax revenue(14).

With regard to the prospects for restructuring, high interest rates have discouraged investment and the creation of new jobs. If firms are unable to pay their taxes they will face forcible restructuring, and almost 2% of the state budget has been set aside for this purpose. However, it seems likely that the government will be under strong pressure to avoid higher unemployment and factory closures. Moreover, Frydman, Wellisz and Kolodko (1990) found that, despite the fall in production, adjustment of output prices meant that in the state sector there was little fall in profitability (97% of the March 1989 level in March 1990). These authors also found that increases in unemployment had not matched the large decline in output, in part because of pressure from unions and Workers Councils to avoid dismissals. They therefore suggest that many expectations about how the stabilisation measures will contribute to the restructuring of Polish industry may be too optimistic.

7.7.2 Hungary

To date the restructuring of the Hungarian economy has been 'gradual and evolutionary, though it is increasingly being affected by the spirit of the times'(15). Despite the New Economic Mechanism of 1968, and a revised reform movement from 1979 which aimed at promoting competition by means of encouraging cooperatives, reducing the restrictions on the private sector, and allowing subcontracting to 'brigades' or teams of workers, in 1987 state enterprises still accounted for 53% of the gross value of assets, and ministries for a further 20%. Private housing absorbed a further 17%, leaving cooperatives with 9% and private enterprise with 2%.

One of the key aspects of the economic programme of Democratic Forum is the creation of a 'social market economy', with the introduction of forint convertibility and continuation of the policy of privatisation. In the first eighteen months of the programme some 150 large state enterprises were to be privatised, while small shops and restaurants were to figure strongly among early privatisations. Foreign investment was encouraged, and it was estimated that by September 1990 there were some 2000 joint ventures in Hungary.

Following the sluggish growth which characterised Hungary throughout the 1980s, GDP fell by 1.5 in 1989. Even greater decline is expected for 1990 and 1991 due to the heavy burden of foreign debt and a worsening of terms of trade following the move to world prices in

CMEA trade from January 1991. In 1990, recognition of 'methodological errors' led to upward revision of the Hungarian hard-currency foreign debt by some $2.5 billion to $20.7 billion for gross debt and $18 billion for net debt at the end of 1989. Unemployment is expected to reach 100,000 by the end of 1990(16).

By September 1990 inflation was running at an annual rate of 30%. This inflation can be attributed to government spending (including large projects such as the Danube dam and the Soviet gas pipeline), lax monetary policy (despite the 1987 reforms designed to introduce a commercial banking system), servicing of the foreign debt, wage increases (which large state enterprises in difficulty were prone to grant) and to forint devaluation(17).

In 1989 hard-currency imports rose in real terms by 7.2% due to a more buoyant internal demand than was expected, and to the easing of licensing and quota requirements on products representing roughly 40% of the value of hard-currency imports(18). At the same time the 5% increase in hard-currency exports in 1989 reflected relatively strong import demand for Hungarian products, two devaluations of the forint and an active export promotion scheme involving tax concessions and subsidies(19).

However, there was an overall current account deficit in convertible currencies of $986 million in the first half of 1989(20). This can be explained by the interest on foreign debt, and because the balance on the travel account was transformed from a surplus of $41 million in 1988 to a deficit of $348 million from January to June 1989, as a result of higher than expected incomes and the liberalisation of regulations relating to foreign travel, access to hard currency and the holding of foreign currency accounts. To remedy this situation, measures such as the imposition of import duties on many private imports and the altering of foreign exchange allowances were introduced in 1989.

Exports in non-convertible currencies fell by 6% in 1989 and imports dropped by 6.9%; and in 1989 Hungary had a surplus in this trade of 532 million roubles(21). Rouble exports to the smaller CMEA countries fell by 4.1% and imports by 7.9% in 1989, casting doubts on the prospects of proposed smaller integration units among Central-East European countries.

The current account rouble surplus with the Soviet Union increased from 450 million roubles in 1988 to 1.6 billion in 1989, when Hungary also had a hard-currency trade surplus with the Soviet Union of $228 million. With the move to world prices in CMEA trade from 1991, Hungary is expected to have dollar deficits with the Soviet Union. Hungary will be allowed to offset these deficits with the rouble surplus which has accumulated up until 1990, using the exchange rate of $1=0.90(22).

7.7.3 Czechoslovakia

Although Czechoslovakia shares the need to renovate and adapt its productive capacity to the world rather than the CMEA market, the economic situation inherited would appear somewhat more favourable than for the other four small Central-East European countries. However, the economic and political outlook is likely to be influenced by growing strains between Czechs and Slovaks. The net foreign debt was only $3.4 billion at the end of 1989. Tight monetary and fiscal policies contributed to low inflation, with retail prices rising only 3.7% in the first half of 1990 compared with the same period in 1988. There is also a strong tradition of engineering (before World War II Czechoslovakia was among the ten most industrialised countries in the world), hence the Czech insistence that what they require from the West is not financial help or loans, but the provision of training programmes, the encouragement of East–West joint ventures, and increased imports of technology and know-how (which the relaxing of Cocom should help to encourage).

Delays in implementing new measures occurred, first, because of a heated debate about whether to try and find a third way between socialism and capitalism (ultimately abandoned) and, second, because of arguments concerning the form to be taken by privatisation and new foreign investment laws. It is also proposed to reform the price system and introduce a convertible currency, possibly by 1991.

Growth has been sluggish in recent years, and though GNP fell by 1% in the first half of 1990(23), this was less than in the other Central-East European countries. As a result Czechoslovakia has so far been able to avoid the social tension associated with higher unemployment. However, slower economic decline might also be due to the fact that Czechoslovakia lags behind Hungary and Poland in the process of economic restructuring. Labour productivity is low and large-scale investment will be necessary to transform predominantly heavy industry concentrated in the state sector into smaller units with greater bias in favour of high technology and services.

Domestic production of brown coal and lignite fell by 11.3% and of hard coal by 12% in the first five months of 1990, partly due to environmental considerations. Czechoslovakia is heavily dependent on Soviet oil and reform of the CMEA trading system from 1991 could increase the dollar cost of energy imports by up to 150%(24). The redirection of much East German trade is also likely to affect Czechoslovakia particularly badly.

In the first half of 1990 Czech non-convertible exports fell by 19.2% in volume terms compared with the same period in 1989, largely because of reduced demand for Czech products in the Soviet Union, Poland and

East Germany(25). Over the same period Czech rouble imports fell by 6.5% in volume terms mainly because of reduced deliveries of Soviet crude oil. In real terms Czechoslovak exports to the West rose by an estimated 8.7% in 1989 and 7.3% in the first half of 1990, while imports rose by 7% in 1989 and 21.4% in the first half of 1990.

7.7.4   *Bulgaria*

In Bulgaria progress towards a market-orientated economy appears slow. The Bulgarian budget deficit grew rapidly in 1990 with a heavy debt burden and over one-quarter of spending going on subsidies. However, in February 1991 consumer prices were liberalised and a privatisation law was passed. The hard-currency foreign debt was some $10 billion at the beginning of 1990, and though it was subsequently reduced by using reserves to make repayments, in March 1990 measures to postpone repayment had to be taken (with, for example, delays of two years in payment of old debts, and planned repayment of short-term debt by 1994). In addition, Bulgaria experienced balance of payments difficulties with the current-account deficit expected to reach $0.6 billion in 1990(26).

7.7.5   *Romania*

Official statistics indicate that Romanian net material product fell by 9.9% in 1989, implying a decline in GNP of an estimated 7–8%(27). According to a preliminary official estimate, industrial output declined by 18% in the first half of 1990 compared to the same period in 1989. Over the first four months of 1990 compared to the same period in 1989 labour productivity fell by 21.7% and centrally financed investment by 46.9%. Food shortages were chronic, while lack of raw materials and energy threatened to close many factories.

Statistics were particularly unreliable up to 1989 and for example, the upward bias in overall growth rate could have been as much as 4% for the 1982–88 period(28).

Over the first four months of 1990, compared to the same period in 1989, rouble exports fell by 38.1% and hard-currency exports by 42.5%. For 1990 a hard-currency current account deficit of some $1–2 billion is expected, and in 1991 further deterioration can be expected with the reform of intra-CMEA trade. Although Romania succeeded in reducing its net foreign debt from $9.3 billion in 1980 to $1.3 billion in 1988, this was only achieved at the cost of excessive deflationary measures. Given the present economic and political situation Romania is likely to encounter difficulties if it attempts to resume large-scale commercial borrowing.

In November it was decided to devalue the leu by 75%, reduce subsidies and to partially liberalise prices. New joint venture legislation was introduced, improving conditions for foreign firms (with, for instance, a tax holiday for the first two years, and incentives for the reinvestment of profits). It was announced that subsidies to enterprises would be reduced, and that half of Romanian industry would be privatised within three years.

The price liberalisation led to some prices increasing by a factor of 2 or 3 and, together with economic decline and shortages, caused widespread public discontent and demonstrations.

7.7.6 The Soviet Union*

The poor economic performance of the Soviet Union during the 1980s is well documented, and since 1989 the situation has deteriorated rapidly, reaching crisis proportions. Stagnation turned into decline; the monetary situation was completely out of control; open, hidden and repressed inflation were increasing, with rationing becoming ever-more widescale; the distribution system virtually collapsed; a large trade deficit emerged; the terms of trade worsened drastically over the period between 1986 and mid-1990; the net foreign debt was $54.6 billion at the end of 1990(29); and the question of economic reform could no longer be separated from the question of division of power between the Union and the Republics.

Although Gorbachev inherited an economic situation on the verge of collapse, the approach based on glasnost and perestroika contributed to its further decline. The reforms succeeded in breaking down the network of tutelage relations on which the command economy was based, without replacing it with a market.

Resistance to reform and fears that it would create social unrest led to vacillation and the adoption of unworkable compromises. For instance, price liberalisation was an essential element of any reform, but the prospect of popular reaction and of releasing hyperinflationary pressures in view of the huge monetary overhang meant that for a long time price increases were announced but not implemented.

Proposals to introduce private property encountered similar hesitation, while attempts to encourage decentralisation, cooperatives and

---

* This section was written before publication of the studies by the EC Commission and IMF/World Bank/OECD/BERD.

East–West joint ventures in the vestiges of a command and shortage economy met with little success, also because they were surrounded by legal loopholes. This meant that, for example, cooperatives had difficulties in obtaining inputs and often had to resort to dubious activities.

Failure to resolve the supply situation and the breakdown of the state distribution network was one of the key stumbling blocks of perestroika. As will be explained below, in a situation of chaos, speculation and theft became increasingly widespread.

Glasnost initiated an awareness of how bad the economic situation was, as well as permitting debate in which expectations were raised, particularly among radical and nationalist groups. One aspect of this was the growing demand for autonomy or independence, not just on the part of the Baltic States, but also by Republics such as Moldavia, Armenia and Georgia. In the case of the Ukraine and Belorussia, the revival of nationalist claims owes much to the publicity (albeit incomplete) given to the Chernobyl accident.

Having gone down in history as the man who lost the smaller Central-East European states, Gorbachev was perhaps understandably reluctant to also take responsibility for dismantling the Soviet Union. Constantly trying to find a rapidly disappearing middle ground between the radicals and Republics requesting more autonomy than he wished to give, and the conservatives concerned to preserve the Union, in late 1990 his choice fell with the latter.

The power base of the conservatives was the army, the KGB and parts of the Communist Party and bureaucracy. In relying on these Gorbachev's probable aim was to restore order so that perestroika could continue. However, in doing so he forfeited the support of many of the authors of reform, including the economists Shatalin, Abalkin and Petrakov, and was forced into reliance on many of the forces most likely to resist further change.

Moreover, it is questionable how feasible the attempt to impose order from above is. As will be shown, the main effect of the first clumsy measures aimed at speculators and 'saboteurs of the economy' was to further discredit the rouble, and to discourage small savers as well as co-operatives and joint ventures on whom hopes of economic recovery rest. Demands for independence or autonomy are coming from so many Republics and autonomous regions that repression on a massive scale would be required to dampen all such claims.

The aim here is to explain how this situation was reached, which first entails a brief account of the Soviet economy, and in particular the deteriorating supply situation; the growing lack of monetary discipline; the link between economic performance and separatist claims; and the collapse of the distribution network. Then follows a short description of the main measures taken in order to illustrate why they proved inadequate.

7.7.7 The Soviet economic situation

According to official statistics (which are notoriously unreliable), growth of net material product fell from 8% in second half of the 1960s to 4% in the late-1970s, and some 3% in the 1980s. The CIA estimates that on average hidden inflation was about 2% per year over the 1980s, while two Soviet economists, Khanin and Selyunin(30), provide the somewhat higher figure of roughly 3%. Aganbegyan (1988, p. 2) argues that Soviet economic growth appears to have ceased from 1978 and again between 1980 and 1985, a situation confirmed by Western observers. This was especially critical in a country which had always pointed to its faster growth rate as one of the main indicators of superiority over the capitalist system. The CIA figures for Soviet military spending show an increase in real terms of about 2% in the early-1980s, which would seem to imply a contraction of the non-military economy.

Official statistics indicate a 2% fall in GNP in 1990 but, according to unofficial estimates, GNP fell by 5% in 1989 and could have fallen by as much as 7% in 1990, with the risk of collapse of the order of 15–20% in 1991(31). Part of this decline is due to growing apathy, absenteeism (of an estimated 200,000 workers on average) and strikes, reflecting the growing disillusion and fear of further degeneration of the situation.

With the exception of the space and military sphere, the technological lag behind the West has also been growing rapidly, while the already poor quality of many products also deteriorated, encouraged by the continuing existence of excess demand. Shmelev(32) reports that, according to optimistic estimates, some 17–18% of Soviet products are of sufficient quality to be exported to the West, while the pessimistic figure is 7–8%. The quality of infrastructure, and of many social services such as health and housing is also poor.

Official statistics indicated an annual inflation rate of 7.5% (or 2% in the state shops) in mid-1990, but according to various Soviet observers, 50% or more would be more realistic (33). Shortages of goods in state shops meant increasing recourse to black or kolkhoz markets, where it is estimated (in so far as such calculations are possible) that prices increased by a factor of four in the first nine months of 1990. In the past, price stability had also been presented as evidence for the superiority over capitalist economies.

During the late-1980s a growing budget deficit began to emerge which was a feature hitherto unknown in the Soviet Union. Official figures were first published in 1985 when the deficit amounted to 18 billion roubles (3% of GDP), but the figure rose to 80 billion for 1988 and 89 billion in 1989 (or 10% of GDP) and could reach 250 billion roubles in 1991. By 1989 the public debt reached an estimated 400 roubles or 44% of GDP(34).

Much of the growing Soviet budget deficit was covered by printing money, and, according to official statistics, the money supply grew by 18.3% in 1989 and by a further 93 billion roubles for the first nine months of 1990. Again, unofficial figures were far higher, indicating that the growth of the money supply might have been as high as 59% in 1989(35). This increase in the money supply added to the monetary overhang which was officially estimated at 170 billion roubles for 1989, though most figures are higher at 250–300 billion roubles or more.

From 1990 the link between economic reform and the power struggle between the Centre, Republics and local authorities became fully apparent. Between 1985 and mid-1990 ethnic clashes led to 1000 deaths, 8500 injuries and 700,000 refugees(36). By mid-1990 four Republics (the Baltic States and Armenia) had declared their independence, while a further nine (out of a total of fifteen) had declared sovereignty, i.e. that their legislation takes precedence over that of the Soviet Union. Even within the Russian Republic, which is composed of sixteen autonomous republics, five autonomous regions and ten autonomous areas, eight of these jurisdictions had declared their sovereignty with respect to Russia.

One of the main complaints of the Republics was that centrally fixed prices led to distortions, especially with regard to the relative prices of the products which they sold to other Republics. For instance, Russia produces 90% of the oil and gas in the Soviet Union, and maintained that sales of these to the rest of the Soviet Union entailed a subsidy of some 70 billion roubles, or $118 billion at the official exchange rate. Azerbaijan claimed that the prices of its exports of oil, vegetables and cotton to other Republics were too low. Those who gained from relatively cheaper imports, such as the Baltic States, none the less requested independence, not only for political reasons and increased chances of Western aid, but on the belief that freer prices would encourage adjustment and reduce their dependence on the other Republics.

To meet this situation (and as a reaction to growing anarchy) individual Republics began to raise prices unilaterally. In order to prevent arbitrage, there was increasing resort to border controls and/or rationing. Uzbekistan and Tadzikistan blocked the export of many products, and in an effort to raise self-sufficiency, Uzbekistan is switching to higher grain production. The Ukraine stopped exports of agricultural products above planned levels and has considered setting up customs posts. Leningrad set up a 'free economic zone' which entailed border controls and the issue of ration cards. Moscow introduced ration cards and special shopping permits in June 1990 following the reaction to the

Ryzkhov reform proposals, and the resentment of farmers in surrounding areas led to a 40% reduction in food supplies(37).

The legacy of central planning and specialisation has rendered the Soviet Union particularly vulnerable to this kind of protectionism. Soviet Republics are heavily dependent on trade with other Republics which on average is equivalent to between one-third and one-half of the GNP of each Republic(38). There is a risk that a vicious circle of growing shortages and protectionism could emerge.

By late-1990 shortages had become chronic, especially in the large cities such as Moscow and Leningrad. The State Commission which monitors the availability of products found that 996 out of 1000 products could not be found in state shops(39). Shortages encouraged hoarding and the deviation of goods from state shops into other retail outlets by legal (purchase for resale) or illegal means. It is estimated that some 20% of products in the state shops disappeared in the passage from the stores to the shelves(40). Theft was facilitated in a situation where the distribution network had broken down.

Disruption of production also contributed to the food shortages, with, for instance, record levels of wastage in the 1990 grain harvest. According to the USDA, Soviet grain production rose from 197.1 million tonnes in 1989 to an estimated 222 million tonnes in 1990, though the official Soviet figure for 1990 was higher at 240 million tonnes(41). The USDA figure for wastage rose from 29 million tonnes in 1989 to 35 million in 1990, but the Soviet agricultural economist, Tikhonov, estimated that only 137–140 million tonnes could be used for consumption. Some 60% of fruit and vegetables also appears to have been lost in 1990(42).

The grain losses can be attributed to heavy rain at the time of harvest, fuel shortages, inadequate transport and storage facilities, and the fact that the decision to raise procurement prices was taken too late. The chaotic harvest also represents another instance of the reforms breaking down the network of vertical relations on which the command economy had been based, without putting anything in its place.

Turning to the Soviet trade balance, as described in Chapter 5, the fall in energy prices meant a loss in foreign exchange earnings estimated at $6–10 billion per year between 1986 and 1988. This, together with lower levels of oil exports and reduced arms sales, helps to explain the Soviet deficit of $5.73 billion with the non-Socialist countries in the first six months of 1990, which was a historic record and five times higher than the deficit for the equivalent 1989 period(43).

Despite the traditional Soviet reluctance to sell gold, it is estimated that gold sales under Gorbachev have tripled, reaching an estimated total of $4 billion by 1990(44). This occurred at a time when gold prices were falling, probably partly in consequence of Soviet sales.

Although a probable increase in energy prices and reduced supplies from the Gulf following the Iraqi War has improved the outlook for Soviet trade, production difficulties are increasingly affecting supplies. Pipelines need replacement while oil supplies in Siberia are becoming harder to extract, and the obsolete equipment is ever more inadequate for the task. Moreover, it has proved impossible to correct the wasteful intensity with which energy and other raw materials are used in the Soviet Union(45).

7.7.8   Measures taken between 1985 and 1989

Initially, from 1985 perestroika took the form of trying to increase the efficiency of the traditional framework by means of 'technocratic fine-tuning'. This aimed at accelerating economic growth by raising investment and gearing it more to economic restructuring. Other measures included revised wage scales, stricter quality controls, and the encouragement of shiftwork; disciplinary campaigns such as the fight against alcoholism and unearned income; and organisational reforms.

In view of the patent failure of these early measures a second phase of perestroika was introduced which aimed at encouraging decentralisation along the lines of the Hungarian model of the 1960s and 1970s. In addition to the property law and the land law described in Chapter 6, the mandatory nature of the five-year plans was ended, though central control of inputs remained largely unchanged. The state's monopoly of foreign trade was ended, and then first a few and subsequently all firms producing goods which could be sold on foreign markets were allowed to participate directly in foreign trade without prior authorisation. Legislation to facilitate East–West joint ventures was passed (as will be described in Chapter 12) and the first steps towards unifying exchange rates were taken. A detailed analysis of all the reforms implemented during this phase is impossible here, but two, the Law on State Enterprises, and that on Cooperatives will be briefly described to illustrate why the limited nature of the reforms doomed them to failure.

The Law on State Enterprises was passed in 1987 with the initial aim of increasing enterprise autonomy. However, in its final form the law was a compromise, attempting to reconcile centralised management and the independence of the enterprise and in the event achieving little of the latter. The concept of self-financing introduced by the law was ambiguous and, for instance, it is difficult to see how financial discipline was to operate in the absence of freeing of prices or direct access to markets. It is doubtful how independent enterprises could be when much of their production still had to be sold to the state at prices which, though more flexible, were still fixed to a large extent. Though state orders were supposed to replace old delivery targets, in practice they operated in the same way and continued to cover some 90% of the production capacity of most enterprises(46).

According to the Law on Cooperatives passed in 1988, cooperatives were to have the same rights as state enterprises and were to be self-managing, self-financing and independent. They were to have property rights, though these did not extend to land. In the first half of 1989 the number of cooperatives in the Soviet Union doubled from 78,000 to 133,000(47) and their labour productivity was reported to be up to ten times higher than production in state enterprises(48). In view of shortages cooperative prices were generally high, and as a result some co-operative members were able to earn huge incomes, in some cases sixty times the average Soviet wage. Ambiguities in the law meant that the status of cooperatives was not clearly defined on a number of issues, particularly relating to contracts and property. Local authorities often opposed the creation of cooperatives, making it difficult to register or obtain premises and supplies. This difficulty in obtaining scarce supplies forced many cooperatives into transactions of dubious legality. A further complaint was that the cooperatives were simply depriving the state sector of workers and supplies. As a result there was widespread popular resentment against what Åslund (1989, p. 175) describes as the phenomenon of 'a relatively small number of clever operators–monopolists quickly skimm(ing) the unbalanced market'.

These measures appeared to be a compromise, less between different political currents than between the desires of the leadership and what was possible in a system characterised by active and passive reform resistance at all levels. Among top politicians the main resistance during this second phase of perestroika came from conservatives such as Ligachev. Lower-ranking bureaucrats resented the challenge to their power, position and/or security and especially the threat of unemployment or transfer. Individuals feared price increases and unemployment and were often hesitant to embark on riskier forms of production, especially when they had little experience of management or entrepreneurial skill.

7.7.9 The reform debate from 1990

Late-1989 was marked by a series of strikes and mounting criticism of the economic situation in the Congress of People's Deputies, and from 1990 the debate became focused on packages designed to reform all aspects of the economy and eliminate its fundamental weaknesses once and for all.

In March 1990 a package of seventeen radical economic reform measures was announced. This was to consist of Polish-type measures including freeing of prices, and gradual introduction of rouble convertibility. With regard to agriculture there was to be a return to the 'prodnalog' or tax in kind introduced by Lenin in 1921 as part of the New Economic Plan (NEP). Once this 'tax' or fixed amount of produce had been paid to the state, all remaining production could be sold freely. In order to tide over the transitional period and render the measures more palatable there would be large-scale recourse to government borrowing in order to finance massive imports of consumer goods. This has been done in the past for imports worth $1 billion, but the figure mentioned in connection with the plan was $20–25 billion.

One difficulty in applying the Polish model with the extreme austerity measures it entails, to the Soviet Union, was that consensus of the kind enjoyed by the Polish government was lacking in the Soviet Union. Moreover, whereas Hungarian and Polish retail prices had been adjusted with a view to the move to a free market, in the Soviet Union they had remained largely fixed. Fear of popular revolt caused the Soviet government to reject the Polish model and present the more moderate *Ryzkhov Plan* for the introduction of a 'regulated market' in May 1990.

This foresaw a preparatory phase up until the end of 1990 in which the basic legislation necessary to introduce a market-orientated economy would be introduced. From January 1991 prices were to be liberalised and over the 1991–92 period the monetary, credit and fiscal systems would be reformed. It would be possible to sell up to 60% of state enterprises in shares to individuals or joint-stock companies. Anti-trust measures were also to be introduced as well as further incentives to foreign direct investment. There was to be a separation of Gosbank as the Central Bank and the development of a commercial banking sector. A stock exchange was to be introduced and there was to be gradual preparation for rouble convertibility.

With regard to prices, the government planned to halve subsidies, causing wholesale prices to rise on average by 46% and retail prices to double(49). It was envisaged that 60% of all food prices would remain fixed by the state, 25% would be controlled and 15% would be free.

Wage indexation was to be introduced and wages would be linked to the qualifications of workers and the quality of their work. There would be new income and company taxes. By way of compensation for the higher cost of living, state expenditure of some 125 billion roubles ($135 at official exchange rates) was envisaged. The measures would include lump-sum transfers, unemployment benefits and retraining schemes. It was estimated that the Plan was likely to increase the budget deficit by at least 50%.

The immediate public reaction to the package was a run on the shops, forcing the authorities to introduce rationing in Moscow, and fully illustrating the imprudence of pre-announcing price increases by seven months. Conservatives attacked the package as a betrayal of socialism, while the radical wing maintained that the measures simply meant additional austerity for an already overstrained population, without offering any guarantee of supply response or that adequate privatisation would be carried out. The measures would also leave responsibility for fixing a large share of consumer prices in state hands.

In the face of the public reaction, in June 1990 Gorbachev dissociated himself from the package, and in September 1990 the *Shatalin Plan* for reform over a period of 500 days was proposed. Within the first 100 days, unfinished construction projects and state-owned vehicles would be auctioned. The sovkhoz and kolkhoz would be dismantled and their land would be divided into plots and divided among agricultural workers. Fifty to sixty state enterprises would be transformed into joint-stock enterprises. A two-tier banking system would be introduced, as well as a single exchange rate for the rouble which would remain the only currency in circulation.

At the same time, draconian stabilisation measures would be introduced to cut the budget deficit to 5 billion roubles and reduce growth in the money supply to zero. This would entail blocking large expenditure programmes, and reducing non-military foreign aid by 75%, defence by 10% and the KGB Budget by 25%. Subject to a limited list of exceptions, subsidies to all loss-making firms would be ended.

By the end of the second phase (day 249) 50% of all shops and restaurants would be sold. Government procurement and negotiation of a large share of prices would continue to avoid a slump in output, while wage indexation would be introduced.

In stage three (days 250–399) privatisation would proceed more rapidly and only certain prices for essentials would remain fixed, so that by the end of phase 4 (day 500) 70% of industrial enterprises and 90% of construction, transport and retail services would be in private hands. There would be measures to increase labour mobility, and hard-currency auctions would become more frequent with the aim of ultimately making the rouble convertible.

The Shatalin Plan differs from the Ryzkhov Plan in its commitment to private property, the degree of decentralisation envisaged and in the proposed sequencing of measures, lending substance to Yeltsin's claim that the two were incompatible.

With regard to private property, the opening sentences of the Shatalin Plan announce the '*de jure* equality of all types of property, including private property' as an essential pre-condition to the functioning of a market-orientated economy.

Also, the Plan envisaged a transfer of state assets to the Republics, which would then be responsible for privatisation. The tax system was to be largely decentralised with even the level of remaining federal taxes being decided by the Republics.

Finally, whereas the Ryzkhov Plan entailed stabilisation and then privatisation, according to the Shatalin Plan these were both to take place simultaneously, with the difficulties (explained above) that this is likely to entail for evaluation of assets. Such a move would be risky given the fact that evidence of mistaken pricing or alleged malpractice in sales of state assets would soon feed discontent, and given the already widespread disdain for 'speculators'.

The sequencing of the Plan is virtually the reverse of the consensus that there should be liberalisation of trade before that of the capital account; of commodity markets before factors markets; and of the labour market before the capital market. As Pitzner-Jorgenson (1990) points out, the Shatalin plan begins with liberalisation of the capital market, with privatisation of state property, and creation of a stock exchange and commercial banking system, and leaves liberalisation of the labour market and trade (through rouble convertibility) largely to later stages of the reform.

In order to maintain the fragile political equilibrium, Gorbachev resisted calls that the Prime Minister, Ryzkhov, should resign because of the drastic economic situation, and was determined to find a compromise between the two proposals. This led to the Presidential guidelines for stabilisation and transition to a market economy agreed by the Soviet Parliament in October 1990. The package is less far-reaching than the Shatalin Plan in the degree of decentralisation envisaged, and in the speed with which privatisation and price reform are to be carried out.

The guidelines were intrinsically linked to the new *Union Treaty* for the Union of Sovereign Soviet States agreed by the Soviet Parliament in December 1990 and submitted for referendum in March 1991. According to this Treaty the Republics would be 'sovereign' but would voluntarily delegate responsibility for certain policies to the centre. The Union Treaty also envisaged reinforced executive powers for the President.

There has been a heated debate as to what the division of power between the centre and Republics should be, with Gorbachev initially requesting authority in eight areas: foreign policy, defence, transport, telecommunications, monetary policy, energy, raw materials and tax gathering.

The Presidential guidelines represented an attempt to resolve this question, establishing the principal guidelines for reform. Each Republic had to decide how these are to be implemented within the framework set out by the President. The reforms stipulate that ownership of most assets is to pass to the Republics, and again there were differences of opinion as to what the exceptions should be, and especially over the proposal that the Republics could use their natural resources, without having the right to their exclusive ownership. The Russian Republic, for instance, declared invalid contracts which result in the export of strategic minerals (including oil, gas, uranium and diamonds) from its territory. The Republics would not be able to mint their own money, and the rouble would remain the only currency.

Given that 90% of assets are still in state hands, the speed of privatisation envisaged by the Shatalin Plan was said to be unrealistic. There seems some justification for this view as the experience of the smaller Central-East European countries illustrates how difficult it can prove to find purchasers for some 46,000 industrial enterprises and 76,000 trading firms. Initially, privatisation would therefore be limited to small firms, particularly those in the service sector, restaurants and construction firms. The reform makes no pronouncement on the privatisation of land and delegates the decision to the Republics, but it does allow for dismantling of collective farms which are no longer viable.

Two-thirds of prices were to be liberalised over a period of eighteen months, though a further third would remain fixed. The social security network would also be more extensive than that foreseen in the Shatalin Plan. The Presidential guidelines were more ambivalent on the question of cuts in subsidies to loss-making firms.

The first major liberalisation of prices took place in April 1991. Prices for bread, meat, and flour were tripled; those for butter, vegetable oil, eggs and soap were doubled, while the prices of other products increased by 60% on average. The state will continue to fix the prices of some 45% of foodstuffs, and basic necessities. There will be partial freeing of prices of products such as furniture, books and clothes, while the prices of some 30% of products, which are considered 'luxuries', are to be liberalised.

The budget deficit is to be cut by some 25–30%, mainly through reductions in spending on the army and KGB, but the precise commitment to the scale of the cuts set out in the Shatalin Plan is missing. Some taxes are to remain central, but the main responsibility is to pass to the Republics. It is questionable how far the guidelines will manage to reduce the budget deficit.

The first reaction to the Presidential guidelines was a letter in *Komsomolskaja Pravda* by Shatalin, Petrakov and other of Gorbachev's closest economic advisors who attacked the measures as 'likely to lead to galloping inflation and the impoverishment of the population'.

After months of vacillation the measures appear too little, too late, and five Republics (the three Baltic States, Moldavia and Georgia) have expressed their unwillingness to sign the Union Treaty. The Russian Parliament has already voted in favour of the Shatalin Plan, and Yeltsin has criticised the Union Treaty as coming from above rather than below.

In the meantime, initiatives 'from below' were proceeding with the diffusion of agreements for political and economic cooperation among the Republics. Attempts were also made to reach agreements with third countries for instance between Russia and Korea, but these met opposition from the Soviet Union.

Parallel to the discussions of the Union Treaty and economic reform, a hard line gradually emerged in an attempt to preserve the integrity of the Union both against the threat posed by separatist tendencies and from the activities of speculators and 'saboteurs of the economy'.

In November 1990 at a request from Gorbachev, Yazov, the Minister of Defence, appeared on television with a warning that the military was unwilling to allow the situation to deteriorate into chaos and that if attacks on the armed forces and their supplies continued, it would be necessary to use force. The subsequent appointment of Boris Pugo, an ex-KGB chief, as Minister for the Interior with a general, Gromov, as his deputy confirmed the direction being taken by policy. In December the KGB chief, Kryuchkov, also appeared on television to warn about the imminent collapse due to 'nationalism, violence and mass disorder', which, he argued, had been encouraged by the subversive activities of extremist and radical groups relying on support from abroad.

Gorbachev's threat to declare a state of emergency, and introduce direct presidential rule in troubled areas such as the Baltic States, Moldavia and the Caucasus led to the resignation of the Georgian, Shevardnadze, in December 1990 as a protest against the 'aggression of the military, and the risk of dictatorship'.

In January 1991 repression in the Baltics began; there was a threat to suspend freedom of the press and it was decided to use the army alongside the police in maintaining order in the main cities.

Increasingly, measures aimed at tackling economic disorder began to compromise the move towards a market economy. A decree was passed to set up special committees to control supplies of foodstuffs at the grassroots level, with legal sanctions envisaged for offenders. Subsequently, it was decided to give the KGB and the Ministry of the Interior authority to check the accounts, documents and inventories of firms and other economic organisations, including East–West joint ventures.

The dual aims of combating speculators and introducing stabilisation as a preliminary to price liberalisation were behind the currency reform of January 1991. This entailed withdrawal of 50 and 100 rouble notes, allowing three days for workers to exchange up to 1000 roubles and pensioners up to 200. Requests for exchange over these amounts were to be examined by special committees, the underlying assumption being that speculators in particular would be hit as much of their business was carried out in these notes, but in the event it seems likely that many speculators were able to avoid the measures and the main impact was on small savers and cooperatives. The measure probably contributed to a further fall in confidence in the rouble, with its value declining from 22.8 roubles for a dollar in the hard-currency auction of 9 January to 25 roubles in the auction of 23 January.

The measure was expected to reduce the monetary overhang by some 40 billion roubles, but new emission would reduce the net effect to 16–18 billion roubles. This would appear a relatively small benefit for the amount of popular resentment encountered. An offer of bonds or treasury certificates could have been used to achieve the same aim of mopping up excess liquidity.

Economic transformation of the Soviet Union has hardly begun, and the balance of power between the Union and the various Republics remains a question to be resolved. The approach currently being adopted by the Soviet leadership to both these issues is not promising and further deterioration of the economic and political situation seems likely.

Notes

1. See Nuti (1990b) for a more detailed account of these questions.
2. For a discussion see the articles in the May 1990 volume of *European Economy*, as well as Daviddi (1990); Nuti (1990b and d); Kaser (1990); and Pitzner-Jorgensen (1990).
3. Rollo *et al.* (1990).
4. As Newbery (1990, p. 90) illustrates.
5. See Hare (1990b) for a discussion of this point.
6. Sachs (1990).
7. For a discussion of this point see Nuti (1990c).
8. See Nuti (1990c) for a full account of these developments.
9. As reported in Chilosi (1990), p. 2.
10. *The Economist*, 26 January 1991.
11. Lafeber and Lafeber-Strazalkowska (1990).
12. *The Economist*, 26 January 1991.
13. Nuti (1990c), p. 174.
14. In Lafeber and Lafeber-Strazalkowska (1990) there is an interesting comparison of the Polish and South American situation.
15. Newbery (1990), p. 69.
16. *The Economist*, 15 September 1990.
17. Laslo Csaba in an interview with *Il Sole 24 Ore*, 14 October 1989.
18. Szalkai (1990), p. 99.
19. Newbery (1990), p. 89.
20. Szalkai (1990).
21. *PlanEcon*, 13 April 1990.
22. All these statistics are taken from PlanEcon Report of 13 April 1990 and 28 March 1990.
23. *PlanEcon*, 14 September 1990.
24. *PlanEcon*, 14 September 1990.

25. All the statistics in this paragraph are taken from *PlanEcon*, 14 September 1990.
26. European Report No. 1586 of 9 May 1990.
27. *Plan Econ*, 22 June 1990.
28. *Plan Econ*, 22 June, 1990.
29. ECE estimates.
30. As reported in Åslund, p. 15.
31. *The Economist*, 6 October 1990 and (21).
32. See Chapter 6 for a discussion of this development.
33. Daviddi (1990b) reports a figure of 49% give by the Vice President of the State Committee for Statistics given to Pravda of 28 January 1990.
34. Daviddi (1990b).
35. *The Economist*, 20 October 1990.
36. *The Economist*, 20 October 1990.
37. *The Economist*, 20 October 1990.
38. *The Economist*, 29 September 1990.
39. *The Economist*, 20 October 1990.
40. *La Repubblica*, 1 December 1990.
41. *Agra Europe,* October 19, 1990.
42. *The Economist*, 1 December 1990.
43. *PlanEcon*, 27 July 1990.
44. Daviddi (1990b).
45. According to the ECE energy intensity was 3.3 times that of western Europe in 1984.
46. *The Economist*, 28 April 1990.
47. *The Economist*, 28 April 1990.
48. Unless otherwise stated, the figures in this paragraph are taken from *Izvestia*, as reported in Åslund (1989), pp. 167–76.
49. The increase would be even greater for energy (82%), metallurgical products (71%) and agricultural commodities (55%). Retail prices were expected to double, with the price of meat rising by a factor of 2.3, fish 2.5, milk and sugar 2, and bread 3. The prices of non-agricultural goods were expected to increase by between 30% and 50%.

8

Western measures to aid the transformation process in Central-East Europe

8.1   Introduction

The economic transformation process in Central-East Europe raises a number of policy options for the West relating to whether to help the transformation process, the form aid should take and the amount of aid to give.

The question of whether to aid the transformation process was decided in July 1989 when, encouraged by President Bush who wished to see the Community emerging as a more active and responsible partner in world leadership, the European Commission chaired a meeting of twenty-four OECD countries(1) to encourage the process of transformation in Hungary and Poland. These rapidly became known as the 'Group of 24' (G-24). Also involved in the programme are the EIB (European Investment Bank), the IBRD (the International Bank for Reconstruction and Development, generally known as the World Bank), the IMF and the OECD. The programme has been likened to a new Marshall Plan despite the substantial differences (described in Nuti, 1990e) between the present situation and that of 1945.

The term 'PHARE' Programme (Economic Reconstruction Aid for Poland and Hungary) has been adopted, though this seems something of a misnomer as aid was subsequently extended to Romania, East Germany (until German unification in October 1990), Czechoslovakia, Bulgaria, the Soviet Union and Yugoslavia. Aid to Romania was temporarily suspended from June 1990 on human rights grounds. The inclusion of Yugoslavia initially encountered opposition from Greece who first wanted the question of transit traffic between the two countries resolved. The Community decided not to grant aid to Albania until some 'Albanian initiative' was forthcoming, but eventually reversed this decision in mid-1991.

The question of extending aid to the Soviet Union was the subject of heated debate. For a long time the United States and the United Kingdom were hesitant and Japan was against financial assistance while Soviet occupation of the Kurile Islands continued. The arguments advanced against aid were that Western contributions would run the risk of being ineffectual given the scale of Soviet needs, as well as a reluctance to help the traditional enemy until there were adequate guarantees that the transformation process was irreversible. It was also maintained that Western aid might act as a disincentive to Soviet measures.

At the June 1990 Dublin Summit it was argued that the EC Commission should carry out a detailed study of Soviet needs before deciding on whether to give aid. However, partly in recognition of the Soviet role in allowing German unification, Germany went ahead unilaterally and offered 5 billion D-mark of government-backed credits. Following an urgent appeal for food aid on the part of Gorbachev in November 1990, Germany immediately responded with consignments, and in December the Community decided in favour of food aid and other forms of financial assistance. The EC(12) also agreed to encourage early entry of the Soviet Union into the IMF and World Bank, and to prepare a new agreement with the Soviets going beyond the 1990 Trade and Cooperation Agreement. The United States agreed to grant emergency aid as well as $1 billion credits for exports of food and other essential items(2).

Following the repression in the Baltic States, in January 1991 the European Parliament voted to suspend this aid (subsequently resumed) and the United States raised the possibility of sanctions.

The Soviet example vindicates the decision of the G-24 to make their aid conditional on progress towards economic and political transformation. The conditions for aid under the PHARE Programme were spelt out in some detail and include: ensuring a state of law, respecting human rights, establishing multipartism, ensuring free elections and instituting a market economy. The Group of 24 maintained that it was not necessary for the Central-East European country to fulfill all these criteria to qualify for aid, but merely to be pointed in the right direction.

In the case of the Soviet Union, the European Community initially also stressed that aid was intended to help the Union counter the separatist tendencies of the Republics. However, as the subsequent behaviour of the Community illustrates, the aim was not to insist on integrity of the Union at any cost.

This chapter attempts to describe and assess the measures taken under the PHARE Programme. The main elements of the transformation process (namely, macroeconomic stabilisation, microeconomic restructuring and systemic change, and social safety nets) will be examined in order to identify the chief risks and obstacles encountered by each to see how Western measures could help to overcome these(3). This enables comparison to be made between what the West could do, and what it has done under the PHARE Programme. Then follows a brief account of why it is in the West's interests to encourage the transformation process, and what the optimal level of aid should be, before drawing conclusions about the effectiveness of the measures taken to date by the Group of 24.

The most lasting form of aid that the West could give to Central-East Europe is to facilitate its reintegration into the world economy by means of improved access to Western markets, for example through trade and cooperation agreements, association agreements or membership of international organisations. However, because these measures also have important implications for the future architecture of Europe and patterns of international relations, they are discussed in more detail in the following chapter.

An additional and unforeseen burden was imposed on the smaller Central-East European countries by the United Nations embargo against Iraq. During the summer of 1990 Hungary, Czechoslovakia, Poland and Bulgaria all called on the Community in its role as coordinator of G-24 assistance for compensation for these losses. For instance, Poland requested $1 billion compensation for having to forego 750,000 tonnes of petrol which Iraq was using to repay its $500 million debt with Poland. That petrol will now have to be obtained from alternative markets at higher world prices.

8.2   Measures to ease the implementation of stabilisation policies

8.2.1 *What the West could do*

Macroeconomic stabilisation is one of the areas where the links between economic, political and social issues are especially tight. The cuts in living standards required by austerity measures, or the possibility of failure to implement such measures resulting in hyperinflation could impose excessive strain on the recently revived faith in democracy in those countries. For instance, the success of Tyminski in the first round of the 1990 Polish presidential election can partly be interpreted as a reaction to the severity of the Balcerowicz package.

In addition to contributing to the social safety nets of those countries (see below), the West could give various forms of financial assistance. In the short run, stabilisation funds or bridging loans could be granted to enable the Central-East European country to overcome a temporary deficit on its current account, or to defend its exchange rate. The concept of multiple equilibria is sometimes used to provide theoretical justification for this type of measure. Longer-term measures could include loans to enable balance of payments difficulties to be overcome and/or structural adjustment to be undertaken; assistance in the introduction of currency convertibility; and debt relief.

Given the level of debt in Poland (at least up until the measures of 1991 described below), Hungary, the Soviet Union and Bulgaria (see Table 7.1), there is little chance of new debt being repaid in the foreseeable future. This would seem to provide a case for aid in the form of grants rather than loans, but there is a bias in favour of the latter as the loans are frequently linked to improving business opportunities for firms of the donor country. The proposal of debt relief for these countries often meets with little support from the IMF or banks, but in many cases it would be simply a recognition of the status quo, as many creditors have already written off these loans (Nuti, 1990a). The value of this debt in secondary markets is at such a discount that, provided collective action by all those involved could be organised, the actual cost of this type of aid would be relatively low(4).

An attack sometimes made on all these types of aid (stabilisation funds, debt relief, etc.) is that they just allow the necessary structural reforms to be delayed, as occurred in the 1970s when untied loans to Eastern European central banks had simply added to foreign debt. The conditionality of PHARE aid is aimed at meeting this difficulty with, for example, the IMF short-term credits requiring certain stabilisation measures be adopted, and the longer-term assistance of the World Bank usually insisting on commitment to certain microeconomic reform measures. However, there has been criticism in some circles that the IMF say in Polish affairs is excessive.

8.2.2 What has been done under the PHARE Programme

At the 1989 Strasburg Summit it was agreed to establish a stabilisation fund for the Polish zloty, and a bridging loan of $1 billion(5) to help Hungary overcome its balance of payments difficulties, provided the two countries reached agreement with the IMF on the measures necessary for economic restructuring. In December 1990 700 million ECU was agreed for Czechoslovakia, again conditional on an IMF agreement. In July 1990 Bulgaria also asked the Community for a short-term bridging loan of some 250–300 million ECU.

In conjunction with other international financial organisations, the

Community began to examine ways of dealing with further requests for stabilisation funds. One proposal made by the EC Commission entailed the Community establishing a reserve facility of some 10 billion ECU, but this met with little support from countries such as the United States or the United Kingdom who felt that the IMF would be a more suitable vehicle for such a measure.

Given the scale of needs, according to the Community, the IMF or World Bank were more suited to give eventual assistance to the Soviet Union for balance of payments purposes or for easing the move towards rouble convertibility.

In February 1990 representatives of Poland's seventeen main creditor countries agreed to favourable terms for rescheduling some $10 billion of the foreign debt (of a total of $41 billion) over fourteen years, with an initial grace period of eight years(6). In April 1991 the Paris Club agreed to debt relief on some 50% of Polish indebtedness which was backed by Western governments, reducing the total from $33.7 billion to $18 billion over a period of five years. Though falling short of the Polish request for 80% remission, this represents the most generous measure agreed by the Paris Club to date.

8.3 Help for economic restructuring and systemic change in Central-East Europe

8.3.1 *What the West could do*

The economic transformation of Central-East Europe entails a number of institutional changes, including the establishment of an independent Central Bank and commercial banking system; the creation of financial markets for shares and bonds; the breaking up of large state enterprises; the introduction of a regulatory system; and an adequate legal framework to deal with private property rights, contracts, company and competition law(7). With its long experience of how these institutions operate, the West has much to offer in helping Central-East Europeans acquire the necessary skills. This could take the form of providing expert advisors, exchanges, participation in Western training courses, or the setting up of training facilities in Central-East Europe.

Production in Central-East Europe must be restructured to overcome technological obsolescence, and so that it reflects consumer requirements to a greater extent. The West could ease this process by encouraging transfer of technology and know-how by means of more relaxed Cocom restrictions and measures to facilitate investment in Central-East Europe, such as help for joint ventures, investment guarantees and double taxation and investment protection agreements with the host

country. Financial backing and advice could also be offered for privatisation and the creation of small and medium enterprises. One of the
main constraints on Central-East European imports of technology and
other products is shortage of hard currency, and Western export credits
could do much towards easing this constraint. Again, training to improve management and marketing skills could be provided. Improved
access to Western markets would also constitute a longer-term incentive. The Central-East European countries would also stand to learn
from the EC experience of industrial policy (especially with regard to
declining industry), regional policy and competition policy.

The failure of much Central-East European production to reflect opportunity costs had particularly adverse implications for the environment. For example, air and water pollution contributed to the average
age at death being seven years less in Czechoslovakia, and twelve years
less in parts of the Soviet Union than in West Europe. Lessons could be
learnt from the Western experience of environmental technology and
policy through training schemes, common projects, cooperation and
joint monitoring.

Aid in overcoming the shortcomings of infrastructure in Central-East
Europe could consist in joint projects, cooperation and investment guarantees and export credits to encourage private initiatives.

8.3.2   *What has been done under the PHARE Programme*

Investment and *industrial modernisation* were to be promoted by a number of measures (see Appendix 8.1). The European Investment Bank,
the European Coal and Steel Community and the Community are to
help finance energy projects in Poland, Hungary, Bulgaria and Romania
(see Appendix 8.1). All these projects have environmental aspects in
enabling a shift to cleaner and less wasteful energy sources. The EIB will
also grant loans of up to 2 billion ECU for infrastructure projects in
Bulgaria, Czechoslovakia and Romania. The World Bank also agreed to
give loans worth some $5–7 billion to the various Central-East Euro-
pean countries over the 1991–93 period.

At the December 1989 Strasburg Summit it was also decided to set up
a European Bank for Reconstruction and Development or BERD (described below). The Community is attempting to increase incentives to
invest in Central-East Europe, such as an improved investment guarantee system, and by providing export credit guarantee arrangements to
supplement those at the national level. In conjunction with the World
Bank there will also be a project to modernise the Hungarian financial
system.

The EC (in conjunction with the World Bank) is to provide financial assistance and technical help for a Polish privatisation agency and will carry out strategic studies of the Polish energy and tourist industries. Measures will also be taken to help Hungarian privatisation and competition agencies. Credits and other forms of financial assistance are to be furnished for small and medium enterprises in both Hungary and Poland. In Hungary this will take the form of funds for providing back-up services and acquiring holdings in small companies, as well as a contribution to the Hungarian Foundation for Enterprise Development. In Poland small and medium enterprises will also be assisted towards access to hard currency to enable them to import equipment and the other products that they require.

The Soviet Union was to receive 400 million ECU in 1991 and 600 million in 1992 for priority areas such as transport and distribution, the food industry, energy, telecommunications and training.

A paper by the Commissioner for Industrial Policy, Martin Bangemann, in July 1990 called for supplements to the PHARE Programme in the area of industrial cooperation. The paper proposed the creation of a new legal, administrative, financial and fiscal environment to facilitate industrial expansion and transformation in Central-East Europe. The programme would be extended to the Soviet Union and would include measures such as increased transparency and exchange of information with regard to investment and market opportunities; promotion of a new legal framework and greater protection of property rights; sectoral projects; assistance for small and medium enterprises and greater cooperation in the area of standardisation.

In February 1990, the EC agreed a programme of 112 million ECU to help Poland and Hungary with *training* in fields such as banking, customs, statistics, economics and scientific research. The British know-how fund covers training projects in management, finance, banking, accounting, commercial law and economics, but also extends to the functioning of democratic institutions and policy for declining industries.

A European Training Foundation for the formation of managers and market experts is to be set up. This would first assist beneficiary countries in identifying the needs and goals of training policy necessary to encourage the process of economic and political transformation. Subsequently, the Foundation would act as a clearing house for exchanges of information on current initiatives and future needs in the context of training.

It was also decided to admit Eastern European citizens to EC training, educational and technology programmes (such as ERASMUS, LINGUA and COMETT). A TEMPUS Programme to encourage cooperation and exchanges between Community and Central-East European universities and to develop the teaching of foreign languages came into operation from July 1990. The EC Commission is responsible for implementation of TEMPUS, but a central coordination office to facilitate its introduction and to select projects is to be set up.

In the context of *agriculture*, as will be discussed below, in addition to food aid, the Commission proposed a large-scale programme lasting a number of years for Poland to furnish inputs such as farm machinery and pesticides, to improve animal feeds, to provide technical assistance, to establish an environmental code corresponding to international standards and to modernise food processing and distribution channels. Credits are also to be granted to help private enterprises in the agricultural and food sectors import equipment.

Hungarian agriculture is to benefit from aid for small farmers, including help in the provision of backup services, credits and improved access to foreign currency. In addition, technical assistance and information services will be provided to increase the possibilities of commercialisation. Assistance for the agricultural sector is also to be given to Bulgaria and Romania.

Access to Western markets is to be encouraged. The EC member states agreed to *eliminate all remaining quantitative restrictions* on imports from Hungary and Poland from 1 January 1990, ahead of the schedules agreed in the respective trade and cooperation agreements. The Community also agreed to extend *GSP* (General System of Preferences) treatment to the two countries from January 1990, and subsequently to Bulgaria, Czechoslovakia, Yugoslavia and (in the short time remaining before unification) the German Democratic Republic. In the case of industrial goods this entailed customs duties ranging from 22% (lorries) to 8% (toys) being reduced to zero, while other concessions related to a number of textile and agricultural products. Access to EC markets was also improved for certain other agricultural and textile products(8).

With regard to *environmental protection*, the Community will give aid to all the smaller Central-East European countries covered by the PHARE Programme for projects which include measures to deal with waste disposal, air and water pollution, and the development of monitoring systems (see Appendix 8.1). The EC will also contribute 2 million ECU towards an initial budget of $10 million to set up a Regional Environment Centre in Budapest. This Centre will also be financed by the United States and various Central-East European countries. It will be responsible for compiling and disseminating data and information on the environment, as well as participating in the global environment monitoring network.

In June 1990 a cooperation agreement was signed between the environmental ministers of the EC and Central-East Europe (including the Soviet Union). Priority was to be given to the security of the twenty-two nuclear installations and the quality of water in Central-East Europe. A

European Environmental Agency to monitor the state of the environment in Central-East Europe and enable exchanges in information was
envisaged.

8.4 Contributions to the social safety nets

8.4.1 *What the West could do*

The austerity implied by the stabilisation policies, and the unemployment and income disparities likely to result from structural and systematic change all call for social security measures. Western aid to help
guarantee certain minimum social needs would seem justified on humanitarian grounds. Medical and food aid are obvious examples of this
type of assistance, though there is a danger that the latter could lead to
market disruption (as in fact occurred in Poland).

There have also been some Central-East European requests for Western contributions to financing their social security systems, and for allowing increased immigration from those countries. It is sometimes
argued that if workers laid off in Central-East Europe were allowed to
work temporarily in the Community, this could also contribute to the
training objective, relieve unemployment and improve the balance of
payments situation by means of capital remissions home.

8.4.2 *What has been done under the PHARE Programme*

One of the main elements of the PHARE Programme has been food
and medical aid for Poland, Romania, Bulgaria and the Soviet Union
(see Appendix 8.1).

As a first step, in 1989 the Group of 24 pledged 336 million ECU in
food aid to Poland(9), of which some 125–130 million ECU was to be
paid from the Community Budget. All the EC food aid was to come
from intervention stocks, except citrus fruit which would come from
preventative withdrawals which would otherwise be destroyed.

Apart from the initial deliveries, all the food aid was to be sold to the
Polish consumers at market prices. The proceeds from these sales were
to be used to set up a counterpart fund for the modernisation of Polish
agriculture. After allowing for transport and distribution costs, this fund
would have an initial capital of 110 million ECU, which could be used to
buy fertilisers, pesticide, tractors and other farm machinery, as well as to
pay labour on small- and medium-size Polish farms. The funds would
also be used to improve the water supply, gas and telecommunications
systems, to modernise distribution channels and to finance a joint

venture between the Deustche Genossenschaftbank and the Bank for Food Economy. The Polish/EC Joint Committee was to supervise the funding of these projects.

Subsequently, the EC pledged a further 200 million ECU in food aid to Poland, and ways of avoiding the shortcomings of the first instalment were considered(10). In particular, the Community was concerned that a request by the Polish food trader, Rolimpex, to export 1 million tonnes of grain (half of which was wheat) did not constitute re-export of part of the 1.5 million tonnes of wheat granted by the EC to Poland over the preceding year(11).

Following the urgent Soviet request for food aid in November 1990, with Gorbachev sending a list of precise requirements(12), there was an immediate public and private response in Germany. This included the consignment of food reserves worth $390 million which had been kept in West Berlin ever since the Cold War years of the early 1950s, ex-GDR army rations and Red Cross packages. In December 1990 the EC voted in favour of 750 million ECU of aid to the Soviet Union, of which 500 million ECU would be in the form of credits to assist Soviet purchases of EC agricultural products and the remaining 250 million ECU would be in the form of food aid. Given the breakdown in the distribution network in the Soviet Union, and prevalence of theft, in some cases the Western donors organised the transportation and distribution of food aid themselves, at times with the help of KGB supervision. The European Parliament voted for suspension of Community aid in January 1991 following repression in the Baltic states, but it was decided to resume aid in March of that year.

8.5 The European Bank for Reconstruction and Development

A European Bank to aid Reconstruction and Development in East-Central Europe (BERD) with headquarters in London is to begin operations from April 1991. The thirty-nine members of the Bank include the OECD countries, the Soviet Union and seven smaller Central-East European countries, other Western countries, the European Investment Bank (EIB) and the EC as an organisation(13).

The Bank is to have capital of some 10 billion ECU, 30% of which is to be paid straightaway, with the rest acting mainly as a guarantee to cover projects. The EC member states, the EC and EIB are to provide 51% of this capital. The United States is to have a 10% stake; Japan, together with Germany, France, Italy and the United Kingdom are each to have a stake of 8.5%, with lower percentages for the smaller EC countries, and a further 6% to be shared between the EC and EIB.

The Central-East European countries are also to provide 13.7% of the capital.

The aims of the Bank were to encourage investment in Central-East Europe, to reduce financial risks, to aid the transformation of these countries into market economies and to accelerate structural change. The essential condition for aid was again that the recipient countries should show themselves to be irreversibly on the road to reform, with the Netherlands and the United Kingdom insisiting on a tight interpretation of this condition.

There was considerable dissent concerning the eligibility of the Soviet Union for loans, with the United States and the United Kingdom arguing that the scale of Soviet needs presented a risk of destabilising the activities of the Bank. As a result it was proposed that no country could take more than 20–30% of the Bank's total lending. It was also decided that for the first three years the Soviet Union could not borrow more than the 6% share of capital it had subscribed. Subsequently, Soviet access on the same terms as other participating countries would require agreement by 85% of all shareholders (which in effect allows a joint veto to Japan and the United States). It was also decided that loans could be granted in dollars or yen as well as ECU.

There were considerable differences among participants as to whether the activities of the Bank should be restricted to the private sector (the US and UK view) or whether aid should also be extended to the state sector, especially where projects to improve infrastructure or telecommunications were concerned (as most EC countries desired). Ultimately, it was decided that 60% of lending to any one country must be to the private sector. Priority is to be given to the promotion of joint ventures and support for small and medium enterprises.

The proposal to set up such a Bank is not new(14), but for many years it received little support. This was partly because of the lack of harmonisation of the export credit and reinsurance policies of the EC member states, but also because it was commonly felt that such a bank would represent an unnecessary duplication and there were fears that it might compete with national institutions.

8.6   Why the West should give aid

One of the main reasons for giving aid to Central-East Europe is Western self-interest. Despite the present relatively low levels of trade, and the adjustment difficulties of Central-Europe, these countries do still represent a potential market of some 450 million consumers. According to a study carried out by four Western research institutes(15), in fifteen years EC exports to Central-East Europe could be greater than those to the

United States. This would represent a trade pattern more similar to that of the pre-War period with, for example, the Central-East European countries accounting for 20% of exports and 16% of imports in European trade in 1937 compared with the equivalent figures of 5% and 4% in 1987(16).

As the statistics in Chapter 11 testify, Western involvement in joint ventures in CMEA countries has been growing rapidly, despite the obstacles encountered. Recovery of the Central-East European economies has to be encouraged in order to exploit these trade and market opportunities.

A study carried out by the Observatoire Français des Conjonctures Economiques(17) suggested that economic changes in Central-East Europe could increase the GDP of the Federal Republic of Germany by 3.45% and that of the EC as a whole by 1.4% by 1993, with retail prices being 0.3% lower in France and 1.5% lower in Germany than would otherwise have been the case in 1993. However, these results should be treated with caution, as their degree of accuracy is rather questionable.

It is frequently claimed that the aid for Central-East European countries is granted at the cost of aid to the needier third world countries, and/or measures to assist the poorer areas of the Community. For instance, this fear was loudly voiced by the African, Caribbean and Pacific (ACP) countries during the negotiations of EC trade concessions under Lomé IV.

However, despite the more deserving claims of the less-developed countries in the longer run, if the opportunity for the transformation of Central-East Europe is missed, the political and economic consequences could be disastrous. The recent changes in Central-East Europe have raised expectations, and failure to deliver the goods could lead to disillusion with the democratic model. The alternatives would seem to be a disintegration into anarchy and chaos on the one hand or a 'Chinese solution' of repression on the other. In either case the West is likely to experience external costs, possibly in the form of large-scale migrations, and/or spillover of ethnic and nationalistic tensions. Soros puts the case very forcefully for the Soviet Union, where the stakes (and also the cost) are highest:

> If and when the disintegration of the Soviet Union turns into civil war, millions die and a few nuclear accidents occur, the benefit of preventing these things from happening will be obvious.

8.6.1   What is the optimal level of aid?

There are considerable variations in assessments of how much aid is necessary, according to the type of aid considered, and who makes the estimate. An inevitable political aspect enters into the making of these calculations, so they should be regarded as maxima, with actual levels of aid granted likely to prove much less. The main danger in giving less aid would seem to be that it might be ineffective.

With regard to Western assessments, in January 1990 Delors suggested that if aid were given to Central-East European countries on the same scale as to the less-developed areas of the Community, a total of 19 billion ECU per year in loans and grants would be necessary for the next five to ten years. Of this 14 billion ECU would be in the form of grants, and the remaining 5 billion in loans. It has been estimated that an additional $25 billion would be necessary to stabilise the Soviet economy(18), though other observers suggest that double that figures might be necessary.

Given the constant comparison with the Marshall Plan, a further estimate voiced is that equivalent to what the United States gave after the second World War, namely on average 1.1% of GDP over three-and-a-half years between 1948 and 1951. This was given to sixteen countries of the then OEEC (Organisation for European Economic Cooperation, which was the precursor of the OECD). It has been estimated that the $12.4 billion given under the Marshall Plan would amount to $65.4 billion in 1989 prices(19). This sum would be equivalent to 0.3% of the present Community GDP, or to 0.1% of the combined GDP of the EC, the United States and Japan.

The estimates from the Eastern side are predictably much higher than those in the West, with, for example the Trzeciakowski Plan calling for $10 billion for Poland alone, while Polish estimates of the food requirements alone of that country for 1990–91 amounted to some $2 billion(20).

8.6.2 *How much has been given under the PHARE Programme?*

The financing of aid is either carried out autonomously by the Community, its member states, other members of the Group of 24 or international organisations, or by some combination of these acting in conjunction. Assistance may also be in the form of grants, loans or guarantees, and this has to be taken into account in arriving at a figure for total aid.

Total aid in grants and loans pledged by the Group of 24 to Poland and Hungary for the following two to three years was $15 billion by October 1990, with a further $6.3 billion for other eligible Central-East European countries(21). Following the increases in December 1990 and the extension of aid to the Soviet Union these figures would have to be revised upwards to at least $25–30 billion. The IMF and World Bank announced that they were prepared to give loans of up to $24 billion over the 1991–94 period, with the first $5 billion being granted in 1991(22).

According to July 1990 statistics, 6 billion ECU out of a total of 11 billion ECU committed were in the form of donations. However, subsequently the share of loans, including rescheduling of debts was expected to rise to some two-thirds(23).

Considering the EC alone, the 1990 budget allocation amounted to 300 million ECU for Poland and Hungary and a further 200 million ECU for the other smaller Central-East European countries. This is in addition to Community funds made available through loans by the EIB, BERD and ECSC.

8.7 Assessment of the PHARE Programme

Though the amount of spending under the PHARE Programme falls short of many estimates of what is needed, there is widespread recognition that 'the amount already mobilized is quite significant and quickly prepared' (Saryusz-Wolski, 1990a).

The comparison of what the West could do and what it has done suggests that the measures taken under the aegis of the PHARE Programme are rather well tailored to the needs of the transformation process. This was facilitated by asking each of the Central-East European countries included in the PHARE Programme to present a memorandum setting out its specific needs. These memoranda were then assessed by EC missions sent to the countries in question.

When extension of the PHARE Programme was decided, the requests of Czechoslovakia, Bulgaria and Yugoslavia coincided largely with the priorities already set out by the Group of 24: improved access to EC markets, GSP treatment, training, technological assistance, technology transfers, the encouragement of joint ventures, cooperation in environmental protection, and help for agriculture (in the case of Bulgaria).

The main areas where Western assistance appears to fall short of Central-East European expectations would seem to be with regard to access to EC markets (discussed in the next chapter) and allowing immigration from Central-East European countries. As a traditional agricultural exporter to the Soviet Union, Hungary also criticised the decision to restrict the granting of export credits to Community agricultural exports to the Soviet Union despite a proposal that Hungarian exports should also benefit from that measure. The Hungarians maintained that they were being placed at a disadvantage. Debt relief was another major lacuna in the Western aid programme until the measure to assist Poland in April 1991, and there would seem a strong case for extending similar measures to Hungary and Bulgaria if requested.

The EC Commission had certain difficulties in coordinating the activities of the Group of 24(24). Rollo *et al.* (1990) provide a matrix of 170 active policy options on the part of the various public and private parties involved in the activities of the Group of 24. This is useful in underlining the dangers of duplication, conflicting action and bureaucratic fatigue.

To meet the need for coordination, the Group of 24 rapidly acquired a structure with regular meetings and working groups on various priority topics. A commitment to implement various undertakings has been established, made up of representatives of the member countries presided over by the EC Commission. From 1990 the Commission also began to publish annual progress reports on the amount of aid given.

Despite these difficulties, the exchanges of information within the G-24 framework are generally considered useful, and have helped to avoid overlaps between measures taken by Western countries. Smaller countries lacking the resources or experience to organise projects on their own have been able to participate more effectively. However, rather than participating in joint projects, many donor countries preferred to operate individually, thereby gaining better press coverage, and frequently trying aid to spending in the donor country. None the less, on balance the experience of the Community in coordinating Western aid measures must be regarded as relatively positive.

Appendix 8.1   Summary of PHARE measures of Group of 24 (a)

1. Food Supplies
Beneficiary: Poland
Donors: EC, the United States, Canada, Australia, Austria, Finland, Norway, Turkey, Italy, Switzerland. Food supplies to the value of 336 million ECU were agreed in 1989, and the EC pledged a further 200 million ECU in 1990.

Beneficiary: Romania and Bulgaria
Donors: EC (6.5 million ECU food and emergency aid to Romania in 1989, 41 million ECU food aid to Romania in 1990, 100 million ECU for Bulgaria and Romania), the United States, Ireland, Austria, Spain, Switzerland.

Beneficiary: Soviet Union
Donors: EC (750 million ECU; US($1 billion export credits for food and other necessary items).

2. Counterpart Fund
Beneficiary: Poland
Main measures: loans for farmers and businessmen; rural development projects; purchase of agricultural machinery; improving the telephone, gas, banking and water-supply networks.
Donors: EC (PLZ 535 billion, likely to increase by 330 by end June 1990); Canada* ($(Can)6–8 million); Austria* (PLZ 15.1); Japan* (PLZ 3 billion); Italy* (l.(It)120 billion); Switzerland* and Norway*.

3. Agricultural Assistance
Beneficiary: Poland
Main measures: Plant and seed protection; deliveries of animal feed; supplies of inputs including secondhand machinery; training; technical assistance; reorganisation of distribution channels; credits for imports of equipment and the modernisation of food processing.
Donors: EC (50 million ECU for plant and seed protection, 20 million ECU for animal feeds); United Kingdom (£(UK)15 million credit for food processing); US ($10 million or ECU 8 million); Canada (ECU 1.4 million for training, 690,000 ECU for management of holdings); Belgium (473,000 ECU for distribution network); Switzerland (17.6 million ECU); Netherlands (0.8 million ECU for stockbreeding); Federal Republic of Germany (4.8 million ECU in secondhand machinery, 4.8 million ECU in technical assistance); Ireland (120,000 ECU for training); New Zealand (technical assistance); World Bank (ECU 80 million for foodprocessing); Austria (690,000 ECU in secondhand machinery for Poland and Hungary); Denmark (955,000 ECU in technical assistance for Poland and Hungary).

Beneficiary: Hungary
Main measures: aid for small farmers; technical cooperation, credits; possibilities for cofinancing; aid in introducing modern technology systems and deliveries of secondhand machinery.
Donors: EC (20 million ECU for small farmers); New Zealand (117,000 ECU for modern technology systems); Netherlands (70,000 ECU); Belgium (141,000 ECU) and World Bank credits to finance imports of inputs and equipment.

Beneficiary: Bulgaria
Donor: EC (16 million ECU, in particular for developing the private sector, the financial sector and processing).

4. Training and Human Resources
Beneficiaries: Poland and Hungary and subsequently Czechoslovakia, Bulgaria, Romania and the Soviet Union.
Main measures: management training; training in banking and finance;

technical training; exchange of scientific and economic knowledge; education and cultural exchanges; help for newly created democratic institutions; unemployment insurance (for Poland); languages; marketing and product control.

Donors: EC (Tempus; European Training Foundation; exchanges); United States ($12 million for newly created democratic institutions; $5 million unemployment insurance in Poland; $10 million in technical assistance; $10 million in student grants; $12 million in exchanges); Belgium and International Labour Office (473,000 ECU for training for Employment Ministries); Belgium (473,000 ECU for training of overseas trading companies); United Kingdom (104 million ECU for know-how fund); Sweden (public administration and technical assistance to Polish mining); Australia* (3.8 million ECU for English and management training also including Czechoslovakia); Germany (3.7 million ECU); Turkey (banking and management courses for Poland); Norway (training especially for Polish Employer's Federation); Italy (marketing and management of joint ventures); Japan (business management and product control); Finland (440,000 ECU including training for the environment and energy saving; statistical training for Bulgaria and banking, forestry and privatisation for Czechoslovakia); Switzerland (30 million Sfr.); Spain (language training); Netherlands (3.5 million ECU); Austria (1.4 million ECU with a further 2.7 million ECU from the Federal Chamber of Commerce and National Bank, and 1.1 million ECU* for other Central-East European countries); Denmark (3.3 million ECU for technical assistance); Canada, United States, France, Italy, the Netherlands (Budapest International Management Centre).

5. Energy and the Environment
Beneficiaries: Poland and Hungary, and subsequently Bulgaria, Romania and the Soviet Union.
Main Measures: improve pollution control systems; reduce emission of polluting gases; combat water pollution; improve waste disposal; preserve or reorganise natural reserves or sites; training; technical assistance; creation of a Budapest Regional Environment Centre.
Donors: EC (22 million ECU for Poland, 24 million for Hungary, 150 million for Bulgaria and Romania*); United States ($10 million for improved air and water supplies in Krakow area and Regional Environmental Centre in Budapest); Belgium (1.5 million ECU for Mazurian Lakes, tree diseases in Poland and monitoring and training in Hungary); Austria (for toxic wastes from coal-fired factories); Sweden (40 million ECU); Switzerland (30 million Sfr.); World Bank (and countries such as the United Kingdom for environmental strategy); EIB (and countries such as the United Kingdom for an electricity project in Hungary and an energy/environment project in Poland).

6. Measures to Assist Stabilisation and Debt Relief
Beneficiaries: Poland, Hungary, Bulgaria and Czechoslovakia.
Donors: Contributions of many of G-24 to a $1 billion stabilisation fund and rescheduling of $10 billion foreign debt for Poland, and $1 billion medium-term loan for Hungary, 700 million ECU for Czechoslovakia if agreement is reached with the IMF*; IMF (standby credits for Poland and Hungary*) 50% debt relief on Polish indebtedness towards official creditors (reducing the total from $33.7 billion to $18 billion in five years), $800 million debt relief for Bulgaria.

7. Improved Market Access
Beneficiaries: Poland and Hungary, Bulgaria, Czechoslovakia and Yugoslavia.
Donors: EC (elimination or gradual reduction of quantitative restrictions, GSP, improved treatment for certain other textiles, steel and agricultural imports).

8. Investment and Economic Reform
Beneficiaries: Poland and Hungary, Bulgaria, Czechoslovakia, Romania, Yugoslavia and the Soviet Union.
Main Measures: Help for joint ventures and other forms of industrial cooperation; export credits and investment guarantees; protection of investment; aid for privatisation; modernisation of the financial system; aid to small and medium enterprises; training; technical assistance; trade policy measures and loans for restructuring.
Donors: EC (9 million for Polish privatisation agency; 5 million for modernisation of Hungarian financial system; 25 million ECU loans for small and medium enterprise in both Hungary and Poland; statistical and technical cooperation; 150 million ECU for energy projects in Bulgaria and Romania; 1 billion for the Soviet Union for priority areas such as transport and distribution, the food industry, energy, and telecommunications); United States (enterprise funds worth $240 million for Poland and $60 million for Hungary; $10 million for other smaller Central-East European countries); the EIB (1 billion ECU loans for Hungary and Poland, 2 billion ECU for infrastructure projects in Bulgaria, Czechoslovakia and Romania); the BERD (10 billion capital); ECSC (loans up to 200 million ECU); EFTA countries (81 million ECU for a Yugoslavian development fund); Canada (733,000 ECU development fund); United Kingdom (2.1 million ECU and 2.25 million to the UNIDO Programme for Poland and Hungary); Switzerland (160 million ECU); Turkey ($250,000 for small-scale industry in Hungary); Italy (creation of a state-supported financing company, Simest spa., with priority for activities in Central-East Europe); Finland; Denmark (38.2 million ECU and 12.7 million ECU to support Danish investment in the area);

New Zealand; Ireland; Norway; Japan (export credits and promotion of investment); Netherlands; Luxembourg (export credits); the World Bank (634 million ECU for Poland and Hungary; structural development loan of $300 million for Poland and $200 million for Hungary).

9. Medical Aid
Beneficiary: Poland
Donors: EC (4 million ECU in 1989); United States ($4 million); United Kingdom; Italy (6 million ECU); Netherlands (4.3 million ECU).

Beneficiary: Romania
Donors: EC (11.5 million ECU emergency aid, 6 million ECU for Romanian orphans, and a further 7.5 billion ECU pledged for 1991) and most of the G-24.

Beneficiary: Bulgaria
Donor: G-24, humanitarian aid.

Beneficiary: the Soviet Union
Donor: the United States and EC member states, emergency medical aid.

Source: Report on progress of coordinated aid from the 24 to Central and Eastern Europe, 3 July 1990, and European Report, various issues.

Notes:
(a) This list does not pretend to be exhaustive, but indicates most of the measures taken or approved by mid-1990.
* measure approved but not implemented at the time of writing.

Notes

1. The EC 12, the EFTA 6, the United States, Canada, Japan, New Zealand, Australia and Turkey.
2. According to the Jackson-Vanik Law, a necessary pre-condition for this measure was that the Soviet Union allow emigration. Although such legislation had not been passed at that time, *de facto* the Soviet Union was allowing some 1000 Jews per day to leave (*La Repubblica*, 6 December 1990).
3. In doing so the structure of this chapter follows that of Rollo *et al.* (1990).
4. See Nuti (1990a) for a detailed discussion of this point.
5. Subsequently there was some disagreement, as the Commission and certain EC member states maintained that a 1 billion ECU (rather than US$) loan had been agreed.
6. Chilosi (1990), p. 6.
7. as discussed in Rollo *et al.* (1990).

8. See Chapters 2 and 6.
9. Although the exact final quantities of this food aid were to be decided by the Commission management committees, the EC Council set out the following guidelines: 500,000 tonnes of bread wheat; 300,000 tonnes of mixed grains; 10,000 tonnes beef, 5000 tonnes olive oil and 20,000 tonnes of citrus fruit.

    The EC had previously given food and medical aid to Poland on a number of occasions over the 1980–85 period.

    The 41 million ECU of food aid for Romania included 62,000 tonnes of maize; 62,500 tonnes of rye; 2,500 tonnes of butter; 2,500 tonnes of olive oil; and 10,000 of beef. Half was to be financed under the new heading of the EC Budget created for aid to Central-East Europe, and the other half by the Guarantee Section of the FEOGA Budget.
10. There were reports of hold-ups in deliveries, and in some cases market disruption. Polish authorities also suggested that in the second consignment there should be more meat and butter, and less olive oil and citrus fruit.

    There was a commitment to deliver this second consignment of aid in the first half of 1990. The Polish government initially announced that for each of the years 1990 and 1991, it would require 200,000–250,000 tonnes of butter; 10,000 tonnes of milk powder; 130,000–150,000 tonnes of vegetable oils; 2.2 million tonnes of wheat; 80,000 tonnes of maize; 500,000 tonnes of barley; and 200,000–250,000 tonnes of sugar each year.
11. *European Report*, 6 July 1990, No. 1601.
12. The list of needs included 500,000 tonnes of meat; 200,000 tonnes of butter; 500,000 tonnes of vegetable oils; and 50,000 tonnes of skimmed milk powder.
13. As *La Repubblica* of 21 November 1989 points out, it is also likely that the Western operators involved in the running and guaranteeing of this bank stand to gain (as occurred in the case of the European Investment Bank).
14. See, for example, Pinder (1974).
15. The institutes were the BIPE, the IFO, Prometeia and Cambridge Econometrics, as reported in Saryusz-Wolski (1990b).
16. These figures are taken from Saryusz-Wolski (1990b).
17. As reported in Saryusz-Wolski (1990b).
18. Nuti (1990a).
19. The figures in this paragraph are taken from an article by Christian Saint-Etienne, *Participazione estera al finanziamento dell'Europa Centrale*, published in *Il Sole- 24 Ore*, 13 December, 1990.
20. Cova (1989), p. 450.
21. According to Horst Krenzler, Director of DG 1 of the EC Commission (*European Report*, 31 October 1990).
22. These figures are taken from *Il Sole-24 Ore*, 5 December 1990.
23. Calculations on the basis of statistics in *Il Sole-24 Ore*, 11 December 1990.
24. Rollo *et al.* (1990, pp. 102–3).

9

The tightening links between the Community and Central-East Europe

9.1 Introduction

With the collapse of the CMEA, the EC rapidly emerged as a pole of attraction for the newly autonomous Central-East European countries. Before going on to explain the reasons for the magnetism of the EC, and to discuss likely developments in the configuration of Europe in the next chapter, it is useful to present here a brief description of the various phases in the tightening of bilateral links between the Community and Central-East European countries.

The Community was quick to respond to the approaches made by Central-East European countries, and the first tangible result of resolution of the political recognition problem in 1988 was the signing of 'first generation' trade and cooperation agreements between the European Community and all these countries. In the first part of this chapter these agreements will be described, and their importance will be assessed.

The trade and cooperation agreements are soon to be replaced by 'second generation' association contracts or 'Europe agreements' with certain Central-East European countries sufficiently advanced in economic and political transformation. These agreements aim at closer political and economic integration with the ultimate objective of creating a free trade area. Though the agreements carry no promise of EC membership, the possibility of eventual accession for countries such as Poland, Hungary and Czechoslovakia has not been excluded.

The demise of the CMEA has put an end to its claim to be treated as an equal bargaining partner with the Community, and in the final part of this chapter it will be shown how bloc-to-bloc relationships are likely to prove minimal and have been vastly overshadowed by the importance of bilateral links between the EC and individual Central-East European countries.

9.2 Trade and cooperation agreements

In September 1988 Hungary signed a trade and cooperation agreement with the Community, and by October 1990 these 'first generation agreements' had been signed between the EC and all Central-East European countries(1). The agreement signed in May 1990 with the German Democratic Republic is probably one of the shortest-lived ever, lasting only until German political unification in October 1990. Following the intervention to quash the protest in University Square in June 1990, the Community held up the Romanian agreement which was eventually signed in October 1990. Statements to the effect that the Community was willing to have relations and even sign a trade agreement with Albania if transformation were undertaken led eventually to discussions from mid-1991.

The agreements all relate to trade and to commercial and economic cooperation and were valid for ten years (five in the case of Poland and Bulgaria). There were separate agreements for textiles and voluntary restraint agreements for steel, with the exception of the German Democratic Republic which was subject to autonomous Community textile and steel regimes. Agricultural products were also excluded from the Czech and Soviet agreements, but not those of the other Central-East European countries. The 1988 Hungarian agreement did not alter existing agricultural agreements or arrangements between the EC and Hungary, but, given the importance of agricultural trade, 'the possibility of giving each other reciprocal concessions on a product by product basis' (2) was to be considered.

All the agreements contained commitments on the part of the Community to progressively liberalise the quantitative restrictions on imports from Central-European countries. Initially, for Poland and Hungary it was envisaged that quantitative restrictions would be dismantled in three phases, depending on the degree of sensitivity of the product, but in the event they were totally eliminated from January 1990. In the case of the Soviet Union, quantitative restrictions on all but the most sensitive products imported by the Community were to be eliminated by 1995, and in 1992 the process of liberalisation was to be assessed.

The *quid pro quo* for elimination of quantitative restrictions was improved access to the Central-East European country's market. This generally also entailed better facilities for businessmen, and more favourable treatment in matters of intellectual property rights. The

Hungarian agreement, for example, included a commitment to give non-discriminatory treatment to the EC in such matters as the application of their import licensing system, their global quota on consumer goods and their procedure for awarding contracts on international competitive tender. In the Soviet agreement there was a commitment to facilitate the transfer of profits and dividends abroad for businesses set up in the Soviet Union.

The Community's commitment to remove quantitative restrictions was accompanied by safeguard clauses to prevent injury to EC producers. In the Hungarian case this entailed a 'supersafeguard' clause allowing the EC to take unilateral action to limit imports or impose a duty if necessary. Poland was also offered a similar 'supersafeguard' clause in exchange for complete elimination of quantitative restrictions, but this was rejected because it was considered to hinder Poland's chances of renegotiating its 'non-market' protocol of accession to GATT. Instead, a GATT safeguard clause was included and the initial reductions in quotas included in the agreement were less far-reaching than those of Hungary. The Soviet agreement included a GATT safeguard clause which allows unilateral action on the part of the EC, but only after consultation.

Each of the agreements entailed the establishment of a joint committee between the Community and Central-East European country to ensure the proper functioning of the agreement, and to seek ways of encouraging trade and cooperation. The latter would include assessing recent trends in trade, making recommendations to overcome problems, identifying new possibilities for trade and cooperation, and exchanging information on macroeconomic plans, forecasts and other matters relating to East–West trade and cooperation. Subsequently, meetings of these joint committees have proved important occasions for negotiating further trade concessions.

The cooperation aspect of the agreements was wide-ranging and, depending on the interests of the Central-European country in question, extended to fields such as industry, agriculture, transport, mineral extraction, energy, science, training, finance, research, tourism, the environment and the encouragement of joint ventures. In the case of the Soviet Union the cooperation also included nuclear research, energy and the safety of nuclear reactors (which explains why the agreement also had to be signed by Euratom).

The Czech case represents an exception in that when the negotiations began in 1983 the initial aim was to sign agreements covering a number of sectors of special interest to that country such as glassware and ceramics. The Community suggested an agreement covering all industrial goods, which was eventually signed in 1988. Only in May 1990 was the agreement extended to cooperation. The exclusion of cooperation from the earlier agreement has to be explained by its timing: the Hungarian precedent had not yet been established, and the more limited agreement offered the prospect of quicker results.

9.3   The significance of the trade and cooperation agreements

Although many of these trade and cooperation agreements will soon be overtaken by events, they are significant on a number of counts. In particular, they represented an early indication of the Community's goodwill and readiness to help these countries by granting improved market access; they reflected a shift in power between the Community and its member states; and they were an important step in the process of evolving closer institutional links between the two parties.

Market access is the form of aid most likely to provide incentives and to benefit the recipient country in the long run, so it is not surprising that it is also the measure which encounters greatest opposition from domestic producers. The most explicit way in which the trade and cooperation agreements improved access to EC markets was through the removal of quantitative restrictions. According to unofficial Commission estimates, quantitative restrictions had covered some 3–5% of trade between the EC and Central-East Europe, depending on the country and year in question. However, this estimate does not provide an accurate indication of the significance of the trade concessions granted to the Central-East European countries in the agreements from 1988. Firstly, the estimate does not take into account what trade might have been in the absence of such restrictions. Secondly, though the liberalisation envisaged by the agreements was only gradual and incomplete, it opened the way for more rapid and extensive concessions in negotiations carried out in the context of the joint committee meetings and the PHARE Programme of aid. Thirdly, though the agreements did not extend to such sectors as textiles or steel there was soon pressure (met to some extent) for more favourable treatment for these sectors. Fourthly, elimination of quantitative restrictions had an important political aspect for countries such as Poland anxious to renegotiate their non-market status in GATT. Finally, and most importantly, the agreements probably represented a 'foot in the door' and, in the case of some of the smaller Central-East European countries, were considered the first step in the gradual creation of a free trade area, if not full membership, with the Community.

Not only do the agreements represent a first concrete response to the demands of the Central-East European countries, they also reflect a change in the balance of power between the Community and its member states. This shift in authority was challenged in the case of the first agreement (with Hungary) but subsequently became less of an issue.

According to the September 1988 Hungarian agreement(3), in addition to being initialled by the EC Commission and signed by the Council (a formality), ratification by the European Parliament was necessary since:

> it appears that certain measures of economic cooperation provided for by the agreement exceed the powers of action provided for in the Treaty and in particular those specified in the field of the common commercial policy

Furthermore, the agreement also contained a specification that it would in no way prevent the EC member states from continuing bilateral economic cooperation with Hungary, even concluding new economic cooperation agreements if appropriate. This formula was initially used for the EC's cooperation agreement with Canada in 1976(4).

On the one hand the EC member states have been allowed to continue their bilateral cooperation agreements, and the Hungarian agreement contains the clause that such agreements appear beyond the competences of the Community listed in the Treaty of Rome. Against this the phrase 'it appears' in the first quotation suggests that the Community has not accepted this definition of its competences, and the mere fact that it signed the agreement represents an extension of its powers. In addition, the agreement contains a clause stating that its provisions should be substituted for those of agreements between the EC member states and Hungary in cases where they are incompatible or identical.

Moreover, there are two ways in which operation of these agreements will increase the strength of the Community vis-à-vis the member states. The first is in the activities of the joint committees, where the member states will have to coordinate their positions and reach a Community line. Secondly, the greater opportunities for direct contacts between the EC and Central-East European countries will improve the flow of information to the Community, making it likely that the consultation procedure becomes a more effective control over cooperation agreements of the member states.

9.4   Second generation association agreements

Certain of the smaller Central-East European countries (notably Hungary, Czechoslovakia and Poland) expressed their interest in possible membership of the EC. The Community initially ruled out accession of these countries before the beginning of the next century, and announced that there would be no new members of any description before 1993. Hungary has set the target date for its accession as 1995(5), when it hoped to become the first Central-East European member of the Community (East Germany aside).

By way of recompense, those Central-East European countries which have made decisive progress in economic and political reform were offered the possibility of *'second generation association agreements'*, which later became known as *'Europe agreements'*. The conditions for eligibility were spelt out and related to the rule of law; the human rights record (including respect for religious and ethnic minorities); political pluralism; free elections; and the liberalisation of the economy.

In September 1990 preliminary discussions for these agreements began with Hungary, Poland and Czechoslovakia, and the Commission announced that it would continue to monitor events in other Central-East European countries where the transformation process was less advanced, with a view to exploratory talks.

Initially it was stressed that these association agreements did not represent a type of pre-membership or preparatory phase for EC membership, and that possible future accession would be decided case by case, regardless of whether the country in question had been an associate or not. The earlier association agreements of Greece, Turkey, Malta and Cyprus specifically mentioned the prospect of membership, but only after long discussion did the Community accept that the possibility of ultimate EC accession would be incorporated into the preamble of the Europe agreements.

The basis of these association agreements was Article 238 of the Treaty of Rome, according to which the 'Community can enter into agreements with a third party State, a union of States or an International Organisation which create an association characterised by mutual rights and duties, by common action and particular procedures'.

The association agreements would replace the existing trade and co-operation agreements and would be aimed at encouraging wider economic integration (and especially freer movement for people, capital, goods and services); higher levels of trade and investment; and greater economic, financial, political and cultural cooperation throughout Europe. The main features of these agreements are set out in Table 9.1.

With regard to the free movement of goods and services the ultimate aim was to create a free trade area. Timetables would be fixed for tariff reductions, but because the Central-East European countries required time to become more competitive, tariff cuts would probably be asymmetric, with the Community proceeding more quickly.

It was expected that in the first phase of liberalisation (due to last five years) the Community would remove all specific quantitative restrictions, and would then gradually reduce non-specific ones. At the same time the Central-East European countries would attempt to gradually eliminate their tariffs on non-sensitive products, and reduce tariffs on

Table 9.1 The main features of association or 'Europe agreements'

1. *Free movement of goods and services* leading ultimately to creation of a free trade area. Timetables would be fixed for reductions in tariffs and quotas, but because the Central-East European countries required time to become more competitive, tariff cuts would probably be asymmetric, with the Community proceeding more quickly. Exceptions would be based on precise criteria (such as the infant industries argument, or the exigencies of restructuring). Introduction of new taxes, tariffs or other restrictive measures affecting trade (including subsidies) would be prohibited.

2. 'Phased introduction' of *free movement of capital and people* with EC measures taken to ease the process (such as encouraging the creation of competitive financial sectors by means of technical cooperation, joint ventures and training).

3. The *approximation of laws* in particular relating to company law, company accounts and taxes, financial services, competition, health and safety regulations, consumer protection, the environment, transport and intellectual and commercial property.

4. The *institutionalisation of political dialogue*, with Association Councils to act as fora for decision and discussion, Association Committees composed of senior officials and Parliamentary Association Committees composed of members of parliament of the associated country, and members of the European Parliament.

5. New and closer forms of *economic, scientific and technical cooperation*, including agriculture, industry, research, transport and information systems.

6. *Cultural cooperation* and exchange of information.

7. *EC financial aid and technical support* in fields such as the environment, transport, telecommunications, agriculture, energy, regional development and tourism. Measures would also be taken to assist small and medium enterprises in Central-East Europe and to encourage and protect investment.

8. *Common projects to improve infrastructure* in particular relating to roads, railways, waterways and gas pipelines.

sensitive products to bring them in line with the GSP. Exceptions to these rules would be based on precise criteria (such as the infant industries argument, or the exigencies of restructuring). Introduction of new taxes, tariffs or other restrictive measures affecting trade (including subsidies) would be prohibited.

During a second period (lasting a further five years) the Community would dismantle all remaining tariffs and quotas. The Central-East European countries would gradually reduce customs duties and restrictive taxes during this period, and although quotas would be allowed, there would be preferential treatment for Community products.

Textiles, ECSC and processed agricultural products would be treated in separate protocols attached to the agreements(6). These three sectors have been the subject of heated debate, with the Central-East European countries accusing the EC of protectionism at a time when they are attempting to liberalise their trade. However, the EC does seem prepared to make certain concessions. Tariffs on textiles will be eliminated over a ten-year period, but the reduction of non-tariff barriers (which are substantial in this sector, as was shown in Chapters 2 and 5) will depend on the outcome of the Uruguay Round negotiations. Tariffs on iron and steel products will be eliminated over a five-year periods. Certain agricultural concessions (for instance on fruit, vegetables and possibly pigmeat for Poland, and poultry for Hungary) are also expected. Sheepmeat and beef are still the subject of contention, with the fall in EC beef prices in 1990–1 being partly attributed to a rise in imports from these countries following the agricultural arrangements which permit limited quotas of calf imports.

Free movement of capital and people was said to require 'phased introduction', though EC measures would be taken to ease the process. As the Albanian and East German examples illustrate, the Community needs to make contingency plans to meet the possibility of widescale requests for immigration from Central-East Europe, and presumably this is partly what the phrase 'phased introduction' above refers to. Substantial Community contributions to the social safety nets of those countries are have been proposed and these could help to alleviate this situation.

As will be shown in the next chapter, the institutionalisation of political dialogue with the Central-East European countries envisaged by the agreements raises complex questions about how far these countries should be allowed to have a say in shaping Community policies which have a direct influence on them.

9.5   The inter-bloc cooperation envisaged by the Joint Declaration

The likely demise of the CMEA has effectively ended the long-standing dispute with the Community as to whether the main links should be at the bloc-to-bloc level, or bilaterally between the EC and individual Central-East European countries.

The 1988 Joint Declaration had called for cooperation between the two blocs in areas of 'mutual interest'. The areas, forms, and methods of cooperation were to be decided in subsequent contacts and discussions between representatives of each side, and specifically, 'on the basis of experience gained', new fields and methods of cooperation could be designated.

During these meetings the continuing EC hesitancy about bloc-to-bloc relationships soon became apparent. The CMEA first wanted to identify areas for cooperation, and only then to discuss the forms and methods, while the Community again raised the question of CMEA competences and maintained that it was necessary to establish what each organisation did and compare their activities before deciding what areas were of 'mutual interest'.

During earlier negotiations (1976, 1978 and 1980), four areas of cooperation between the two blocs had been identified: standardisation; presentation of statistics; environmental questions; and macroeconomic forecasts. The Soviet Union wanted to see cooperation in science and technology, transport and energy policy added to this list.

The EC raised the point that cooperation in some of these areas was already underway elsewhere so there was a risk of duplicating the work of wider, more complete fora such as the ECE (Economic Commission for Europe), the IAEA (International Atomic Energy Agency) and the CSCE. Alternatively, certain questions might be better addressed at the bilateral level between the EC and individual Central-East European countries. Furthermore, it is difficult to see how European-wide cooperation on transport or the environment could be carried out excluding such countries as Austria, Switzerland, Yugoslavia, and those of Scandinavia (Maslen, 1988).

The importance of links with the organisation for coordination and information likely to succeed the CMEA has long since been overshadowed by that of the bilateral relations between the Community and individual Central-East European countries. The CMEA claim to be treated as an equal bargaining partner is a thing of the past.

9.6   Conclusions

The EC response to requests on the part of Central-East European countries for closer ties has been relatively rapid and generous, probably mainly in view of political considerations. The main areas in which the EC has not met Central-East European expectations would seem to be with regard to labour mobility (and the possibility of allowing large-scale migration from these countries) and the conditions of access to EC markets for agricultural, textile, iron and steel products and Polish coal. Although the EC has granted some real, if limited, trade concessions to the Central-European countries in these sectors, many non-tariff barriers remain, leading to charges of EC protectionism. The prospects of trade liberalisation in these sectors depend on the outcome of the Uruguay Round negotiations. However, as the negotiations themselves illustrate, the difficulties are immense, particularly given the sensitive nature of these sectors (as the fall in Community beef prices illustrates) and the strength of producer lobbies in the EC and elsewhere.

Despite the interest expressed by some of the smaller Central-East European countries in EC membership, the transitional and poor state of their economies suggests that full integration would be premature. A greater degree of economic convergence would seem an essential precondition and, as will be shown in the next chapter, this will be even more the case with the move towards EC economic and monetary union. The Europe agreements can be regarded as an attempt to solve the dilemma of wanting to meet the requests of these countries despite the practical difficulties of doing so. Association would enable substantial steps towards economic and political integration to be taken, while allowing time for the necessary transition to occur.

Notes

1. A trade agreement was signed with Czechoslovakia in December 1988, and trade and cooperation agreements with the Soviet Union in December 1989, and Bulgaria and the German Democratic Republic in May 1990.
2. Article 6 of the Agreement.
3. P.1 of the Agreement with Hungary (EC Commission (88) 1332 final of September 1988).
4. OJ 260/76.
5. European Report No. 1605 of 18 July 1990.
6. European Report No. 1611, August 1990.

10

New forms of association and integration in Europe

10.1   Introduction

By 1990, with the increasingly evident strength of the EC, and the virtual demise of the CMEA, it was clear that the old order in Europe was dead and various proposals and initiatives for a new Europe began to take shape. These can be divided into three categories: the process of creating an expanded, reinforced Community; proposals for the evolution of a pan-European organisation; and a number of schemes to set up smaller integration units involving Central-East European countries. These proposals were not necessarily considered as alternatives, but as options which could coexist and reinforce each other.

The first part of this chapter is concerned with the changing configuration of the Community in view of the widening and deepening that is taking place and the implications of these processes for Central-East Europe. The widening of the EC, or enlargement to include new members, relates not just to Central-East Europe (as described in the last chapter) but also to other European countries interested in accession and to the attempt of the EC and EFTA (European Free Trade Association) countries(1) to create a common European Economic Area (EEA). The possibility of certain Central-East European countries developing closer ties with the EFTA and/or the European Economic Area are being explored. As will be shown in the first part of this chapter, this widening of the Community in other directions affects the Central-East European countries both by altering the nature of the EC they want closer links with, and by changing the costs and benefits of membership.

The 'deepening' of integration (with the creation of the Single

Market, political union, economic and monetary union and European political cooperation) explains why Central-East Europe and other European countries have been attracted to the EC, while at the same time the prospects of an enlarged community have added urgency to the need to strengthen its institutions. There will therefore be a brief account of this deepening process, concentrating on how it affects the Central-East European countries.

Then follows a short discussion of some of the proposals to create a pan-European organisation, and of the possible role and usefulness of smaller integration units involving Central-East European countries. A comparison of these initiatives with those linked to the Community reveals the latter to be more concrete and further advanced.

10.2   Central-East Europe and the changing configuration of the EC

10.2.1   *The widening of the Community*

The association or membership of the EC on the part of Central-East European countries will be affected by other enlargements of the Community. The number of applicants that the EC has to deal with will affect the timing of accessions, especially if the perceived chances of membership are altered by other countries joining. For example, the integration of East Germany into the Community is said to have altered perceptions as to when Austria should accede (with Italy, together with Germany, Belgium and Denmark all supporting early Austrian entry). The Hungarians maintain that Austrian entry would in turn strengthen their case.

Enlargement of the EC also affects the size of expected costs and benefits of membership or association with the Community. The benefits relate to the opportunities for economies of scale, increased competition, changed business strategies, and so on, while the costs arise from the additional time, energy, expense and compromises necessary to reach common positions and take decisions, and the likelihood that the level of economic convergence among member states will be lower.

Formal applications for EC membership have been made by Austria, Malta, Cyprus and Turkey(2). Negotiations are also going ahead between the EC and the EFTA countries to create a *European Economic Area* (EEA), also referred to as a European Economic Space (EES) in earlier negotiations(3).

There have been various suggestions (from, for example, Norway and the Soviet Union) that Central-East European countries could be included with the EFTA countries in the European Economic Area.

There have also been approaches by the Central-East European countries directly to EFTA. For example, in June 1990 declarations of cooperation in the areas of trade, tourism, transport and the environment were signed between the EFTA countries and Poland, Hungary and Czechoslovakia. These countries also expressed interest in accession to EFTA and Polish adherence was expected by 1991(4).

The aim of the European Economic Area would be to extend the four fundamental freedoms of the EC's internal market (freedom of movement of labour, capital, goods and services) to the EFTA countries. A free trade area has existed between the two blocs since 1984.

As the timing and aim suggest, to a large extent the European Economic Area can be regarded as an attempt to minimise the possible negative repercussions and share in the gains of the Single Market. At the same time the relaxing of East–West tensions meant that countries such as Austria, Sweden or even Finland began to consider neutrality as less of an obstacle to closer links, or even membership with the EC. Somewhat ironically, this coincided with the EC's increasing coordination of 'political and economic' aspects of security, first sanctioned in the Single European Act. With the move to political union, the difficulties with neutrality may re-emerge for some countries. An interesting question for speculation is whether the Central-East European countries would figure among these.

Negotiations between the EC and EFTA ran into two main areas of difficulty relating to: (a) how much of the existing body of EC legislation, or *acquis communautaire* the EFTA countries would have to accept; and (b) the degree to which they should be allowed to participate in EC decision-making.

The Community insisted that exemptions from EC law should be minimal, temporary and justified on grounds of fundamental national interest. Against this the EFTA countries were asking for derogations in at least twelve areas, and, according to an article in the Swedish press there were twenty-two areas where one or more EFTA countries were seeking derogations(5).

The debate about involvement in the decision-making process is of direct relevance to Central-East Europe seeking closer links with the Community, whether or not these countries are included in a European Economic Area, or the EFTA. During the early stages of negotiations it seemed likely that EFTA countries would be offered a share in 'decision-shaping', but not the decision-making of the EC. This was subsequently watered down to 'exchanges of information' before the EC took decisions, in view of growing apprehension about the likely strain on EC institutions if EFTA countries were consulted on all measures. The EFTA countries were increasingly concerned that major issues of joint interest would be decided by the Community alone(6).

Given these rather substantial differences there would seem to be a strong risk of negotiations breaking down, but the EC has a major incentive not to allow this to occur, namely that it would simply encourage certain of the EFTA members to request EC membership. Austria has already applied, Sweden is considering doing so, and in Finland the question of membership is being discussed, though as a distant possibility. Norway has already been accepted once, in 1972 (along with Denmark, the United Kingdom and Ireland) when membership was rejected in a referendum. In October 1990 the Norwegian government fell, over foreign ownership of property, banks and firms which membership of the Community (or possibly even the European Economic Area) would permit. There is, however, a strong likelihood that the Central-East European countries would be acceding to a club of far more than twelve.

10.2.2 The deepening of the Community

The question which then arises is what kind of Community these additional European countries will belong to or be associated with, and in particular, how are decisions in a wider and deeper Community to be taken. Attempt is made to answer this question here by describing the main areas where deepening is taking place, and the implications of this process for Central-East Europe.

10.2.3 The Single Market

The roots of the Single-Market project are to be found in the mid-1980s when the EC member states were becoming increasingly concerned about the growing lag between their economic performance, and that of Japan or the United States. Over the 1979–85 period, the EC share in world markets for manufactured goods as a whole fell by 1.4% compared with a 0.7 rise for the US and a 5.7% increase for Japan over the same period(7). In particular the Community seemed especially weak in high technology industries such as electrical and electronic equipment, information technology and office automation. For example the sectors in which demand is growing strongly accounted for 22.4% for EC industry, 27% for the United States and 28% for Japan in 1985(8).

The solution was perceived as a return to and completion of the original objectives of the Community set out in the Treaty of Rome: namely to implement the freedom of movement of labour, capital, goods and services throughout the Community. The removal of tariffs on intra-EC trade was thought to be a major factor contributing to a quadrupling of intra-EC trade during the first decade of the Community, with intra-EC trade growing twice as fast as world trade over that period(9). If the Community could now eliminate non-tariff barriers such as those arising from specifications and regulations; frontier controls; public procurement; capital movements and differences in national tax systems the European economy could perhaps reacquire a new dynamism reflecting the increased possibilities for economies of scale, technological progress, competition and European business strategies.

These views were set out in the 1985 Cockfield White Paper, calling for a Single European Market from 1985 and listing some 300 measures necessary to achieve this aim. The commitment of the EC member states was formally embodied in the Single European Act which came into force from July 1987. In addition to the Single Market, this Treaty also pledged the EC member states to a revived integration effort in fields such as monetary policy, technology, social, regional and external policy, as well as introducing certain institutional reforms such as the increased use of the majority voting rule in the Council of Ministers.

Four aspects of the Single Market were of particular concern to the Central-East European countries. The first were the quotas discussed in Chapter 2 which were one of the reasons why the frontier controls between EC member states had persisted.

Secondly, there was the fear shared by many third countries that a 'Fortress Europe' might emerge. The controversial Cecchini Report on the 'Costs of non-Europe' appeared to assuage these fears. The Report suggested that in the medium term, assuming a passive macroeconomic policy (i.e. that the additional growth expected to result from completion of the Single Market did not lead to more expansionary policy), the external balance of the European Community could improve by up to 1% of GDP; intra-EC trade could grow by 10%; the GDP of the Community could grow by an additional 4.5% while inflation would be 6% lower. Assuming a more expansionary macroeconomic policy, reflecting the improvement in EC performance, the GDP gain could be as high as 7%, while inflation would be 4.5% lower. It should be pointed out that these are among the most questionable and questioned results of the Cecchini Report (which also entailed a wide range of industry case studies and business surveys). None the less, a view which encounters a great deal of support is that the more vigorous and confident Community enabled by the Single Market would be in a stronger position to grant trade concessions to third countries.

If it is accepted that completion of the Single Market contributes to growth of the Community, and if this growth is reflected in higher import demand, the Central-East European countries might find the conditions for exporting to the EC eased. Against this the slower price increases suggested by the Cecchini Report would imply lower export earnings for the Central-East European exporter, while their difficulty in producing goods of a sufficient quality might impede improvement in their performance on EC markets.

The question of quality of their products underlies the third concern of Central-East European countries with regard to the Single Market namely that measures taken with regard to specifications and regulations could close European markets for many of their products. In addition to promoting better functioning of EC standardisation bodies and more exchanges of information, the Community has adopted two policy instruments to enable completion of the Single Market in this context. The first is the principle of 'mutual recognition', whereby products lawfully marketed or produced in any member state can have access to the whole Community, provided they are not damaging to health, safety or the environment. The second is the 'new approach' to harmonisation, whereby the Community only fixes the essential requirements, and in many cases the detailed specifications are worked out by institutes concerned with standards. There have been numerous contacts between the Community and Central-East European countries to inform the latter of measures being taken in this context in order to minimise possible negative effects and allow the Central-East European countries time to make the necessary adjustments where possible. Moreover, operating in a single European space with harmonised norms and standards might simplify matters for certain Central-East European exporters, or even allow them to benefit from economies of scale.

Fourthly, it seems likely that measures to compensate the less-favoured areas of the Community will ultimately be agreed, and there is a risk that these could mean less funds available for Central-East Europe. Saryusz-Wolski (1990) found a relatively high degree of similarity in the commodity structure of exports of the five smaller Central-East European countries, and Greece, Spain and Portugal. He argues that if the Single Market has adverse effects on the wage levels and employment levels in the more vulnerable sectors and areas of the Community, there might be renewed demands for protection of sensitive industries prevalent in these areas (such as textiles and footwear), and for restrictions on immigration from Central-East Europe.

10.2.4 *Economic and monetary union*

Various aspects of EC economic and monetary union are relevant to the Central-East European countries interested in closer links with the Community. These include the question of compensation for less-favoured areas which again arose, and the ability of all member states to proceed with integration at the same pace. The timing of commitment to economic and monetary union (agreed at the Dublin Summit of June 1990) was also significant, coinciding with the unification of Germany and the German desire to show that it remained firmly anchored in the European Community. Only subsequently did the profound misgivings of the Bundesbank emerge.

The three phases in the route towards economic and monetary union were set out in the 1989 Delors Report and entailed the following:

1. The freeing of capital movements and increased economic and monetary cooperation. The deadline (which has been met) was set as July 1990.
2. A European central bank or Eurofed would be created but national governments would remain responsible for monetary policy. There would, however, be greater coordination of monetary policies through the Eurofed, and of fiscal policies through the Council of Financial Ministers (Ecofin).
3. Exchange rate changes between EC member states would be impossible and the Eurofed would be responsible for interest-rate policy.

At the Rome Summit of October 1990, eleven member states (excluding the United Kingdom) agreed to go ahead with the second phase from January 1994, conditional on a certain degree of convergence being attained. A possible date for commencement of the third phase was three years later. The objectives for the third phase were agreed and entailed a single currency, the 'strong and stable ECU', and a 'new monetary institution comprising Member States' central banks and a central organ exercising full responsibility for monetary policy'.

In December the statute for this 'new monetary institution', the Eurofed, was approved (again with British reservation). The Bundesbank insistence on guarantees concerning the commitment of the Eurofed to price stability and its independence from national governments and EC institutions was met.

Despite the commitment of the other eleven member states to substituting national currencies with the ECU, Britain remained in favour of the 'parallel-currency' approach with the introduction of a 'hard ECU' alongside existing national currencies. This would be managed so that it would never be devalued, and could ultimately develop into a single European currency 'in the very long term if peoples and governments so choose' (John Major, speaking in 1990).

The head of the Bundesbank, Poehl, expressed concern at the risks of moving too quickly towards currency union, pointing to the example of German economic and monetary union. Unable to alter the exchange rate, GDR adjustment has had to take place through unemployment and this has implied a heavy burden on public spending. A possible solution favoured by Poehl was for EC member states to progress with economic and monetary union at different speeds. This could, for instance, entail certain countries (such as Benelux, France and Germany) going ahead with Phase 2, and the others following only when they had reached the appropriate stage of convergence. Such a solution would allow a certain leeway to the smaller Central-East European countries interested in EC membership, but this solution was opposed by most of the EC member states(10).

Initially, Delors refused the requests of countries such as Greece, Ireland, and Portugal that EMU should be directly linked to additional aid through the Regional and Social Funds, and pointed out that in any case such funds were due to double over the 1988–93 period. This position was probably partly to avoid antagonising counties such as Germany who would have to bear the additional budget contributions required. It was also argued that in the long run the poorer countries would stand to benefit most from EMU, because the lower intererst rates and inflation likely to result would encourage higher levels of trade and investment. Subsequently, Delors proposed possible short-term loans for countries having difficulty adjusting to economic and monetary union, and it seems likely that a compromise on regional measures will be reached.

10.2.5 Political union

The key to resolving the tensions resulting from a deepening and widening of the Community would seem to lie in political union. However, although agreement was reached on the main objectives of political union at the December 1990 Summit, differences remain as to how these are to be achieved(11). The objectives agreed on included the following:

1. filling the 'democratic deficit' by making the EC institutions more politically accountable;
2. developing a common foreign and security policy;
3. defining a European citizenship;
4. developing the political dimension of the Community and extending its powers into other fields of integration (for instance with regard to social, energy and environmental policy); and
5. strengthening the Community's capacity for action, possibly by extending the use of majority voting in the Council, or even by making it a general rule.

The question of a common foreign and security policy is of particular relevance to the Central-East European countries. Formally, the Community is responsible for the common commercial policy and international trade negotiations, while 'external relations' are decided in a separate institutional framework, European Political Cooperation (EPC). In practice, the dividing line between the two is often blurred. European Political Cooperation dates from 1970 and only received statutory backing in the Single European Act. It operates chiefly through the EC foreign ministers' meetings at regular intervals in their role of EPC, and has a relatively small Secretariat. Decisions have to be taken unanimously. The EPC procedure has been criticised as being relatively ineffectual in the past, while its system of six-month presidencies is sometimes said to undermine continuity.

With the need to work out a coherent, common approach to Central-East Europe, the traditional distinction between EPC and the European Community increasingly began to break down. From 1989 national officials of the EC member states had to collaborate and work ever more closely with Community officials responsible for policy towards Central-East Europe. *De facto* the Community has already begun to play a more active role, at least in this area of foreign policy.

10.2.6   *A Europe* 'à la carte' *or of 'concentric circles'*

The Poehl solution of a Europe of differing speeds to meet the strains of economic and monetary union finds its echo in a wider context, as a means of meeting the possible trade-off between the deepening and widening processes of the Community. These schemes are often referred to as a *'Europe à la carte'*. Possibly the most elaborate version is that put forward by the President of the EC Commission, Delors, in November 1989, when he referred to a Europe organised in concentric circles. This could consist of an inner circle of those present EC members which are most committed to integration; a second circle of less enthusiastic EC members (with the United Kingdom as a possible candidate); a third of the EFTA countries organised with the EC in the European Economic Area (EEA); and finally there would be the associated countries including certain Central-East European countries.

A difficulty with this scheme is that many countries do not seem content with the position ascribed to them in the 'outer circle' and are clamouring for a place in the inner core.

10.3   Accession to other 'European' organisations

In addition to an interest in having closer ties with the EC and EFTA, all the Central-East European countries have attempted to tighten their links with other organisations such as the Council of Europe and the

CSCE (not to mention the IMF and GATT for those countries which were not already members, and the OECD in a few cases). The motive for Central-East European countries approaching various organisations is probably multiple: to increase their chances of establishing solid ties with the West by trying as many channels as possible; in some cases to use membership of other organisations as a means of strengthening the case for EC accession; to avoid being left out of anything going in a type of bandwaggon effect; and to 'deliver the goods' at home by showing that successes in international relations have been achieved.

Bulgaria, Czechoslovakia, Poland and Yugoslavia already have 'special guest' status with the *Council of Europe*, and Hungary became a member in November 1990. It is envisaged that Poland and Yugoslavia might be able to join during 1991, while conditions would be created for the membership of certain other smaller Central-East European countries, especially Czechoslovakia. The exclusion of Romania, at least for the time being, was explained in terms of its unstable situation and the apparent lack of guarantees on the part of the Romanian government. It has been suggested that if the United States and Canada were also involved, the Council could provide an appropriate forum for East–West debate and especially for discussion of the third Helsinki Basket (that dealing with human rights).

A view frequently expressed is that the CSCE (Conference on Cooperation and Security in Europe) with its thirty-five members including the United States and Canada would be a suitable vehicle for the architecture of a new Europe. In the past, talks on disarmament between NATO and the Warsaw Pact have taken place under the aegis of the CSCE, so in the changed international environment a transformed CSCE has been proposed not only as a forum for disarmament, but also as a body which could replace the Warsaw Pact and NATO. This idea does not appear to have much support in the United States.

According to even more ambitious schemes, such as that presented by Havel at the Bratislava Summit of April 1990, the CSCE could ultimately become a 'European Confederation of free and independent states'. The definition of 'Europe' here is taken to include the United States and Canada. This suggestion is not too different from the 'Common European House' sometimes proposed in Soviet circles.

In the event, the conversion of the CSCE has been more limited, and more concrete. It was decided to institutionalise the CSCE, transforming it from a conference into a genuine international organisation with a general secretariat, an Assembly of Europe and annual ministerial meetings. The fact that each country retains a veto limits progress to the pace of the slowest. There is also to be a Conflict Prevention Centre in Vienna and an office in Poland to gather information on elections.

In April 1990 a comprehensive document, which effectively amounts to a charter for East–West trade and cooperation, was agreed within the CSCE framework. This document entails a formal commitment on the part of Central-East European countries to move towards multiparty democracies and market-orientated economies in view of what is recognised as the link between improved economic performance and market forces. The importance of free enterprise and of private property, including intellectual property rights was recognised. The Central-East European countries are to move towards convertibility and free trade *inter alia*, rendering it easier for Western businessmen to expatriate profits. Monetary and fiscal measures to promote sustainable growth and allow free markets to function are also to be encouraged.

10.4 New associations among Central-East European countries

It is sometimes argued that the reintegration of Central-East European countries into the world trading system might be assisted by creating new smaller integration units among the Central-East European countries. One such unit, the *Pentagon* has actually been created, and there have been discussions about creating an integration area between Hungary, Poland and Czechoslovakia, a northern *Triangle* and a *Central European Payments Union*.

In November 1989 Italy, Austria, Hungary and Yugoslavia met to form a *Quadrilateral* designed to promote the 'process of greater unity in Europe', and Czechoslovakia subsequently also joined what became the *Pentagon*. Poland is expected to join, and contacts are likely to be established with the Soviet Union, Romania and Bulgaria. Bavaria, Baden Württemberg and the Ukraine have asked to participate in certain projects, in particular those relating to transport. The initiative also extends to contacts among members of parliament and trade unionists from the countries involved.

The members of the Pentagon (or parts of them) share certain characteristics of 'Mitteleuropa' as well as having links which historically were based on notions of the balance of power in Europe. The project received the active backing of the Italian Foreign Minister, de Michelis, in part to revive the importance of this part of Europe (de Michelis comes from Venice) as well as to create a more active foreign policy role for Italy.

The aims of the organisation include the improvement of transport connections, cooperation on research and the reduction of customs controls. Attention has also been given to the problem of emigration, especially with the prospect of the opening of the Soviet frontier. There have been discussions of projects including the development of motorway links between Trieste, Zagreb and Budapest; a Slovak–Austrian hydroelectric project, and an 800-mile pipeline through Italy and Austria to transport Algerian natural gas(12). There has also been a division of responsibilities among the countries involved. Italy is to deal with transport, Yugoslavia with telecommunications and Czechoslovakia with culture and tourism. Hungary is to be responsible for the promotion of small and medium enterprises, given the large number of these springing up in Hungary. In view of its geographical location, close to some of the worst polluting areas in Central-East Europe, Austria has agreed to accept responsibility for environmental measures and energy programmes. Considerable doubts arise as to the ability of Yugoslavia, Hungary or Czechosloakia to make substantial financial contributions to these programmes.

At the Bratislava Summit of April 1990 between Czechoslovakia, Poland, Hungary, Italy, Austria and Yugoslavia, there was a proposal to establish a *Triangle* in the north composed of Czechoslovakia, Poland and Sweden to match the Quadrilateral in the south. The possible inclusion of the Baltic States was also raised.

It was suggested that links between the Triangle and Pentagon might enable a free trade area to be created from the Baltic to the Adriatic. In some versions this was envisaged as primarily a political entity, permitting a multilateral system of security and cooperation which could possibly replace the CMEA.

A further proposal, often called the Lubbers' Plan after the Dutch Prime Minister, entails establishing a *European Energy Community*. This would cover issues such as access to energy, joint research efforts and technology exchanges. The uncertain situation in the Soviet Union has meant that progress on this initiative has been slow.

The proposal to create a *Central European Payments Union* (CEPU) echoes the European Payments Union (EPU) introduced in Western Europe in 1950 which enabled most of the countries involved to pass from bilateralism to convertibility in less than ten years(13).

The European Payments Union was a clearing system for the debits and credits arising among its seventeen member states. If any country had a balance of payments deficit, part of what was owed would be settled in gold or convertible currencies, while automatic lines of credit existed for the rest. These took the form of payments in dollars from a fund constituted by the United States. As the deficit grew, so did the share to be paid in convertible currency and the interest on the credit so there was an incentive to correct imbalances by devaluation. The proposed CEPU would function along the same lines, using the ECU and with an ECU fund established by the Community.

Matejka (1990b, pp. 21–4) criticises this proposal, arguing that whereas the EPU covered the settlement of most of the transactions of the member states involved, a CEPU formed with Hungary, Poland and Czechoslovakia would cover only between 7% and 12% of any member's total trade. If the scheme were extended to include the Soviet Union the share of trade covered would rise, but the CEPU would be likely to break down. This is because in the absence of properly functioning markets, devaluation would do little to correct the imbalance so the CEPU mechanism would not provide the required incentive. If, however, economic transformation were taking place, major disequilibria could be expected which, in the case of the Soviet Union, would require financial assistance on a scale beyond that likely to be offered by the CEPU.

10.5 Conclusions

There has been much debate generally about the usefulness or role of integration units among Central-East European countries which could replace the CMEA. On the one hand it is argued that forty years of the socialist international division of labour has left a certain legacy of contacts and trading arrangements, as well as separate technological development, so there is space for such associations. However, the collapse in trade between these countries does not augur well for their prospects. Moreover, new integration initiatives require expense in terms of money, time and organisational effort, resources in short supply in Central-East European countries already undertaking a huge adjustment process. It is perhaps significant that only those integration units involving Western countries have so far come into operation, and that one of the main question marks hanging over the Pentagon is the ability of Hungary, Yugoslavia and Czechoslovakia to contribute financially. Given the dependence of these countries on the West for assistance in areas such as technology and training to ease the transformation process, it is doubtful how far association between them could resolve their basic needs. There is also a certain reluctance to join what simply might be considered a 'poor man's club'.

As the appeal to the CSCE Charter following Soviet repression in the Baltic illustrated, pan-European organisations can fulfil certain functions enabling discussions and exchanges of view to take place. However, inevitably, the heterogeneous and wide membership of a 'common European House' or 'European Confederation' implies a more limited role than that of an integration unit like the Community.

The question which then arises is whether the widening of the EC will provoke the same effect, compromising the effectiveness and ability to operate of the EC. The key to resolving this tension between widening and deepening would seem to lie in whether political union can be successfully implemented. At the same time, though for political reasons there are strong motives for proceeding with the widening process, the Community would seem justified in the care with which it fixes the timetable.

Notes

1. The EFTA countries are Switzerland, Austria, Norway, Sweden, Iceland, and Finland.
2. Austria is concerned that its application should be the first to be considered, and would like to begin preparatory talks as early as possible so that even if the 1993 deadline could not be brought forward, formal negotiations could be completed within a few months.

     The Cypriot application has been made by the Nicosia government without consulting the leadership of the Turkish-occupied part of the island, thus accession would seem to raise some tricky legal questions. Aside from the question of Greek opposition, the Community has suggested that the Turkish application in 1987 to join the EC may have been premature in view of the human-rights record and economic situation of the country.
3. According to European Report No. 1607 of 26 July, the word 'space' was rejected as not being sufficiently concrete or 'down to earth'.
4. According to Menato (1990).
5. These included: agricultural policy; forestry; fishing; banking independence; foreign investments; pesticides; worker safety; the environment; health measures; dangerous substances; transport; administrative services; company law; and the free movement of people. It seems likely that flexibility in applying EC law will be allowed on some issues, such as purchase of real estate, or regulations relating to health, safety or the environment where many EFTA countries have higher standards than the EC. However, Switzerland's request for a derogation with regard to the free movement of people has met opposition, and there has been heated debate over agricultural policy. Not only is agricultural support in the Scandinavian countries mainly in the form of direct subsidies, with a strong emphasis on structural and social policies, but, according to the OECD, measures of producer subsidy equivalents (PSE) per capita were extremely high for these countries; in the case of Norway and Finland they even exceeded EC levels. The EC requested better access to EFTA agricultural markets, but stressed that any agreement with EFTA would be circumsubscribed by the wider context of GATT negotiations.
6. The Community would also favour a stronger EFTA organisation which could present a unified position and enable the evolution of a 'two pillar' approach between the blocs, while the EFTA countries would prefer a joint EC–EFTA surveillance body.
7. Emerson *et al.* (1988), p. 15.
8. Emerson *et al.* (1988) p. 13.
9. Pinder (1988), p. 94.
10. *The Economist*, 7 July 1990.
11. For instance, there were differences as to whether to fill the 'democratic deficit' by involving national parliaments more actively in EC decision-making (favoured by France and the United Kingdom), and about what

increase in powers the European Parliament should have (with Germany, opposed by France, suggesting that it could initiate legislation). France (unlike Germany) would prefer a greater role for the European Council in new areas of policy. Germany also favoured majority voting in the Council in more areas than did France. Countries such as Italy and Belgium would like to transfer some of the powers of the Western European Union (WEU) to the Community in order to develop a common security and defence policy, while France favoured a more gradual approach, and Ireland (on grounds of neutrality) and the United Kingdom prefer more limited measures.

12. *The Economist*, 25 August 1990, and *La Repubblica*, 1 December 1990.
13. See Matejka (1990b) for a comparison of the European Payments Union and the proposed Central European Payments Union.

11
East–West interfirm cooperation and joint ventures

11.1 Introduction

Encouraged by official policy and easier legislation in Central-East European countries, and by export credits and investment guarantees in the West, since 1987 there has been a virtual boom in the number of East–West joint ventures. As shown in Table 11.1, the number of East–West joint ventures in the CMEA countries signed each year grew from five in 1981 to sixteen in 1986 and ninety-one in 1987 and then jumped so that by October 1989 there was a total of 2120(1). This tendency appears to have accelerated still further during 1990, and, according to the ECE, there were 5070 foreign investment projects in Central-East Europe (excluding the German Democratic Republic) by June 1990; 1800 of these were in the Soviet Union, 1600 in Hungary, 1550 in Poland and eighty-five in Czechoslovakia.

Joint ventures have emerged as the most dynamic, and now most prevalent, form of East–West cooperation. The share of joint ventures in total cooperation agreements rose from 1% in the late-1970s to 90% in the first seven months of 1989 (see also Table 11.2).

Joint ventures are sometimes envisaged as a means of offering something to everyone: the Western partner can benefit from entry to Central-East European markets and cheaper labour costs, while the Eastern partner can obtain Western technology and know-how. The aim here is to see how far this picture corresponds with reality and to explain the growing preference for joint ventures over other forms of industrial cooperation. This will involve presenting definitions and statistics, describing the relevant legislation and attempting to indicate the objectives and shortcomings of both joint ventures and other forms of industrial cooperation agreements.

Table 11.1 Registration of new East–West joint ventures in CMEA countries

	Bulgaria	Czech.	Hungary	Poland Polonia[a]	Other	Romania	USSR
1972	–	–	–	–	–	1	–
1973	–	–	–	–	–	3	–
1974	–	–	2	–	–	1	–
1975	–	–	1	–	–	1	–
1976	–	–	–	–	–	2	–
1977	–	–	–	14	–	1	–
1978	–	–	–	–	–	–	–
1979	–	–	1	5	–	–	–
1980	–	–	1	57	–	–	–
1981	1	–	4	–	–	–	–
1982	1	–	3	78	–	–	–
1983	1	–	10	448	–	–	–
1984	4	–	8	142	–	–	–
1985	1	–	14	–	–	–	–
1986	–	–	16	–	–	–	–
1987	7	2	50	–	13	–	19
Total by 15 October 1989	25	45	600[c]		400	5[b]	936

Notes:
[a] The Polonia enterprises are usually small-scale businesses established and operated by foreigners of Polish origin.
[b] Four of the earlier agreements had gone out of operation.
[c] Data from *The Economist*, 21 October 1989.
Source: ECE.

Table 11.2 Registration of industrial cooperation agreements by Central-East European countries (yearly averages)

1966–70	4
1971–75	34
1976–80	93
1981–85	93
1986	87
1987	113
1988	135
1989*	58

* January–July.
Source: ECE.

11.2 A definition of joint ventures

There are various definitions of joint ventures according to whether a broader or narrower coverage with respect to other forms of industrial cooperation is intended. In the following an ECE definition is taken (2), according to which a joint venture has the following essential features:

1. an agreement between the parties on 'common long-term business objectives, such as production, sales, maintenance, repair, research co-operation, consultations, financing';
2. a pooling of assets (such as money, plant, machinery or management) between the parties to achieve these objectives;
3. these pooled assets are characterised as 'capital contributions' by the parties;
4. management organs separate from the management of the two parties are set up to pursue the common objectives;
5. both parties share in the profits and risks arising from pursuance of the common objectives.

11.3   The objectives of setting up joint ventures

As is to be expected, the East and Western partners generally have different objectives in setting up joint ventures. At a 1988 symposium in Varna(3) a group of experts attempted to identify the main objectives on either side. The main objectives for the Western partner were:

(a) Market expansion and penetration
(b) Improvement of production capacities and reduction of production costs
(c) Sale of equipment and services to the joint venture
(d) Increased sales and profits
(e) Prestige

Joint ventures were seen as a way round the traditional obstacles to expanding in these markets, and especially lack of currency convertibility, and foreign trade monopolies. With regard to production costs, Western businessmen were particularly attracted by the cheap, relatively well-educated labour supply, and the nearness of the smaller Central-European countries to major EC markets.

The main motives of the East European partner were identified as:

(a) Technology acquisition and modernization
(b) Convertible currency generation through sales of exports and import substitution
(c) Access to improved management and organisational techniques
(d) Introduction of new and better products into the domestic market
(e) Access to Western capital and investments.

In addition there are a number of objectives which are common to both, such as increasing production, turnover, raising profits, reducing costs, and possibly sales on third markets.

In considering objectives the time scale also has to be taken into account. For example, while sales of equipment to the joint venture is essentially a short-run objective, market penetration relates more to the longer run.

Conflicts between the objectives of both parties may also arise, since, for instance, the Western aim of market penetration may be in contradiction with the Eastern aim to earn hard currency.

11.4 Legislation relating to joint ventures in Central-East European countries

From 1986 onwards the central role of East–West joint ventures in promoting economic restructuring, and especially in encouraging foreign trade, appeared in repeated policy statements of Central-East European countries committed to reform. In order to promote joint ventures, the Western partner was to be granted increasingly greater freedom to operate. For this purpose, between 1986 and 1988, with the exception of the German Democratic Republic (which, as discussed in the next chapter, had no joint venture legislation until 1989) and Romania (which had legislation from 1971 but the situation under Ceausescu offered little incentive to Western firms), all the Central-East European countries introduced or amended their legislation concerning joint ventures with foreign participation. In many cases these legislative reforms went ahead in progressive stages and, for example, the Soviet Union passed laws on joint ventures in 1987 and again in 1991.

It is extremely difficult to keep up to date on this new joint venture legislation in Central-East European countries(4), but by July 1990, up to 100% foreign ownership was allowed in all Central-East European countries except the Soviet Union, where the maximum was 99%. Measures to ease the repatriation of profits had been taken, though in most cases limitations remained. For example in Czechoslovakia repatriation was only possible if the joint venture had adequate foreign currency reserves, and joint ventures were obliged to offer 30% of foreign currency proceeds to the state. In Romania, repatriation of profits in local currency could be transferred abroad in convertible currency up to a maximum of 8% of the share of foreign capital. In the Soviet Union the main problem is earning profits in convertible currency. In Poland there were requirements to lodge zloty profits with local banks, with conversion into hard currency only allowed at the time of repatriation. Tax incentives are offered in the Soviet Union, Hungary and Poland (in priority sectors) and many Central-East European countries have signed double taxation and investment protection agreements with the main Western partners involved. In most cases the new legislation has also entailed more freedom in fixing wages and prices.

As will be explained below, many difficulties remained, but the Western response to the official encouragement and changes in legislation in Central-Eastern countries was reflected in vastly raised expectations and interest in the possible gains from this type of economic operation, leading to the explosion in the registration of joint ventures from 1987.

11.5   Statistics on East–West joint ventures in Central-East European countries

The information on the order of magnitude of all East–West joint ventures in Central-East European countries is piecemeal and incomplete, but an ECE estimate in October 1989 placed the total foreign participation of all Western countries at $2.2 billion, though it has subsequently grown. According to ECE data (ECE, 1988a) in over half of all the cases registered the Western partner was a multinational. Table 11.3 sets out estimates of the capital involved for some of these joint ventures.

The average share of foreign participation in joint ventures in Central-East European countries is relatively similar, ranging from 44.7% for Hungary, 43.8% for Poland, 41.5% for the Soviet Union and 40.6% for Czechoslovakia(5).

The sector most often involved in these joint ventures was manufacturing, accounting for 65% of joint ventures in Poland, 61% in Hungary, 49% in the Soviet Union and 45% in Czechoslovakia. Trade, hotels and

Table 11.3   Joint ventures in the USSR, Poland and Czechoslovakia by origin of foreign partner

	USSR		Poland		Czechoslovakia	
	Foreign capital ($ million)	no.	Foreign capital ($ million)	no.	Foreign capital ($ million)	no.
EC	620.4	327	16.2	112	30.2	17
EFTA	321.4	247	4.8	38	11.8	11
Japan	190.6	86	–	–	–	–
USA	36.6	49	4.1	13	–	–
LDCs	1.7	1	0.2	4	–	–
CMEA	181.6	88	0.7	5	13.4	6
Other	201.2	109	2.0	10	7.8	4
Total	1620.8	929	28	182	63.2	38

Data as at 1 October 1989 for the USSR and Czechoslovakia and at 1 May 1989
Source: ECE.

restaurants, and business services are also important, though to a varying extent in these countries.

In the Soviet Union only twenty-three joint ventures were registered
at the beginning of 1988, but by January 1990 this figure had reached
1274 of which 191 were with the Federal Republic of Germany, 146 with
Finland and 143 with the United States(6). Following the $2 billion deal
signed between Combustion Engineering of the United States and the
Soviet oil and chemicals ministry, and a joint venture with FIAT to build
a $1.4 billion plant at Yelabuga, it is estimated that by late-1989 total
capital pledged for joint ventures in the Soviet Union amounted to some
$6 billion(7). In 1990 the growing trend continued, and a further deal
with FIAT meant that this joint venture alone would entail total capital
of some 5000 million lire in order to produce an estimated 900,000 cars a
year. The Italian group Ferruzzi–Montedison also signed three deals
involving investments worth slightly over $2 billion in November 1989.
The largest of these entailed converting some 500,000 hectares near
Stavrapol into a modern agricultural enterprise covering the entire
cycle.

Two big US consortia were formed to do business with the Soviet
Union. One includes Chevron, Eastman Kodak, RJR Nabisco, Johnson
and Johnson, and Arthur Daniels Midland, while among the members of
the second are Hewlett-Packard and Colgate–Palmolive. Both have met
considerable obstacles, in particular resulting from non-convertibility of
the rouble(8).

There was slightly more diversification in the origin of the Western
partner for the Soviet Union than for the smaller CMEA countries,
though West European countries represent the majority in all cases.
Using a sample of 936 joint ventures in the Soviet Union in October
1989, the ECE estimated that in 35.2% of all cases the parent company
of the foreign partner was from the EC, 26.6% from the EFTA (and
especially Finland); 9.3% from the United States; 1.9% from Japan;
5.3% from less developed countries, and 9.6% from other CMEA countries (see Table 11.3). Of the EC countries (see also Table 11.4), most
Soviet partners came from the Federal Republic of Germany (15%),
followed by Italy and the United Kingdom (5.7% each).

In Hungary the number of joint ventures rose from 130 at the end of
1987 to some 600 in 1989, though many of these are tiny(9). According to
the ECE, in June 1989 the EC accounted for 34.8% of the then 178
operating joint ventures in Hungary and other Western European countries (especially Austria (27.5%), Switzerland (10.1%) and Sweden (5.6))
for a further 47%. Of the joint ventures with EC countries most were with
the Federal Republic of Germany (20.7% of all joint ventures) followed
by the Netherlands (4.5%) and the United Kingdom (2.8%).

Between 1985 and the end of the first quarter of 1989 total capital

invested in Hungarian joint ventures grew from 3.6 to 27.8 billion forints, while the share of foreign capital grew from $44.1 to $263.3 over the
same period. In 1989 a group of Western financiers and the National
Bank of Hungary set up the First Hungary Fund to raise $50 million
initially for direct equity investment in Hungary. The average size of
foreign investment in Hungary rose to some $2.2 million between 1988
and mid-1989 as compared with the average size of $1.5 million for
foreign investment in all joint ventures. If foreign investment is measured by the amount of capital invested, rather than the number of joint
ventures, in 1989 the Republic of Korea occupied first position ($95
million), followed by the Federal Republic of Germany ($28.6 million)
and with the Netherlands in fifth place ($9.8 million).

Manufacturing is the main industrial sector involved, accounting for
60% of joint ventures in Hungary and 38.2% of total capital. Financial
services (28%) and hotels and restaurants (17.7%) are the next most
important sectors in terms of total capital. In addition, there are large
numbers of relatively small joint ventures in business services and transport and communication.

The number of joint ventures authorised by the Polish Foreign Investment Agency grew from thirteen in January 1988 to some 400 by mid-
October 1989. These Polish statistics do not include the *Polonia* enterprises, which are over 700 small enterprises set up over the past
decade using capital provided by Poles living abroad, and which it is
difficult to consider as fully fledged joint enterprises.

The cumulative foreign capital contribution at current exchange rates
rose from $4.4 million at the end of 1987 to $28 million by June 1989.

On the basis of a sample of 182 joint ventures in Poland in June 1989,
the ECE estimated that in 82% of all cases the partner came from
Western Europe, and in 61.5% from the EC. The Federal Republic of
Germany is the main EC country involved (27.5% of all cases), followed
by the United Kingdom (21.4%).

The first (five) joint ventures in Czechoslovakia were registered in
1987, a further eleven were registered in 1988 and by October 1989 the
total had reached forty-five. The foreign contribution to statutory capital
increased from $23.7 million in 1987 to $63.2 million in mid-October
1989 at current exchange rates. Of a sample of thirty-eight, the ECE
estimates that the most frequent Western partners are from the EC
(45%) and EFTA (29%). Among the EC partners most came from
France (13.2%), followed by the Federal Republic of Germany (10.5%).

The increase in East–West joint ventures over the January 1988–June
1989 period was slower for Bulgaria (fifteen to twenty-five), while of the
nine joint ventures signed in Romania between 1971 and 1977, four went
out of operation and between 1978 and 1989 no new joint ventures were
signed.

11.6 Problems with joint ventures in Central-East European countries

Difficulties for East–West joint ventures may arise from conflicting objectives, and adjustment to different operating conditions (management, wage and price fixation and accountancy, and so on). However, the Western partners often maintain that the problem is less one of adaptation than of the effectively difficult operating conditions in Central-East European countries. The reasons for these adverse conditions can be divided into the following three main (though interrelated) categories:

1. loopholes in the legislation of Central-East European countries;
2. system-endemic features because of the incomplete transformation of the Central-East European country into a market economy;
3. the macroeconomic situation of the East European country, and especially an investment and risk climate which is not always favourable.

These difficulties are especially rife in the Soviet Union, given the uncertain economic and political situation. Of the 936 joint ventures registered by October 1989, it is estimated that only 150 were operative, and of these only very few were attracting Western technology. Many operations are in the service sector, such as in hotels or shops. Encouraged by official policy, Western partners have set up so-called joint ventures when what in fact are involved are other, more limited, forms of industrial cooperation.

In part, the small share of successfully operating joint ventures may be due to the inevitable time lag involved in setting up a new enterprise. However, as mentioned above, legal loopholes also represent an obstacle. For instance, it is still not clear how much profit it will be possible to take out in hard currency, while the unanimous approval required by the board meetings on 'fundamental questions' remains a considerable check on the Western partners' freedom of action.

Western partners also frequently complain of poor infrastructure, with totally inadequate road, rail and telephone networks, and port authorities which are incapable of storing goods safely or delivering them on time. A further complaint relates to bureaucratic delays which in some cases have been rendered worse by perestroika adding to confusion and blurring of responsibility. Negotiations are often lengthy, for instance taking fourteen years for the project to set up the famous McDonald's restaurant in Moscow. Although in theory joint ventures should receive priority in receiving inputs, in practice bottlenecks, poor quality and irregular deliveries continue. This explains why, for example, to set up a restaurant involving $4.5 million capital, McDonald's invested a further $40 million in vertical integration in the Soviet food industry. Many Western firms prefer joint ventures which get around the convertibility question by providing services for foreigners, such as Pan Am's 40% stake and ITT's 10% through Sheraton in two Moscow hotels. Others are extremely wary of any joint ventures which involve heavy capital investment or the 'commitment of too much money too fast'(10).

Though not immune to these difficulties, joint ventures in Hungary have been able to realise sales per employee that are three times higher than the average for Hungarian industry(11). This is partly because Hungary has a longer experience of joint ventures (and their enabling legislation) and economic reform than many of its neighbours, as well as relatively favourable banking and financial conditions. As in the case of Poland, uncertainties still remain with regard to the overall economic situation.

11.7   East–West joint ventures in EC countries

Table 11.4 sets out statistics for the number of East–West joint ventures in EC countries in 1987. The main Western host country of these joint ventures is the Federal Republic of Germany (68), followed by the United Kingdom (61) and then Austria (49). The choice of Western country is influenced by historical links and geographical considerations, and reflects the overall pattern of East–West trade. The Central-East European country with the greatest number of joint ventures in the EC is the Soviet Union (79), followed by Poland (50) and Hungary (43).

Table 11.4   East–West joint ventures domiciled in EC countries at October 1987

	Bulgaria	Czech.	GDR	Hungary	Poland	Romania	USSR	Total
Belgium	2	3	6	1	5	0	13	30
Denmark	0	0	2	1	1	0	2	6
France	4	3	3	3	8	6	12	39
FRG	12	3	0	20	15	7	11	68
Greece	2	0	1	1	1	2	2	9
Ireland	1	0	0	0	0	0	0	1
Italy	5	3	4	5	2	5	8	32
Lux.	0	0	1	1	0	0	1	3
Neth.	1	1	3	2	3	0	2	12
Portugal	0	0	0	0	1	0	0	1
Spain	1	0	1	3	2	1	5	13
UK	6	9	10	6	12	5	13	61
EC(12) Total	34	22	31	43	50	26	79	275

Source: ECE.

According to an ECE publication (1988a), except in the banking and financial sectors, the average size of these joint ventures in the West is relatively small, roughly in the order of $500,000.

In general, the EC member states tend to welcome foreign direct investment as a means of creating employment, introducing new technologies, products or skills, or furthering the aims of regional policy in less-favoured areas. In no EC countries are there any limits on the share of foreign ownership allowed in sectors open to foreign investment. There are slight variations in the sectors excluded according to country, but they may include armaments, explosives, atomic energy, telecommunications and certain public utilities. In some EC countries there may be residency restrictions on non-EC nationals.

Though the Treaty of Rome does not contain special provisions for joint ventures, the latter are subject to EC competition law and the 'rules applying to undertakings' set out in Articles 85–90 of the Treaty.

The main objective of Central-East European partners is export promotion and, according to the ECE (ECE, 1988a), joint ventures accounted for some 15–30% of CMEA exports to the West, and in some sectors, such as machinery and equipment, oil and oil products, they accounted for 30–80% of these exports.

Roughly half of these joint ventures are marketing companies dealing with advertising, marketing research, warehousing, and so on. These commercial activities enable the Eastern partner to develop marketing skills, and may help to improve the quality and competitiveness of Eastern goods offered on Western markets. The Soviet Union is an exception in that only a small share (20%) of joint ventures in the West are involved in these activities. A large share of Soviet joint ventures operate in the service sector, and especially in banking, transport and travel, sectors which are also important (though to a lesser extent) for other Central-East European countries. Hungary is also an exception in that more of its investment in the West is concerned with manufacturing and assembling than is the case for other Central-East European countries.

11.8 Industrial cooperation agreements

There is no commonly accepted definition of what is meant by interfirm industrial cooperation. Most of the early literature quotes the working definition of the 1973 ECE Analytical Report (p.2):

> Industrial cooperation in an East–West context denotes the economic relationships and activities arising from
> (a) contracts extending over a number of years between partners belonging to different economic systems which go beyond the straightforward sale

or purchase of goods and services to include a number of complementary or reciprocally matching operations (in production, in the development and transfer of technology, in marketing, etc.) and from

(b) contracts between partners which have been identified as industrial cooperation contracts by governments in bilateral or multilateral agreements.

The definition then goes on to exclude specifically 'arrangements under which repayment of equipment or technology transfer . . . takes the form of deliveries of related goods', as well as arrangements involving agricultural products.

However, this definition is plainly inadequate since its conditions are not even met by the later examples of the various types of industrial cooperation agreement described in the Analytical Report itself, many of which do not extend 'over a number of years', while others involve agricultural products (p. 94) or repayment in unrelated products (p. 97).

It is not surprising, then, that in later publications the ECE altered its definition. In 1976 as a result of a meeting of a group of experts under the auspices of the ECE, the following definition was put forward(12):

> a contractual economic relationship between two or more enterprises of different nationalities, extending over a longer period, whereby a community of interest is established for the purpose of complementary activities relating to the supply of licenses and equipment, development of new technologies, the exchange of information on, and the use of, those technologies, production and marketing with provision for settlement in kind of the whole or part of the obligations arising from cooperation activities.

However, a considerable number of problems remain. In particular it is difficult to understand what is meant by the phrase 'community of interest' or even the word 'cooperation' in this context. This point is made by Professor Carl Macmillan who argues that the term 'cooperation' may even be misleading since it is not always appreciated that what is at issue is not a function or an activity, but an institutional relationship(13). These ambiguities are also reflected in the ECE studies. The criteria of what constitutes an industrial cooperation agreement, and the breakdown of these agreements according to the forms they take, vary from one ECE publication to the next, making comparison over time very difficult.

Unfortunately, it is difficult to see how these problems could be avoided as the permutations taken by cooperation agreements are seemingly endless and, furthermore, are evolving over time. The ECE definitions probably represent the best attempt to meet these problems in that they do at least point to the main (or most typical) features of cooperation agreements. However, given that exceptions remain, these characteristics should neither be regarded as necessary nor sufficient. They can be listed as follows:

1. A transfer of technology from one partner to the other. Technology transfer is here taken to include the sale of licences, equipment and components, and the training of personnel.
2. If trade is involved, there must be at least partial payment in kind.
3. That typically, though not invariably, the time period involved is greater than that of a one-off sale.

The ECE also provides a list of some of the forms which interfirm cooperation may take, including: licensing; supply of plant or equipment with payment in resultant products; coproduction and specialisation; sub-contracting; joint tendering or joint projects involving third parties; general cooperation contracts; and management contracts. This list is not intended to be exhaustive, but it does indicate something of the nature of interfirm cooperation.

According to the ECE, licensing is emerging as the most common form of cooperation contract (accounting for 40% of a 1988–89 sample). The share of coproduction and specialisation fell from 50% in the pre-1988 ECE sample to 20% in the 1988–89 sample, and the ECE suggests that it is being replaced by the form of cooperation closest to it in complexity, namely joint ventures. Moreover, the ECE reports that when joint ventures are not considered appropriate, there is a growing tendency to use less comprehensive forms of cooperation such as licensing. This increasing use of joint ventures is largely to be explained by the active encouragement on the part of Central-East European countries, which is reflected in the more favourable legislation described above.

11.9 Statistics on interfirm cooperation agreements

Partly as a result of these definitional problems, but also because of commercial confidentiality, precise statistics about interfirm cooperation agreements are not available. The ECE estimates are probably the most complete.

As Table 11.2, which is based on these estimates, illustrates, after a relatively slow growth in the 1960s, on average ninety-three East–West industrial cooperation agreements were signed each year over the 1975–85 period. There was a slight fall in 1986 (eighty-seven agreements), but the number of new cooperation agreements was 113 in 1987 and 135 in 1988, so that a total of 1512 was reached by the end of July 1989.

Information about the value of undertakings is not available for industrial cooperation contracts.

Of the 1512 East–West industrial cooperation agreements in July 1989, the most frequent host country was Hungary (35% of the total), followed by the Soviet Union (32%), Bulgaria, Czechoslovakia, the German Democratic Republic and Poland, in that order.

Between 1988 and mid-1989, 84% of all Central-East European industrial cooperation contracts were signed with West European partners, and 63% with EC member states (see Table 11.5). The EC share rose to 84.6% in the case of the German Democratic Republic, and never fell below 57.1% (Poland). The United States accounted for a further 10.6%, and Japan for 2.8% of all industrial cooperation agreements over this period. In descending order the main Western partners were the German Federal Republic, Austria, Italy, the United States and the United Kingdom, which together accounted for 67% of all agreements.

Certain preferences emerge when industrial cooperation agreements are broken down by country involved, and these are probably explained by factors such as traditional links, and geographical proximity. Austrian agreements tended to be concentrated in Hungary and Bulgaria; the Soviet Union with Finland and Sweden; the Federal Republic of Germany with the German Democratic Republic, even before unification, and France with Hungary.

The agreements generally involved the manufacturing sector (90%) and, in the case of Czechoslovakia, Poland and the German Democratic Republic were exclusively in that sector. 'Business activities' (including research and development and computer services) accounted for a further 5%.

Within manufacturing, most cooperation contracts related to transport equipment (10%), coal and petroleum products and the chemical, rubber and plastic industries (17% taken together). Clothing and footwear (9%) were also important.

Table 11.5 Industrial cooperation agreements by host country and origin of Western partner (per cent)

	Bulgaria	Czech.	GDR	Hungary	Poland	Romania	USSR	CMEA
EC	62.1	64.3	84.6	60.3	57.1	0	61.3	62.7
Other Western Europe	27.6	14.3	7.7	22.1	14.3	0	22.6	21.2
Japan	3.4	0	0	4.4	14.3	0	3.2	3.6
USA	6.9	14.3	7.7	10.3	14.3	0	6.5	8.8
LDCs	0	7.1	0	1.5	0	0	1.6	1.6
Other	0	0	0	1.5	0	0	4.8	2.1

Source: ECE.

Turning to individual countries, the agreements involving Poland and the Soviet Union were concentrated in the transport equipment and the engineering sectors. Bulgaria was especially active in engineering equipment, the food industry and leather and footwear. Hungary had an above-average share in chemicals and transport equipment, while Czechoslovakia was more active in food production and chemicals.

With regard to EC partners, the Federal Republic of Germany and France were active in engineering industries, the Federal Republic of Germany and Italy in transport equipment, the United Kingdom in chemicals, and the Federal Republic of Germany, France and Italy in clothing, leather and footwear.

11.10 Tripartite cooperation agreements

During the early 1980s much importance was attached to tripartite co-operation agreements. These, which took the form either of protocol or framework agreements or legal business contracts among the partners(14), were described by the UNCTAD (1984, p. 2) as:

> the way in which enterprises from both socialist countries and developed market-economy countries are jointly carrying out industrial projects or other forms of joint operation in a developing country in cooperation to a greater or lesser extent with local companies and/or authorities. . . . In tripartite cooperation partners from all three groups of countries are responsible signatories and actively participate in the cooperation. In the cooperation in third countries the client is the passive recipient of the undertaking who takes over the project when it is finalized. In practice, however, this distinction is rather difficult to make.

This type of cooperation was envisaged, *inter alia*, as a means of encouraging the international division of labour, and the industrialisation and development of the Southern partners. For instance, the UNCTAD (1984, p. 29) argued:

> A developing country is enabled to receive the highest possible technology at the lowest cost when building up its infrastructure or production capacity. The development process and industrial infrastructure is strengthened, not only through the direct transfer of the technology included in the new production plant, but also through the transfer of know-how gained during the active participation in the project execution.
>
> The know-how adopted by managers and workers in the developing country is enriched by often diversified expertise and working methods implemented by the project participants from the different groups of countries.

However, this form of cooperation was never very widespread.

Gutman (1981) estimated that by the end of 1979 some 230 business contracts and 119 protocol agreements had either been completed or were in progress, though he has been accused of some double-counting. Gutman found the EC countries and the Federal Republic of Germany in particular to be the most important Western partners. According to the UNCTAD Secretariat, there were over 300 business contracts completed or in progress at the end of 1982, and a further thirty protocol agreements over the 1980–82 period. M. Gomez (1984) maintained that tripartite cooperation agreements accounted for 4–10% of all East–West interfirm cooperation contracts in 1980, or less than 1% of all world trade.

The limited scale of these arrangements seems largely to be the result of the huge practical obstacles involved: complicated and lengthy negotiations; the need to adjust to differences in legislation, business practices, technology and technical standards, working mentality and methods; the difficult geographical and environmental conditions, and so on. It has also been argued that the correct term is 'tripartite cooperation *in* developing countries', rather than *with* them, as these countries rarely participated in the management of such projects and often did little more than provide local labour, raw materials or a market.

With the present difficulties of the Central-East European countries and the huge task of economic transformation, this form of cooperation has largely fallen into the background. For example, speaking of the Ministry for Cooperation with Less Developed Countries, in April 1990 the then GDR Minister for the Interior said that its chief function was to undo rather than sign new agreements of this type(15).

Notes

1. Unless otherwise stated the data in this chapter are taken from the ECE which probably has the most complete data base on this topic.
2. ECE (1988a), page 2.
3. International Council for New Initiatives in East–West Cooperation and International Institute of Applied Systems Analysis Task Force on Joint Ventures, Varna Symposium, September 1988.
4. For a detailed though somewhat dated account of this legislation see ECE 1988b.
5. Unless otherwise stated, the statistics presented in this section are taken from the ECE and are based on a sample of 1327 joint ventures in the Soviet Union, Poland, Hungary and Czechoslovakia.
6. *The Economist*, 24 February 1990.
7. *The Economist*, 6 January 1990.
8. *The Economist*, 24 February 1990.
9. *The Economist*, 21 October 1989.
10. *The Economist*, 24 February 1990.

11. *The Economist,* 21 October 1989.
12. ECE (1976), p. 5.
13. Stretching the case considerably, one could perhaps paraphrase Voltaire's famous statement about the Holy Roman Empire. Industrial cooperation agreements are not 'industrial' because they often involve agricultural goods or commodities; as MacMillan argues, frequently they could not be classed as 'cooperation' in the more usual sense of the word, and finally they are not always 'agreements' in view of the disputes which arise with the Western partners complaining about delays and the poor range and quality of goods being offered, while the Eastern partners sometimes complain that obsolete technology has been offloaded on them.
14. See S.M. Senior Nello (1985a) and the bibliography therein for a more detailed account.
15. *La Repubblica,* 11 April 1990.

12

The implications of German Unification for the EC

12.1 Introduction

The East German case shares many elements of the transformation of other Central-East European countries, but is occurring at a vastly accelerated rate and with social safety nets that would be inconceivable elsewhere. The language and cultural affinity with the Federal Republic of Germany and, in some cases, contacts already in place through trade and industrial cooperation to some extent ease the transformation process.

None the less, the obstacles should not be underestimated and it is precisely the speed of change which creates strains. Total unemployment in united Germany was 1.9 million on average in 1990, with unemployment and reduced working hours concentrated in the East. The possibility of labour moving to the West led to rapid wage increases at a time of widespread bankruptcies in the five Länder. It is proving difficult to introduce many changes (such as privatisation, new legislation relating to property rights and competition, and the breaking of bureaucratic power) at a sufficiently rapid pace. Continual upward revision of the cost of unification led to three supplementary budgets in 1990.

Integration into the EC is occurring with the minimum transition period and number of derogations possible. As will be shown, even before unification the Special German Provisions of the Treaty of Rome had led to the German Democratic Republic being referred to as the thirteenth member of the Community. It seems likely that when the short-run adjustment difficulties are overcome, unification will contribute even further to German economic and monetary dominance in Europe, but the reaction of the other EC members, aimed at ensuring that a united Germany is firmly rooted in the Community, would seem correct.

After considering the main economic aspects of the integration of East Germany into the EC, this chapter will give an indication of the estimated costs of German unification. Then follows a brief description of the privileged relation that the German Democratic Republic had with the Community, even prior to 1990 as a result of the Special German Provisions of the Treaty of Rome. The final section of the chapter deals with the implementation of various EC policies (the CAP, Regional Policy, Competition Policy, environmental measures, and so on) in the five Länder.

12.2 Economic aspects of German unification

Following the 'fall' of the Berlin Wall in November 1989 the process of German unification has assumed an ever quicker pace. At first this speed was caused by the need to stem immigration from the East, which reached 340,000 in 1989 and 120,000 in the first two months of 1990 alone. It was also a response to the poor performance of the Christian Democrats in the Rhine–Westphalia elections in May 1990, with successful and rapid completion of German unification offering a possibility for recapturing votes. Subsequently, much of the pressure came from the East Germans themselves, who faced much higher costs of economic transition than initially expected, and saw in political union (with the Federal Republic paying the bill) a solution.

In July 1990 Kohl was able to overcome the last obstacle to German unification, namely Soviet hesitancy about having a united Germany in NATO. This was achieved by proposing that the nature of NATO be altered and the role of the CSCE be increased. Kohl also took the initiative in encouraging Western measures to assist the Soviet Union by leading the way with a German offer of 5 billion D-marks of state-guaranteed credits and subsequently by the provision of food aid. In addition, he accepted limits being imposed on the military strength of a united Germany and agreed to pay the costs of Soviet troops in East Germany, provided a deadline was fixed for their withdrawal.

German political unification took place in October 1990 via the 'quick route' permitted by Article 23 of the FRG Basic Law. This enabled the German Democratic Republic simply to be absorbed into West Germany, in contrast with Article 146 which would have required negotiation of a new pan-German constitution.

A treaty on economic, monetary and social union came into force from 1 July 1990. This envisaged the extension of the Federal Republic's 'social market economy' to the five Länder, and the replacement of the

Ostmark with the D-mark (with the Bundesbank *de facto* becoming the central bank for all Germany). The exchange rate of one-for-one was to be used for all prices and wages, as well as for 4000 Ostmarks per head (6000 for pensioners and 2000 for under fifteens). It was estimated that the one-for-one rate would apply to some 64 billion Ostmarks out of GDR personal savings and cash of some 180 billion Ostmarks, or GDR bank liabilities and cash of 275 billion(1). A two Ostmark for one D-mark would be used for other assets and liabilities denominated in Ostmarks, and of three-for-one for non-residents.

The introduction of a 'social market economy' would entail price reform and elimination of subsidies, bringing the monetary and fiscal systems into line with those of the Federal Republic, and the creation of an economic and legal environment to encourage free enterprise, privatisation of the state sector and the freedom of movement of workers, capital, goods and services.

The scale of this task is immense. The GDR capital stock was run down (the Soviets took much GDR capital to the Soviet Union after the War), and infrastructure was poor, requiring massive investment for housing, roads, railways, air transport and the Baltic seaports. Trade was heavily concentrated (65%) in bilateral exchanges with CMEA countries. Two-thirds of the GDR GNP was in manufacturing, mining and energy as compared with 35% for the Federal Republic(2). Comparisons are difficult to make, but it is estimated that GDR labour productivity was 40% of the FRG level(3). Experience of markets and marketing was lacking, and environmental measures were urgently required.

Although after the Second World War about 40% of industry remained in private hands, subsequently the state gradually increased its holdings. In 1972 the remaining 'Mittelstand' (small companies) were nationalised and from 1980 transformed into the large and diffuse 'Kombinate' which covered various economic activities. In March 1990 a Treuhandanstalt (trusteeship) was established to privatise the 8000 formerly state-owned enterprises. Its function was to establish which firms could be privatised without significant changes, which needed restructuring and which would go bankrupt.

On the basis of a survey of 3000 firms, the ex-GDR Economics Minister, Gerhard Pohl, suggested that only 30% of these firms would be capable of surviving in a market economy, 50% would need restructuring and 20% would go bankrupt. Many businessmen found these figures optimistic(4), and later estimates indicated that possibly only 15% could survive without significant changes, 40% required restructuring, and 45% would fail.

Recovery seemed to come first for the services, as indicated by the fact that GNP for the five Länder fell by only 30% compared with the

50% fall in industrial production during the third quarter of 1990(5). It is estimated that of the new firms established in 1990, 45% were retail outlets and restaurants, etc., leading to the term 'snack-bar economy'(6).

The wage differential between East and West Germany narrowed rapidly, with wages rising by between 50% and 80% in many industries in the East over the nine months to April 1991. Many economists attribute the speed of this wage convergence to the one-to-one conversion rate, but even with a less favourable rate for the Ostmark, free migration from East to West would have meant that wages were likely to converge.

Investment by West German and foreign firms fell short of initial expectations, partly because of the narrowing wage differential, but also because of uncertainty about property rights, poor infrastructure, and the unfavourable economic situation in the five Länder. Up until March 1990 many FRG industrialists appeared interested in expanding into East Germany, but a poll carried out by the 'Frankfurter Allgemeine Zeitung' in April 1990 indicated that the interest was becoming more selective. While many service industries which rely on a physical presence intended to extend their activities in the five Länder(7), many manufacturers (such as BASF) decided that it would not be necessary(8).

The scale of certain takeovers is enormous. For example, in the insurance sector, Allianz took over 51% of the GDR state monopoly insurance company(9). The Deutsche Bank bought an 85% stake in the former GDR state banking monopoly, Deutsche Kreditbank. The latter also formed a joint venture (Commerzbank) with the Dresdner bank. Lufthansa made a bid for 26% of the East German state airline, Interflug.

With regard to improving GDR infrastructure, the FRG Bundesbahn and Bundespost planned to extend their activities to the East, while a merger between the Bundesbahn and the Reichsbahn was due to take place in 1991(10). It is estimated that investment of 100 billion D-marks would be necessary for East German track, and 30 billion D-marks for rolling stock. SEL (Standard Elektrik Lorenz) was to contribute to the modernisation of the telephone system.

The ground was to some extent already prepared for certain of these FRG initiatives. The Democratic Republic represented an exception in not having legislation on joint ventures until 1989, but it had a moderately successful tradition of industrial cooperation, in particular with FRG firms(11).

Despite a slight slowing of orders towards the end of the year, in 1990 the GNP of the united Germany grew by 4.6%, exceeding forecasts. In 1989 there was an increase of 3.9%, and growth of at least 3% is expected in 1991(12). This would seem to confirm the results of a study carried out by the economic research institutes(13) according to which

German unification would add 0.75% to the expected FRG growth rate in 1990 and 1.5 to the 1991 forecast, increasing overall growth of the EC by some 0.5%. Inflation was 2.7% in 1990 and has been forecast at 3% for 1991.

The main impulse for this expansion came from the five Länder and the increased demand was particularly accentuated in two sectors: foodstuffs and consumer durables. The adjustment of patterns of food consumption to those of the rest of Germany contributed to a 20% increase in production of the German food industry in 1990(14), while purchases of consumer durables rose by 12% during the year, causing output of these products to reach a record 10% of GNP(15).

In 1990 775,000 work posts were created in Germany. Total unemployment in the five Länder was 642,000 or 7.3% of the labour force (compared with 6.8% for the FRG) in December 1990. A further 1.8 million workers were on 'kurzarbeit' or short time (which in 60% of all cases amounted to no working hours) in an East German workforce of roughly 8 million. It is estimated that by the end of 1991 the total unemployment rate in the five Länder could reach 40–50%. Migration to the West also appeared to continue, with, for instance, some 11,000 moving in just the first two weeks of October 1990.

The pressure of demand in East Germany and recession in many Western industrialised countries explains why the German trade surplus fell from 134.7 billion marks for the Federal Republic alone in 1989 to 110 billion marks for a united Germany in 1990, with a further fall expected for 1991.

As will be shown below, the costs of unification were larger than initially expected, contributing to a German budget deficit which was expected to rise to some 140–150 billion marks or 5% of total German GNP in 1991. This compares with an FRG deficit of only 30 billion marks or 0.5% of FRG GNP in 1989.

The response of the Bundesbank to this situation was to raise interest rates, causing protests on the part of other Western partners, and especially the United States, which was concerned about recession, and other EMS members who feared the consequences of divergent monetary policies. Subsequently Kohl was also forced to renege on his 1990 election promise that taxes would not be increased as a result of German unification, and in 1991 a temporary increase in income tax by 7.5% on average and higher levels of taxation for petrol and tobacco was announced. It is estimated that these measures could add some 0.5–1.0% to the inflation rate.

Once the initial difficulties are overcome, the outlook is relatively favourable, and in the medium term East German growth could reach some 10% per year. East Germany offers investment opportunities and a relatively well-educated labour force to a Federal Republic which in

1989 had a current account surplus of 104 billion D-marks and an increase in tax revenue of 47 billion D-marks because of its rapid economic growth. The contacts and experience in exporting to CMEA countries may also enable East Germany to act as a springboard for exporting to Central-East Europe.

12.3 The integration of East Germany into the European Community

Community support for unification was first offered in December 1989 with a political declaration in favour of peace in Europe 'in which the German people can find their unity again by means of free self-determination'. At the same time it was stressed that German reunification should respect the relevant Treaties, and the Helsinki Final Act. To reassure its partners, at the same Summit the FRG government pledged its commitment to a revived process of European integration which included the European Social Charter (approved by all EC member states except the United Kingdom) and the agreement to set up the intergovernmental conference on economic and monetary union during 1990. This attitude was confirmed at the June 1990 Dublin Summit when the conference on political union within the year was also agreed.

Given the special case of reinstatement of the Democratic Republic into a unified Germany on the basis of Article 23, there was no need to apply Article 237 of the Treaty of Rome which relates to the accession of other states to the Community. As a result a formal application or negotiations of conditions of accession were not necessary. None the less, given the difficulties raised by this 'widening' of the Community, the Commission prepared a Report, which was discussed at the April 1990 Dublin Summit, suggesting that integration should take place in the following three phases:

1. An interim adaptation phase would begin with the introduction of German economic and monetary union. During this phase as much as possible of the legislation necessary for integration into the Federal Republic and the Community would be implemented.
2. There would be a transitional phase beginning with the unification of the two states during which Community law would apply on GDR territory, apart from temporary derogations decided in the Council on the basis of EC Commission proposals.
3. The ultimate phase would require full application of Community laws.

It was initially anticipated that a large part of the integration of East

Germany into the Community would occur during the interim adjustment phase, before political unification took place. In the event, bringing political union forward to October 1990 meant that this phase lasted
only three months. During this time the Democratic Republic benefited
from Community aid under the PHARE Programme.

From 1 July a customs union between the EC eleven and the Democratic Republic came into operation, which entailed the suspension of all
tariff barriers, customs duties, and quantitative restrictions on GDR
products entering the EC, provided EC products had free access to
GDR markets. In its trade with non-EC countries, the Democratic Republic was to apply the Common External Tariff, and extend the GSP to
those countries already receiving this preferential treatment from the
EC. Limited derogations were envisaged to avoid adverse economic
consequences for the Democratic Republic and to allow existing trade
arrangements between it and third countries to continue.

Once FRG products became freely available, there appeared to be a
virtual collapse of sales of East German products as consumers were
convinced that their quality was inferior. For instance, GDR food products (particularly eggs, milk and dairy products) began to build up in
cold stores. In the first quarter of 1990 FRG deliveries of agricultural
and food products to the Democratic Republic rose by 81% compared
with the same period a year earlier (to 279 million D-marks), while
GDR deliveries to the Federal Republic rose by only 7% (to 180 million
D-marks; see also Table 12.1)(16). In response to this situation, the
GDR Parliament passed a law by which import licences were required
for FRG deliveries of many agricultural products (17) to the Democratic
Republic, but in practice these proved ineffective. At the same time,
sales of GDR products to the Soviet Union, Poland and Romania were
organised(18).

A package of 'interim measures' to facilitate the integration of East
Germany into the Community was introduced from October 1990. Because the date for unity was brought forward from December, special
powers had to be granted to the EC Commission to implement these
measures until the due legislative process could be completed. The time
limit set for most of the transitional arrangements was the end of 1992,
though, as will be shown in more detail below, there were certain technical adjustments and exceptions, such as a delay in the application of EC
air and water (but not nuclear) standards.

Existing trade arrangements with CMEA countries could be continued until the end of 1991, with the option of renewing them for a
further year. The importance of this is evident when it is recalled that,
for instance, in 1987 some 42.4% of GDR trade was with the Soviet
Union, and roughly 65% with CMEA countries, much of which was
covered by agreements.

Table 12.1 Agricultural trade between the FRG and the GDR (million D-marks)

	Deliveries by the FRG*			Purchases by the FRG*		
	Total	Agricultural	Ag. as % total	Total	Agricultural	Ag. as % total
1975	3922	26	0.7	3342	399	11.9
1976	4269	34	0.8	3877	419	10.8
1977	4343	19	0.4	3960	410	10.4
1978	4575	28	0.6	3900	387	9.9
1979	4711	26	0.6	4587	418	9.1
1980	5293	26	0.6	5580	413	7.4
1981	5575	27	0.5	6051	465	7.7
1982	6382	181	2.8	6639	476	7.2
1983	6947	166	2.4	6872	503	7.2
1984	6408	39	0.6	7744	483	6.2
1985	7901	70	0.9	7636	468	6.1
1986	7454	38	0.5	6844	385	5.6
1987	7367	33	0.5	6677	386	5.8
1988	7234	45	0.6	6789	402	5.9

* Because the FRG considers this internal trade, the words 'exports' and 'imports' are not used.
Source: Handel, Gastgewerbe and Reiseverkehr, Statistiches Jahrbuch, Bundesrepublik Deutschland.

Various implications of German unification for the Community can be distinguished as follows:

1. The impact on the prospects for EC political union and the possible changed weight of Germany in EC institutions: with the exception of representation in the European Parliament, such changes have not so far been requested, but are likely to be considered within the intergovernmental conferences concerned with institutional reform. The initial reaction of most of the other member states has been to increase the obligations of EC membership in order to ensure that an enlarged Germany is firmly rooted in Western Europe.

2. The consequences for the EC Budget in view of the extra expenditure that will be required from the CAP, Regional and Social Funds, European Coal and Steel Community and European Investment Bank: there has been a commitment to avoid other less-favoured areas of the Community (especially in Greece, Portugal, Ireland and Spain) being adversely affected by these measures.

3. The effect on the German and Community economies and the repercussions for EC economic and monetary union.

4. The implementation of EC measures in East Germany, including those relating to competition; the Common Commercial Policy; the internal market; the CAP; the introduction of VAT; the environment; fisheries; transport; structural policies, and the ECSC.

5. The timetable for admitting other new members into the

Community may be affected. Despite the decision that there should be no new members until at least January 1993, the integration of East Germany has altered many perceptions of Austrian prospects of accession. In Hungary it is argued that Austrian accession would also alter Hungarian prospects.

12.4 Possible costs of German unification

The Federal Republic accepted the total cost of integrating the East up until January 1991, and subsequently there was to be a 'correction' of the 1991 Community Budget to allow for the extra funds required for East Germany.

In May 1990 the FRG government voted in favour of a *Fund for German Unity* which envisaged 115 billion D-marks for East Germany between 2 July 1990 and the end of 1994. Of this, 20 billion would be financed by the Federal Budget, while the rest would be raised on the capital market: 22 billion of these marks would be available in 1990; 35 billion in 1991; 28 in 1992; and 10 in 1994. A further 3 billion marks per year would be available for unemployment benefits and pensions in 1990 and 1991(19).

The budgetary allocation for 1990 proved a serious underestimate, and three supplementary budgets had to be introduced during the year. On some estimates, the internal cost of unification in 1990 was 100 million D-marks, which is over 4% of GNP, and the costs are expected to be even higher in 1991(20). A further 15 million D-marks were needed to finance the withdrawal of Soviet troops from the five Länder, as well as at least 3 million D-marks to ensure that existing East German trade commitments were fulfilled with regard to the Soviet Union. The total cost of restructuring was estimated as high as 500 billion D-marks(21).

It has been estimated that German unification could add some 4–6 billion ECU to expenditure on the EC Budget over the 1991–92 period(22). About 3 billion ECU would be necessary from EC structural funds (the Social Fund, Regional Fund and FEOGA Guidance Section) for less-developed areas in the five Länder. Preliminary figures suggest that German unification could increase the FEOGA budget by some 1.3 billion ECU in 1991(23).

According to calculations made by a senior member of the EC Court of Auditors(24), the total cost of application of the CAP in East Germany could be in the order of 8 billion ECU. Half of this might be borne by the Federal Republic of Germany, but the extension of EC agricultural market support systems to Eastern Germany could add 2 billion ECU to the Guarantee Section of the FEOGA Budget, while restructuring of farms could cost a further 2 billion each year for ten years, or 20 billion ECU.

It is estimated that East Germany could pay some 500 million ECU in contributions to the Community in 1991 (though this seems somewhat optimistic), but that economic difficulties would reduce the German contribution by some 1.5 billion ECU in 1992 (25). By 1993 a contribution of 500 million ECU is again expected.

12.5 The special German provisions

Although the task of integration of East Germany into the EC is formidable, the special German provisions of the Treaty of Rome meant that even before 1989 the Democratic Republic was sometimes already considered to be the thirteenth member of the EC *de facto*. These provisions reflected the FRG view that internal German trade was not foreign trade so trade between the Federal and the Democratic Republics was never subject to the Community customs regulations applicable on goods coming from third countries. In practice this meant that imports from the Democratic Republic were not subject to the Community tariff or quota system or to the levies on agricultural products coming from third countries. However, they were subject to controls, licensing procedures and quotas imposed independently by the Federal Republic. In principle, the FRG authorities forbade all trade with the Democratic Republic which was not explicitly allowed. In practice, as John Garland has said (1985, p. 3): 'some commodities receive general approval, some require ad hoc approval on a case-by-case basis and some are subject to stringent quotas'.

It is estimated that FRG controls covered some 35% of industrial goods and 86% of agricultural goods in 1981(26). GDR agricultural goods sold in the Federal Republic were subject to the market regulations of the Federal Agricultural Agency.

The institutional framework for trade between the Federal Republic and the Democratic Republic was established by the 1951 Berlin agreement, although there were subsequent modifications on a number of occasions. The agreement was signed by 'currency areas' on both sides to allow the inclusion of Berlin and to avoid the problem of recognising the Democratic Republic politically. In this way the FRG principle that although there were two German states there was only one German nation was respected.

According to the Berlin agreement, contracts for trade between the Federal and Democratic Republics were concluded in western D-marks but clearing was in a special unit of account, the VE (Verrechsnung-seinheiten), which was equivalent to the Western D-mark. Conversion into the GDR mark was exclusively the responsibility of the GDR authorities. All payments were carried out between the two central banks rather than between buyers and sellers directly.

As a result of this bilateral clearing, in the long run trade flows in both directions had to balance. To prevent disruption of trade because of temporary imbalance, a 'swing' credit was created. This was an interest-free loan to be used by either side, but in the event it acted as a virtually permanent interest-free loan for the Democratic Republic. The consequent savings on interest payments for the Democratic Republic were estimated at over 50 million D-marks annually from 1970(27).

12.6   Application of EC policies in the five Länder

12.6.1   *The CAP*

As part of the *acquis communautaire* the Common Agricultural Policy was to apply in the Democratic Republic from 3 October 1990, though with certain transitional measures. EC market support structures such as intervention agencies were set up, and, as described above, during the interim adjustment period a customs union with the Community had already came into operation. The speed with which such changes were introduced is largely to be explained by the potential for speculation which could otherwise have arisen.

East Germany has soil and climatic advantages over the Federal Republic and was once known as the Kornkammer or granary of Germany. Furthermore, a legacy of collective farming has left the East with a more favourable farm structure as many FRG farms are small and part-time. The average size of East German farms is 4600 hectares. Members of GDR cooperative farms had certain property rights and were able to employ labour. With unification, two sets of question arise, one relating to land ownership, and the other to the division of the cooperatives into smaller more workable units.

GDR agriculture suffered from an excess labour force and in May 1990 the then Agricultural Minister, Pollack, suggested that possibly 50% of the 800,000 collective farmers in the Democratic Republic would have to change job by 1996. In part this was because a large number of workers on the cooperatives carried out supplementary activities such as building construction and maintenance, machinery repair, child care and so on. Pollack also estimated that some 20% of collective farms would not survive the changes, and a further 50% would require subsidies(28). In August 1990 Pollack was forced to resign following physical attacks by farmers fearing unemployment, and suffering from the cuts in subsidies, the collapse in sales and a freeze on farm credit following German economic and monetary union(29).

Provided land holdings do not become too fragmented, the potential for expansion of East German agriculture is substantial. It is estimated that the application of CAP rules (and especially of higher agricultural prices), together with the introduction of more modern methods and improved inputs, could increase East German agricultural output of certain products by as much as 20–30%(30). For example, cereal yields are some 20% below FRG levels and an increase in yields even to FRG levels would entail East German production of 8% or more of the current EC (12) grain production(31).

A major FRG trader, Toepfer, envisaged East Germany being transformed from a major net grain importer to a net exporter in the space of two to three years(32). This view was confirmed by the USDA who argued that if East German yields were raised to West German levels, the five Länder could be exporting some 3 million tonnes of grains in a few years(33). Over the 1986–89 period the average GDR harvest was 11 million tonnes, leaving 2–3 million to be imported. The share of grain in feedstuffs amounted to some 68.3% in the Democratic Republic compared with some 19.3% in the Federal Republic where cheap cereal-substitutes are used extensively. In 1988 GDR imports of manioc were only about 27,000 tonnes, rising to 284,000 tonnes in 1989.

It was agreed that the EC stabiliser or maximum guaranteed quantity for grain would not be altered to take account of GDR production in 1991, even though any price reductions and penalties would also apply there. In effect, this amounted to postponing what is likely to prove a controversial question.

From April 1991 a milk quota of 6.3 million tonnes will be applied in East Germany, implying a decline in production of some 20% over 1989 levels. Transitional measures will also entail a 7.8% fall in deliveries between July 1990 and March 1991 compared with 1989–90 levels. The East German dairy herd, estimated at some 1.98 million head in 1989 is expected to fall by 500,000 by April 1991. In part this is because environmental considerations suggest that large herds of 1000 head or more would be better reduced to levels of 300–500.

In 1991 the milk quota for the united Germany will amount to 28.13 million tonnes, with a Community quota of 104.32 million tonnes, implying that Germany is the third world producer, behind only the Soviet Union and the United States. As a result of German unification, in 1991 the milk quota available per capita in the EC will rise from 301 kg to 304 kg(34).

Despite frequent shortages, East Germany has a potential surplus in milk production. The relatively high consumption figures in the past also reflected high levels of wastage. In the next three to four years it seems likely that yields will be raised considerably as a result of improved herd management, culling of poor cows, and the use of better breeds and feeds.

The EC Commission proposed a sugar quota of 870,000 tonnes for East Germany in 1991, which would mean that a united Germany producing 3.5 million tonnes of sugar would be the largest producer in the Community. The other EC members challenged the level of this quota on the grounds that subsidies and losses had raised the GDR consumption figure, and that if East German sugar consumption were in line with West Germany (33.5 kg per capita rather than 40 kg), total consumption would reach only 600,000 tonnes(35).

A set-aside scheme was also agreed for the five Länder which would involve 350,000 hectares or 6% of agriculturally productive land in the five Länder. The aim was to withdraw many outdated structures from agriculture in order to concentrate on increasing the efficiency of those remaining.

There were also to be structural grants to facilitate the dismantling of collective farms and the creation of private farms. Financial assistance would also be given for improvements in processing plants, abattoirs, the marketing system and environmental conditions. Modernisation of the food-processing industry is one of the most fundamental requirements for the transformation of East German agriculture. It is estimated that some 50% of equipment in the food-processing industry is over 20 years old, while more than a third is at least 40 years old.

EC veterinary and plant health legislation was not to apply in East Germany until the end of 1992 in order to allow time for adaptation to EC standards. However, conformity to EC norms was a necessary condition for East German products to be sold in the Community.

12.6.2 *Regional policy and measures to improve infrastructure*

The EC has pledged a contribution of possibly 1 billion ECU per year from its structural funds to assist industrial restructuring and systemic change. Measures are likely to include aid to small and medium enterprises; a decentralisation programme, and the establishment of regional development agencies. There are also likely to be contributions to training programmes and unemployment benefits from the European Social Fund, and East Germany will be eligible for loans from the EIB, Euratom, and the ECSC.

Difficulties arise in drawing up criteria for eligibility, partly because of lack of reliable statistics, but also because the indicator of average unemployment levels in previous years cannot be used to identify specific priority areas. Certain derogations and deviations from usual EC rules are therefore likely over a two to three year period.

Community funds will be used to improve infrastructure, and in particular to develop road and rail links. Though most of the funds to develop telecommunications are expected to come from the Federal Republic, there may also be a Community contribution.

12.6.3 *Energy and the environment*

The scale of air and water pollution, and inefficient treatment of waste renders the alignment of East Germany to EC environmental measures especially urgent.

A policy of self-sufficiency had meant that 70% of GDR energy needs and 85% of its electricity (compared with 19% in the Federal Republic and 9% in the EC) was met by extremely polluting brown coal(36). This was produced in antiquated power plants, leading, for instance, to levels of sulphur dioxide per capita of 310 kg compared with 30 kg in the Federal Republic(37).

A further 10% of energy requirements was met by nuclear power, much of which is generated near Greifswald. Following a visit by FRG experts, three of the plant's four generators were closed when grave defects were found in their operation.

Partly as a result of inefficient technologies in industry, energy consumption per capita was an estimated 7000 kilowatt hours per person, compared with the FRG average of 6400 kwh(38). Thirty per cent of rivers are polluted and 45% can no longer be used to supply drinking water. Over the past ten years the Democratic Republic has also received industrial waste from the Federal Republic, Switzerland and the Netherlands.

Measures are therefore required to reduce dependence on brown coal; to improve safety standards of nuclear plants; to correct the wasteful use of energy; and to improve environmental conditions. Alternative energy sources will have to be found and the Federal Republic has signed agreements for shipments of 2 billion cubic metres of natural gas from 1992–2023, as well as for electricity. Studies are being carried out to see which existing plant can be adapted, and which will have to be closed because the level of pollution is too high. The removal of energy subsidies should help to encourage conservation. Though the main provisions of the Euratom Treaty with regard to safeguards, standards and so on came into operation in the five Länder from October 1990, a number of transitional arrangements (i.e. temporary exemptions) have had to be made in the applications of other aspects of EC environmental law.

12.6.4 *Competition policy, company law and the Single Market*

Though the aim is to keep the number of derogations to a minimum, the implementation of EC competition policy in the five Länder with regard to monopolies and state aids seems likely to create difficulties, in particular during the interval while the Kombinate system is being dismantled(39).

The EC was also concerned that the various measures to aid East German restructuring should conform to Community competition law, and should not discriminate between different firms or EC member states. In particular, the huge takeovers by the FRG banks and public utilities have raised concern in the EC Commission. A rigid interpretation of competition as set out in Article 85 of the Treaty seems likely in the German case, especially with regard to takeovers, state subsidies and investment incentives.

FRG legislation concerning banking, insurance and capital markets, as well as company law has been extended to the five Länder.

Turning to the Single Market, FRG legislation introducing Community Directives on the liberalisation of public procurement came into effect in East Germany from July 1990. The Commission has considered transitional measures for technical harmonisation, but reintegration with the Federal Republic requires rapid adjustment in this context. Moreover, with the exception of specifications relating to toys and pressure vessels, most standards will not become mandatory at the Community level until 1993. East Germany has already begun to adopt the specifications of the FRG standardisation institute, the Deutsches Institut für Normung.

12.6.5 *Other sectors presenting specific difficulties for the application of Community measures*

One area in which German unification seems likely to pose specific difficulties for the Community is in the *steel* sector. The Democratic Republic produce 8 million tonnes of steel per year and ranked fourth among Central-East European producers. Roughly 40% of this steel was produced using outdated processes such as continuous casting and, as a result, the quality is lower than that of EC countries(40).

Over the last ten years the EC steel sector has undergone drastic rationalisation to eliminate excess production, with the number of jobs being reduced from 800,000 to 400,000. The entry of 8 million tonnes of East German steel would cause market imbalance, and thus restructuring and reduced East German production is necessary. The Community expects the Federal Republic to finance much of the adjustment.

Since unification, the East German fishing fleet has been able to fish FRG total allowable catches and quotas, in addition to previously existing GDR fishing rights. Because the FRG quota was underutilised, the fear of excess capacity was not realised. None the less, the East German fleet is one-and-a-half times that of the Federal Republic, as well as being old and less productive, thus restructuring will be necessary.

The GDR shipbuilding industry employed 30,000 and accounted for 4% of world trade. Roughly 70% of production was exported to the Soviet Union. Given the low productivity of these yards and a situation of excess capacity, restructuring will have to be carried out(41).

Notes

1. *The Economist*, 30 May 1990.
2. *The Economist*, 30 June 1990.
3. *The Economist*, 30 June 1990.
4. *The Economist*, 30 June 1990.
5. Official German statistics as reported in *Il Sole-24 Ore*, 5 February 1991.
6. *Il Sole-24 Ore*, 5 February 1991.
7. The retailers Edeka and Hertie are planning takeovers, and other major chain stores such as Deutsche Spar and Horten intend to open large retail outlets in East Germany. The Dresdner Bank and Commerzbank are also opening branches, while in the tourism sector, Steigenberger, the hotel group, and Lufthansa plan extensive operations in East Germany (as reported in *The Economist*, 30 June 1990).
8. The outlook for manufacturing is more mixed. Many of the large FRG car manufacturers, such as Volkswagen (based close to the East German border), Opel and Daimler-Benz will set up plants in East Germany. In the engineering sector, firms such as AEG, Mannesmann, Thyssen, Krupp, Metallgesellschaft and Kloeckner-Humbolt-Deutz have entered into joint ventures. However, many other firms such as Siemens plan simply to extend their distributon network there (as reported in *The Economist*, 31 March 1990).
9. See *The Economist*, 16 March 1991 for a description of the difficulties associated with this takeover.
10. A pan-German timetable is expected before then (as reported in *The Economist*, 30 June 1990).
11. Tirapolsky and Globokar (1984) provide some indication of the scale of FRG–GDR interfirm industrial cooperation at the time. They maintain that cooperation dates from the early-1970s, with the first really large contract being signed in 1976 for a value of 1.1–1.2 billion D-marks by the chemical firm, Friedrich Uhde GmbH, a subsidiary of the Hoechst group. The authors quote a list kept by the CEDUCEE which indicates that over the 1970–83 period most inter-German industrial cooperation occurred in the chemical industry (with contracts valued at 2 billion D-Marks), followed by the metallurgical sector (with contracts of 1 billion D-Marks). Despite the importance of the electrotechnical and light industry for the GDR economy, a study by the DIW (in Pohled ed., 1977, p. 253) estimates

that there were contracts worth only 300 million D-Marks for this sector over the 1970–82 period. In addition to these large turnkey projects, writing in 1984, Tirapolski and Globokar suggested that there may have been other agreements worth 400 million D-Marks. By November 1989 there were also large-scale indusrial cooperation projects involving Volkswagen, AEG, Salamander (which produces shoes in the East), Veba (the energy group), and Thyssen (8).

12. These forecasts were given by Otto Schlecht, the Under Secretary for Economics, as reported in *Il Sole-24 Ore*, 12 January 1991.
13. The DIW of Berlin, the HWWA of Hamburg, the IFO of Munich, the IWW of Kiel and the RWI of Essen.
14. *Il Sole-24 Ore*, 5 February 1991.
15. *Il Sole-24 Ore*, 12 January 1991.
16. *Agra Europe*, 14 September 1990.
17. Including meat products, dairy products, sugar and sugar products, cereal products and vegetables.
18. In particular there was a deal worth 1 million D-marks of exports to the Soviet Union, including 140,000 tonnes of beef and 100,000 of pork. There were also exports of 30,000 tonnes of beef and 10,000 tonnes of live animals to Romania (*Agra Europe*, 14 September, 1990).
19. *La Repubblica*, 17 April 1990.
20. *The Economist*, 22 September 1990.
21. *The Economist*, 30 June 1990.
22. European Report No. 1608, 1990.
23. European Report, No. 1624, 23 October 1990.
24. *Agra Europe*, 18 April 1990.
25. *Agra Europe* 18 April 1990.
26. Irmer Report of the European Parliament (1982), p. 26.
27. Garland, J. (1985), p. 5.

A study carried out by the German DIW (in Pohled ed. 1977, p. 253) concluded that the special provisions involved transfers from the FRG government to the Democratic Republic and to FRG businessmen involved in trade with the Democratic Republic, but stated that quantification of these transfers was extremely difficult.

The other EC member states repeatedly expressed fears that the special German provisions might lead to competitive distortions, market disruption or potential abuses. For instance a possible abuse might relate to the question of 'country of origin' by which GDR products could be mistaken for those produced in the Federal Republic and re-exported to other EC countries. Another problem might be that of 'back door entry', by which other Central-East European countries could put their goods on EC markets via the Democratic and Federal Republic.

A European Parliament Report (the Irmer Report (1982), pp. 26–7) considered the possibility of such abuses as relatively small scale. In 1981 the EC Commission put the sum of GDR exports being re-exported to other EC states at 44 million D-Marks compared with total imports from the Democratic Republic of 4,066 million D-Marks, and total FRG exports to other EC countries of 130,566 million D-Marks at the time (as reported in *Agra Europe*, 23 March 1990). The estimates of these re-exports are based on FRG statistics, as the Community had no checks on this trade, nor did it have any legal redress which is the responsibility of the FRG customs. Cases of abuse have been difficult to prove, and those that have been discovered were both minimal and infrequent.

28. *Agra Europe,* 18 May 1990.
29. *The Economist,* 28 July 1990.
30. *Agra Europe,* 9 March 1990.
31. *Agra Europe,* 9 March 1990.
32. *Agra Europe,* 23 March 1990.
33. *Agra Europe,* 6 July 1990.
34. All these statistics are taken from *Agra Europe,* 12 October 1990.
35. *Agra Europe,* 28 September 1990.
36. *The Economist,* 23 June 1990.
37. European Report No. 1608, 1990.
38. All the statistics in this paragraph are taken from European Report No. 1608, 1990.
39. The scale of the task is considerable, given, for instance, the 65,000 employees in the Kominat producing cotton, 30,000 for textile machinery, 28,000 for machine tools, and 40,000 for footwear.
40. European Report 6 March 1990, and No. 1608 of 1990.
41. European Report No. 1608.

13

Conclusions: The outlook for economic relations between the European Community and Central-East Europe

It is extremely difficult to make predictions about future developments in Central-East Europe and their links to the European Community, but here an attempt will be made to consider four fundamental questions, namely:

1. Is the economic and political transformation of Central-East Europe irreversible?
2. Are the aid measures taken by the West to promote the transformation of Central-East Europe adequate and appropriate, and in particular was it a mistake to extend aid to the Soviet Union?
3. What are the prospects for East–West trade and joint ventures in Europe, and what is to become of the 'special mechanisms' used by the West in its trade with non-market economies?
4. What is the likely future configuration of Europe?

13.1 Is the transition process irreversible?

In trying to assess the prospects of irreversibility of the transformation process, it is essential to distinguish according to the Central-East European country in question. East Germany undoubtedly represents an extreme case, with change proceeding at breakneck speed, though even here the burden in terms of social unrest and budgetary cost was substantially underestimated. As a result of the additional public spending, and fears of inflationary pressures, German interest rates were raised considerably, leading to complaints on the part of other Western industrial countries that they were being forced to bear part of the cost of

German unification. Despite these difficulties, and uncertainty about the time required and scale of bankruptcies and unemployment involved, few would question the irreversibility of the process.

This would also appear to be the case for Poland, Hungary and Czechoslovakia, where indeed one of the main aims of the privatisation processes currently underway is precisely to ensure that change cannot be reversed. However, it is difficult not to conclude that a long and difficult process is just at its beginning, exacerbated by the higher energy prices that these countries will have to pay. It is estimated that the use of world prices in intra-CMEA trade from January 1991 could increase the energy bill of the smaller Central-East European countries by some 90–120%. Moreover, Iraq had foreign debts with all three countries which were being repaid in the form of oil exports. Further falls in production and rising unemployment can be expected before improvements begin.

In Bulgaria and, to an even greater extent, Romania the liberalisation of prices and radical policies to meet the underlying economic weakness have led to social protest, while the political situation would seem to be somewhat precarious, reflecting the difficulty of introducing democracy overnight in countries where there was no longer a democratic culture.

In the Soviet Union, after five years of patently unsuccessful attempts to reform the system from within, radical programmes for the transition to a market economy were finally proposed in 1990. However, fear of social unrest and the need to reach political compromise led to a rather watered down and inconsistent version of these proposals eventually being adopted. The incomplete nature of these measures, the vacillating reform debate and the resistance to implementation of change at all levels meant that perestroika actually worsened the economic situation and discredited the reform movement in the opinion of much of the population.

Peristroika succeeded in breaking down the vertical hierarchy of a command economy without replacing it with a market. The announcement and non-implementation of price increases until April 1991 encouraged hoarding, adding to the growing shortages. Monetisation of an increasing budget deficit contributed to an enormous monetary overhang, undermining confidence in the rouble and rendering price reform ever more difficlut. Republics began to reform their price systems autonomously, closing their borders and again contributing to the deteriorating supply situation. The system of multiple retail networks with state shops where goods were cheap but in scarce supply, and cooperative and black markets where goods were plentiful but expensive encouraged purchase for resale, and theft. On some estimates 20% of products was 'disappearing' between the stores and the shelves in state shops. Legal loopholes in the measures aimed at decentralisation and the creation of cooperatives encouraged dubious activities, and provided opportunities for speculators. Widespread apathy, absenteeism and a wave of strikes further contributed to the fall in production.

At the same time glasnost permitted an awareness of how bad the situation actually was, and created expectations among radical and separatist groups. Gorbachev attempted to cling to a rapidly disappearing middle ground between Republics and radicals demanding more autonomy than he was prepared to give, and the conservatives who were determined to preserve the integrity of the Union. In late 1990, his choice fell with the latter whose power base lay with the army, KGB and parts of the Communist Party and bureaucracy. His choice was probably influenced by the experience of 'losing' the smaller Central-East European countries and fears of a domino effect if he gave in to the claims of any separatist group. Gorbachev's presumed aim was to restore order so that perestroika could continue, but forfeiting the support of many reformers and relying on the forces most opposed to change, it is doubtful how far this will be possible. None the less it seems probable that some form of market-orientated economy will emerge. It is also open to question whether priority for the Union can be imposed in the face of claims, not just on the part of the Baltic States, but also from Republics such as Moldavia, Georgia, Armenia and even Russia. The situation is complicated by the fact that boundaries do not coincide with ethnic groups. Whatever the outcome, it is no longer possible to separate the question of economic change from that of nationalities.

13.2 Western aid measures

On balance, the measures taken by the Group of 24 Western countries to aid the transformation process in Central-East Europe would seem timely and relatively well adapted to the needs of the recipient country, thanks also to the practice by which each Central-East European country must write a memorandum of its requirements. The assistance given was fairly substantial, especially when it took the form of disposal of unwanted EC agricultural surpluses as food aid. The EC also proved rather effective in coordinating the measures of Western countries.

The main areas in which there would seem to be scope for further measures appear to be in the context of trade concessions (discussed below) and contingency plans to meet possible requests for immigration on a massive scale.

In April 1991 the Paris Club agreed to substantial debt relief for Poland, meeting the claim that the level of indebtedness was such that it was threatening the transformation process. There would seem to be a strong case for extending such measures to Hungary and Bulgaria if requested. As Nuti (1990b) points out, to some extent this would simply be a recognition of the status quo as the value of this debt on secondary markets is extremely low.

The question of immigration is extremely sensitive, especially given the potential scale of requests if the situation in the Soviet Union deteriorates and people are allowed to leave. Clearly, this is not a question to be faced by the EC alone, but in conjunction with countries such as Israel, the United States, Canada and Australia.

Distinction does, however, have to be made for those countries likely to sign association agreements (i.e. Hungary, Czechoslovakia and Poland), and who are potentially EC members. An essential element of these agreements is the 'phased introduction' of free movement of labour. Even allowing the right to work temporarily in the Community could make a crucial contribution to the recovery of these countries, by containing unemployment figures, allowing training to take place, and improving the balance of payments through workers' remittances.

The question of aid to the Soviet Union remains extremely controversial. Withdrawal of aid could force Gorbachev into even greater reliance on the conservative forces opposed to reform, reducing the chances of perestroika still further. Even with this risk, however, it is difficult not to conclude that aid should be conditional on progress towards economic and political transformation. This is one of the few ways in which the West has shown its reaction to the violation of civil liberties in the Baltic States.

13.3 Prospects for trade

Early indications suggest that the collapse in intra-CMEA trade will be far more rapid than was initially envisaged. This is perhaps surprising given the large percentage of intra-CMEA in the total trade of these countries (55% of exports and 58% of imports in 1988) and the reliance of the smaller Central-East European countries on energy imports from the Soviet Union.

However, the Soviet Union was unable to take full advantage of the higher prices for its energy exports following the adoption of world prices in intra-CMEA trade because of production difficulties and growing domestic consumption. At the same time the smaller Central-East European countries were reluctant to continue exporting to the Soviet Union because of Soviet payment difficulties.

Ultimately, the extent to which Central-East European countries can switch to East–West trade will depend on their success in economic restructuring. This is the key both to improving export supply response and enabling essential imports to continue. The imports required relate not just to technology but also to consumer goods which can provide the necessary incentives.

East–West joint ventures have experienced a boom since 1987 in response to official encouragement on the part of Central-East European countries and easier enabling legislation. However, here also the situation varies to a great extent according to the country in question, depending *inter alia* on the overall economic climate of the host country.

Despite the high degree of uncertainty the huge Soviet market has attracted a large number of joint ventures (possibly 2000 by the end of 1990), but many of these were not fully operational. Those that were tended to be concentrated in the service sector and in particular in activities such as tourism, hotels, restaurants and transport where hard currency could be earned directly and where repatriation of profits was less of a problem.

In countries such as Hungary, Poland and Czechoslovakia, in some cases joint ventures have been able to realise the objectives of both sides, for instance enabling the Eastern partner to obtain know-how, and the Western firm to penetrate the Central-East European market; but the operating difficulties should not be underestimated.

As argued in the first half of this book, the EC (like other Western countries) used various mechanisms in its trade with Central-East Europe, including anti-dumping measures, quotas, safeguards, voluntary export restraints, tariffs, and variable levies. The way in which these were applied on trade with 'non-market economies' was said to place the Central-East European countries at a disadvantage vis-à-vis other exporters to the Community. With the economic transformation of Central-East Europe, what then are the chances of liberalisation of this trade?

Some of the mechanisms used against non-market economies have already been adjusted, with, for example, the reduction or elimination of quotas, the granting of GSP and other trade concessions, enabling at least the smaller Central-East European countries to move to a higher position in the 'hierarchy' of EC trade preferences. Depending on the degree of transformation reached it seems likely that some of these countries will be reclassified as market-orientated ecomomies for the purpose of anti-dumping rules.

However, with regard to other measures, the key to international trade liberalisation lies in the GATT negotiations. Even with a successful outcome to the Uruguay Round, there are certain sectors (notably agriculture, textiles and steel) in which excess supply would seem to preclude completely free trade, and the prerogative of being affected by 'special trade mechanisms' is likely remain not just for non-market economies, but for all exporting countries. In such sectors the main hope for international trade negotiations would seem to be in encouraging the substitution of domestic policies with fewer adverse implications on world trade, ensuring a more 'equitable' division of world markets, and convincing countries to undertake massive economic restructuring.

13.4 The new configuration of Europe

With the collapse of the CMEA and the revival of the EC integration process in the late 1980s, the newly autonomous smaller Central-East European countries found a pole of attraction in the Community, which responded by offering trade and cooperation agreements and subsequently association agreements to those countries that were sufficiently advanced in transformation. The possibility of ultimate accession in some cases has not been excluded.

Though there has been discussion of the creation of a European Confederation or 'Common European House', possibly building on the CSCE or Council of Europe, and of forming new integration or association units among Central-East European countries, the initiatives associated with the EC are undoubtedly the most far-reaching and furthest advanced.

Widening of European Community membership is also likely to occur in other directions, though the questions of who and when have yet to be decided. Negotiations for the creation of a European Economic Area with the EFTA are also going ahead. The problem then becomes how the deepening of the Community is to be reconciled with the widening. Both the Single Market and economic and monetary union would seem to require increased transfers to less-favoured areas, especially in an enlarged Community, while a 'Europe of differing speeds' may be the price to pay for the required degree of convergence to enable economic and monetary union to go ahead. The difficulties of decision-making in a larger Community will have to be resolved in the context of political union. It remains to be seen whether the European integration process can maintain the momentum required for such far-reaching changes.

Bibliography

Adams, F.G. and Klein, S.A. (eds.) (1978) *Stabilizing World Commodity Markets: Analysis, Practice and Policy,* Lexington Books, London and Toronto.

Aganbegyan, A.G. (1988) *The Economic Challenge of Perestroika,* Indiana University Press, Bloomington and Indianapolis.

Amann, E. and Marin, D. (1989) 'Barter in international trade', Paper presented at a meeting of the Working Group of Comparative Economic Systems, European University Institute, 5 May.

Anderson, K. and Tyres, R. (1984) 'European Community grain and meat policies: Effects on international prices, trade and welfare', *European Review of Agricultural Economics,* vol. 11, pp.367–94.

Åslund, A. (1989) *Gorbachev's Struggle for Economic Reform,* Pinter Publishers, London.

Avery, G. (1988) 'Agricultural policy: The conclusions of the European Council', *Common Market Law Review,* vol. 25, pp.523–39.

Balassa, B. (1967) 'Trade creation and trade diversion in the European Common Market', *Economic Journal,* vol. 77, pp.1–22.

Balassa, B. (ed.) (1975) *European Economic Integration,* North Holland/ American Elsevier, Amsterdam, Oxford and New York.

Balassa, B. (1988) 'Agricultural policies and international resource allocation', *European Review of Agricultural Economics,* vol.15, pp.159–71.

Bale, M.D. and Lutz, E. (1979) 'The effects of trade interventions on international price instability', *American Journal of Agricultural Economics,* vol.61, no.3.

Barizza, F. (1984) *Il commercio della Comunità Economica Europea con il resto del Mondo,* Il Mulino, Bologna.

Basevi, G. (1990) 'Transferimenti verso i paesi dell'Europa Orientale e implicazioni per l'unificazione monetaria ed economica della Comunità Europea'. *Note Economiche,* vol.2, pp.308–21.

Bel, J. (1988) 'Les relations entre la Communauté et le Conseil d'Assistance Economique Mutuelle', *Revue du Marché Commun,* no. 318, pp.313–16.

Bertsch, G.K. (1985) 'Technology transfer and technology controls: A synthesis of the Western–Soviet relation', Paper presented at a colloquium on 'East–West Trade and Financial Relations', European University Institute, 4–6 June.

Beseler, J.F. and Williams, N. (1986) *Anti-Dumping and Anti-Subsidy Law: The European Communities*, Sweet and Maxwell, London.

Bolz, K. and Pissula, P. (1986) 'GATT's role in East–West trade', *Inter-economics*, March–April, pp.102–6.

Brada, J.C. (1989) 'The Soviet Union and the GATT: A framework for Western policy', *Soviet Economy*, vol.5, no.4, pp.360–71.

Brada, J. and Wädekin, K.-E. (eds.) (1988) *Socialist Agriculture in Transition*, Westview Press, Boulder, Colorado.

Brus, W. and Laski, K. (1989) *From Marx to the Market: Socialism in Search of a System*, Clarendon Press, Oxford.

Buckwell, A.E., Harvey, D.R., Thomson, K.J. and Parton, K.A. (1982) *The Costs of the Common Agricultural Policy*, Croom Helm, London and Canberra.

Bureau of Agricultural Economics (1985) *Agricultural Policies in the European Community: Their Origins, Nature and Effects on Production and Trade*, Policy Monograph No.2, Australian Government Publishing Service, Canberra.

Burniaux, J-M. (1988) 'Effetti intersettoriali della liberalizzazione della PAC', pp.75–107 in Tarditi, S., Thomson, K.J., Pierani, P. and Croci Angelini, E. (1988) *Liberalizzazione del commercio agricolo e Comunità Europea*, Istituto Nazionale di Economia Agraria, Il Mulino, Bologna, and in English as *Agricultural Trade Liberalization and the European Community*, Oxford University Press.

Chapman, S. (1986) 'The economic relations between the EEC and the CMEA: A survey of problems and prospects', *Comunità Internazionale*, no.3, pp.421–49.

Chilosi, A. (1990a) 'Poland's programme of economic transformation: How has the West helped and what else should it do?' Paper presented at a NATO conference, Brussels, April.

Chilosi, A. (1990b) 'Il processo di trasformazione economica ed istituzionale nell'Est europeo: il caso polacco', *Note Economiche*, vol.2, December, pp.359–87.

Chiusano, V. (1985) *Dossier CEE-Comecon*, Centre Européen du Kirchberg, Luxembourg.

Choi, Ying Pik, Chung, Hwa Soo and Nicolas, Marian (1985) *The Multi-Fibre Arrangement in Theory and Practice*, Frances Pinter, Dover, NH.

Clavaux, F.J. (1969) 'The import elasticity as a yardstick for measuring trade creation', *Economia Internazionale*, vol.22, pp.602–12.

Clayton, E. (1985) 'Rising demand and unstable supply: The prospects for Soviet grain imports', *American Journal of Economics*, vol.67, pp.1044–8.

Cline, W.R. (1987) *The Future of World Trade in Textiles and Apparel*, Institute for International Economics, Washington D.C..

Club de Bruxelles (1988) *Trade Relations between the EEC and Eastern Europe*, European News Agency, Brussels.

Colman, D. (1988) 'The CAP in conflict with trade and development', *European Review of Agricultural Economics*, vol.15, pp.123–35.

Cook, E. (1985) 'Soviet agricultural policies and the feed–livestock sector', *American Journal of Agricultural Economics*, vol.67, pp.1049–54.

Cova, C. (1989) 'La CEE at la Pérestroika', *Revue du Marché Commun*, no.330, September–October.

Crane, K. and Kohler, D.F. (1985) 'Removing export-credit subsidies to the Soviet bloc: Who gets hurt and by how much?' *Journal of Comparative Economics*, vol.9, pp.371–90.

Cristofoli, A.M. (1981) 'L'export ungherese di prodotti agricoli e alimentari', *Est Ovest*, no.1, pp.25–9.

Csaba, L. (1990) 'External implications of economic reforms in the European centrally-planned economies', *Soviet and East European Trade*, Summer, pp.81–105.

Csaki, C. (1990) 'Policy reform and structural changes in Hungarian agriculture', Paper presented at a conference on 'New Tendencies in Agricultural Policies and in Trade Relations in Europe' organised by the INEA (Istituto Nazionale di Economia Agraria), 19 April, Rome.

Csikos-Nagy, B. and Young, D.G. (eds.) (1986) *East–West Economic Relations in the Changing Global Environment*, Macmillan, London.

Csizmadia, E. and Székely, M. (1986) *Food Economy in Hungary*, Académiai Kiado', Budapest.

Cutler, R.M. (1987) 'Harmonizing EEC–CMEA relations: Never the twain shall meet?' *International Affairs*, vol.63, no.2, pp.259–70.

Daviddi, R. (1988) The Evolution of Soviet Foreign trade. An Attempt to Assess Soviet Dependence on Foreign Trade, PhD thesis, European University Institute, Florence.

Daviddi, R. (1990a) Tensioni inflazionistiche, deficit di bilancio ed eccesso di liquidità in Unione Sovietica. Une prima riflessione, Banca Toscana, *Studi e Informazioni*, pp.167–73.

Daviddi, R. (1990b) 'Riforme strutturale e politiche di stabilizzazione in Unione Sovietica', Paper presented at the XXXI Annual Meeting of the Società Italiana degli Economisti, Rome, 2–3 November, 1990.

Davis, C. and Charemza, W. (eds.) (1989) *Models of disequilibrium and shortage in centrally-planned economies*, Chapman and Hall, London and New York.

Denton, R. (1987) 'The non-market economy rules of the European Community's anti-dumping and countervailing duties legislation', *International and Comparative Law Quarterly*, vol.36, pp.198–239.

de Puifferrat, J. (1984) 'La CEE et les pays de l'Est', *Revue du Marché Commun*, no.273, January, pp.25–30.

Dietz, R. (1985) 'Differences between intra-CMEA and world market prices: Some of their implications', Paper presented at the conference on 'East–West Trade and Financial Relations', European University Institute, 4–6 June, 1985.

Di Leo, R. (1986) 'La politica agraria di M. Gorbachev', *La Questione Agraria*, no.24, pp.59–83.

Dûchene, F., Szczepanik, E. and Legg, W. (1985) *New Limits on European Agriculture: Politics and the Common Agricultural Policy*, Croom Helm, Beckenham, Kent.

EC Commission, *The Agricultural Situation in the European Community*, various years, Brussels.

EC, First, Second, Third, Fourth and Fifth Annual Reports of the Commission of the EC on the Community's Anti-Dumping and Anti-Subsidy Activities, respectively: COM(83)519, COM(84)721, COM(86)308, COM(87)178 and COM(88)92, Brussels.

EC Commission (1990) 'Stabilisation, libéralisation et dévolution des competences. Evaluation de la situation économique et du processus de réforme en Union Sovietique', *Economie Européenne*, no.45, December, Brussels.

ECE (United Nations Economic Commission for Europe) (1988a) *East-West Joint Ventures. Economic, Business, Financial and Legal Aspects*, United Nations, New York.

ECE (United Nations Economic Commission for Europe) (1988b) *East–West Joint Ventures*, United Nations, New York.

ECE (United Nations Economic Commission for Europe) (1988c) *Economic Bulletin for Europe*, vol.40, no.3. Pergammon Press, Oxford.

ECE (United Nations Economic Commission for Europe) (1989a) *East–West Joint Ventures News*, no.2, July.

ECE (United Nations Economic Commission for Europe) (1989b) *Economic Bulletin for Europe*, vol.41, United Nations, Geneva.

ECE (United Nations Economic Commission for Europe) (1989c) *Promotion of Trade through Industrial Cooperation. Statistical Survey of Recent Trends in East-West Industrial Cooperation*, United Nations, Geneva.

ECE (United Nations Economic Commission for Europe) (1990) 'Economic transformation in Hungary and Poland'. Reports prepared by a group of independent experts, *European Economy*, March 1990, Brussels.

El Agraa, A.M. (1985) *The Economics of the European Community*, Philip Allan, Hemel Hempstead.

Emerson, M. *et al.* (1988) *The Economics of 1992: The EC Commission's Assessment of the Economic Effects of Completing the Internal Market*, Oxford University Press, p.304.

European Parliament Document 425/74, The Klepsch Report, *Report on the European Community's Relations with the East European State-Trading Countries and Comecon*, European Parliament, Luxembourg.

European Parliament Document 129/77 of 8 June 1977, Cousté Report, *Report on the Harmonization of Export Credit Systems*, European Parliament, Luxembourg.

European Parliament Document 89/78 of 11 May 1978, Schmidt Report, *Report on the State of Relations between the EEC and East European State Trading Countries and Comecon*, European Parliament, Luxembourg.

European Parliament Document 51/79 of 11 April 1979, Jung Report, *Report on the EEC's relations with the Comecon in the field of maritime shipping*, European Parliament, Luxembourg.

European Parliament (1981), *Debate on the Report of the European Parliament's Anti-Dumping Activities*, Working Document I-422/81, European Parliament, Luxembourg.

European Parliament Document 846/81 of 8 January 1981, Aigner Report, *Report on Exports of Community Agricultural Products to the USSR and State-Trading Countries*, European Parliament, Luxembourg.

European Parliament Document 1-424/81 of 28 August 1981, De Clercq Report, *Report on Relations between the EEC and East European State-Trading Countries and the CMEA*, European Parliament, Luxembourg.

European Parliament Document 1-531 of 28 July 1982, Irmer Report, *Report on the Relations between the European Community and the East European State-Trading Countries and the CMEA (Comecon)*, European Parliament, Luxembourg.

European Parliament Document A 2-111/85 of 7 October 1985, Bettiza Report, *Report on Relations between the European Community and the Countries of Central and Eastern Europe*, European Parliament, Luxembourg.

European Parliament Document 1-1482/83 of 24 March 1984, Delorozoy Report, *Report on Export Credit Subsidies*, European Parliament, Luxembourg.

European Parliament Document A2-187/86 of 19 December 1986, Seeler Report, *Report on Relations between the European Community and the Council for Mutual Economic Assistance (CMEA) and the East European Member States of the CMEA*, European Parliament, Luxembourg.

European Parliament Report of 14 June 1988, Ercini Report, *Report on the Proposal from the Commission of the EC to the Council (COM(88)) 333 Final for a Draft Decision on the Conclusion of the Joint Declaration on the Establishment of Official Relations between the EEC and CMEA*, European Parliament, Luxembourg.

European Parliament Document of 18 July 1988, Hänsch Report, *Report on Political Relations between the European Community and the Soviet Union*, European Parliament, Luxembourg.

European Parliament Report of 20 October 1988, Zarges Report, *Report on the Proposal from the Commission of the EC to the Council (SEC(88) 1332 final – Doc.C 2 158/88) for a Decision on the Conclusion of an Agreement on Trade and Commercial and Economic Cooperation between the EEC and the Hungarian People's Republic*, European Parliament, Luxembourg.

European Parliament Document EN (1988) 2110 E, M. Toussaint, *Restraints on Strategic Exports and US–EC Technology Transfer,* Report to the Committee on External Economic Relations, August, European Parliament, Luxembourg.

European Parliament Document EN (1989) A 2.31/89/A, M. Toussaint, *Second Report on Restraints on Strategic Exports and US-EC Technology Transfer*, Report to the Committee on External Economic Relations, March, European Parliament, Luxembourg .

European Parliament (1990) *The Eastern European Countries* 1/5/1990, European Parliament, Luxembourg, pp.1–146.

Eurostat (1990) *Echanges CE-CAEM, 1979–87*, European Parliament, Luxembourg.

Evans, A. (1990) 'The application of EC anti-dumping rules to third countries in Europe, *World Competition*, vol.13, pp.5–17.

Fallenbuchl, Z. (1983) *East–West Technology Transfer. Study of Poland 1971–1980*, OECD, Paris.

Feld, W.J. (1984) 'The CMEA and the European Community: A troubled courtship', *Journal of European Integration*, vol.7, nos.2–3, pp.197–219.

Ford Runge, C. and Stanton, G.H. (1988) 'The political economy of the Uruguay Round negotiations: A view from Geneva', *American Journal of Agricultural Economics*, December, pp.1146–55.

Franklin, D. (1983) *The Prospects for East–West Trade: Policies, Indebtedness, Exports*, Economist Intelligence Unit Special Report No. 154, London.

Frantseva, I. (1988) *Otnosheniya SZV–EC: istoria, sovremennost, perspektivi. (CMEA–EC Relations, History, Present Situation, Prospects)*, International Economic Relations Series, Information Office on Capitalist Countries in Europe and North America, Moscow.

Frantseva, I. (1990) 'The future of CMEA–EC relations and economic reforms in Eastern Europe and the USSR', Paper presented at the First Conference of the European Association for Comparative Economic Studies, Verona, 27–29 September.

Friessen, C.M. (1976) *The Political Economy of East–West Trade,* Praeger Publishers, New York.

Frohberg, K., Fischer, G. and Parikh, K. (1988) 'Effetti internazionale della liberalizzazione della PAC', in Tarditi, S., Thomson, K.J., Pierani, P. and Croci Angelini, E. (1988) *Liberalizzazione del commercio agricolo e Comunità Europea,* Istituto Nazionale di Economia Agraria, Il Mulino, Bologna, and in English as *Agricultural Trade Liberalization and the European Community,* Oxford University Press.

Frydman, R., Wellisz, S. and Kolodko, G.W. (1990) 'Stabilization in Poland: A progress report', Paper for a conference on 'Exchange Rate Policies of Less-Developed Market and Socialist Economies', Berlin, 10–12 May 1990.

Gale Johnson, D. and McConnell Brooks, K. (1983) *Prospects for Soviet Agriculture in the 1980's,* Indiana University Press, Bloomington and Indianapolis.

Garland, J. (1985) 'GDR–FRG relations', Paper presented at a conference on 'East–West Trade and Financial Relations', European University Institute, 4–6 June.

Gati, C. (1990) *The Bloc that Failed.* Indiana University Press, Bloomington and Indianapolis.

Giroux, A. (1984) 'La difficile mutation de l'agriculture soviétique', *Le Courrier des Pays de l'Est,* no.285, June, pp.3–21.

Giroux, A. (1986) 'Gorbatchev et l'agriculture: cinq ans pour convaincre', *Le Courrier des Pays de l'Est,* no.305, April, pp.3–21.

Giroux, A. (1989) 'Le Plenum de mars 1989 sur l'agriculture sovietique: un compromis', *Le Courrier des Pays de l'Est,* no.338, March 1989, pp.65–9.

Glibert, F. (1983) 'Réassurance et Coassurance des risques politiques', *Droit et Practique du Commerce International,* Tome 9, no.2, pp.261–76.

Gomez, M. (1984) 'La coopération industrielle tripartite: mythe ou réalité', *Le Courrier des Pays de l'Est,* no.284, May.

Graziani, G. (1982) *Comecon, domination et dépendences,* Maspero, Paris, 1982.

Graziani, G. (1987) 'La CEE e il Comecon: Concorrenza e Complementarità', in Parboni, R. and Wallerstein, I. (eds.) (1987) *L'Europa e l'economia politica del sistema-mondo,* Franco Angeli, Milan.

Graziani, G. (1990) 'Le joint venture in Unione Sovietica. Aspetti economici', *Note Economiche,* vol.2, pp.461–89.

Grosfeld, I. (1990) 'Prospects for privatisation in Poland', *European Economy,* March, pp.139–50.

Groux, J. and Manin, P. (1984) *The European Communities in the International Legal Order,* Office for Official Publications of the EC, Luxembourg.

Guth, E. and Aeikens, H. (1980) *Implications of the Second Enlargement for the Mediterranean and ACP Policies of the European Community,* European Information Development X/235/80, EC Commission, Brussels.

Gutman, P. (1981) 'Tripartite industrial cooperation and East Europe' in a compendium of papers submitted to the Joint Economic Committee, US Government Printing Office, Washington, D.C..

Gwiazda, A. (1990) 'The revival of countertrade in East–West economic cooperation', *World Competition,* vol.13, no.3, pp.65–74.

Hardt, J. (ed.) (1977) *East European Economies post-Helsinki,* US Joint Economic Committee, US Government Printing Office, Washington D.C..

Hare, P. (1989) 'The economics of shortage in the centrally planned economies' in Davis, C. and Charemza, W. (eds.), *Models of Disequilibrium and Shortage in Centrally-Planned Economies*, Chapman and Hall, London and New York, pp.49–82.

Hare, P.G. (1990a) 'Reform of enterprise regulation in Hungary – from 'tutelage' to market' *European Economy*, May, pp.35–54.

Hare, P.G. (1990b) 'From central planning to market economy: Some microeconomic issues', *The Economic Journal*, 100, June, pp.581–95.

Harris, S., Swinbank, A. and Wilkinson, G. (1983) *The Food and Farm Policies of the European Community*, John Wiley and Sons, Chichester.

Hartford, K. (1987) 'Socialist countries in the world food system: The Soviet Union, Hungary and China', *Food Research Institute Studies*, vol.xx, no.3, pp.181–243.

Hartmann, M. and Schmitz, P.M. (1988) 'EC agricultural reform policy – the beginning of a new form of protectionism?' *Intereconomics*, July–August, pp.151–8.

Hedlund, S. (1984) *Crisis in Soviet Agriculture*. Croom Helm, London and Sydney, p.228.

Hillman, A.L. (1990) 'Macroeconomic policy in Hungary and its microeconomic implications', *European Economy*, March, pp.55–66.

Hine, R.C. (1985) *The Political Economy of European Trade: An Introduction to the Policies of the EEC*, Harvester Wheatsheaf, Hemel Hempstead.

Hirsch, S. (1988) 'Anti-dumping actions in Brussels and East–West trade', *The World Economy*, vol.11, no.4, pp.465–84.

Holzman, F.D. (1974) *Foreign Trade under Central Planning*, Harvard University Press.

Holzman, F.D. (1976) *International Trade under Communism: Politics and Economics*, Macmillan, London.

Honma, M. and Hayami, Y. (1986) 'Structure of agricultural protection in industrial countries', *Journal of International Economics*, vol.20, pp.115–29.

House of Commons Paper 51, Session 1988/89 of 26 January 1989, Trade and Industry Second Report, *Trade with Eastern Europe*.

Huerni, B. (1989) 'European integration: West and East', *Intereconomics*, July–August.

IMF, World Bank, OECD and BERD (1990) *The Economy of the USSR*, The World Bank, Washington, D.C..

Jackson, J.H. (1988) 'Consistency of export-restraint arrangements with the GATT', *The World Economy*, vol.11, no.4, pp.485–500.

Jampel, W. and Lhomel, E. (1989) 'L'industrie agro-alimentaire en Europe de l'Est', *Le Courrier des Pays de l'Est*, no.338, March, pp.3–32.

Johnston, B.F. (1989) 'The political economy of agricultural development in the Soviet Union and China', *Food Research Institute Studies*, vol. XXI, no. 2, pp.97–137.

Josling, T.E. (1980) *Developed-Country Agricultural Policy and Developing-Country Supplies: The Case of Wheat*, Research Report 14, International Food Policy Research Institute, Washington.

Josling, T. (1981) 'Price, stock and trade policies and the functioning of international markets,' pp.161–84, in A. Valdés (ed.) *Food Security for the Developing Countries*, Westview Press, Boulder, Colorado.

Kaser, M. (1990) 'The technology of decontrol: Some macroeconomic issues', *The Economic Journal*, vol.100, June, pp.596–615.

Keller, C., Matejka, H. and Nyiri, K. (1990) *European Integration and East–West Relations. Papers presented to the Sixth Swiss-Hungarian Roundtable 12–16 September 1988*, Graduate Institute of International Studies, Geneva.

Koekkoek, K.A. and Mennes, L.B.M. (1986) 'Liberalising the multi fibre arrangement: Some aspects for the Netherlands, the EC, and the LDCs', *Journal of World Trade Law*, vol.12, no.2 March–April, pp.142–67.

Koester, U. (1982) *Policy Options for the Grain Economy of the European Community: Implications for Developing Countries*, Research Report 35, International Food Policy Research Institute, Washington.

Koester, U. and Schmitz, P.M. (1982) 'The EC sugar market policy and developing countries', *European Review of Agricultural Economics,* vol.9, pp.183–204.

Koester, U. and Terwitte, H. (1988) 'Breakthrough in agricultural policy, or another policy failure?' *Intereconomics,* May–June, pp.103–8.

Kokushkina, I. (1990) 'Market of the countries which belong to the CMEA: Conditions for creation and trends of development', Paper presented at the First Conference of the European Association of Comparative Economic Studies, Verona, 27–29 September.

Kornai, J. (1980) *The Economics of Shortage*, North Holland, Amsterdam.

Kornai, J. (1986a) 'The soft budget constraint', *Kyklos*, vol.39(1).

Kornai, J. (1986b) 'The Hungarian reform process: Visions, hopes and realities', *Journal of Economic Literature*, vol.24, no.4, pp.1687–1737.

Kostecki, M. (1979) *East–West Trade and the GATT System*, Trade Policy Research Centre, Macmillan, London.

Kostecki, M. (1987) 'Export-restraint arrangements and trade liberalization', *The World Economy*, vol.10, no.4, pp.425–53.

Koves, A. (1983) '"Implicit subsidies" and some issues of economic relations within the CMEA (remarks on the analysis made by Michael Marresse and Jan Vanous)', *Acta Oeconomica*, vol.31, no.1/2, pp.126–36.

Kristoff, B. and Ballinger, N. (1989) 'Agricultural trade liberalization in a multi-sector world model', *Agricultural Economics*, vol.3, pp.83–98.

Lafeber, F.N. and Lafeber-Strazalkowska, D.B. (1990) 'Poland's future: Europe or Latin America', Paper presented at the First Conference of the European Association for Comparative Economic Systems (EACES), Verona, September 17–29.

Lavigne, M. (1985) *Economie internationale des pays socialistes,* Arman Collin – Collection U, Paris.

Lavigne, M. (1990) 'Per un nuovo raggruppamento regionale nell'Europa dell'Est', *Politica Internazionale*, nos.5–7, May–July, pp.120–6.

Levcik, F. and Stankovsky, J. (1979) *Industrial Cooperation between East and West*, M.C. Sharpe Inc., White Plains, New York.

Levcik, F. and Skolka, J.V. (1984) *East–West Technology Transfer. A Study of Czechoslovakia*, OECD, Paris.

Litvak, L.A. and McMillan, C.H. (1974) 'Intergovernmental co-operation agreements as a framework for East–West trade and technology transfer', in C.H. McMillan (ed.) (1974) *Changing Perspectives in East–West Commerce*, Lexington Books, London and Toronto, pp.151–172.

Lhomel, E. (1989) 'Les productions agricoles en Europe de l'Est', *Le Courrier des Pays de l'Est*, no.336, January, pp.3–28.

Littmann, E.L. (1989) 'Agricultural policies in the USSR: Problems, trends and prospects', *Journal of Agricultural Economics*, vol.40, no.3, September, pp.290–301.

Lodge, J. (ed.) (1985) *The European Community and the Challenge of the Future,* Pinter Publishers, London.

Lysén, G. (1987) 'EEC–CMEA/Eastern Europe legal aspects on trade and co-operation', *Legal Issues of European Integration*, no.1, pp.83–110.

Maciejewski, W. and Nuti, D.M. (1985) 'Economic integration and prospects for East–West trade', Paper presented at a conference on 'East–West Trade and Financial Relations', European University Institute, 4–6 June.

Mahé, L.P. and Moreddu, C. (1988) 'Analisi di alcune politiche di liberalizzazione del commercio agricolo', in Tarditi, S., Thomson, K.J., Pierani, P. and Croci Angelini, E. (1988) *Liberalizzazione del commercio agricolo e Comunità Europea*, Istituto Nazionale di Economia Agraria, Il Mulino, Bologna, pp.121–46, and in English as *Agricultural Trade Liberalization and the European Community*, Oxford University Press.

Majmudar, M. (1988) 'The multifibre arrangement (MFA IV) 1986–1991: A move towards a liberalized system?' *Journal of World Trade Law*, vol.22, no.2, pp.109–25.

Malle, S. (1990) 'Il processo asimmetrico delle riforme', *Politica Internazionale* nos.5–7, May–July, pp.105–19.

Marer, P. and Tabaczynski, E. (eds.) (1981) *Polish–US Industrial Cooperation in the 1980s*, Indiana University Press, Bloomington.

Marer, P. (1984) 'The political economy of Soviet relations with Eastern Europe', in Meiklejohn Terry, S. (ed.), *Soviet Policy in Eastern Europe*, Yale University Press, New Haven and London, pp.155–88.

Marrese, M. (1988) 'The CMEA's dilemma: More intra-CMEA trade or more trade with the West', unpublished manuscript, Northwestern University, Evanston, Illinois.

Marrese, M. and Vanous, J. (1983) *Soviet Subsidization of Trade with Eastern Europe: A Soviet Perspective*, University of California, Institute of International Studies, Berkeley.

Marsh, P. (1978) 'The development of relations between the EEC and CMEA', in Shlaim, A. and Yannopoulos, G.N. (eds.) (1978), *The EEC and Eastern Europe*, Cambridge University Press, pp.25–71.

Maslen, J. (1983) 'The European Community's relations with the state trading countries 1981–1983', *Yearbook of European Law*, vol.3, pp.323–46.

Maslen, J. (1986) 'The European Community's relations with state trading countries of Europe 1984–1986', *Yearbook of European Law*, vol.6, pp.335–56.

Maslen, J. (1988) 'A turning point: past and future of the European Community's relations with Eastern Europe', *Rivista di Studi Politici Internazionali*, Anno LV, no.4, October–December, pp.557–86.

Matejka, H. (1988) 'EEC–CMEA relations: The aftermath of the declaration of June 25th, 1988', in C. Keller, H. Matejka and K. Nyiri (eds.) (1990), *European Integration and East–West Relations. Papers presented to the Sixth Swiss-Hungarian Roundtable 12–16 September 1988*, Graduate Institute of International Studies, Geneva, pp.19–34.

Matejka, H. (1990a) 'Central planning, trade policy, and how centrally planned economies fit into the GATT framework, *Soviet and East European Foreign Trade*, Spring, vol.26, no.1, pp.36–65.

Matejka, H. (1990b) 'East–West European integration', Paper presented at the Fourth World Congress for Soviet and East European Studies, Harrogate, UK, 21–26 July, 1990.

Matthews, A. (1985) *The CAP and Less Developed Countries*. Gill and Macmillan, Dublin.

McClatchy, D. and Cahill, S. (1988) 'Cross commodity trade effects of agricultural policies: Some implications for the GATT', Paper presented at the xxth conference of the International Association of Agricultural Economists (IAAE), on 'Agriculture and Governments in an Interdependent World', Buenos Aires, August.

McIntyre, R.J. (1988) 'The small enterprise and agricultural initiatives in Bulgaria: Institutional invention without reform', *Soviet Studies*, vol.XL, no.4, October, pp.602–15.

McMillan, C.H. (ed.) (1974) *Changing Perspectives in East–West Commerce*, Lexington Books, London and Toronto.

McMillan, C.H. (1981) 'Trends in East–West industrial cooperation', *Journal of International Business Studies*, Fall, pp.53–67.

McMillan, C.H. (1986) in Csikos-Nagy, B. and Young, D.G. (eds.) (1986) *East–West Economic Relations in the Changing Global Environment*, Macmillan, London.

Menato, G. (1990) 'New relations between the EEC and Eastern European countries', Paper presented at a Summer School organised by the European University Institute, Florence, 25 June–5 July.

Michelmann, H.J. *et al.* (eds.) *The Political Economy of Agricultural Policy and Trade*, Westview Press, Boulder, Colorado, forthcoming.

Moyer, H.W. and Josling, T.E. (1990) *Agricultural Policy Reform: Policy and Processes in the EC and USA,* Harvester Wheatsheaf, Hemel Hempstead.

Neville-Rolfe, E. (1989) *EC Aid to Poland,* Economist Intelligence Unit European Trends, No.4.

Newbery, D.M. (1990) *Tax Reform, Trade Liberalisation and Industrial Restructuring in Hungary,* 'Economic transformation in Hungary and Poland', *European Economy*, March, pp.67–95.

Norall, C. (1986) 'New trends in anti-dumping practice in Brussels, *The World Economy*, vol.9, no.1, pp.97–111.

Nuti, D.M. (1986) 'Hidden and repressed inflation in Soviet-type economies: Definitions, measurement and stabilisation', *Contributions to Political Economy*, vol. 5, pp.37–82.

Nuti, D.M. (1988) *Economic Relations between the European Community and CMEA,* EUI Working Paper No.88/360, European University Institute, Florence.

Nuti, D.M. (1990a) 'The case for Western aid to Central East Europe', Paper presented at a conference on 'An East European Recovery Programme', European University Institute, Florence 19–20 February 1990.

Nuti, D.M. (1990b) 'The pace of change in Central and East Europe', Paper presented at a conference on 'An East European Recovery Programme', European University Institute, Florence 19–20 February 1990.

Nuti, D.M. (1990c) *Internal and International Aspects of Monetary Disequilibrium in Poland,* in 'Economic Transformation in Hungary and Poland', *European Economy*, March, pp.169–82.

Nuti, D.M. (1990d) 'Seguenza e credibilità delle riforme nelle economie post-communiste'; *Note Economiche*, vol. 2, pp.225–41.

Nuti, D.M. (1990e) 'Un piano di aiuti per accelerare la transizione', *Politica Internazionale,* nos.5–7, May–July, pp.143–9.

OECD (1987) *National Policies and Agricultural Trade*, OECD, Paris.

OECD (1989) *PSE and CSE Tables 1979–1989,* OECD, Paris.

O'Keeffe, D. and Schermers, H.G. (eds.) (1982) *Essays in European Law and Integration,* Kluwer-Deventer, The Netherlands.

Olechowski, A. and Sampson, G. (1980) 'Current trade restrictions in the EEC, the United States and Japan', *Journal of World Trade Law,* May–June, vol.14, no.3, pp.220–31.

Olechowski, A. and Yeats, A. (1982) 'The incidence of nontariff barriers on socialist country exports', *Economia Internazionale,* vol.XXXV, no.2, May, pp.277–45.

Paarlberg, R.L. (1986) 'Responding to the CAP. Alternative strategies for the USA', *Food Policy,* May, pp.153–73.

Padoan, P.C. (1990) 'Cooperazione Est-Ovest. La Comunità Europea tra competizione globale e bilateralismo', *Note Economiche,* vol.2, pp.291–307.

Parboni, R. and Wallerstein (eds.) (1987) *L'Europa e l'economia politica del sistema-mondo,* Franco Angeli, Milan.

Patterson, E.R. (1986) 'Improving GATT rules for nonmarket economies', *Journal of World Trade Law,* vol.20, no.2, pp.185–205.

Pelkmans, J. (1984) *Market Integration in the European Community,* Martinus Nijhoff Publishers, The Hague, Boston and Lancaster.

Pelkmans, J. and Gremmen, H. (1983) 'The empirical measurement of static customs union effects', *Rivista Internazionale di Scienze Economiche e Commerciali,* vol. XXX, no.7, pp.612–22.

Peters, G. (1989a) *The Interpretation and Use of Producer Subsidy Equivalents,* Erasmus Discussion Papers on European Integration No.3, University of Siena.

Peters, G. (1989b) *Measuring Government Intervention in Agriculture for the GATT Negotiations: A Note on Scwartz and Parker,* Erasmus Discussion Papers on European Integration No.4, University of Siena.

Pinder, J. (1974) 'A Community policy towards Eastern Europe', *The World Today,* vol.30, no.3, March, pp.291–9.

Pinder, J. and Pinder, P. (1975) *The European Community's Policy towards Eastern Europe,* PEP, Chatham House, London.

Pinder, J. (1979) 'Integration in Western and Eastern Europe: Relations between the EC and CMEA', *Journal of Common Market Studies,* vol.XIX, December.

Pinder, J. (1986) 'The political economy of integration in Europe: Policies and institutions in East and West', *Journal of Common Market Studies,* vol.XXV, no.1, September, pp.1–14.

Pinder, J. (1988) 'The single market: a step towards European union' in Lodge, J. (ed.) (1988) *The European Community and the challenge of the future,* Pinter Publishers, London.

Piontek, E. (1987) 'Anti-dumping in the EEC – some observations by an outsider', *Journal of World Trade Law,* vol.21, no.4.

Pissula, P. (1990) 'Experiences of the centrally planned economies in GATT', *Soviet and East European Foreign Trade,* Summer, vol.26, no.2, pp.3–15.

Pitzner-Jorgensen, F. (1990) 'Economic reforms and East–West trade and cooperation', Paper presented at the First Conference of the European Association for Comparative Economic Studies (EACES), Verona, 27–29 September.

Pohled, R. (ed.) (1977) *Handbook of the Economy of the German Democratic Republic,* Saxon House, London.

Pomfret, R. (1988) *Unequal Trade: The Economics of Discriminatory International Trade Policies,* Basil Blackwell Ltd, Oxford and New York.

Portes, R. (1990) 'Introduction', *European Economy,* May, pp.11–17.

Pouliquen, A. (1987) 'La modernisation structurelle d'une agriculture privée en économie socialisée: le tournant polonais', *Revue d'Etudes Comparatives Est-Ouest*, vol.XVIII, no.4, December.

Pouliquen, A. (1990) 'Principali elementi ed insegnamenti delle decisioni centrali relativi al perestroika agricola in Unione Sovietica', *Rivista di Politica Agraria*, June 1990, pp.23–40.

Prieb, H., Scheper, W. and Von Urff, W. (eds.) (1984) *Agrarpolitik in der EG–Probleme und Perspektiven*, Nomos Verlagsgesellschaft, Baden-Baden.

Prodi, R. (1990) 'Impresa privata, impresa pubblica: strutture istituzionali e performance: Il problema della privatizzazione nell'Est', Paper presented at the XXXI Annual Meeting of the Società Italiana degli Economisti, Rome, 2–3 November.

Ray, J.E. (1986) 'The OECD "Consensus" on export credits', *The World Economy*, September, vol.9, no.3, pp.295–309.

Riishoj, S. (1985) 'The Soviet Union and Western European economic integration. Negotiations between the EEC and Comecon', Paper presented at a conference on 'East–West Trade and Financial Relations', European University Institute, 4–6 June.

Robson, P. (1987) *The Economics of International Integration*, Allen & Unwin, London.

Rollo, J.M.C. with J. Batt, B. Granville and N. Malcolm (1990) *The New Eastern Europe: Western Responses*, Chatham House Papers, Royal Institute of International Affairs, Pinter publishers, London.

Ronnas, P. (1989) 'Turning the Romanian peasant into a new socialist man: An assessment of rural development policy in Romania', *Soviet Studies*, vol. XLI, no.4, October, pp.543–59.

Saccomandi, V. (1988) 'Situazione agricola internazionale e riforma della PAC', *La Questione Agraria*, vol.29, pp.3–31.

Sachs, J. (1990) 'What is to be done?', *The Economist*, 13 January, pp.21–6.

Sampson, G. and Yeats, A.J. (1977) 'An evaluation of the Common Agricultural Policy as a barrier facing agricultural exports to the EEC', *American Journal of Agricultural Economics*, February, pp.99–107.

Sampson, G.P. (1987) 'Pseudo-economics of the MFA – a proposal for Reform', *The World Economy*, vol.10, no.4, pp.455–68.

Sarre, F. (1988) 'Article 115 EEC Treaty and trade with Eastern Europe', *Intereconomics*, September–October, pp.233–40.

Sarris, A.H. and Freebairn, J. (1983) 'Endogenous price policies and international wheat prices', *Amercian Journal of Agricultural Economics*, vol.2, no.65, pp.214–24.

Sarris, A.H. (1988) 'Politiche dei prezzi e distorsioni internazionali: il caso del frumento', in Tarditi, S., Thomson, K.J., Pierani, P. and Croci, Angelini, E. (1988) *Liberalizzazione del commercio agricolo e Communità Europea*, Istituto Nazionale di Economia Agraria, Il Mulino, Bologna, pp.237–61, and in English as *Agricultural Trade Liberalization and the European Community*, Oxford University Press,

Saryusz-Wolski, J. (1989) 'Divergence et convergence de l'integration regionale en Europe: La CEE et le Comecon. Les aspects comparatifs', Paper presented at the VI AISSEC (Associazione Italiana per lo Studio dei Sistemi Economici Comparati) Conference, Urbino, 12–14 October 1989.

Saryusz-Wolski, J. (1990a) 'Western response to European recovery programme', Paper presented at the conference on 'An East European Recovery Programme', European University Institute, Florence, 19–20 February, 1990.

Saryusz-Wolski, J. (1990b) 'The dynamics of European integration: structural adjustment of Central-East European economies in transition', Paper presented at the First Conference of the European Association of Comparative Economic Studies, Verona, 27–29 September.

Schiavone, G. (1982) *East–West Relations: Prospects for the 1980s*, Macmillan, London.

Schiavone, G. (1985) 'Cocom and multilateral export controls: Economic, strategic and institutional issues', Paper presented at a colloquium on 'East–West Trade and Financial Relations, European University Institute, Florence.

Schmitz, P.M. (1984) *Handelsbeschränkungen und Instabilität auf Weltshaftsagrarmärkten*. Weltwirtschaftliche Studien des Instituts für Europäische Wirtschaftspolitik der Universität Hamburg, Göttingen.

Schmitz, P.M. (1985) 'International repercussions of EC agricultural policy', *Intereconomics*, November–December, pp.261–7.

Schreiber, T. (1985) 'Les relations entre le Caem et la CEE', *Le Courrier des Pays de l'Est*, no.296.

Schwartz, N.E. and Parker, S. (1988) 'Measuring government intervention in agriculture for the GATT negotiations', *American Journal of Agricultural Economics*, December, pp.1137–45.

Segrè, A. (1989a) 'Les échanges agro-alimentaires dans les relations est-ouest', *Est-Ovest*, no.2, ISDEE-Trieste, pp.53–77.

Segrè, A. (1989b) 'La politica agraria in Unione Sovietica verso il mercato', *Rivista di Politica Agraria*, no.1, March 1989, pp.17–27.

Segrè, A. (1989c) 'Crisi dell'agricoltura e riforme in Unione Sovietica', Acts of the VI Conference of the Associazione Italiana per lo Studio dei Sistemi Economici Comparati, Urbino, 12–14 October, pp.881–93.

Segrè, A. (1990a) 'Le ultime misure di politica economica e agraria in URSS, il commercio estero e le nuove prospettive per l'Italia', *Rivista di Politica Agraria*, June, pp.41–53.

Segrè, A. (1990b) 'Le statistiche agricole sovietiche e i problemi legati alla loro interpretazione', *Rivista di Politica Agraria*, June, pp.81–91.

Sellekaerts, W. (1971) 'The effects of the EEC on her members' imports from the communist countries of Eastern Europe', *Southern Economic Journal*, January, vol.37, no.3, pp.323–33.

Sellekaerts, W. (1973) 'How meaningful are empirical studies on trade creation and diversion?', *Weltwirtschaftliches Archiv*, vol.109, pp.519–51.

Selyunin, V. and Khanin, G.I. (1987) 'Lukavaya tsifra (lying statistics)', *Novy Mir*, vol.63, no.2, February, pp.219–41.

Senior Nello, S.M. (1985a) *EC–East European Economic Relations: Cooperation Agreements at the Government and Firm Levels*, European University Institute Working Paper no.85/183, Florence.

Senior Nello, S.M. (1985b) 'Reform of the EC agrimonetary system: A public choice approach', *Journal of European Integration*, vol.IX, pp.55–79.

Senior Nello, S.M. (1989) *Recent Developments in Relations between the EC and Eastern Europe*, EUI Working Paper No. 89/381, European University Institute, Florence.

Senior Nello, S.M. (1990a) 'Some recent developments in EC–East European economic relations', *Journal of World Trade*, February.

Senior Nello, S.M. (1990b) 'Agricultural trade between the European Community and Central-East Europe', Paper presented at a conference organised by the INEA on 'Trends in Agricultural Policies and Trade Relations in Europe', Rome, 19 April 1990.

Shlaim, A. and Yannopoulos, G.N. (eds.) (1978), *The EEC and Eastern Europe*, Cambridge University Press.

Shmelev, N. (1988) 'Novye trevogi', *Novy mir*, vol.63, no.6; pp.142–58, June.

Sorbini, M. and Segrè, A. (1989) *Politica agraria e commercio internazionale nei paesi del Comecon. Evoluzione, problemi e bibliografia*, ISDEE, Trieste, p.207.

Soros, G. *Opening the Soviet System*, Weidenfeld and Nicolson, London and New York, forthcoming.

Stoeckel, A. (1985) *Intersectoral Effects of the CAP: Growth, Trade and Unemployment*. Occasional Paper No.95, Bureau of Agricultural Economics, Australian Government Publishing Service, Canberra.

Szalkai, I. (1990) *The elements of policy for rapidly redressing the Hungarian balance of payments*, in 'Economic Transformation in Hungary and Poland', *European Economy*, March, pp.97–106.

Taylor, K.C. (1977) 'Import protection and East–West trade: A survey of industrialised countries' practices', in Hardt, J. (ed.) (1977) *East European Economies post-Helsinki*, US Joint Economic Committee, US Government Printing Office, Washington, D.C..

Tangermann, S. (1989) 'Evaluation of the current CAP reform package', *The World Economy*, vol.12, no.2, June, pp.175–88.

Tangermann, S., Josling, T.E., and Pearson, Scott (1987) 'Multilateral negotiations on farm-support levels', *The World Economy*, vol.10, no.3, pp.265–80.

Tanner, C. and Swinbank, A. (1987) 'Prospects for reform of the common Agricultural Policy', *Food Policy*, November.

Tarditi, S., Thomson, K.J., Pierani, P. and Croci Angelini, E. (1988) *Liberalizzazione del commercio agricolo e Comunità Europea*, Istituto Nazionale di Economia Agraria, Il Mulino, Bologna, and in English as *Agricultural Trade Liberalization and the European Community*, Oxford University Press.

Meiklejohn Terry, S. (ed.) (1984) *Soviet Policy in Eastern Europe*, Yale University Press, New Haven and London.

Taylor, K.C. (1977) 'Import protection and East–West trade: A survey of industrialised countries' practices', in Hardt, J. (ed.) (1977) *East European Economies post-Helsinki*, Joint Economic Committee, US Government Printing Office, Washington, D.C..

Tirapolski, A. and Globokar, T. (1984) 'Les relations économiques entre les deux Allemagnes', *Le Courrier de Pays de l'Est*, no.287, September.

Tosi, D. (1987) 'Le relazioni della CEE con i paesi dell'Est europeo: Aspetti generali e recenti sviluppi', *Est-Ovest*, no.4, pp.59–75.

Tosi, D. (1989) 'Sul funzionamento del sistema Cocom e sulle possibilità d'intervento della Comunità Economica Europea', *Est-Ovest*, pp.45–61.

Tracy, M. 'The political economy of agriculture in the European Community', in Michelmann *et al.* (eds.), *The Political Economy of Agricultural Policy and Trade*, Westview Press, Boulder, Colorado, forthcoming.

Turnovsky, S.J. (1978) 'The distribution of welfare gains from price stabilization: A survey of some of the theoretical issues', in Adams, F.G. and Klein, S.A. (eds.) (1978) *Stabilizing World Commodity Markets: Analysis, Practice and Policy*, Lexington Books, London and Toronto.

UNCTAD (1980) *Report of Committee of Commodities at its Ninth Session* (TD/B/C.1/(IX)/Misc.3), UNCTAD, Geneva.

UNCTAD (1986) *Document ST/TSC/6*, 25 June, 1986, UNCTAD, Geneva.

Valdés, A. (1981) *Food Security for the Developing Countries*, Westview Press, Boulder, Colorado.

Valdés, A. and Zietz, J. (1980) *Agricultural Protection in OECD Countries: Its Cost to Less-Developed Countries*. Research Report 21, Food Policy Research Institute, Washington.

Van Bael, I. and Bellis, J-F. (1985) *EEC Anti-Dumping and Other Trade Protection Laws*, CCH Editions Ltd, Bicester, UK.

Van Brabant, J.M. (1988) 'Planned economies in the GATT framework: The Soviet case', *Soviet Economy*, vol.4, no.1, pp.3–33.

Van Brabant, J.M. (1989) *Economic Integration in Eastern Europe: A Handbook*, Harvester Wheatsheaf, Hemel Hempstead.

Van Brabant, J.M. (1990) 'The Soviet Union and the international trade regime: A reply', *Soviet Economy*, vol.5, no.4, pp.372–7.

Vandoren, P. (1988) 'Mise en oeuvre de la politique anti-dumping de la CEE contre les importations en provenance des pays à commerce d'état', *Revue du Marché Commun*, no.316, April.

Velo, D. (1986) 'The prospects of cooperation between the EEC and Comecon', *Journal of Regional Policy*, no.3, July–September, pp.383–93.

Verny, S. (1988) 'The EEC and the CMEA. The problem of mutual recognition', *Soviet and East European Foreign Trade*, vol.24, no.2, summer, pp.6–25.

Von Urff, W. (1984) 'External pressure on the CAP: Emerging conflicts between trade policy and development policy', Paper presented at a Colloquium 'Can the CAP Be Reformed', organised by ISEA and TEPSA, 8–10 March, Wageningen.

Von Urff, W. and Weinmueller, E. (1984) 'Aussenwirtschaftliche Aspekte der EG-Agrarpolitik', in Priebe, H., Scheper, W. and Von Urff, N. (eds.) *Agrarpolitik in der EG – Probleme und Perspektiven*, Nomos Verlaggesellschaft, Baden-Baden.

Wädekin, K.E. (1982) 'Soviet agricultural dependence and the West', *Foreign Affairs*, Spring, 1982.

Wädekin, K.E. (1989) 'The re-emergence of the Kolkhoz principle', *Soviet Studies*, vol.XLI, no.1, January, pp.20–38.

Wädekin, K.E. (1990) 'Fattori di crisi dell'economia agro-alimentare sovietica', *Rivista di Politica Agraria*, June, pp.13–22.

Wallace, W.V. and Clarke, R.A. (1986) *Comecon, Trade and the West*, Frances Pinter, London.

Wellenstein, E. (1982) 'The relations of the European communities with Eastern Europe', in O'Keeffe, D. and Schermers, H.G. (eds.) (1982) *Essays in European Law and Integration*, Kluwer-Deventer, The Netherlands, pp.197–208.

Wetter, T. (1985) 'Trade policy developments in the steel sector, *Journal of World Trade Law*, vol.19, no.5, pp.485–96.

Whetten, L.L. (1982) 'Scope, nature and change in inner-German relations', *Foreign Affairs*, Spring.

Wilczyński, J. (1969) *The Economics and Politics of East–West Trade*, Macmillan, London.

Wilczyński, J. (1980) 'Institutional framework of relations between the EEC and CMEA: The EEC viewpoint', *Foreign Trade*, Spring.

Williamson, O.E. (1986) *Economic Organization: Firms, Markets and Policy Control*, Harvester Wheatsheaf, Hemel Hempstead.

Wolf, T.A. (1990) 'Macroeconomic adjustment and reform in planned economies', *Soviet and East European Foreign Trade,* Summer, pp.47–62.

Woolcock, S. (1982) 'East–Trade: US policy and European interests', *World Trade*, February.

Wülker-Mirbach, M. (1990) 'New trends in countertrade', *OECD Obsever,* vol.163, April–May, pp.13–16.

Yannopoulos, G.N. (1985a) 'The European Community's Common External Commercial Policy; Internal contradictions and institutional weaknesses', *Journal of World Trade Law,* vol.19, no.5, September–October, pp.451–65.

Yannopoulos, G.N. (1985b) 'The impact of the European Economic Community on East–West trade in Europe', Paper presented at a conference on 'East–West Trade and Financial Relations', European University Institute, 4–6 June.

Yannopoulos, G.N. (1986) 'Patterns of response to EC tariff preferences: An empirical estimation of selected non-ACP associates', *Journal of Common Market Studies,* vol.XXV, no.1, September, pp.15–30.

Young, C. (1972) 'Association with the EEC: Economic aspects of the trade relationship', *Journal of Common Market Studies,* December, pp.120–35.

Zaleski, E. and Wienert, H. (1980) *Technology Transfer between East and West,* OECD, Paris.

Index

accession protocols, 29–31, 203, 206–7, 219–21
ACP countries, 96, 113, 192
ad valorem tariffs, 88, 97, 109
agricultural agreements, 36, 114, 202, 207–8
agricultural aid, 188, 194, 196
'agricultural arrangements', 114
agricultural trade, 107
    CAP (impact), 137–45
    CAP mechanisms, 108–10
    CAP and third countries, 135
    concessions, 113–15
    main features, 130–5
    other measures, 110–13
    outlook for trade, 145–7
    protection levels, 135–7
    smaller countries, 122–30
    Soviet, 116–22
    transformation (features), 116
agriculture, 41, 174, 188, 194, 196
    exports, 22, 130–5
    Germany, 248–9, 252–4
    imports, 130–5, 143–5
agrimonetary system, 146
aid, *see* Western aid
Aigner Report (1981), 142
analogue country, 50, 55–7, 59–60
anti-dumping, 4, 28, 38–9, 41
    comparative advantage, 59–60
    legislation, 48–54
    procedures, 54–9
    statistics, 50–4
anti-monde, 99–100
association agreements, 10, 24, 146, 201, 205–8, 210, 263, 265

association and integration, 211
    configuration, 5, 212–19, 265
    new associations, 221–3
    other organisations, 219–21
austerity policies, 86, 122, 126, 146, 160, 162–3, 174, 183
autonomous trade policy, 32–4

Balcerowicz Programme, 162, 183
bandwaggon effect, 44, 220
Bank for European Reconstruction/ Development, 63, 186, 190–1, 194
banking and banks, 175, 185, 190
    BERD, 63, 186, 190–1, 194
    EIB, 8, 181, 186, 190, 194, 249, 254
    see also central banks; commercial banking
bankruptcy, 159, 160, 261
Banque Française, 66
barter, 86, 87, 88, 118
Basic Law (of FRG), 243
Berlin, 243, 251
big bang (Poland), 9, 155, 160–1
bilateral agreements, 19, 31–2, 75
    cooperation, 28, 42–6, 205
    sectoral, 37–40, 49
bilateral links (tightening), 201
    inter-bloc cooperation, 208–9
    second generation, 205–8
    trade and cooperation, 202–5
bilateral relations, 4, 19–22, 24, 44, 73, 88, 222
black economy, 118, 162, 169, 261
border controls, 170, 215
Bratislava Summit, 220, 222

Brezhnev, L., 18, 64
Bucharest Formula, 73
budget deficits, 3, 6, 156, 159, 163, 166, 169–70, 174–5, 177
Bulgaria, 128–9, 166, 195–9
Bundesbahn, 245
Bundesbank, 217, 244, 246
Bundespost, 245
Bush, George, 181
buy back, 86

Cairns group, 128, 146
capital mobility, 207, 217
capitalism, 15, 16, 18, 165
carry-forward/carry-over, 37
Ceausescu regime, 41, 75, 129, 229
Cecchini report, 215
Central-East Europe
    agriculture, 107–47
    association/integration, 211–24
    bilateral links, 201–10
    central-planning system, 5–9
    economic transformation, 1, 5, 87–8, 155–79
    economic transformation (aid), 181–99
    interfirm cooperation, 226–40
    new configuration, 5, 265
    non-market economies, 2–5
    smaller countries, 82–3, 122–30
    statistics, 8–9
    see also trade relations (until 1989)
central-planning system, 4–9
Central Banks, 68, 87, 174, 185, 217, 244–6, 252
Central European Payments Union, 221, 222–3
ceteris paribus conditions, 100
CIA, 6, 7, 8, 169
CMEA, *see* Council for Mutual Economic Assistance
COCOM, *see* Coordinating Committee for Multilateral Export Controls
Cold War, 62, 190
collective farms, 119–20, 130, 177, 252, 254
COMETT programme, 187
commercial banking, 66, 185, 245
Common Agricultural Policy, 9, 17, 18, 32, 36, 103
    impact, 141–5
    implications of German unification, 249–50, 252–3
    third countries, 107–10, 135, 137–41
    variable levies, 89, 109, 115
Common Commercial Policy, 17, 27–8, 31–3, 42, 43, 97, 249
Common European House, 10, 220, 223, 265
Common External Tariff, 98, 248
Common Fisheries Policy, 36

Common Market effect, 100–3
Communist Party, 23, 168, 262
community interest, 58–9, 236
company law, German, 256
comparative advantage, 59–60
compensation, 86–8, 110, 216
competition, 89–93, 256
competitive effect, 100–3 *passim*
Conference on Security and Cooperation, 10, 18, 122, 209, 220–1, 223, 243, 265
Conflict Prevention Centre, 220
consumer cooperatives, 118
consumer durables, 2, 246
consumer goods, 72, 81, 263
convergence, 217–18, 265
cooperation, *see* interfirm cooperation; trade and cooperation agreements
cooperation agreements, 4, 17, 20, 26, 188–9
    agriculture, 110, 112, 146
    bilateral, 28, 42–6, 205
    industrial, 86–7, 226–8, 235–40
    inter-bloc, 208–9
cooperative farms, 116, 120–1, 127–8, 252
cooperative markets, 261
cooperatives, 162, 167–8, 172–3
Coordinating Committee for Multi-lateral Export Controls, 5, 62–6, 81, 185
coordination, information and, 3
coproduction, 42, 87, 237
Council of Europe, 10, 219–20, 265
Council of Financial Ministers, 217
Council of Ministers, 108, 110–11, 115, 215, 218
Council for Mutual Economic Assistance (CMEA)
    agriculture, 110–13, 130–5, 141–7
    central planning, 5–9
    EC trade, 71–85, 94–6, 100–5, 141
    EC trade mechanisms, 26–46
    historical background, 15–24
    Joint Declaration, 5, 10, 15–16, 21, 24, 208–9
    reasons for attitude change, 22–3
counterpart fund, 189, 196
counterpurchase, 86, 88
countertrade, 57, 71, 85–8
countervailing duties, 109
Craxi, Bettino, 21
currency convertibility, 4, 7, 71, 75, 87, 158, 161–2, 165, 174–5, 184–5, 222, 228–9
currency reform, 178–9
customs duties, 109, 188, 207, 221, 248
customs union, 9, 51, 98–105, 248, 252
Czechoslovakia, 128, 165–6
    agreement, 202, 203–4
    PHARE aid, 196–7, 198–9

Davignon Plan, 39

debt, 4, 6–7, 87, 262–3
  PHARE programme, 184–5, 194, 198
decentralisation, 120–1, 155–6, 167, 172,
  175–6, 254, 261
decision-making, 28, 213, 265
deficiency payments, 109
Delors, Jacques, 193, 217, 218, 219
demand, 100, 102
democracy, 218, 261
Deutsche Bank, 68, 245
Deutsche Genossenschaftbank, 190
devaluation, 156, 161, 164, 222–3
Dillon Round, 99
disarmament, 220
Dublin Summit, 182, 217, 247

Economic Commission for Europe, 8, 74,
  76, 85, 209, 226, 228, 230, 231, 232,
  235–7
economic and monetary union, 7, 210, 212,
  216–19, 247, 249, 253, 265
economic reform (PHARE), 198–9
economic reforms (trade relations)
  economic transformations, 155–79
  German unification, 242–57
  interfirm cooperation, 226–40
  new forms of association, 211–24
  outlook, 260–5
  tightening links, 201–10
  Western aid, 181–99
economic relations (outlook), 260–5
economic restructuring, 157–9, 161, 185–9
economic transformation, 87, 181–99
economic transformation process
  individual countries, 161–79
  introduction, 155–6
  macroeconomic stabilisation, 156–7
  microeconomic restructuring, 157–9
  sequencing measures, 160–1
  social safety nets, 159–60
  speed of transformation, 160
economies of scale, 2, 59, 212, 216
energy, 197, 222, 255
  prices, 6–7, 71, 73–6, 129, 132, 171–2,
  261, 263
environment, 186–9, 197, 222, 255
ERASMUS programme, 187
Euratom, 203, 254, 255
'Europe à la carte', 219
Europe agreements, 201, 205–8, 210
European Agricultural Guarantee and
  Guidance Fund, 110
European Bank for Reconstruction/
  Development, 63, 186, 190–1, 194
European Coal and Steel Community, 39,
  95, 186, 194, 207, 249, 254
European Community, 7–8
  association/integration, 211–24
  CMEA relations, 15–24

CMEA trade (products), 94–6
  German unification, 242–57
  Joint Declaration, 5, 10, 15–16, 21, 24,
  208–9
  links (tightening), 201–10
  new configuration, 5, 212–19, 265
  protectionism (measures), 48–60
  wider context, 62–8
  see also agricultural trade;
  trade mechanisms, EC (to 1988);
  trade relations (until 1989)
European Confederation, 10, 220, 223
European Court, 62
European Economic Area, 99, 211–14, 219,
  265
European Energy Community, 222
European Environmental Agency, 189
European Free Trade Association, 77, 79,
  91, 93, 96, 99, 103–4, 144–5, 211–14,
  219, 265
European Investment Bank, 8, 181, 186, 190,
  194, 249, 254
European Payments Union, 222–3
European Political Cooperation, 212, 219
European Social Charter, 247
European Social Fund, 254
European Trade Council, 44
European Training Foundation, 187
evidence accounts, 86
ex-post residual-imputation approach,
  99–100, 102
exchange rate, 100, 172, 175, 184, 217, 244,
  245
export-restraint, 4, 34, 40–1, 89, 114
export-supply management, 40
Export Administration Act (US), 64
export credit guarantees, 44, 63, 66, 74, 186
export credits, 4–5, 9, 28, 62–3, 66–8, 74,
  88
export price, 57–8
export refunds, 109, 141–2
exporters, competition from, 89–93
exports, 4
  agricultural, 22, 130–5, 141–3
  controls, 5, 62–6, 81, 185
  licensing, 64, 65–6, 89
  product groups, 88–9
  Soviet, 6, 22–3
  technology, 6, 63–6, 76, 88, 159, 185,
  236, 237, 239
  see also trade relations (until 1989)

FEOGA, 110, 250
financial aid, 182–4, 188–91, 193–4
first generation agreements, 201–2
fiscal policy, 217, 221
fishing fleet (Germany), 257
floor prices, 109
food aid, 113, 122, 142–3, 145, 182, 189–90,
  195, 243, 262

food consumption, German, 246
Food Programme (Soviet), 20
food supply, Polish, 125–7
food supply, Soviet, 117–19, 120, 122, 170–1
foreign policy, 5, 7–8, 218–19, 221
'Fortress Europe', 215
Four-Power Agreement, 21–2
Frankfurter Allgemeine Zeitung, 245
free trade area, 98, 201, 204, 213, 222

GATT, 20, 23, 36, 67, 86, 88, 104, 158, 204, 220
   agriculture, 108, 110, 128, 142–3, 146–7
   aims, 28–31
   anti-dumping, 49–51, 53, 57
   autonomous trade policy, 32–4
   Dillon/Kennedy Rounds, 99
   safeguards, 28, 30, 38, 203
   Uruguay Round, 28–9, 35, 38, 146, 147, 208–9, 264
General System of Preferences, 96, 113, 115, 188, 194, 207, 248, 264
German unification, 10–11, 65, 260
   application of EC policy, 252–7
   economic aspects, 243–7
   integration into EC, 247–50
   possible costs, 250–1
   special provisions, 242–3, 251–2
glasnost, 7, 8, 167–8, 262
gold sales, Soviet, 171
Gorbachev, M., 3, 6–7, 21, 23, 64, 75, 120, 122, 128, 167–8, 171, 175–8, 182, 190, 262, 263
'grey area', 29, 35, 40
Group of 24, 8, 75, 181–3, 189, 193, 194, 195
guidance price system, 39

Hänsch Report (1988), 66
hard-currency shortages, 3–4, 6, 22, 63, 75, 88, 122–3, 132–3, 146, 156–7, 164, 166
Helsinki Final Act, 220, 247
historical background, 15–24
human resources (PHARE), 196–7
human rights, 220, 263
Hungary, 127–8, 163–4, 187
   agreement, 21, 202–5
   see also PHARE programme

immigration, 189, 262, 263
imports
   agricultural, 130–5, 143–5
   autonomous policy, 32–4
   licensing, 60, 203
   quotas, 22, 32–40, 89, 203, 215, 251
   textile, 36–7
   see also anti-dumping; sectoral trade agreements; trade relations (until 1989)

industrial compensation, 86–8, 216
industrial cooperation agreements, 86–7, 226–8, 235–40
industrial modernisation, 186–7
industrial trade agreements, 35
inflation, 110, 125–6, 156, 161–2, 164–5, 167, 169, 218, 246
information, coordination and, 3
infrastructure, 119–20, 186, 207, 233, 239, 244–5, 254–5
injury, threat and, 58
integration
   of East Germany, 247–50
   new configuration, 5, 212–19, 265
   process, 16–17, 19, 22, 28, 100
   see also association and integration
inter-bloc cooperation, 208–9
interest rates, 6–8, 217–18, 246, 260
interfirm cooperation, 226–7
   industrial agreements, 235–7
   statistics, 237–9
   tripartite agreements, 239–40
internal trade creation, 98
International Bank for Reconstruction and Development, 181
international division of labour, 16–17, 72, 223, 239
International Monetary Fund, 8, 85–6, 162, 181–2, 184–5, 193, 220
intervention prices, 109
intra-CMEA trade, 71–7, 141, 263
investment, 29, 218, 245, 246
   agricultural, 117, 123, 128
   BERD, 63, 186, 190–1, 194
   guarantees, 63, 6
   joint ventures, 10, 65, 163, 165, 226, 230–2, 234–5
   PHARE programme, 185–7, 198–9
   Soviet Union, 172, 174
   technocratic fine-tuning, 155, 172
Irmer Report (1982), 54

joint-stock agribusiness firms, 116, 128
joint-stock companies, 159, 174–5
joint committees, 4, 32, 41–2, 45, 112, 190, 203–5
Joint Declaration, 5, 10, 15–16, 21, 24, 208–9
joint ventures, 8, 42, 245, 264
   agricultural, 112–13, 122
   definition, 227–8
   economic transformation, 159, 163, 167–8, 172, 178
   investment, 10, 65, 163, 165, 226, 230–2, 234–5
   legislation, 229–30
   objectives, 228–9
   problems, 233–4
   statistics, 230–2

trade analysis, 85–8
Western aid, 185, 191–2

Kennedy Round, 99
KGB, 168, 175, 177–8, 190, 262
know-how, 23, 64, 72, 76, 88, 159, 239, 264
kolkhoz farms, 119–22 *passim*, 175
kolkhoz markets, 118, 169
Kombinate system, 244, 256
Krushchev, N., 16, 18
'kulaks', 122

labour costs, 54, 59–60, 226
labour mobility, 158, 175, 207, 209, 242, 263
Länder, 242–6, 250, 252–7
land policies, 116, 120–2, 127, 175
less-developed countries, 27, 29, 79, 88, 141, 144, 192, 240
less-favoured areas, 34, 235, 249, 265
licensing, 237, 251
    exports, 64, 65–6, 89
    imports, 60, 203
'like product', 49, 55–7, 58
LINGUA programme, 187
Lomé Agreements, 96, 113, 192
Lubbers' Plan, 222

McDonald's (in Moscow), 233–4
macroeconomic stabilisation, 12, 156–7, 161, 183–5
majority voting, 215, 218
market-management measures, 109
market-share analysis, 89–93, 108, 144–5
market access, 27, 30, 35–6, 103
    PHARE, 146, 188, 198, 204
market disruption, 30, 37, 60
marketing (joint ventures), 235
Marshall Plan, 16, 193
medical aid, 189, 199
microeconomic restructuring, 157–9
military spending, 6, 7, 169, 177
minimum price system, 39
monetary policy, 215, 217, 221
money supply, 3, 6, 170
mortality rates, Soviet, 117
Moscow Formula, 73
Most Favoured Nation status, 19, 28, 30–1, 45, 67, 96–7
Multifibre Agreement, 33, 36–8, 97
mutual interest, 15, 42, 208–9
mutual recognition, 20–1, 23, 216

National Bank of Hungary, 232
nationalism, Soviet, 168, 178
NATO, 15, 63, 220, 243
New Economic Mechanism, 127, 163
New Economic Plan, Soviet, 174
newly industrialised countries, 48, 72, 93

'no preference' countries, 9, 97
nominal protection rate, 135–6
non-discrimination, 29, 30
non-market economies, 1–3, 49–50, 264
non-recognition, 16, 18, 20–1
non-tariff barriers, 27–8, 88–9, 209, 215
normal value, 49–50, 55–9
normalisation of relations, 22, 23

OECD, 17, 28, 62, 88, 136–40, 145
    export credits, 9, 66–8
    see also Group of 24
OEEC,193
offsets, 86–7
oil industry, 39, 71, 73–6, 165
orderly market arrangements, 40

'parallel-currency' approach, 217
Paris Club, 185, 262
peasant farms, 120, 127, 254
Pentagon unit, 221, 222, 223
perestroika, 23, 167–8, 233
    agriculture and, 117, 120–2
    future (outlook), 261-3
    measures taken (1985–9), 172–3
PHARE programme, 63, 68, 204, 248
    agriculture, 126, 146
    assessment of, 194–9
    financing aid, 193–4
    measures used, 181–90
Poland, 125–7, 162–3, 232
    agreement, 202, 203, 204
    big bang, 9, 155, 160, 161
    see also PHARE programme
Polish Foreign Investment Agency, 232
political union, 7, 212, 218–19, 223–4, 243, 247–9, 265
pollution, 186, 188–9, 222, 255
population trends, Soviet, 117–18
preferences, *see* trade preferences
price effect, 100, 101, 103
price liberalisation, 158, 161, 167, 174–5, 177–8, 261
price systems, 2–4, 7, 39, 165–6, 169–70, 261
prices, 73–4
    agricultural, 108–11, 116, 118–21, 125–7, 129, 135, 137–41, 147
    normal value, 49–50, 55–8
private farms, 120, 127, 254
privatisation, 261
    agriculture, 122, 129
    aid initiatives, 186, 187
    economic transformation, 158–9, 161–3, 165–7, 175
    Shatalin Plan, 122, 175–6, 177
procurement policies, 87, 119, 171, 215, 256
product groups, 94–6
production costs, 228

property rights, 167, 172–3, 175, 221, 252
    agriculture, 116, 121–2, 128, 130
protectionism, 26–7, 88–9, 135–7
    anti-dumping, 4, 28, 38–9, 41, 48–60,
      264
    grey areas, 29, 35, 40
    other EC laws, 60
    'rebound', 39
    safeguard measures, 4, 26, 28, 30, 38,
      60, 203
    see also quotas; tariffs
Pugo, Boris, 178

Quadrilateral unit, 221, 222
quantitative restrictions, 4, 41, 188, 248
    agreements, 202–4, 206
    agriculture, 110, 113, 127
    autonomous policy, 32–4
    GATT, 28, 30–1
quotas, 26, 110, 114
    import, 22, 32–40, 89, 203, 215, 251

rapprôchement, 16, 18–20, 24
rationing, 118, 167, 170–1, 174
reciprocity, 29–30, 86, 112
reference price, 109
reform debate (from 1990), 173–9
Regional Environmental Centre, 188
Regional Fund, 218, 249, 250
regional policy, 235, 254–5
regulation theory, 28, 174
Reichsbahn, 245
research, 221, 222
resettlement programme, 129
resource allocation, 2–3
restrictive competences, 43
Rolimpex, 126, 190
Romania, 129, 166–7
    agreement, 23, 41, 202
    PHARE aid, 195–9
Rome Summit (1990), 217, 218
Ryzkhov Plan, 174, 175–6

safeguards, 4, 26, 28, 30, 38, 60, 203
seasonal barriers (CAP), 110
second generation association agreements,
    146, 201, 205–8, 210
sectoral trade agreements, 21, 26, 28, 34–40,
    49
Seeler Report (1982), 65
sequencing of measures, 160–1
services, 85
set-aside (under CAP), 110, 254
Shatalin Plan, 122, 175–6, 177
Shevardnadze, E., 178
shipbuilding (Germany), 257
Single European Act, 213, 219
Single Market, 99, 256, 265
    agriculture and, 108, 112, 146

aims (and projects), 214–16
completion, 22, 32, 62, 66, 211–13
small and medium enterprises, 186, 187, 191,
    222, 254
Social Funds, 218, 249, 250
social market economy, 163, 243-4
social safety nets, 159–60, 183, 189–90, 208,
    242
social security, 177, 189
socialism, 2, 16–17, 18, 72, 165, 175, 223
'soft budgetary constraints', 3
Soviet Union, 22–3, 202, 203
    agriculture, 116–22, 132–3
    aid for, 195–9, 263
    EC-USSR trade structure, 80–1
    economic situation, 169–72
    military spending, 6, 7, 169, 177
    rationing, 118, 167, 170–1, 174
sovkhoz farms, 116, 119–22, 175
special preferences (CAP), 110
'special trade mechanism', 264
specialisation, 42, 237
specialised preferences, 96–7
stabilisation, 178
    macroeconomic, 126, 156–7, 161, 183–5
    PHARE programme, 189, 198
state farms, 116, 119, 121, 128
state shops, 118, 169, 171, 261
steel sector, 38–40, 202, 207–8, 256
Strasburg Summit, 184, 186
subcontracting, 87, 163, 237
subsidies, 38, 49, 60
    agriculture, 109, 116, 125–9, 135–7, 146
    export credit, 4–5, 9, 28, 62–3, 66–8, 74,
      88
    Soviet (to others), 7, 73
supply-side diversion, 99, 100
Support Measurement Unit, 137
support-price system, 108–11, 135
'swing' credit, 252
swing provision (quotas), 37
switch trading, 87
systemic change, 157–9, 185–9, 254

takeovers, 245, 256
target price, 58, 109–9
tariffs, 251
    ad valorem, 88, 97, 109
    Common External, 98, 248
    reductions, 4, 28–9, 115, 206–7
    see also customs union; GATT
taxation, 157, 163, 174–6, 229–30, 246
technical agreements, 35
technocratic fine-tuning, 155, 172
technology, 23, 48, 60, 72, 223, 226, 228,
    235, 263
    transfer, 6, 63–6, 76, 88, 159, 185, 236,
     237, 239
TEMPUS programme, 187–8

territorial clauses, 21
textile industry, 33, 36–8, 97, 202, 207
Third World, 62, 192
threshold price, 109
trade
  concessions (agriculture), 113–15
  controls, 65–6
  creation, 98, 100–2, 104
  destruction, 98
  diversion, 98, 100–1, 103–4, 107, 146
  embargoes, 5, 23, 63, 75
  intra-CMEA, 71–7, 141, 263
  liberalisation, 33, 137–41, 158, 264–5
  links (tightening), 201–10
  prospects for, 263–5
trade agreements, 20, 28, 41–3, 46, 188
  agricultural, 110, 112, 14
  bilateral, 19, 31-2, 75–6
  sectoral, 21, 26, 28, 34–40, 49
Trade Agreements Act (USA), 60
trade and cooperation agreement, 4, 24, 182,
    165
  first generation, 201, 202
  individual countries, 202–5
  significance, 204–5
trade mechanisms, EC (until 1988)
  autonomous trade policy, 32–4
  Common Commercial Policy, 31–2
  cooperation agreements, 42–6
  export-restraints, 40–1
  GATT, 28–31
  introduction, 26–8
  Romanian agreements, 41
  sectoral agreements, 34–40
trade policy, autonomous, 32–4
trade preferences, 27, 96–7, 103–4
  GSP, 96, 113, 115, 188, 194, 207, 248,
    264
trade protection, *see* protectionism
trade relations (until 1989), 4–5
  competition, 89–93
  countertrade, 85–8
  customs union, 98–105
  EC trade preferences, 96–7
  export protection, 88–9
  intra-CMEA, 71–7, 141, 263
  product groups, 94–6
  share of member states, 83–5
  statistical survey, 77–9
  structure of trade, 80–3
  trade in services, 85

training, 165, 223, 254, 263
  PHARE, 185, 186–7, 196–7
transition process (irreversible), 260–2
transport, 109, 221, 222
Treaty of Rome, 16, 21, 27–8, 42, 98, 205–
    6, 214, 235, 247
  Article 113, 19, 31, 34, 43–6, 67
  special German provisions, 242–3, 251–
    2
Triangle proposal, 221, 222
tripartite cooperation agreements, 239–40
Trzeciakowski Plan, 193
tutelage relations, 157, 160, 167

UK–Soviet agreement (1974), 45
UNCTAD, 20, 38, 89, 143, 239–40
unemployment, 158–60, 189, 217, 261, 263
  benefits, 156, 174, 250, 254
  Germany, 242, 246, 252
  individual countries, 162–5, 173
Union Treaty, Soviet, 176, 177–8
United Nations, 183
  UNCTAD, 20, 38, 89, 143, 239–40
Uruguay Round, 28–9, 35, 38, 146–7, 208,
    209, 264
USDA, 127, 129, 171, 253

variable/annual premiums, 109–10
variable levies, 53, 88–9, 109, 115
voluntary export restraints, 4, 34, 38, 40, 89,
    114
voucher schemes, 159

wages, 157–8, 162–3, 174, 245
Warsaw Pact countries, 5, 62–4, 220
welfare effect of customs union, 98
Western aid, 5, 8, 113, 181–2, 248
  economic restructuring, 185–9
  European Bank (BERD), 63, 186, 190–
    1, 194
  outlook, 262–3
  PHARE programme, 194–9
  reasons for aid, 191–4
  social safety nets, 189–90
  stabilisation policies, 183–5
working parties, 42–3, 112
World Bank, 8, 181–2, 184–6, 193

Yaoundé agreements, 97
Yeltsin, Boris, 175, 177
Yugoslavia (PHARE aid), 109–9